MW01004946

Spanish

With Ease Series

by Francisco Javier ANTÓN MARTÍNEZ

Adapted for English-speaking learners by
Paul Gerard Pickering

Illustrated by J.-L. GOUSSÉ

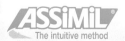

ASSiMiL®
The intuitive method

B.P. 25
94431 Chennevières-sur-Marne Cedex
FRANCE

© ASSIMIL 2014
ISBN 978-2-7005-0551-1

ASSiMiL

Language-learning courses

- Accompanied by optional audio files on CD or in MP3 format
- Now also available as e-courses

Assimil Series

Beginner – Intermediate

Arabic
Brazilian Portuguese**
Chinese With Ease Volume 1
Chinese With Ease Volume 2
Writing Chinese With Ease
Dutch With Ease
New French With Ease*
German
Hebrew
Hungarian With Ease
Italian With Ease
Japanese With Ease Volume 1
Japanese With Ease Volume 2
Writing Japanese With Ease
Russian*
Spanish
Yiddish

For Kids

Sing Your Way To French

Advanced

Using French

Phrasebooks

French
Italian
Polish
Russian
Spanish

* **e-course** (downloadable) available on www.assimil.com
** Available soon

Contents

Introduction

Spanish is a major international language that is spoken as a mother tongue by more than 400 million speakers, and as a second language by hundreds of millions of others. It is the most studied second language in the world, and its use continues to grow. It is an official language of the European Union and the United Nations (together with English, Arabic, Chinese, French and Russian).

Spanish is a Romance language, belonging to the Latin branch of the Indo-European family of languages. It is closely related to two other languages spoken in Spain, Galician and Catalan, as well as to Portuguese, French and Italian. It shares some similarities, to a greater or lesser degree, with other Indo-European languages such as English, German, Greek, Russian and even Sanskrit.

Since taking its first tentative steps as a literary language around the 11th and 12th centuries, Spanish has made many contributions to global cultural heritage. Its two most well-known figures, Don Quixote and Don Juan, are universal characters that span all eras.

Spanish is the official language of Spain as well as the majority of Latin American countries. After English, it is also the language most spoken in the United States. Despite the wide range of accents and regional idiomatic differences, the basic vocabulary and unified grammar of Spanish give it a common foundation that allows Spanish speakers all over the world to understand each other.

This simultaneous unity and diversity gives Spanish remarkable richness. Even inside the borders of Spain, accents and expressions are markedly different from one region to another. Equally, over history Spanish has absorbed influences from other languages, in particular from Arabic. In the same way, in Latin America, Spanish has adopted many words and expressions deriving from indigenous languages. Very often, regional speech overlaps more in accordance with geography than with national boundaries; the Spanish spoken on the Caribbean coast of Colombia, for example, is closer to that of Venezuela than to that of Colombia's Pacific coast.

Aside from its cultural importance, the extent of the Spanish language makes it impossible to ignore at a commercial level.

Latin America is a global region of growing economic potential. Speaking Spanish is increasingly good for business!

One final point regarding terminology: Spanish is also referred to as 'Castilian'. There are political reasons for this that we won't attempt to analyze here, but the historical reason is that the language originated in the former kingdom of Castile. Over time, it became the dominant language of the whole of Spain, which is why nowadays Spanish and Castilian are considered synonymous terms, at least from a linguistic point of view.

And now … **¡manos a la obra!** *Let's get to work!*

Some tips

- Try to make time to study each day for about half an hour. Regular practice is one of the keys to learning a language. If you're short of time one day, maybe listen to or reread the lesson from the day before or repeat an exercise, even if only for a few minutes. At the same time, don't try to overstretch yourself by going too quickly; just one lesson a day is sufficient. As with most things, it's better to do just a bit each day than to try to do a lot at once, followed by nothing.
- The first lessons are always a difficult hurdle. Don't get discouraged! As with learning anything new, everyone initially tends to think that the difficulty lies with the material or task being tackled. In fact, in most cases, this feeling stems from the adjustments that we have to make in order to overcome a kind of natural resistance to something new. Just relax and approach the language in a spirit of openness; you'll see that you'll quickly acquire a taste for your daily foray into Spanish.
- Trust us. Our method is based on the progressive assimilation of the language; the lessons aim to follow a process similar to the acquisition of one's first language. You'll come across an expression or a point of grammar several times before fully grasping it. The method is not based on trying to teach the language by memorizing rules, but to allow you to understand it in context using real examples.
- Read the dialogues in the lessons aloud, using the recordings to help you, if you have them. Try to imitate the intonation

and accent, fine-tuning these as you progress. The more you practice, the more you will be able to shed your inhibitions and feel confident when speaking. This will prepare you for real-life conversations to come!

- Review what you've learned regularly. If you're having difficulty remembering a word or understanding some grammatical point, don't panic! Give yourself time and keep moving forward. Just note the item that is giving you trouble and come back to it occasionally. Chances are that the stumbling block will resolve itself over the course of the lessons.
- Supplement your studies by taking every opportunity to immerse yourself in Spanish language and culture: watch Spanish films, read the Spanish press, listen to songs in Spanish ... this will all help you to learn the language even more quickly.
- Enjoy yourself! This is also an essential part of our course. The lessons are designed to entertain as well as to educate, with amusing stories, cartoons and interesting cultural information.

The Assimil method

Comprehension: the first wave

The first 50 lessons concentrate on comprehension and assimilation of the language. The main goal is to try to understand what you read, and, if you have the recordings, hear.

We recommend the following:

1) **Listen to the recording of the lesson**, which is very important for acquiring good pronunciation. It is possible to use the course without the recordings, but that's rather like reading the lyrics to a song without knowing the music!
2) **Read the lesson carefully.** Don't be embarrassed to read out loud, line by line, using the phonetic transcriptions to approximate the pronunciation. Check the English translation to help you understand what you're reading.

3) **Listen to the recording again** and repeat every line aloud. Imitate the speaker's accent and intonation as best you can. The text in the first few lessons is recorded twice, with the speakers enunciating slowly. The speech speeds up gradually with each lesson until it reaches a normal pace in the later lessons.
4) **Read the notes**, which provide important explanations about points of grammar, as well as additional information on vocabulary.
5) **Do the exercises**, which give you a chance to practice what you've just learned.

After every six lessons, a review lesson summarizes all the main grammatical points introduced in that set of lessons, as well as additional information where necessary. Devote just as much time to these as to the other lessons to consolidate your learning.

Many of the lessons also contain extra cultural information that will enrich your learning and stir your interest. In addition, at the end of the book you'll find a grammatical appendix and index, a two-way glossary (Spanish–English and English–Spanish) and a glossary of expressions, all of which allow you to easily check things you come across in the lessons.

Consolidation: the second wave

This is what we call the 'active phase'. Beginning from lesson 50, you will continue to study new lessons in the same way as before, but at the same time you will go back to review a previous lesson, starting with lesson 1. This time, however, instead of translating the first exercise in each lesson from Spanish to English, try to translate it in the other direction: that is, into Spanish. This will consolidate your learning, as well as allow you to see how much you've progressed.

Don't forget to learn the numbers in Spanish. The ordinal numbers are given at the beginning of every lesson, and the cardinal numbers with the page numbers at the bottom of each page.

So, the keystones to this method are regular effort in small doses, gradual progress and enjoying yourself while learning; these will allow you to acquire a good command of Spanish painlessly!

Pronunciation

1 Introduction

Spanish pronunciation is really not very difficult – it has the huge advantage of being phonetic, i.e. words are pronounced as they are spelled. In general (and in contrast to English):

- every letter is pronounced
- a letter is almost always pronounced in the same way.

As we go along, we will point out the very rare exceptions to these two general principles.

The Spanish alphabet has 29 letters: 5 vowels, 1 semi-consonant and 23 consonants.

The following sections contain some simple tips along with phonetic transcriptions in English that will help you become fluent in the sounds of Spanish. (The syllables that carry the stress are shown in bold.)

2 The vowels

There are five vowels, each corresponding to one sound:

Spanish vowel & pronunciation	Our transcription	Example
a (as in *father*)	*ah*	**la patata** *[lah pah-**tah**-tah] the potato*
e (usually like *ey* in *they*, but sometimes shorter, like *e* in *bet*)	*ay; e*	**el tomate** *[el to-**mah**-tay] the tomato*
i (as in *bee*)	*ee*	**sí** *[see] yes*
o (as in *no*, but shorter)	*o*	**no** *[no] no*
u* (as in *food*)	*oo*	**unidad** *[oo-nee-**dahd**] unit*

* The **u** is not pronounced in the combinations **gue**, **gui** or **que**, **qui**: e.g. **guerra** *[**gay**-rra]* *war*; **que** *[kay]* *that, what*; **quinto** *[**keen**-to]* *fifth*. However, if the **ü** has two dots, it is pronounced: **lingüista** *[leen-**gwee**-stah]* *linguist*; **pingüino** *[peen-**gwee**-no]* *penguin*. (The **g** before a **u** is hard, as in *gun*.)

In vowel combinations, each vowel retains its own sound (but see section 8 on 'Pronouncing vowel combinations'). So, **ai** is *[ah-ee]*, **au** *[ah-oo]*, and **eu** *[ay-oo]*: **aislar** *[ah-ee-**slar**]* *to isolate*; **autor** *[ah-oo-**tor**]* *author*; **deuda** *[day-**oo**-dah]* *debt*.

3 The semi-consonant *y*

Like in English, the letter **y** can represent two different sounds:

- a vowel sound, which is pronounced like the Spanish **i** *[ee]* when at the end of a word or on its own: **hoy** *[oy]* *today*; **y** *[ee]* *and*.
- a consonant pronounced like *y* in *yes* when at the beginning of a word or a syllable: **ya** *[yah]* *already*; **mayor** *[mah-**yor**]* *older, greater, major*.

4 The consonants

b	*[b]* as in *bar*, but slightly softer, with the lips a bit less tightly closed: **bien** *[bee-**en**]* *well*; **deber** *[day-**bayr**]* *to have to, must*.
c	• *[k]* as in *can* before **a**, **o**, **u**: **café** *[kah-**fay**]* *coffee*; **comer** *[ko-**mayr**]* *to eat*; **cuerpo** *[**kwayr**-po]* *body*. • *[th]* as in *thing* before **e** or **i**: **cenar** *[thay-**nahr**]* *to have dinner*; **cine** *[**thee**-nay]* *cinema*. (Note that in some parts of Spain and most of Latin America, this **c** is pronounced as an *[s]*.)
ch	*[ch]* as in *cheek*: **chocolate** *[cho-ko-**lah**-tay]* *chocolate*. Until recently, **ch** was considered a distinct letter in the Spanish alphabet.
d	similar to *[d]* as in *dad*: **dar** *[dahr]* *to give*, but slightly softer. It is often pronounced like a soft *th*, especially at the end of a word, when it is pronounced only very slightly or sometimes not at all.

f	*[f]* as in *flamenco*: **en efecto** *[en ef-**ayk**-to] in effect.* Note that there is no double **f** in Spanish, and **f** also replaces the English *ph*: **fotografía** *[fo-to-grah-**fee**-ah] photograph.*
g	• hard *[g]* as in *get* before **a**, **o**, **u**: **gato** *[**gah**-to] cat*; **gota** *[**go**-tah] drop*; **agua** *[**ah**-gwah] water*, **guía** *[**ghee**-ah] guide.* • guttural *[h]* before **e** or **i**, like the Spanish **j**: **general** *[hay-nay-**rahl**] general*; **giro** *[**hee**-ro] turn, spin.* (In some regions of Spain and most of Latin America it is pronounced non-gutturally, like the *h* in *horse*.)
h	is always silent: **hacer** *[ah-**thayr**] to make*; **hoy** *[oy] today.* Note that with the exception of some proper nouns, the combinations *ph*, *rh* and *th* do not exist in Spanish: e.g. **rinoceronte** *[ree-no-thay-**ron**-tay] rhinoceros.*
j	guttural *[h]* or *[kh]* like the *ch* in the Scottish word *loch*, a sound made at the back of the throat: **jota** *[**ho**-tah] the letter j*; **jugar** *[hoo-**gahr**] to play*; **reloj** *[rray-**lokh**] watch, clock.*
k	*[k]* as in *kind*: **kilo** *[**kee**-lo] kilogram.*
l	*[l]* as in *lemon*: **libro** *[**lee**-bro] book.*
ll	*[y]* as in *yes*: **malla** *[**mah**-yah] mesh*; **pollo** *[**po**-yo] chicken*; **paella** *[pah-**ay**-yah].* Note that this is not a double **l**, but a distinct letter. We've given the *[y]* pronunciation, as this is what you're most likely to hear in many parts of Spain, as well as throughout Latin America (and is the easiest for English speakers to pronounce!). However, in some regions it is pronounced like the English *[j]* sound. Careful: it is never pronounced like a single *[l]*!
m, n	*[m]* as in *map*, *[n]* as in *nod*: **mano** *[**mah**-no] hand.*
ñ	*[ny]* as in *canyon*: **España** *[es-**pah**-nyah] Spain*; **señor** *[say-**nyor**] sir, Mr.* The **n** with a **tilde** *[**teel**-day]* (~) is a distinct letter in the Spanish alphabet: the letter **eñe** *[**ay**-nyay].*

p	*[p]* as in *prawn*: **aplaudir** *[ah-plah-oo-**deer**]* *to applaud*; **oportunidad** *[o-por-too-nee-**dad**]* **opportunity**. There is no double **p** in Spanish.
q	*[k]* as in *king* – the **q** is always followed by a silent **u**: **que** *[kay]* *that*, *what*; **queso** *[**kay**-so]* *cheese*; **quiosco** *[kee-**os**-ko]* *kiosk*.
r	The Spanish **r** is rolled, a sound made by trilling the tip of the tongue against the roof of the mouth. • *[r]* – a single **r** between two vowels or at the end of a word is a short, single vibration, producing a soft sound almost like an **l**: **pero** *[**pay**-ro]* *but*; **toro** *[**to**-ro]* *bull*; **hablar** *[ahb-**lahr**]* *to speak*; **beber** *[bay-**bayr**]* *to drink*; **flor** *[flor]* *flower*. • *[rr]* – **r** at the beginning of a word, after **l**, **n** or **s**, or when doubled, is a more heavily rolled, longer trill: **repita** *[rray-**pee**-tah]* *repeat*; **alrededor** *[ahl-rray-day-**dor**]* *around*; **honrado** *[on-**rrah**-do]* *honest*; **Israel** *[ees-rrah-**el**]* *Israel*; **perro** *[**pay**-rro]* *dog*.
s	*[s]* as in *ghost* (always like 'ss', never like the 'z' sound in *goes*): **saber** *[sah-**bayr**]* *to know*; **cosa** *[**ko**-sah]* *thing*; **mes** *[mes]* *month*. Note that there is no double **s** in Spanish.
t	*[t]* as in *ten*, but slightly softer, with the tongue touching the top teeth: **patata** *[pah-**tah**-tah]* *potato*. Note that there is no double **t** in Spanish.
v	identical to *[b]*, with some regional exceptions – most Spanish speakers barely distinguish between them: **lavar** *[lah-**bahr**]* *to wash*.
w	In Spanish, **w** only appears in words borrowed from other languages, mainly German and English. • *[b]* – in words of Germanic origin, it is pronounced like a **v** *[b]*: **walkiria** *[bahl-**kee**-ree-ah]* *Valkyrie*. • *[oo]* – in words of English origin, it is pronounced like the letter **u** *[oo]*: **whisky** *[oo-**ee**-skee]* *whisky*.

x	• *[ks]* as in *a<u>x</u>e* in most cases: **taxi** ***[tah**-ksee]* *taxi.* • *[s]* as in *<u>s</u>un* before a consonant or at the beginning of a word in colloquial Spanish (although **x** is also correct): **exterior** *[es-tay-ree-**or**/eks-tay-ree-**or**]* *exterior*; **extra** *[**es**-trah/**eks**-trah]* *extra*; **xilófono** *[see-**lo**-fo-no/ksee-**lo**-fo-no]* *xylophone.*
z	*[th]* as in *<u>th</u>ing*: **caza** *[**kah**-thah]* *hunt*; **zumo de manzana** *[**thoo**-mo day mahn-**thah**-nah]* *apple juice*; **feliz** *[fay-**leeth**]* *happy*; **paz** *[pahth]* *peace.* (Note that in some parts of Spain and in Latin America, the **z** is pronounced as an *[s]*.)

5 Letters unique to the Spanish alphabet

The letters **ch**, **ll** and **ñ** are letters specific to the Spanish alphabet.

Until recently, in dictionaries they were placed separately after **c**, **l** and **n** respectively. In 1994, the **Asociación de Academias de la Lengua Española** decided to merge **ch** words under 'c' and **ll** words under 'l' in line with the universal Latin alphabet. Thus, words beginning with **ch** are now found where they would be in any English dictionary.

The letter **ñ** is still placed between **n** and **o**.

6 The Spanish alphabet

Letter	Name	Pronunciation
a	**a**	*ah*
b	**be**	*bay*
c	**ce**	*thay*
ch	**che**	*chay*
d	**de**	*day*
e	**e**	*ay*
f	**efe**	***ay**-fay*
g	**ge**	*hay*
h	**hache**	***ah**-chay*
i	**i**	*ee*

j	**jota**	***ho**-tah*
k	**ka**	*kah*
l	**ele**	***ay**-lay*
ll	**elle**	***ay**-yay*
m	**eme**	***ay**-may*
n	**ene**	***ay**-nay*
ñ	**eñe**	***ay**-nyay*
o	**o**	*o*
p	**pe**	*pay*
q	**cu**	*koo*
r	**erre**	***ay**-rray*
s	**ese**	***ay**-say*
t	**te**	*tay*
u	**u**	*oo*
v	**uve**	***oo**-bay*
w	**uve doble**	***oo**-bay **do**-blay*
x	**equis**	***ay**-kees*
y	**i griega**	*ee gree-**ay**-gah*
z	**zeta/ceta**	***thay**-tah*

The letters **b**, **v**, **w**, **y** and **z** also go by other names, depending on region. So, for example, Argentinians don't say **uve** *[**oo**-bay]* for the letter **v**; instead, they say **ve corta** *[bay **kor**-tah]* ('short v') to distinguish from **be larga** *[bay **lar**-gah]* ('long b'), which is the name they usually give to the letter **b**. However, the names in our table are the ones most widely used in the Spanish-speaking world.

7 Accentuation

Accentuation – that is, where the stress falls in a word – is important in Spanish, and gives the language its musicality. Spanish also has written accents on certain vowels; these almost always indicate where the word stress is placed.

• **Word stress**

All Spanish words of more than one syllable have one syllable on which the stress is placed, meaning that this syllable is emphasized when speaking. This is frequently the second-to-last syllable, but not always.

To indicate where the emphasis goes in a word, we will put the stressed syllable in bold: **palabra** *[pah-**lah**-brah]* *word*; **sílaba** *[**see**-lah-bah]* *syllable*; **acento** *[ah-**thayn**-to]* *accent.*

• **Written accents**

Each of the five vowels in the Spanish alphabet can take a written accent [´]. There can only be one written accent per word. When a written accent is placed on a vowel, this is the syllable that bears the stress: **árbol** *[**ahr**-bol]* *tree*; **ésta** *[**es**-tah]* *this one* (f.); **aquí** *[ah-**kee**]* *here*; **¿cómo?** *[**ko**-mo]* *How?*; **útil** *[**oo**-teel]* *useful.*

Written accents can be used to indicate word stress that would otherwise not be obvious. They can also be used to distinguish between two words that are spelled in the same way. We'll look at the rules for written accent placement as we progress.

8 Pronouncing vowel combinations

Vowel combinations can be pronounced in two different ways in Spanish. Sometimes each of the vowels is distinctly pronounced, and sometimes the vowels are combined to form a single sound, which is called a diphthong. We've included a few examples, but don't get too hung up about this. Just use the phonetic pronunciations in the lessons to guide you, along with the recordings.

Vowel combinations pronounced as diphthongs

In the following examples, although each vowel is pronounced, it sounds like one syllable when spoken at a normal pace:

aire *[**ah**-ee-ray]* *air*, **hay** *[**ah**-ee]* *there is/there are*: the sounds in *[ah-ee]* combine, resembling the long *i* in *fire.*

viaje *[bee-**ah**-hay]* *trip, voyage*: the sounds in *[ee-ah]* combine, resembling *ya* in *yahoo.*

nieve *[nee-**ay**-bay]* *snow*: the sounds in *[ee-ay]* combine, resembling *yay.*

viuda *[bee-**oo**-dah]* *widow*: the sounds in *[ee-oo]* combine, resembling *you.*

ruido *[rroo-**ee**-do]* *noise*, **muy** *[**moo**-ee]* *very*: the sounds in *[oo-ee]* combine, resembling *wee.*

fuerte *[foo-**ayr**-tay]* *strong*, **puerta** *[poo-**ayr**-tah]* *door*: the sounds in *[oo-ay]* combine, resembling *way*.

Certain words even contain triphthongs, i.e. a string of three vowels pronounced as a single syllable:
buey *[boo-**ay**-ee]* *ox*: the sounds in *[oo-ay-ee]* combine, resembling *way*.
estudiáis *[es-too-dee-**ah**-ees]* *you* (informal plural) *study*: the sounds in *[ee-ah-ee]* combine, resembling 'yice' (imagine a combination of *yes* and *nice*).

Vowel combinations pronounced as two distinct syllables
In these examples, each vowel is pronounced distinctly as a separate syllable, the sounds are not blended together.
teatro *[tay-**ah**-tro]* *theatre*: **te-a-tro**.
país *[pah-**ees**]* *country*: **pa-ís**.
fiesta *[fee-**ays**-tah]* *party*: **fi-es-ta**.
euro *[ay-**oo**-ro]* *euro*: **e-u-ro**.

One last thing to note is that because the **h** in Spanish is silent, when it occurs between two vowels these can be pronounced as a diphthong: for example, **ahijado** *[ah-ee-**hah**-do]* *godchild* ends up sounding like 'I-had-o'; and **prohibir** *[pro-ee-**beer**]* *to forbid* like 'proy-beer'.

In our phonetic transcriptions in the lessons, we've often used hyphens to help you sound out the individual sounds, but just remember that when spoken at a normal pace, the vowels often blend together. The good news is that in Spanish, even in diphthongs, a vowel always retains the same pronunciation – it's not like in English, in which vowel combinations can completely change the way the vowels are pronounced.

So now you're ready to get started! Although the information we've given here is not exhaustive, it will give you a good grounding in Spanish pronunciation. You can come back to consult it at any time as you go through the lessons. You don't need to learn it by heart; you'll pick it up as you go along. As we've mentioned, the stressed syllable is in bold in the lessons so that you learn the correct intonation of Spanish words. **¡Buena suerte!** Good luck!

Before beginning your first lesson, be sure to read the introduction carefully. It provides important information about pronunciation and how to make the most of your learning.

1 Lección primera *[lek-**thee-on** pree-**may**-rah]*

Un aperitivo

1 – **Bue**nos **dí**as ①, **u**na **ta**pa ② de tor**ti**lla, por fa**vor**.
2 – Sí. Ah**o**ra **mis**mo.

Pronunciation
*oon ah-pay-ree-**tee**-bo **1 bway**-nos **dee**-ahs **oo**-nah **tah**-pah day tor-**tee**-yah por fa-**bor 2** see. ah-**o**-rah **mees**-mo*

Pronunciation notes
To ease your way into Spanish, we'll provide some reminders about pronunciation in the first few lessons. Whenever you need to, you can also refer to the pronunciation section in the introduction.

Remember:
Title The Spanish **o** is pronounced similarly to the *o* in the English words *note*, *home*, etc.
1 • In Spanish, **b** and **v**, with some regional exceptions, sound similar to the English letter *b*.

Notes

① **Buenos días** is a polite way to greet someone that is equivalent to the now obsolete English greeting *Good day.* In Spanish it is used in the morning – in the afternoon, the greeting is **buenas tardes** *good afternoon*, and after sundown, **buenas noches** ▸

To help you learn the meaning of the Spanish words and match them with their translations more easily, the literal translations of certain expressions are given in parentheses and italics. The square brackets [ ] indicate words that are needed in English, but do not appear in the Spanish.

First lesson 1

A snack *(appetizer)*

1 – Good morning *(Good days)*, a [Spanish] omelette tapa *(tapa of omelette)*, please *(by favour)*.
2 – Yes. Right away *(Now even)*.

• The Spanish **r** is trilled softly when it is between two vowels or at the end of a word: it is pronounced by placing the tip of the tongue against the palate and making it vibrate slightly. It is rolled more strongly at the beginning of a word, or if it is doubled (**rr**) or comes after the letters **l**, **n** or **s**. More about this later.

▸ *good night*. Note that these greetings all use the plural form, unlike in English.

(2) **un aperitivo** *a snack* or *an appetizer*; **una tapa** *a tapa*. **un** and **una** are the Spanish equivalents of the indefinite article *a/an*. In Spanish, nouns are classed as either masculine or feminine (even nouns that have nothing to do with biological gender): **un** is used with masculine nouns and **una** with feminine nouns. **tap**a is a feminine noun; **aperitiv**o is a masculine noun. One rule for working out the gender of a Spanish noun is if the word ends in **-o**, it is masculine; if the word ends in **-a**, it is feminine. Of course, as with any rule, there are some exceptions, but not too many. We'll introduce them gradually! Here's the first one: **un día** *a day*.

3 ¡A**quí tie**ne! ③
4 – **Gra**cias. A**diós**.
5 – ¡Eh! Son dos **eu**ros. ④ ☐

*3 ah-**kee tee-ay**-nay 4 grah-thee-ahs. ah-**dee**-os 5 ¡ay! son
dos **ay-oo**-ros*

Notes

③ **¡Aquí tiene!** ('Here, have!') *Here you are!* Note that **tiene**, *he/
she/it has*, is the third-person singular present tense of the verb
tener *to have*. We will come back to this important verb in the
review (lesson 7).

④ **Son dos euros.** *That's* (They-are) *two euros.* **Son**, [*they*] *are*,
is the third-person plural present tense of the verb **ser** *to be*.
Unlike in English, Spanish verbs do not have to be preceded ▸

* * *

Ejercicio 1: Traduzca – Translate

❶ ¡Buenos días! ❷ Una lección. ❸ Por favor.
❹ Gracias. ❺ Adiós.

* * *

Ejercicio 2: Complete – Fill in the missing words
(Each dot corresponds to one letter.)

❶ Translate, please.
Traduzca, Por. favor.

❷ Right away.
Ahora Mismo.

❸ Thank you.
. Gracias

❹ Here you are – one euro.
Aquí tiene Un eu. .

❺ Here you are – a [Spanish] omelette.
Aquí tien. Una tortilla.

3 Here you are *(Here, have)*!
4 – Thank you. Goodbye.
5 – Hey! That's *(They-are)* two euros.

Pronunciation notes

3 The '**u**' in the letter combination **qu** is silent, so this is pronounced like an English *k*, not like 'kwuh'.
4 In most of Spain, the letter **c** before **e** or **i** is pronounced like the English *th* in the word *thing* (in Latin America, it is pronounced like *s*). Otherwise, it is pronounced like the English letter *k*.

by a subject pronoun (*I*, *you*, *he*, *she*, *it*, *we*, *they*) because each verb form has a different ending that gives all the necessary information about who is performing the action. Context and intonation also give clues.

* * *

Answers to Exercise 1 (Translation)

❶ Good morning! ❷ A lesson. ❸ Please. ❹ Thank you. ❺ Goodbye.

* * *

Answers to Exercise 2 (Missing words)

❶ – por favor ❷ Ahora mismo ❸ Gracias ❹ Aquí – un euro ❺ – tiene una –

Everywhere in Spain, **tapas** *are truly an institution. They are small portions of different kinds of dishes served as snacks or appetizers, or even as a meal. Traditionally, they are served with a drink. Most bars and restaurants display what tapas are on offer at the counter. That makes it easy to choose what you want just by pointing, which is handy because the names of tapas can vary from one place to another, and plus, almost every bar has its* **especialidad de la casa** speciality of the house. *If you want a larger portion to share between two or three people, ask for* **una ración**.

Spaniards love to go for tapas (**ir de tapas**), *moving from one bar or café to the next and sampling the different specialities on offer. Traditionally, each person in the group pays for a round.* Enjoy your meal! **¡Buen provecho!**

¡Hola!

1 – ¡**Ho**la! Yo ① soy **Pe**dro.
2 Y tú, ¿**có**mo te **lla**mas? ②
3 – Me **lla**mo ③ **Cla**ra.
4 Soy fran**ce**sa, ¿y ④ tú?
5 – Soy espa**ñol** ⑤, de **Cór**doba.

Pronunciation

***o**-lah* **1** *¡**o**-lah! yo soy **pay**-dro* **2** *ee too ¿**ko**-mo tay **yah**-mahs?* **3** *may **yah**-mo **klah**-rah* **4** *soy frahn-**thay**-sah ¿ee too?* **5** *soy es-pah-**nyol** day **kor**-do-bah*

Pronunciation notes

Remember:
Title The letter **h** is always silent in Spanish.
1 The letter **y**, between vowels or before a vowel, is pronounced like the consonant *y* in the English word *year*.
1, 2 At the end of a word, or on its own, the letter **y** is pronounced like *ee* as in *feel*.

Notes

① Although Spanish verbs do not need to be preceded by the subject pronoun (e.g. **yo** *I*), it can be included for emphasis or contrast: *My name is* ... **Me llamo** …, **Yo me llamo** … *My name is* … Compare lines 1, 2, 3, 4 and 5 in the dialogue.

② You will surely have noticed the inverted question mark (¿) that introduces a question in Spanish. It may look odd, but it is a useful way to indicate that what follows is a question, because questions in Spanish can be formed in exactly the same way as statements. The auxiliary verb *Do/does ...?* used in English to form a question (or a negative statement) is not used in Spanish. More on this later. The inverted exclamation mark, as in line 1, follows the same principle. Topsy-turvy! ▸

Hello!

1 – Hello! I'm Pedro.
2 And you *(informal)?* What's your *(informal)* name *(how yourself you-call)*?
3 – My name is *(Myself I-call)* Clara.
4 [I] am French, and you?
5 – [I] am Spanish, from Cordoba.

2, 3 The double **ll** forms a letter by itself (**elle** *[**ay**-yay]*) that is usually pronounced like the *y* in *year*.
5 The letter **ñ** (**eñe** *[**ayn**-yay]*) is also unique to the Spanish alphabet. This letter sounds like the *ny* in the English word *canyon*. The symbol over the letter **ñ** is called a **tilde** *[**teel**-day]*.

Don't forget, any time you want to review how to pronounce something, just go to the pronunciation section in the introduction for a full explanation!

▸ ③ **me llamo** *[I] am called* ('[I] call myself'), is the first-person present of **llamarse** *to be called*. It consists of the verb **llamar** *to call*, which belongs to the group of verbs ending in **-ar**, plus a reflexive pronoun (in this case, **me**). This is called a reflexive verb, which we'll find out more about later.

④ **y** is a word in Spanish! It means *and*. While we're on the subject of *y*, in certain English–Spanish cognates (words that are related in two different languages because they share the same origin), the Spanish word often has *i* instead of *y*: **sílaba** *syllable*; **física** *physics*; **estilo** *style*, etc. Remember that the *i* is pronounced *[ee]*: *[**see**-lah-bah], [**fee**-see-kah], [es-**tee**-lo]*. English and Spanish share many similar words.

⑤ To say you are English, American or Canadian, for example: **soy inglés** (m.)/**inglesa** (f.), **soy americano** (m.)/**americana** (f.) or **soy canadiense** (m./f.). Note that nationalities and languages are not capitalized in Spanish.

2 **6** ¿Cuál es tu (6) **nú**mero de te**lé**fono (7)?

6 kwahl es too ***noo****-may-ro day tay-****lay****-fo-no*

Notes

(6) **tú**, spelled with an accent (lines 2 and 4), corresponds to *you* when referring to one person (singular) in an informal context (in Spanish, a different form of *you* is needed in plural or formal contexts – more on this later!). Without a written accent, **tu** is the informal possessive adjective *your*.

* * *

Ejercicio 1: Traduzca – Translate

❶ ¡Hola, buenos días! ❷ ¿Cómo te llamas? ❸ ¿Y tú? ❹ Me llamo Pedro. ❺ Yo soy español.

* * *

Ejercicio 2: Complete – Fill in the missing words

❶ Hello!
¡ . . . . !

❷ What's your *(informal)* name?
¿ . . . . te llamas?

❸ My name is Clara.
. . . . Clara.

It's not unusual to hear Spaniards greet strangers with **¡Hola!** *or* **¡Buenos días!** *at a bus stop or in a bar, for example. It's always difficult to generalize, but for the most part Spaniards are easygoing, sociable and friendly, and they make contact easily. Obviously, in the centre of Madrid or Barcelona at* **una hora punta** rush hour, *people are in a hurry to get home or to their jobs, just like in any big city. But if you ask for directions, even under somewhat stressful circumstances, they will almost always take the time to reply, often with a smile.*

As we briefly mentioned, Spanish has a formal and an informal mode of address: traditionally, **usted** you (formal) *is used with*

6 What *(Which)* is your *(informal)* telephone number?

⑦ Note here the phrase **número de teléfono**. In English, two nouns can be placed together (e.g. *telephone number*) when the first is used to describe the second. These so-called compound nouns are not used in Spanish. Instead, the two nouns are linked by the preposition **de** *of*. You have already seen this structure in the first lesson: **tapa de tortilla** *omelette tapa*. This can even be the case with certain compound nouns that in English are combined into one word, e.g. *toothpaste* = **pasta de dientes**, literally, 'paste of teeth'.

* * *

Answers to Exercise 1

❶ Hello, good morning! ❷ What's your name? ❸ And you? ❹ My name is Pedro. ❺ I'm Spanish *(m.)*.

* * *

❹ I'm Australian *(f.)*.
. . . . . . australiana.

❺ What's your *(informal)* telephone number?
¿ . . . . . . tu número de . . . . ?

Answers to Exercise 2

❶ Hola ❷ Cómo – ❸ Me llamo – ❹ Yo soy – ❺ Cuál es – teléfono

those you don't know; however, it is increasingly common in Spain to use **tú** you (informal) *in these situations, especially among young people. Today, ordinarily, the use of* **tú** *does not imply any misplaced familiarity or lack of respect, but we recommend using* **usted** *in circumstances that require politeness, unless the person you are addressing uses* **tú** *first. Note that* **usted** *uses the third-person singular form of the verb:* **¿Cómo se llama?** What's your name? (formal). *In written Spanish,* **usted** *and* **ustedes** *are also often replaced by the abbreviations* **Ud.** *and* **Uds.** *(sometimes written* **Vd.** *and* **Vds.***) respectively.*

3 Lección tercera *[lek-**thee**-on tayr-**thay**-rah]*

¿Qué tal? ①

1 – ¡**Bue**nos **dí**as ②! ¿Qué tal?
2 – Muy ③ bien, ¿y tú?
3 – Yo he dor**mi**do ④ muy bien.
4 – ¿**Quie**res desayu**nar** ⑤?

Want

Pronunciation

kay tahl ***1*** *¡**bway**-nos **dee**-ahs! ¿kay tahl?* ***2*** *moo-ee bee-en ¿ee too?* ***3*** *yo ay dor-**mee**-do moo-ee bee-en* ***4*** ***kee-ay**-rays day-sah-yoo-**nahr***

Pronunciation notes

Pronouncing vowels in another language is often tricky – even more so when there are two or more vowels one after the other! Spanish, like English, has a number of diphthongs, which can be thought of as 'gliding vowels' – the combination of two vowels

Notes

① **¿Qué tal?** *How are you? How's it going?* is a Spanish expression you'll hear everywhere, sometimes preceded by **hola** or **buenos días**. It allows you to make contact in any situation, at home or in the office, with family members or friends, in a shop or with someone you've just met. It has no verb, so it allows you to avoid the dilemma about whether to use **tú** or **usted**!

② The word **días** *days* combines a weak vowel, **i**, with a strong one, **a**. In this case, the spoken accent (stress) falls on the weak vowel, so it needs a written accent. Each vowel is pronounced distinctly rather than blended together.

③ When the letter **y** comes at the end of a word after a vowel, it is equivalent to an **i** and is considered a weak vowel. In diphthongs composed of two weak vowels, the second is dominant. So in the word **muy** *very* (transcribed as *moo-ee),* the diphthong **uy** is blended together and pronounced almost like the English word *we.* ▸

How are you *(What such)*?

1 – Good morning! How are you?
2 – Very well, and you *(informal)*?
3 – I *(have)* slept very well.
4 – [Do you *(informal)*] want to [have] breakfast?

pronounced together. For example, in English the vowel sounds made by *ai*, *aw* and *oy* are diphthongs.

In Spanish, a diphthong is formed by combining a strong vowel, **a**, **e** or **o** (one way to remember the strong vowels is the mnemonic device 'aero', which contains all three) with a weak vowel, **i** or **u**, or even by combining two weak vowels. However, each vowel retains its pronunciation; the weak vowel simply has a slightly less pronounced sound. In our transcriptions, we've used hyphens to separate the sounds to help you pronounce them, but keep in mind that when spoken at a normal speed, they should flow together.

④ **he dormido** *I have slept*, *I slept* is an example of one of the ways to form the past tense in Spanish, using the auxiliary (helping) verb **haber** *to have* + a past participle (what in English is sometimes called the '*-ed* form'). This is the first-person singular present tense: **(yo) he** … *(I) have* … In English there is no distinction between *to have* in its auxiliary or its independent form (in which it means 'to possess'), but in Spanish, two totally different verbs are used for these purposes. More regarding this in the review (lesson 7).

⑤ **quieres** *you* (informal) *want* is the second-person singular present tense of **querer** *to want*. **desayunar** *to have breakfast* is a regular verb belonging to the first group (verbs ending in **-ar**). The verb **ayunar** means *to fast*, so **desayunar** literally means 'to de-fast' or 'to break the fast'. Along the same lines, the noun **el desayuno** means *the breakfast*. Although in English it is rare to use *breakfast* as a verb, in Spanish it's perfectly correct: **(yo) desayuno** *I [have] breakfast*.

5 – **¡Claro!** ⑥

***5 klah**-ro*

Notes

⑥ **¡Claro!** *Of course! Certainly!* is a word used constantly. It can also be used to mean *That's it!* or *You're right!* You'll also hear it in expressions that reinforce the sense of conviction: **¡Claro que sí!** *Absolutely right! Definitely!* Used as an adjective, **claro** means *clear. Is that clear?* **¿Está claro?**

* * *

Ejercicio 1: Traduzca

❶ ¿Qué tal? ❷ ¡Muy bien! ❸ He dormido bien. ❹ ¿Quieres una tapa? ❺ ¡Claro!

* * *

Ejercicio 2: Complete

❶ Very well!
¡ . . . . !

❷ Is that clear?
¿ . . . . . claro?

❸ Of course it is!
¡ . . . . . que sí!

❹ I (have) slept.
. . dormido.

❺ Do you *(informal)* want …?
¿ . . . . ?

5 – Certainly!

* * *

Answers to Exercise 1

❶ How are you? ❷ Very well! ❸ I slept/have slept well. ❹ Do you want a tapa? ❺ Certainly!

* * *

Answers to Exercise 2

❶ Muy bien ❷ Está – ❸ Claro – ❹ He – ❺ Quieres

In these first lessons, we've put a lot of emphasis on pronunciation; we know it takes some getting used to. If you have the recordings, listen to them as often as you can. Repeat each phrase, pronouncing each syllable separately, slowly at first and then gradually speeding up to speak more fluently and naturally. Spanish pronunciation is not too difficult. It just takes a bit of practice!

4 *In Spain, the traditional* **desayuno** *varies from region to region, and in addition many families have their own customs. But one favourite found in* **churrerías** *throughout the country is the famous* **chocolate con churros**, *which consists of a cup of thick hot chocolate accompanied by 'churros' – ridged, cylindrical doughnuts sprinkled with sugar. This sweet breakfast is especially popular on Sundays and holidays. During the week, although*

4 Lección cuarta *[lek-**thee-on kwahr**-tah]*

Una buena idea

1 – La ① a**mi**ga de **A**na ha ② telefone**a**do ③.
2 – ¿Qué que**rí**a?
3 – Invi**tar** a ④ los **ni**ños ⑤ a meren**dar**.

Pronunciation
oo**-nah **bway**-nah ee-**day**-ah* **1** *lah ah-**mee**-gah day **ah**-nah ah tay-lay-fo-nay-**ah**-do* **2** *kay kay-**ree**-ah* **3** *een-bee-**tahr** ah los **nee**-nyos ah may-ren-**dahr

Notes

① **la amiga** *the friend* (fem.); **el desayuno** *the breakfast*. **la** and **el** correspond to the English definite article *the*: **la** is used with feminine nouns and **el** is used with masculine nouns. Note also that in Spanish, possession is shown by using 'of' ('the friend of Ana') – there is no equivalent to apostrophe plus *s*.

② This is another example of the auxiliary verb **haber** *to have*, which is used with a past participle to indicate an action that happened in the past. This form is called the present perfect. We have already seen **he** … *I have* ... Here we have **ha** … *he/she/it has* ... or *you have* ... (formal sing.). Note that in Spanish, this verb form is sometimes used where in English we might use the simple past: for example, *called* rather than *has called*. ▸

desayuno *is often eaten at home, you'll notice that Spaniards love to* **desayunar** *in cafés or bars, either before beginning their workday or for a coffee break between 10:30 and noon, which is truly a national institution. First thing in the morning,* coffee *(***café***) and* fresh-squeezed orange juice *(***zumo de naranja***) are staples, with a croissant or sometimes* a sandwich *(***un bocadillo***).*

Fourth lesson 4

A good idea

1 – Ana's friend *(The friend[f.] of Ana has)* called.
2 – What did she want *(What she-wanted)*?
3 – To invite *(to)* the children over for a snack *(to snack)*.

Pronunciation note

3 Remember: between two vowels or at the end of a word, the **r** has a soft sound, produced by making the tip of the tongue vibrate against the roof of the mouth.

③ To create the past participle (the equivalent of the *-ed* form of a verb that comes after a form of **haber** in the present perfect), verbs ending in **-ar** replace the ending with **-ado**:
telefonear, **ha telefoneado** *to telephone, has telephoned*
llamar, **ha llamado** *to call, has called.*
By the way, you can say either **telefonear** or **llamar por teléfono** *to telephone / to call on the* (by) *phone*.

④ **invitar a los niños** *to invite the children*. When the direct object (the noun that receives the action of the verb in a sentence) is a person, it is usually introduced by the preposition **a** *to*: *I called Ana.* **He llamado a Ana.**

⑤ To form the plural of a noun ending in an unstressed vowel, just add an **-s**: **niño**, **niños** *child, children*; **amiga**, **amigas** *friend, friends* (fem.). It's as easy as that!

4 – ¡Estu**pen**do!
5 Podemos **ir**nos ⑥ al ⑦ **ci**ne. □

***4** es-too-**pen**-do **5** po-**day**-mos **eer**-nos ahl **thee**-nay*

Notes

⑥ **ir** *to go*; **irse** *to go* (oneself), *to go off, to go away, to leave*; **irnos** *to go off* (ourselves). **Irse** is an example of a reflexive verb, which is a verb that reflects its action back on the doer by including a pronoun. With an infinitive (e.g. *to go*), the pronoun is attached after the verb. With a conjugated verb, the pronoun usually comes before the verb: remember **me llamo**? Don't try to memorize everything now; we'll come back to this again later! ▸

* * *

Ejercicio 1 – Traduzca

❶ Clara ha telefoneado. ❷ ¿Qué quieres? ❸ Ir al cine. ❹ Una buena idea. ❺ ¿Y los niños?

* * *

Ejercicio 2: Complete

❶ Do you *(informal)* want to call the children?
¿ . . . . a los niños?

❷ Certainly!
¡ . . . . !

❸ We can have breakfast.
. . . . . . desayunar.

4 – Great!
5 [We] can go to the cinema *(We-can to-go-ourselves to-the cinema)*.

▸ ⑦ **a** + **el** = **al** *to the*. When the preposition **a** *to* is combined with the masculine article **el** *the* it contracts to **al**, which is easier to pronounce. However, this only occurs with the masculine article. If the noun is feminine, the preposition **a** and the feminine article **la** are not contracted: **a la casa** *to the house*.

* * *

Answers to Exercise 1

❶ Clara phoned/has phoned. ❷ What do you want? ❸ To go to the cinema. ❹ A good idea. ❺ And the children?

* * *

❹ Great!
¡ . . . . !

❺ Good idea!
¡ . . . . !

Answers to Exercise 2

❶ Quieres llamar – ❷ Claro ❸ Podemos – ❹ Estupendo ❺ Buena idea

Lección quinta *[lek-thee-on keen-tah]*

¿Adónde ① vas ②?

1 – Per**do**ne ③, ¿**sa**be ④ us**ted** ⑤ **dón**de es**tá** la **ca**lle de la Zar**zue**la?
2 – Sí. Es ⑥ la pri**me**ra a la de**re**cha.
3 – **Gra**cias.
4 – De **na**da.
5 – ¡Ay!

Pronunciation
*ah-**don**-day bahs **1** payr-**do**-nay ¿**sah**-bay oos-**ted** **don**-day es-**tah** lah **kah**-yay day lah thahr-**thway**-lah? **2** see. es lah pree-**may**-rah ah lah day-**ray**-chah **3** **grah**-thee-ahs **4** day **nah**-dah **5** ah-ee*

Notes

① If *where* refers to a verb indicating movement, it is **adonde** or **a donde**. Otherwise, it is simply **donde** (sometimes **en donde**), as in line 1. When used as a question word, it needs a written accent: **¿Dónde está Luis?** *Where is Luis?*

② **vas** *you* (informal) *go* is the second-person singular present tense of **ir** *to go*. Note that in Spanish, the present tense can be used to express something happening now, for which English often uses the present continuous form (*to be* + -ing): so **vas** here means *you are going*.

③ **¡Perdón!** (noun) **¡Perdone!** (verb) *Sorry! Excuse me!* The latter form, used in this dialogue, is the formal command of **perdonar** *to pardon, forgive*. We'll find out more about commands later.

④ **sabe** is the third-person singular present of **saber** *to know*. It means *he/she/it knows* or, as here, *you know* (formal sing.). The third-person singular is used in formal situations, such as this one where the speaker is addressing a stranger. ▶

Where are you going?
(To-where you-go[informal]?)

1 – Excuse me *(Pardon)*. [Do] you *(formal)* know where La Zarzuela street is?
2 – Yes. [It]'s the first on the right.
3 – Thank you.
4 – Don't mention it *(Of nothing)*.
5 – Oh!

Pronunciation notes
Title The Spanish **d** is often pronounced like a lightly spoken *th*, but a **d** at the end of a word is only pronounced very slightly (or sometimes not at all).
1 In most of Spain, the letter **z** is pronounced like the English *th* as in *thing*. In Latin America, it is pronounced like *s*.
2 **ch** is pronounced as in the English word *church*.

▸ (5) **usted** is the singular formal or polite form of *you*. The word **usted** could have been omitted here because the verb in the third-person already indicates the polite form of *you*. Its use simply reinforces the politeness.

In the same way that the third-person singular is used to address one person formally, when addressing more than one person formally, the third-person plural is used, and **usted** *you* becomes **ustedes** *you* (plural).

Note that **tú**, the singular informal *you*, becomes **vosotros** (m.)/**vosotras** (f.) when addressing more than one person informally. This use is restricted to Spain. In other Spanish-speaking countries, **ustedes** is used for all plural forms of *you*.

(6) **es** *he/she/it is* or *you* (formal sing.) *are* is the third-person singular present tense of **ser** *to be*.

6 – ¡Cui**da**do! El se**má**foro es**tá** ⑦ en **ro**jo. □

*6 ¡kwee-**dah**-do! el say-**mah**-fo-ro es-**tah** en **rro**-ho*

Pronunciation notes

6 • r at the beginning of a word is strongly rolled, so we transcribe it as *rr.*

Notes

⑦ **está** *he/she/it is* or *you* (formal sing.) *are* is the third-person singular present tense of **estar** *to be*. Ah, yes! Both **ser** and **estar** mean *to be*. So which to use? Don't worry, as we go along, we'll explain this particularity of the Spanish language. However, if you're in a hurry to know more, go straight to lesson 7!

* * *

Ejercicio 1 – Traduzca

❶ ¡Perdón! ❷ ¿Sabe usted…? ❸ ¿Dónde? ❹ Es aquí. ❺ La primera calle.

* * *

Ejercicio 2: Complete

❶ Where do you *(informal)* want to go?
¿. . . . . quieres . . ?

❷ Excuse me *(formal)*.
. . . . !

❸ Don't mention it.
. . . .

6 – Careful! The traffic light is *(at)* red.

• In Spain, **j** is pronounced as a guttural sound at the back of the throat, similar to the *ch* in the Scottish *loch*. In Latin America, it is pronounced simply as **h**, which is how we transcribe it.

* * *

Answers to Exercise 1

❶ Sorry!/Excuse me! ❷ Do you know...? ❸ Where? ❹ It's here. ❺ The first street.

* * *

❹ He's on the phone.
. . . al . . . .

❺ Careful!
¡ . . . . !

Answers to Exercise 2

❶ Adónde – ir ❷ Perdone ❸ De nada ❹ Está – teléfono ❺ Cuidado

A bit of history: in days gone by, courtesy and good manners required that those of a higher rank be addressed as 'your grace'. In Spain, this era of **hidalgos**, *or* noblemen, *gave rise to the expression* **vuestra merced** *(the literal translation of 'your grace'). If more than one person was addressed, the plural was used:* **vuestras mercedes**. *In the former, the third-person singular form of the verb was used; in the latter, the third-person plural.*

So what remains of this form of courtesy today? Firstly, the girl's name 'Mercedes', also made famous, as chance would have it, by the celebrated make of car. Secondly, in Spanish, the linguistic particularity of employing the third person, singular or plural, for polite address is still used. Lastly, over time the expression itself has through use been simplified to today's pronouns **usted** *and* **ustedes**.

6 Lección sexta *[lek-**thee-on seks**-tah]*

Dos pérdidas

1 – ¡De**pri**sa, el auto**bús** va a sa**lir** ①!
2 – ¿**Tie**nes **suel**to? ②
3 – Sí, es**pe**ra.

Pronunciation

*dos **payr**-dee-dahs **1** day **pree**-sah el ow-to-**boos** bah ah sah-**leer** **2** **tee-ay**-nays **swel**-toh **3** see es-**pay**-rah*

Notes

① **salir** has several meanings: *to leave*, *to go out*, *to set off* are the most common.

Congratulations! You've reached the end of a lesson that covers quite a few important points. We'll come back to them as we go on to help you get to grips with them. You'll see that mastering the language is just a matter of time and repetition. For now, it's enough just to understand the sentences and repeat them aloud. The rest will come before you know it!

Sixth lesson 6

Two losses

1 – Quick, the bus is going to leave!
2 – Do you have any change *(You[informal]-have change)*?
3 – Yes, wait *(informal)*.

El tren sale de la estación de Atocha.
The train leaves from Atocha station.
Hoy vamos a salir. *Today we are going to set off.*

② **dinero suelto** *loose change*. **Tener dinero suelto** (literally, 'to have money loose') is often shortened to **tener suelto** *to have change*, as the word **dinero** *money* is understood.

4 – Yo he olvi**da**do co**ger** ③ el mone**de**ro.
5 – ¡Oh, no! ¡**Ten**go ④ un agu**je**ro en el bol**si**llo!
6 – ¡**Va**ya ⑤, lo ⑥ **he**mos per**di**do ⑦! □

4 *yo ay ol-bee-**dah**-do ko-**hayr** el mo-nay-**day**-ro* ***5*** *¡o no! ¡**ten**-go oon ah-goo-**hay**-ro en el bol-**see**-yo!* ***6*** ***bah**-yah lo **ay**-mos payr-**dee**-do*

Pronunciation notes
Remember:
4 g, before **e** or **i** (as in **coger**), has the same guttural sound as the Spanish **j**. As with **j**, we transcribe it as *h*.
5 Before **a**, **o** or **u** the Spanish **g** has the same sound as in *get*.

Notes

③ **coger** *to get, to pick up, to take*. Note that **cojo** *I get/pick up/take* is spelled with a **j**. This spelling change allows the verb to maintain the same sound. **Cojo el metro.** *I take the metro/underground.* **Coges el autobus.** *You* (informal) *take the bus*. A word of warning: in some Latin American countries, it is better to avoid using **coger** as it has a vulgar meaning. It is replaced by **tomar** (*to take* when referring to means of transportation) or by **agarrar** (in the sense of *to get hold of*).

④ **tengo** *I have*, from **tener** *to have*. Remember that, depending on the context, *to have* can be either **haber** or **tener**. But it's quite simple: **haber** is always an auxiliary verb, e.g.: **he olvidado** *I have forgotten*. The verb **tener** expresses possession: **No tengo dinero.** *I don't have [any] money.* ▸

* * *

Ejercicio 1 – Traduzca

❶ ¡Deprisa! ❷ Coger el metro. ❸ ¡Espera! ❹ Sí, tengo dinero. ❺ He perdido el autobús.

4 – I've forgotten to bring *(take)* my *(the)* wallet.
5 – Oh, no! I have a hole in my *(the)* pocket!
6 – Oh dear, we've missed it *(it[m.] we've lost)*!

HE PERDIDO EL AUTOBÚS.
350

⑤ **¡Vaya!** is often used in the sense of *Oh dear! Oh no!* It is also the formal command of the verb **ir** *to go*: **¡Vaya!** *Go [away]!*

⑥ What's this **lo** doing here? In this sentence it's the direct object *it* (masc.), referring back to the bus. In Spanish, the direct object pronoun usually goes in front of a conjugated verb, not after it, as in English. Just pointing it out – we'll be coming across this again!

⑦ **perder** means both *to lose* and *to miss*: **perder la llave** *to lose the key*; **perder el autobús** *to miss the bus*. So the title of the lesson, **Dos pérdidas**, is a play on words, as both meanings apply to the situation in the dialogue. And remember: **no perder la cabeza** *not to lose your head!*

* * *

Answers to Exercise 1

❶ Quick! ❷ To take the metro. ❸ Wait! ❹ Yes, I have money. ❺ I missed/have missed the bus.

Ejercicio 2: Complete

❶ I don't have [any] change.
No . . . .

❷ I've forgotten the street number *(the number of the street).*
. . . . el número de la . . . . . .

❸ Do you *(informal)* have [any] money?
¿. . . . . ?

❹ Where is the wallet?
¿. . . . . el monedero?

❺ Oh dear!
¡. . . . !

---

7 Lección séptima *[lek-**thee-on sep**-tee-mah]*

Repaso *[rray-**pah**-so]* / Review

This lesson summarizes the main grammatical points you've seen in the six preceding lessons. Don't feel you have to memorize everything; just read the information at your own pace. If you feel the need, you can go back to the relevant lesson before continuing.

It's completely normal to have questions – in fact, it's a good sign. Don't attempt to master everything at once; you've only just started! The most important thing isn't knowing the rules, but being able to express yourself.

1 Pronunciation

Luckily, in Spanish there's no great mystery: all the letters are pronounced (except **h**) and virtually always in the same way. To get the hang of it, separate each syllable and pronounce each vowel clearly.

Answers to Exercise 2
❶ – tengo suelto ❷ He olvidado – calle ❸ Tienes dinero ❹ Dónde está – ❺ Vaya

Each member country of the Eurozone chooses its own designs for its national coins. For the first issue of its coins, Spain featured the head of King Juan Carlos I for the 1 and 2 euro **monedas** coins, *the portrait of Miguel de Cervantes, the father of Spanish literature, for the 10, 20 and 50 cent coins, and the Santiago de Compostela Cathedral, a jewel of Baroque architecture and one of the world's most famous pilgrimage sites, for the 1, 2 and 5 cent copper-coloured* **monedas**.

¿Qué tal? *You are already beginning to establish a good base in Spanish. To consolidate what you've learned, lesson 7 will provide a general review of some of the main points. See you soon!*

Seventh lesson 7

To review the pronunciation rules, go back to the introduction at the beginning of the book and read through the section on pronunciation again. Practice by repeating the examples aloud.

2 Accent placement

There are two kinds of accents in Spanish: spoken accent (where the stress is placed in a word – that is, which syllable is emphasized) and written accent.

• Spoken accent: In the dialogues and phonetic transcriptions, we indicate in **bold** where the word should be stressed when speaking.

• Written accent: An accent can be used with any of the five Spanish vowels: **está** *is*; **teléfono** *telephone*; **aquí** *here*; **adiós** *goodbye*; **tú** *you* (informal).

When a vowel has a written accent, this is the syllable that should be stressed. We'll come back to this again later. (In the fill-in-the-missing-word exercises in each lesson, don't forget to include the written accent if one is required.)

3 Grammatical gender

Like all languages of Latin origin (and many other languages), all Spanish nouns have a gender. Apart from certain words such as *he/she*, *his/her* or *actress/actor*, in English we don't need to think much about gender. In contrast, in Spanish, the gender of a noun, either masculine or feminine, makes a difference to some of the other words used in the sentence: for example, the articles, as mentioned below, as well as other words.

For the time being, it's enough to keep this major difference in mind. One fairly easy rule to remember is that Spanish nouns ending in **-o** are generally masculine, while those ending in **-a** are generally feminine: **el desayuno** *the breakfast*; **la merienda** *the snack*. So far you've seen only one exception to this rule: **el día** *the day*.

4 Articles ('the', 'a', 'an')

4.1 Definite articles

Spanish is more complicated than English when it comes to the word *the* …

• With singular masculine nouns, the definite article is **el**, and with singular feminine nouns it is **la**: **el día** (masc.) *the day*; **la tortilla** (fem.) *the Spanish omelette*.

• With plural nouns, the definite articles are **los** (masc.) and **las** (fem.): **los niños** *the children*; **las calles** *the streets*.

4.2 Indefinite articles

• The Spanish words for *a/an* are **un** (with a masculine noun) and **una** (with a feminine noun): **un euro** *a euro*; **una española** *a Spanish woman*.

• The equivalents of the indefinite article *some* are **unos** (masc.) and **unas** (fem.).

5 Forming the plural

As a general rule, to make a word plural:

• add the letter **-s** to words that end in a vowel:

número *number* → **números**

• add **-es** to words ending in a consonant:
lección *lesson* → **lecciones**.

6 Forming questions

In English, we use the helping verb *do/does* to form questions. Spanish does not – to form a question, you simply invert the subject and the verb, introducing the question with the upside-down question mark: **¿Sabe usted?** *Do you know?* literally, 'Know you?' Or you can simply turn a statement into a question by changing the intonation, without changing the word order: **¿Roberto vive en Barcelona?** *Does Roberto live in Barcelona?*

7 Conjugating verbs ar: ado ir = ido
er = ido

Spanish has three groups of verbs that each conjugate a bit differently: verbs ending in **-ar**, verbs ending in **-er** and verbs ending in **-ir**.
• The past participle (i.e. the *-ed* form used with the verb *to have* in English) of verbs of the first group ends in **-ado**: **llamar** → **llamado** *to call* → *called*. The good news is that there are no exceptions in this group!
• The past participle of verbs of the second and third group ends in **-ido**: **tener** → **tenido** *to have* → *had*; **dormir** → **dormido** *to sleep* → *slept*. We will introduce the exceptions gradually.

Remember that the subject pronoun is often not included in Spanish when conjugating the verb: **Tengo** *[I] have.*

8 *Haber* ('to have ...') and *tener* ('to have')

• The auxiliary (helping) verb **haber** is used with a past participle to form compound tenses, just like the English verb *to have ...* **Haber** usually has no meaning on its own; it is almost always used with another verb. (Note: in Spanish, the present perfect is sometimes used where in English we might use the simple past, so we've indicated both meanings.)
He desayunado. *I ate/have eaten breakfast.*
Pedro no ha llamado. *Pedro did not call/has not called.*
Ana ha ido al cine. *Ana went/has gone to the cinema.*

7 Present tense of the auxiliary verb **haber**:

yo	**he** …	*I have* …
tú	**has** …	*you have* … (informal sing.)
él, ella **usted**	**ha** …	*he/she/it has* … *you have* … (formal sing.)
nosotros, nosotras	**hemos** …	*we have* … (m., f.)
vosotros, vosotras	**habéis** …	*you have* … (informal plural) (m., f.)
ellos, ellas **ustedes**	**han** …	*they have* … (m., f.) *you have* … (formal plural)

• The verb **tener** expresses the idea of possession:
Tengo dinero. *I have money.*
No tengo tu número de teléfono. *I don't have your phone number.*

Present tense of the verb **tener**:

yo	**tengo**	*I have*
tú	**tienes**	*you have* (informal sing.)
él, ella **usted**	**tiene**	*he/she/it has* *you have* (formal sing.)
nosotros, nosotras	**tenemos**	*we have* (m., f.)
vosotros, vosotras	**tenéis**	*you have* (informal plural) (m., f.)
ellos, ellas **ustedes**	**tienen**	*they have* (m., f.) *you have* (formal plural)

9 *Ser* and *estar* ('to be')

• **ser** is used to describe essential, inherent characteristics that are independent of the immediate circumstances of the subject.
Soy español. *I am Spanish.*
Es un niño. *He's a child.*
Ella es muy simpática. *She is very nice.*

Present tense of the verb **ser**:

yo	**soy**	*I am*
tú	**eres**	*you are* (informal sing.)
él, ella **usted**	**es**	*he/she/it is* *you are* (formal sing.)
nosotros, nosotras	**somos**	*we are* (m., f.)
vosotros, vosotras	**sois**	*you are* (informal plural) (m., f.)
ellos, ellas **ustedes**	**son**	*they are* (m., f.) *you are* (formal plural)

• **estar** is used to describe a state or condition of something in time or space; that is, things bound by circumstances – the moment, the place, the physical or emotional state, etc.:
¿Dónde están los niños? *Where are the children?*
Están en el cine. *They are at the cinema.*
El dinero está en el monedero. *The money is in the wallet.*
Estamos en huelga. *We are on strike.*
Estoy cansado. *I am tired.*

Here's a tip: if *to be* expresses location, **estar** is always used. (Exception: if *to be* can be replaced by *to take place*, **ser** is used.)
Where is the telephone? (i.e. where is it located)
¿Dónde está el teléfono?
Where is the party? (i.e. where is it being held, taking place)
¿Dónde es la fiesta?

Present tense of the verb **estar**:

yo	**estoy**	*I am*
tú	**estás**	*you are* (informal sing.)
él, ella **usted**	**está**	*he/she/it is* *you are* (formal sing.)
nosotros, nosotras	**estamos**	*we are* (m., f.)
vosotros, vosotras	**estáis**	*you are* (informal plural) (m., f.)
ellos, ellas **ustedes**	**están**	*they are* (m., f.) *you are* (formal plural)

7 Diálogo recapitulativo / Review dialogue

Here is a review dialogue that goes over some of the main things you've seen in the previous six lessons.

If you have the recordings, just listen to each line and repeat it. Reading aloud is vital for practicing the pronunciation. You'll be surprised at your progress and your ability to remember!

1 – ¡Hola!
2 – Buenos días. ¿Qué tal?
3 – Bien, gracias. ¿Y tú?
4 – Muy bien.
5 – ¿Quieres ir al cine?
6 – ¡Estupendo! Es una buena idea.
7 – Podemos invitar a Pedro.
8 – ¡Claro!
9 – Aquí tengo su número de teléfono.
10 – ¿Sabes? ¡He olvidado coger dinero!

Traducción / Translation

1 Hello! **2** Good morning. How are you? **3** Fine, thank you. And you? **4** Very well. **5** Do you want to go to the cinema? **6** Great! It's a good idea. **7** We can invite Pedro. **8** Of course! **9** I have his telephone number here. **10** You know [what]? I've forgotten to bring [any] money!

You've now completed the first seven lessons, and hopefully the basics are already beginning to fall into place. Great work!

8 Lección octava *[lek-**thee-on** ok-**tah**-bah]*

Después del ① teatro

1 – ¿Qué has **he**cho hoy?
2 – He **i**do ② al te**a**tro.
3 – ¿Y qué tal ③ la **o**bra?
4 – El pri**mer** ④ **ac**to **e**ra ⑤ ma**lí**simo ⑥.
5 – ¿Y el se**gun**do?
6 – Toda**ví**a ⑦ pe**or**.

Pronunciation
*days-**pways** del tay-**ah**-tro **1** kay ahs **ay**-cho oy **2** ay **ee**-do ahl tay-**ah**-tro **3** ee kay tahl lah **o**-brah **4** el pree-**mayr ahk**-to **ay**-rah mah-**lee**-see-mo **5** ee el say-**goon**-do **6** to-dah-**bee**-ah pay-**or***

Notes

① **de + el = del**. The phrase **después de** means *after*. If the following noun is masculine, the masculine article before the noun contracts with **de** to form **del**: **después del teatro** *after the theatre*. However, if the noun is feminine, the feminine article before the noun is not contracted: **después de la cena** *after the dinner*. Compare this with the similar construction **a + el = al**: **He ido al teatro** (line 2), which you first saw in lesson 4.

② **he ido** *I went/have gone*. As we have noted, the present perfect is formed with the auxiliary verb **haber** *to have* ... followed by the past participle. Remember that this tense sometimes translates into the English simple past tense:
¿Qué has hecho? *What did you do/have you done?*
He ido al teatro. *I went/have been to the theatre.*

③ In colloquial speech, when the expression **¿Qué tal?** *How are you?* or *How's it going?* is followed by a noun, the verb often remains understood:
¿Y qué tal (ha estado) la obra? *And how (was) the play?*
¿Qué tal (va) tu trabajo? *How (is) your job (going)?*

After the theatre

1 – What did you *(informal)* do today?
2 – [I] went to the theatre.
3 – And how was the play?
4 – The first act was very bad.
5 – And the second?
6 – Even worse.

DESPUÉS DEL PRIMER ACTO

④ The word **primero** *first*, just like **uno** *a*, *one*, loses its final **o** before a masculine singular noun. This is called 'apocope' (see the section on this subject in review lesson 14).
Es el número uno. *It's the number one.*
but **un aperitivo** *a snack.*
Eres el primero. *You are the first.*
but **el primer acto** *the first act.*

⑤ This is the past (imperfect) tense of **ser** *to be*. This verb tense will be discussed later, but note that this is an irregular form.

⑥ **malo** *bad*; **malísimo** *very bad.*
Adding the suffix **-ísimo**, **-ísima** to the end of an adjective intensifies, or emphasizes, it. In English, this idea is usually translated by the adverb *very*, **muy**. Note that we can just as easily say **muy malo** *very bad.* Or on a more positive note: **una salsa muy buena** or **buenísima** *a very good sauce.*

⑦ **todavía** – this useful word translates variously into English as *even*, *still* or *yet*, depending on the context.

Ejercicio 1 – Traduzca

❶ ¿Qué has hecho aquí? ❷ He hecho un agujero. ❸ Después del primer acto. ❹ Era una idea muy buena. ❺ Ana no ha llamado todavía.

* * *

Ejercicio 2: Complete

❶ She went/has gone to the cinema.
. . . . . al . . . . . .

❷ Do you *(informal)* want to take the bus?
¿. . . . . autobús?

❸ We went for a snack.
. . . . a merendar.

---

9 Lección novena *[lek-**thee-on** no-**bay**-nah]*

No hay que confundir la velocidad con el tocino ①

1 Un re**cién** ② ca**sa**do **vuel**ve ③ son**rien**te del ④ tra**ba**jo:

Pronunciation
*no a-ee kay kon-foon-**deer** lah bay-lo-thee-**dah**d kon el to-**thee**-no **1** oon rray-**thee-en** kah-**sah**-do **bwayl**-bay son-**rree-en**-tay del trah-**bah**-ho*

Notes

① The expression **confundir la velocidad con el tocino** (literally, 'to confuse speed with bacon') is perhaps best translated by *to compare apples and oranges*.
no hay que → *one must not*: more about this soon. ▸

Answers to Exercise 1

❶ What have you done here? ❷ I made/have made a hole. ❸ After the first act. ❹ It was a very good idea. ❺ Ana has not called yet.

* * *

❹ After the snack, we came here.

. . . . merienda . . . . . venido aquí.

❺ We came by bus.

. . . . autobús.

Answers to Exercise 2

❶ Ha ido – cine ❷ Quieres coger el – ❸ Hemos ido – ❹ Después de la – hemos – ❺ Hemos venido en –

Ninth lesson 9

You mustn't compare apples and oranges

1 A newly *(recently)* married [man] comes home from work smiling *(returns smiling from-the work)*:

② **recientemente** *recently* becomes **recién** before a past participle. It is most often translated by *newly* or *new*:
los recién casados *the newlyweds*
un recién nacido *a newborn.*

③ **vuelve** *he/she/it returns* or *you return* (formal sing.), from **volver**, here means *comes home*. This is a verb that you will come across quite frequently! Note the change in the verb stem from **o** to **ue**. We will see other stem-changing verbs soon.

④ As we've seen, the preposition **de** followed by the masculine singular article **el** contracts to **del**: **Vengo del cine.** *I'm coming from the cinema.* This very common preposition can mean either *of* or *from.*

2 – ¡Da **gus**to ⑤ **ver**te vol**ver** con**ten**to del tra**ba**jo!
3 Te **gus**ta ⑥ **mu**cho tu tra**ba**jo, ¿ver**dad**? ⑦
4 – ¡Mi a**mor**, por fa**vor**!
5 ¡No con**fun**das la **i**da ⑧ con la **vuel**ta! □

***2** dah **goo**-sto **bayr**-tay bol-**bayr** kon-**tayn**-to del trah-**bah**-ho **3** tay **goo**-stah **moo**-cho too trah-**bah**-ho ¿bayr-**dad**? **4** mee ah-**mor** por fah-**bor** **5** no kon-**foon**-dahs lah **ee**-dah kon lah **bwayl**-tah*

Notes

⑤ **da gusto** (literally, 'gives pleasure') is translated by *it's nice, it's a pleasure.* **Gusto** is a much-used noun that is also often used in the sense of *taste* – for example, **tener buen gusto** *to have good taste.*

⑥ **te gusta** *you like, it pleases you, it appeals to you.* The most natural-sounding equivalent of **gustar** in English is *to like*, but 'to please', 'to appeal to' is the more direct translation, and helps to explain why the verb does not conjugate according to the person speaking, but according to the object being spoken about. Because of this, **gustar** normally has only two present-tense endings: singular or plural. If you're referring to just one thing, use **gusta**; however, if you're referring to more than one thing, the verb needs to agree with the plural noun and becomes **gustan**:
Me gusta tu proyecto. *I like your plan.*
('Your plan appeals to me.')
Me gustan tus proyectos. *I like your plans.*
('Your plans appeal to me.')

⑦ **la verdad** *the truth.* **Es verdad.** *It's true.*
The expression **¿Verdad?** means *Right?* However, it is often translated into English by what is called a 'tag'. In this example, ▸

* * *

Ejercicio 1 – Traduzca

❶ Estoy muy contenta. ❷ María vuelve en autobús. ❸ ¿Es verdad? ❹ ¡No confundas! ❺ ¿Te gusta el teatro?

2 – It's nice *(Gives pleasure)* to see you *(informal)* come home *(return)* happy from work!
3 You like your job a lot *(To-you[informal] it-appeals much your job)*, don't you *(true)*?
4 – My love, please!
5 Don't confuse *(informal) (the)* going with *(the)* returning!

the 'tag' would be *don't you?* You needn't worry about this right now; we'll remind you when it comes up again. English tags depend on the verb used in the sentence, but Spanish simply uses **¿Verdad?** or **¿Sí?** or **¿No?**
Vuelves en un momento, ¿no?
You're coming back in a moment, aren't you?
Vuelves en un momento, ¿verdad?
You're coming back in a moment, right?

⑧ **ida** (literally, 'gone') comes from the verb **ir** *to go*, but is used here as a noun. **ida y vuelta** [the] *going and* [the] *returning* (This also means *return ticket* – e.g. for a train.) Also, **idas y venidas** *comings and goings*. Note that the Spanish expression is back-to-front!

* * *

Answers to Exercise 1

❶ I'm very happy *(f.)*. ❷ María is returning by bus. ❸ Is it true? ❹ Don't confuse [things]! ❺ Do you like the theatre?

Ejercicio 2: Complete

❶ You *(informal)* like your job, right?
.. .. tu ...., ¿.......?

❷ He is very happy!
¡Está ... .!

❸ I like Seville a lot.
Sevilla .. ..

10 Lección décima *[lek-**thee-on day**-thee-mah]*

Una cita ①

1 – ¿Nos **ve**mos ② **es**te fin de se**ma**na?

Pronunciation
__oo__-nah __thee__-tah 1 nos __bay__-mos __es__-tay feen day say-__mah__-nah

Notes

① **una cita** *a date*, *meeting*, *appointment*. Although commonly used, **cita** often has a formal connotation. **Tengo cita con la maestra de mi hija.** *I have a meeting with my daughter's teacher*. Between friends it is more frequent to use **quedar** *to meet* or *to arrange to meet* (but see note 3). For a doctor's appointment, Spaniards say **coger cita** or **tomar cita** (literally, 'to take date').
He tomado cita con el médico. *I have an appointment with the doctor*. ('I have taken date with the doctor.')
He quedado con mis amigos. *I'm meeting my friends*. ('I have arranged to meet with my friends.')

② Here we have another reflexive verb, **verse** (remember **llamarse** in lesson 2?), and some explanation is now necessary to avoid confusion. Reflexive verbs are used in several ways in ▸

❹ She's a friend of the newlyweds.
Es una . . . . . de los . . . .

❺ Do you *(informal)* like it?
¿. . . . . . . ?

Answers to Exercise 2
❶ Te gusta – trabajo – verdad ❷ – muy contento ❸ – me gusta mucho ❹ – amiga – recién casados ❺ Te gusta

Tenth lesson 10

A meeting

1 – [Will] we see each other *(Us we-see)* this weekend *(end of week)*?

Spanish, and the current case differs from that of **llamarse** *to be called, to call oneself.* The reflexive can be used to indicate: a) *myself, yourself, himself, oneself,* etc: **Yo me lavo.** *I wash myself.* b) the passive voice: **Yo me llamo Pedro.** *I am called Pedro.* c) or reciprocity, that is, *each other*: **nos vemos** *we [will] see each other* (or in colloquial English, *I'll see you)*; **nos llamamos** *we [will] call/ring each other.* (Note also in both these examples the use of the present tense to express the future.)

2 – Po**de**mos que**dar** ③ **pa**ra el ④ **sá**bado por la **no**che ⑤.
3 – ¿A qué **ho**ra que**da**mos?
4 – ¿Te pa**re**ce bien a la **ho**ra de **siem**pre?
5 – ¡**Va**le! ⑥
6 – De **to**das **for**mas, nos lla**ma**mos.
7 – ¡De a**cuer**do! □

2 *po-****day****-mos kay-****dahr pah****-rah el* ***sah****-bah-do por lah* ***no****-chay* ***3*** *ah kay* ***o****-rah kay-****dah****-mos* ***4*** *tay pah-****ray****-thay bee-en*

Notes

③ **quedar** has many different meanings. In its reflexive form, **quedarse**, the commonest meaning is *to stay, remain*. When not reflexive, it can mean *to be left*: **¿Cuánto tiempo nos queda para llegar?** *How long do we have before we arrive?* ('How much time is left for us to arrive?'). In colloquial language, **quedar**, sometimes followed by **para** *for*, means *to arrange to meet*, *to meet* or simply *to see each other*: **Hemos quedado para el lunes.** *We've arranged to meet on Monday* or *We're meeting on Monday.*

④ In Spanish, when talking about a specific day of the week, the definite article is needed: **el sábado pasado** *last Saturday.* Note also that lower case is used for the days of the week and the months of the year. ▸

* * *

Ejercicio 1: Traduzca

❶ Este fin de semana he ido al cine. ❷ He quedado con mi amigo. ❸ Te llamo después del teatro. ❹ ¿Te parece bien? ❺ Nos llamamos por la tarde.

2 – We can arrange to meet *(for the)* Saturday *(during the)* night.
3 – At what time [will] we meet?
4 – Is the usual time OK with you *(To-you[inf.] seems good at the hour of always)*?
5 – Okay!
6 – Anyway *(Of all forms)*, we'll call each other *(us we-call)*.
7 – Agreed *(Of agreement)*!

*ah lah **o**-rah day **see-em**-pray **5 bah**-lay **6** day **to**-dahs **for**-mahs nos yah-**mah**-mos **7** day ah-**kwayr**-do*

⑤ Spanish sometimes uses prepositions where English omits them. Note also that the preposition **por** is used with the three standard divisions of the day: **por la mañana** *in the morning*; **por la tarde** *in the afternoon* and **por la noche** *in the evening* or *at night*.

Be very careful with the word **mañana** (with no preceding article), which means *tomorrow*, as opposed to **la mañana** *the morning*. For example: **Nos vemos mañana por la mañana.** *I'll see you tomorrow morning.*

⑥ **¡Vale!** ('It is worth') is a colloquial expression meaning *Okay!* **De acuerdo** means *Agreed!* or *All right!*

* * *

Answers to Exercise 1

❶ This weekend I went to the cinema. ❷ I'm meeting *(I've arranged to meet with)* my friend. ❸ I'll call you after the theatre. ❹ Is that okay with *(Does that seem good to)* you? ❺ Let's call each other in the afternoon.

Ejercicio 2: Complete

❶ At what time did he/she call?
¿. ... . ha llamado?

❷ At the usual time.
. .. . de ....

❸ Anyway, it's a good idea.
.. .., es una buena ..... .

❹ I agree.
Estoy .. ..

❺ Do you *(informal)* have change?
¿Tienes .... ?

---

11 Lección once *[lek-**thee-on on**-thay]*

Cuestión ① de apreciación o ... todo es relativo

1 – ¡He per**di**do el ② tren!
2 – ¡Qué **ma**la **pa**ta! ③

Pronunciation
*kways-**tee-on** day ah-pray-thee-ah-**thee-on** o ... **to**-do es rray-lah-**tee**-bo **1** ay payr-**dee**-do el tren **2** kay **mah**-lah **pah**-tah*

Notes

① We should note that *question* in the interrogative sense is **(la) pregunta**. For example: **hacer una pregunta** *to ask* ('to make') *a question*. The *question* in this title is in the sense of *matter*, *issue* or *problem* and can be translated by **(la) cuestión**, **(el) asunto**, **(el) tema** or **(el) problema**:
Es cuestión de vida o muerte. *It's a question of life or death.* ▸

Answers to Exercise 2

❶ A qué hora – ❷ A la hora – siempre ❸ De todas formas – idea ❹ – de acuerdo ❺ – dinero suelto

* * *

In Spain, **la tarde** the afternoon, *begins after the midday meal, around 2:00 or 3:00 pm, and basically continues until sunset. However,* **la tarde** *can continue into what for us is considered evening. If you meet someone at 7:00 or 8:00 pm, it's quite normal to be greeted with* **¡Buenas tardes!**, *which can mean* Good afternoon! *or* Good evening! *according to the context. If it is later at night, use* **la noche**, *which can be translated by* the night *or* the evening. **¡Buenas noches!** *means* Good evening! *when it is a greeting, but* Good night! *when you are saying goodbye at the end of the night.*

¡Hasta mañana! See you tomorrow!

Lesson eleven 11

A question of appreciation or … everything is relative

1 – I missed my *(the)* train!
2 – What bad luck! *(What bad foot!)*

② In Spanish, the possessive adjective (e.g. *my*, *your*, etc.) is used much less than in English; if the context allows the possessor to be identified, it's usually replaced by the article.
He olvidado la cartera. *I've forgotten my* (the) *wallet.*

③ **pata** means *leg* (referring to an animal or furniture) or *paw*, but it also occurs in many colloquial expressions.
tener mala pata *to have bad luck*
¡Mala pata! *Tough luck!*

3 – Lo he per**di**do por **po**co ④.
4 ¡Por un mi**nu**to!
5 – ¡Ah, **bue**no! ¡No es tan ⑤ **gra**ve!
6 Con la **ca**ra ⑥ que has **pues**to…
7 ¡cre**í**a que lo ha**bí**as ⑦ per**di**do por **u**na **ho**ra!

__3__ lo ay payr-__dee__-do por __po__-ko __4__ por oon mee-__noo__-to __5__ ¡ah __bway__-no…! ¡no es tahn __grah__-bay! __6__ kon lah __kah__-rah kay ahs __pways__-to __7__ kray-__ee__-ah kay lo ah-__bee__-ahs payr-__dee__-do por __oo__-nah __o__-rah

Notes

④ **por poco** *by [a] little*, *only just*. But the placement of this phrase can change the meaning … before a verb, **por poco** often means *almost*, *nearly*: **Por poco pierdo el tren.** *I almost missed the train*. Note that the present tense tends to be used with this expression, even to refer to an action in the past (although in line 3, the past tense is used).

⑤ The adverb **tanto** *so*, *so much* changes to **tan** before an adjective or adverb. **Estoy tan contento.** *I am so happy*. (More on this in review lesson 14.)

⑥ **la cara** *the face*. Expressions using this word include: **Tienes buena cara.** *You look well*. And **poner buena cara** *to put on a brave face* or, just the opposite, **poner mala cara** *to balk [at something]*.

* * *

Ejercicio 1: Traduzca

❶ He perdido la cartera. ❷ ¡Mala pata! ❸ Todo es relativo. ❹ Tienes muy buena cara. ❺ ¿Quieres hacer una pregunta?

3 – I just missed it *(It I-have missed by little).*
4 By one minute!
5 – Oh well! That's not so bad!
6 From the look on your face *(With the face that you-have put)…*
7 I thought that you had missed it by an hour!

⑦ We draw your attention to **creía** *I thought* and **lo habías perdido** *you had missed it.* The verbs **creer** and **haber** here are in the imperfect tense, which is a tense used to describe things that happened in the past. We'll find out more about this tense soon (see also **quería** in lesson 12, exercise 2). For the time being, just note that these are the typical imperfect tense endings of **-er** verbs. Also notice the position of the direct object pronoun **lo** *it* (i.e. the train). As we have already mentioned, Spanish generally places object pronouns in front of the conjugated verb.

* * *

Answers to Exercise 1

❶ I've lost my wallet. ❷ Bad luck!/That's unlucky! ❸ Everything is relative. ❹ You look very well. ❺ Do you want to ask a question?

Ejercicio 2: Complete

❶ What's the problem?
¿. . . . es . . . .?

❷ Good question!
¡. . . . .!

❸ Do you *(informal)* have a minute?
¿Tienes . . . .?

❹ We've lost an hour.
. . . . una . . . . . .

❺ It's not so bad!
¡No es . . . .!

---

12 Lección doce *[lek-**thee-on do**-thay]*

Proyectos de futuro ①

1 – **Pa**ra ② ca**sar**me ③ yo nece**si**to encon**trar** un **hom**bre

Pronunciation
*pro-**yek**-tos day foo-**too**-ro **1 pah**-rah kah-**sahr**-may yo nay-thay-**see**-to en-kon-**trahr** oon **om**-bray*

Notes

① This is another example of how a noun phrase in English, e.g. *future plans*, must be constructed in Spanish with **de** *of*. Look at the notes on this in lesson 7 if you need a reminder.

② The use of prepositions varies greatly from one language to another – despite being short words, they can be the hardest to get right! You can master which one to use in which context only through practice. Let's start with **para** and **por**.
para *for the purpose of, in order to* (a future purpose)
por *for the sake of, because of* (a preceding cause) ▸

Answers to Exercise 2
❶ Cuál – el problema ❷ Buena pregunta ❸ – un minuto ❹ Hemos perdido – hora ❺ – tan grave

You may have noticed that we have changed the lesson numbers from ordinal numbers to cardinal numbers. We'll explain the reason for this change later when we look at numbers in more detail (in lesson 21). For the time being, just take note and don't forget to read and repeat the names of the numbers on each page. That way, you'll have a good idea of how to count in Spanish before we get there!

Lesson twelve 12

Future plans *(Projects of future)*

1 – To marry *(For to-marry-me)*, I need to find a man [who is]

▸ **Para coger el autobús necesito dinero.**
In order to take the bus I need money.
Lo he hecho por ella. *I did it for her.* (i.e. for her sake)

③ **casarse** *to marry, to get married* is another example of a reflexive verb, used to indicate that the action of the verb is happening to the subject. In line 1, the reflexive pronoun is **me** *me, myself* as the woman is referring to herself: **para casarme**, 'in order for me to get married'. As we've already briefly mentioned, with an infinitive, the pronoun is attached to the end of the verb. (Otherwise pronouns in Spanish usually come before the conjugated verb.) If a couple says they are getting married, the pronoun changes to **nos** *us, ourselves*:
Vamos a casarnos. *We are going to get married.*
Nos casamos. *We're getting married.*

2 **bue**no, **gua**po, **ri**co y **ton**to.
3 – ¿Y por qué **tie**ne que ④ ser **ton**to?
4 – **Por**que ⑤ si no es **bue**no, **gua**po y **ri**co,
5 yo no me casa**ré** con él;
6 y si no es **ton**to,
7 es él quien no se casa**rá** ⑥ con**mi**go ⑦. □

***2 bway**-no **gwah**-po **rree**-ko ee **ton**-to **3** ee por kay **tee-ay**-nay kay sayr **ton**-to **4 por**-kay see no es **bway**-no **gwah**-po ee **rree**-ko **5** yo no may kah-sah-**ray** kon el **6** ee see no es **ton**-to **7** es el kee-en no say kah-sah-**rah** kon-**mee**-go*

Notes

④ **tengo que** *I have to*; **tienes que** *you* (informal) *have to*; **tiene que** *he/she/it you* (formal) *has/have to*, etc. To form the equivalent of *to have to*, in the sense of an obligation, **tener** *to have* is followed by **que** + an infinitive.
tengo que llamar *I have to call*
tiene que trabajar *he/she has to work.*

⑤ **¿por qué?** *why*, literally, 'for what?' (line 3), but **porque**, one word with no written accent, *because* (line 4).
¿Por qué no nos vemos mañana?
Why don't we see each other tomorrow?
Porque tengo que trabajar. *Because I have to work.*

⑥ **se casará** is an example of the future tense (third-person singular) of **casarse**. For the time being, simply note this typical future tense ending; in most cases the ending is simply ▸

* * *

Ejercicio 1: Traduzca

❶ ¿Cuál es tu proyecto? ❷ Vamos a casarnos. ❸ Necesito verte. ❹ ¿Pedro ha ido contigo? ❺ De todas formas, te llamo.

2 good, handsome, rich and stupid.
3 – And why does he have to be stupid?
4 – Because if he isn't good, handsome and rich
5 I won't marry *(with)* him;
6 and if he isn't stupid,
7 he is the one *(it-is he)* who won't marry *(with-)* me.

added to the infinitive. We've already seen another way of forming the future, using **ir** *to go*: **él va a casarse conmigo** *he is going to get married to me.* Note also the use here of one of those tricky prepositions: in Spanish, you get married *with* (**con**) someone, not *to* someone.

⑦ **conmigo** *with me*; **contigo** *with you.* Note that the pronoun in this case is attached to the preposition. We'll talk about prepositional pronouns in more detail in review lesson 14.
Ha desayunado conmigo. *He/she had breakfast with me.*
Estoy contigo. *I am with you.*

* * *

Answers to Exercise 1

❶ What is your plan? ❷ We're going to get married. ❸ I need to see you. ❹ Has Pedro gone with you? ❺ Anyway, I'll call you.

Ejercicio 2: Complete

❶ Your *(informal)* friend is very handsome.
.. amigo .. ..

❷ She's not stupid.
.. ..

❸ He has [a] future.
....

13 Lección trece *[lek-**thee-on tray**-thay]*

Hombre precavido vale por dos

1 – Una ra**ción** de **se**tas ①, por fa**vor**.
2 – ¿Una ra**ción** de **se**tas?
3 ¡Es**tá** bien ②, **pe**ro ense**gui**da ③ le **trai**go ④ la **cuen**ta ⑤!

Pronunciation
***om**-bray pray-kah-**bee**-do **bah**-lay por dos **1 oo**-nah rrah-**thee-on** day **say**-tahs por fah-**bor** **2 oo**-nah rrah-**thee-on** day **say**-tahs **3** es-**tah** bee-en **pay**-ro en-say-**ghee**-dah lay **trah-ee**-go lah **kwen**-tah*

Notes

① **las setas** *wild mushrooms*, although **los champiñónes** is commonly used to refer to mushrooms that aren't wild. No one wants to eat **una seta venenosa** *a poisonous mushroom*. Note in line 5 the reference to **las setas** – in Spanish, the definite article is often used to refer to things generally in contexts where in English the article is left out. We see another example of this later in the same line: **las cosas**.

② **¡Está bien!** ('It's fine!') is often used to mean *All right! Agreed! That's fine!*

❹ Why have you *(informal)* done it today?
¿... ... lo has ....?

❺ Because I wanted to go to the cinema.
...... quería .. al ..... .

Answers to Exercise 2
❶ Tu – es muy guapo ❷ No es tonta ❸ Tiene futuro ❹ Por qué – hecho hoy ❺ Porque – ir – cine

---

Lesson thirteen 13

Forewarned is forearmed
(Man warned is-worth for two)

1 – A serving *(portion)* of [wild] mushrooms, please.
2 – A serving of mushrooms?
3 Very well, but I'll bring you the bill immediately *(but immediately to-you[formal] I-bring the bill)*!

③ **enseguida** or **en seguida** *immediately* has the same meaning as **ahora mismo** *right now* (see lesson 1).

④ **le traigo** 'to you I bring' *I'll bring you* – **le** is a third-person indirect object pronoun that here refers to *you* (formal). Don't forget, the object pronoun goes before the conjugated verb. This is also an example of the present tense being used to refer to the future.
¿Le traigo la cuenta? *[Shall I] bring you the bill?*
¿Le traigo un té? *[Shall I] bring you a [cup of] tea?*

⑤ **la cuenta** *the bill* – always a useful word to know!
La cuenta, por favor. *The bill, please.*
pedir la cuenta *to ask for/request the bill.*
Another meaning of **cuenta** is *account* or *count*: **una cuenta corriente** *a current account.*

4 – ¿**Có**mo? ¿**Ten**go que pa**gar an**tes de que me **sir**va?
5 – ¡**Mi**re! ⑥ ¡Con las **se**tas **nun**ca ⑦ se **sa**be **có**mo ⑧ a**ca**ban las **co**sas! □

***4** ¿**ko**-mo? ¿**ten**-go kay pah-**gahr ahn**-tays day kay may **seer**-bah? **5** ¡**mee**-ray! ¡kon lahs **say**-tahs **noon**-kah say **sah**-bay **ko**-mo ah-**kah**-bahn lahs **ko**-sahs!*

Notes

⑥ **¡Mire!** *Look!* is used colloquially as a kind of filler exclamation that can have various meanings depending on the situation. For example, *Listen …*, *Hey!* or *Well …* It is the formal singular command of **mirar**; the informal would be **¡Mira!** We'll be looking more at how the imperative is formed later.

⑦ Negative words such as **nunca**/**jamás** *never* can go in front of the verb, replacing the **no** that is normally used to negate a statement. However, the negative **no** is needed as well if such words come <u>after</u> the verb. Compare: ▸

* * *

Ejercicio 1: Traduzca

❶ ¿Qué quieres comer? ❷ Voy a pedir un café con leche. ❸ Tengo que pagar. ❹ ¿Vas a pedir la cuenta? ❺ ¡Ahora mismo!

* * *

Ejercicio 2: Complete

❶ I like wild mushrooms.
. . . . las . . . . . .

❷ I'm going to ask for a serving.
. . . a . . . . . una . . . .

❸ That's fine!
¡ . . . . bien!

4 – What? I have to pay before being served *(before that me you-serve[formal])*?
5 – Look! With mushrooms, one never knows how things will end *(how finish the things)*!

No cojo nunca el autobús. *I never take the bus.*
Nunca cojo el autobús. *I never take the bus.*
Note also that **nunca jamás** means *never ever* or *never again.*

⑧ **¿Cómo?** *What?* or *How?* when used as an interrogative (line 4) or exclamation always takes a written accent. The accent must also be used if the question is indirect. Don't confuse it with **como**, with no written accent, which is the first-person present tense of **comer** *to eat.* Additionally, **como** can mean *like* or *as*. We will see these different uses again later. By the way, you've now seen several interrogative pronouns that can be translated as *what*. This can be a bit tricky, but one tip is that **cuál** is usually used before **ser** (*What is …?*) or to suggest a selection from among a group (in the sense of *which*), and **qué** is used in most other situations.

* * *

Answers to Exercise 1

❶ What do you want to eat? ❷ I'm going to ask for a coffee with milk. ❸ I have to pay. ❹ Are you going to ask for the bill? ❺ Immediately!

* * *

❹ I must finish the lesson.
. . . . la lección.

❺ Immediately.
. . . .

Answers to Exercise 2

❶ Me gustan – setas ❷ Voy – pedir – ración ❸ Está – ❹ Tengo que acabar – ❺ Enseguida

14 **Ración** *(literally, 'ration') basically means* portion *or* serving. *In Spain, it belongs to the culture of* going for tapas, **ir de tapas**, *which was discussed in lesson 1. When you go out for tapas, you can order different serving sizes as well as different types of food.* **Un pincho** *is a bite-size tapa on a toothpick,* **una tapa** *is a small snack-sized plate, and* **una ración** *is a fairly large serving that can either be a meal in itself, or shared between two or three people over a drink.*

Tapas originally come from Andalusia, where traditionally a drink (very often sherry) was served accompanied by a small appetizer, for example, cured meat or olives. The saucer was placed over the

14 Lección catorce *[lek-**thee-on** kah-**tor**-thay]*

Repaso

1 *Al* and *del*: contraction of prepositions and definite articles

When the masculine definite article **el** follows the prepositions **a** or **de**, the words contract to form **al** and **del** respectively.
ir al cine *to go to the cinema*
hablar al autor *to speak to the author*
el primer día del mes *the first day of the month*
la salida del tren *the departure of the train*

There are no other contractions of this type – the feminine definite article does not contract with the preposition.

2 Apocope

Apocope, from the Greek for 'cutting off', is the loss of the final vowel or syllable at the end of a word. In Spanish, it occurs in some 15 or so adjectives and adverbs, most of which lose their final vowel when they come before a singular masculine noun.

glass as a kind of lid to protect against flies, hence the name **tapa**, *which literally means 'cover'. The custom gradually spread, and inventive bar owners enlarged their selection of tapas. While tapas used to be offered free with your drink, today you usually have to pay for them. This convivial tradition of sharing food with friends, colleagues or family in a relaxed atmosphere is so popular that tapas have now spread to other parts of the world.*

¡Que aproveche! Enjoy your meal!

Lesson fourteen 14

You already know some of them:

• **uno** *one*; **primero** *first*; **bueno** *good* and **malo** *bad* are adjectives that drop the final **o** before a masculine singular noun:
un día *one day*
primer mes *first month*
un buen café *a good coffee*
un mal día *a bad day.*

Note that apocope occurs even when an adjective comes in between (see **un** in the last two examples).

Now compare:
Tengo un sello. *I have a stamp.* but **Tengo uno.** *I have one.*
Es un buen coche. *It's a good car.* but **Es bueno.** *It is good.*
And in the feminine: **una buena máquina** *a good machine.*

• **tanto**, **tanta**, **tantos**, **tantas** *so much/many, as much/many* used before a noun becomes **tan** *so, as* before an adjective or adverb:
No tomes tantas galletas. *Don't eat so many cookies.*
No es tan grave. *It's not so bad.*

• **recientemente** *recently* becomes **recién** before a past participle (the *-ed* form):
un recién nacido *a newborn.*

14 To conclude our first look at apocope in Spanish, let's add to the list the adjective **grande** *big, great*, which generally becomes **gran** before a singular noun, masculine or feminine:
un gran hombre *a great man*
una gran mujer *a great woman.*

Note that the position of the adjective, which in these examples comes before the noun, can change its meaning. Although in Spanish most adjectives used in a literal sense come after the noun they modify, adjectives used figuratively are placed in front.
un hombre grande *a tall man*
un gran hombre *a great man* (in terms of importance).

3 Intensifiers: adding emphasis to an adjective

The suffix **-ísimo** (m.), **-ísima** (f.), which replaces the final vowel of an adjective or is added to an adjective ending in a consonant, is a way to intensify or emphasize a description:
una idea buenísima *a very good idea*

We find the same concept in the Italian musical term *pianissimo*, which means 'very softly and quietly'. In English, this is expressed using an adverb such as *very*, *extremely* or *most*. This is also possible in Spanish using the adverb **muy** *very* – we recommend this option because certain **-ísimo/-ísima** forms are irregular.

4 Using an article with the days of the week

In Spanish, if the day of the week is specified, it is preceded by the definite article **el** *the*:
el lunes pasado *last Monday*
el próximo miércoles *next Wednesday*
el jueves catorce *Thursday the fourteenth.*

Note that the article stands in for the English preposition *on*:
el viernes = *on Friday.*
Comí con mi amiga el sábado. *I ate with my friend on Saturday.*
Voy a verte el domingo. *I'll see you on Sunday.*

The plural article **los** expresses the idea of habitual action when

used with the days of the week:
Los domingos desayunamos en familia.
On Sundays, we have breakfast as a family.
Voy a verle los jueves. *I'm going to see him on Thursdays.*

In the same way, **todos los domingos** means *every Sunday* ('all the Sundays') and **todos los jueves** *every Thursday.*

And what about Tuesdays? See the end of this lesson!

5 Irregular past participles

As we've seen, the present perfect tense is formed using the auxiliary verb **haber** followed by the past participle (*-ed* form). All **-ar** verbs have a regular past participle ending in **-ado**:
hablar *to speak, talk* → **hablado** *spoken, talked.*

However, this is not the case with verbs ending in **-er** and **-ir**, some of which have irregular past participles (regular **-er** and **-ir** past participles end in **-ido**). You'll just have to learn these exceptions as you go along. So far, you've already come across **puesto** *put, set* (from **poner** *to put, to set*) and **hecho** *done, made* (from **hacer** *to do, to make*). Other useful ones to remember are **visto** *seen* (from **ver** *to see)* and **dicho** *said, told* (from **decir** *to say, to tell*). Here are some in context:
He puesto la mesa. *I have set the table.*
¿Qué has hecho hoy? *What have you* (informal) *done today?*
Ha visto el semáforo. *He/she has seen the traffic light.*
¿Qué han dicho? *What have they said?*

If you add to this list **escrito** *written* (from **escribir** *to write*) and **abierto** *opened* (from **abrir** *to open*), you will already have almost half of the most frequently occurring irregular past participles under your belt. Congratulations!

That's enough about past participles for now, but we take the opportunity to remind you that (in Spain, though not in Latin America) the present perfect tense is often used instead of the simple past (preterite) (**Lo he perdido.** *I missed it.* or *I have missed it.*) and also that the object pronoun – for example, **lo** – appears <u>before</u> the conjugated auxiliary verb.

6 *Hay* ('there is', 'there are')

Hay is a very useful word meaning *there is* or *there are*. It is actually an irregular form of the verb **haber** *to have*, *to be* (in the sense of *to occur*). It is used in both singular and plural contexts.
Hay un tren en la estación. *There is a train at the station.*
Hoy hay setas. *Today there are wild mushrooms.*

However, the expression **hay que** followed by an infinitive means *one must* (lesson 9, note 1).
No hay que confundir … *One mustn't confuse …*
Hay que tomar el tren. *You have to take the train.*

7 Pronouns following a preposition

When pronouns are used after prepositions (e.g. *with him*, *for you*), in general, the subject pronouns are used:

* * *

Diálogo recapitulativo

1 – ¿Qué has hecho hoy?
2 – He ido a trabajar; y después…
3 he ido de tapas.
4 ¡Necesito ver a los amigos!
5 Y tú, ¿qué has hecho?
6 – Quería ir al teatro porque me gusta mucho;
7 pero he perdido el autobús.
8 – ¡Qué mala pata!
9 – ¿Te parece si quedamos para ir al teatro el domingo?
10 – ¡Está bien!

Hablo con él. *I'm speaking with him.*
Yo voy por usted. *I'm going for you.* (i.e. for your sake)

Two exceptions are the pronouns **mí** *me* and **ti** *you* (informal), which are used after all prepositions apart from **con** *with*.
No llores por mí. *Don't cry for me.*
Esto es para ti. *This is for you* (informal).

After **con**, the preposition combines with the pronoun for *me* or *you* to become **conmigo** *with me* or **contigo** *with you*:
Tu vas conmigo. *You* (informal) *are going with me.*
Yo voy contigo. *I'm going with you.*

See the grammatical appendix for the full list of Spanish personal pronouns.

* * *

Traducción

1 What did you do today? **2** I went to work, and then … **3** I went for tapas. **4** I need to see my friends! **5** And you, what did you do? **6** I wanted to go to the theatre because I enjoy it a lot; **7** but I missed the bus. **8** What bad luck! **9** How about if we arrange to go to the theatre on Sunday? **10** That's fine!

Taking its name from the Roman god of war, Mars, **el martes** Tuesday *is no different linguistically speaking from any other day of the week. However, symbolically, Tuesday is considered an unlucky day in Spanish culture, rather like Friday the 13th in the English-speaking world. Likewise, if* **el martes** *coincides with the* 13th, **trece**, *of the month, those who are superstitious are particularly wary of unfortunate events befalling them. This bad reputation has given rise to the proverb:* **En martes, ni te cases ni te embarques.** 'On Tuesday, neither marry nor embark.'

15 Lección quince

¿Cuál es tu profesión ①?

1 – ¿En qué tra**ba**jas ②?
2 – Soy profe**so**ra ③ de espa**ñol pa**ra extran**je**ros.
3 Y tú ④, ¿a qué te de**di**cas ⑤?
4 – Soy ⑥ escri**tor**,
5 **pe**ro en mis **ra**tos **li**bres tra**ba**jo en un **ban**co.

Pronunciation

*kwahl es too pro-fay-**see-on** **1** en kay trah-**bah**-has **2** soy pro-fay-**so**-rah day es-pah-**nyol** **pah**-rah es-trahn-**hay**-ros **3** ee too ¿ah kay tay day-**dee**-kahs? **4** soy es-kree-**tor** **5** **pay**-ro en mees **rrah**-tos **lee**-brays trah-**bah**-ho en oon **bahn**-ko*

Pronunciation note

2 Before a consonant, **x** is often pronounced simply as an *s*.

Notes

① **la profesión** *the profession*, *job*, *trade* (**el oficio**). The word **profesión** is more common for professional jobs, while **oficio** is used for more manual or mechanical jobs.

② Like **llamar** *to call* or **desayunar** *to have breakfast*, **trabajar** *to work* is a regular verb of the first conjugation (**-ar** verbs). Read aloud the first-, second- and third-person singular forms of the present tense:
yo trabajo *I work*; **tú trabajas** *you* (informal) *work*; **él/ella/usted trabaja** *he/she/you* (formal) *work(s)*.

③ Most titles or professions have both a masculine and a feminine form: *teacher* – **el profesor, la profesora**; *writer* – **el escritor, la escritora**; *prime minister* – **el primer ministro, la primera ministra**.

What *(Which)* is your profession?

1 – What do you do for a job? *(In what you-work [informal]?)*
2 – I'm [a] Spanish teacher *(teacher[f.] of Spanish for foreigners)*.
3 And you *(informal)*? What do you do? *(To what yourself you-dedicate?)*
4 – I'm [a] writer *(m.)*,
5 but in my spare time *(moments free)* I work in a bank.

④ **tu** (no written accent) *your* (informal): **tu profesor** *your teacher*; **tu profesión** *your profession* or *your job, trade*.
tú (with accent) *you* (informal): **(tú) trabajas** *you work*; **¿y tú?** *and you?*

In Spanish, there are some ten pairs of monosyllabic words whose literal meaning or grammatical function is differentiated by a written accent. In addition to the two in this lesson, you already know **el** *the* and **él** *he, him*: **el trabajo** *the work, job*; **él trabaja** *he works*; **¿y él?** *and him?*

⑤ **dedicar** *to dedicate, to devote.*
dedicarse *to dedicate oneself, to devote oneself to* or *to be engaged in doing something.* **¿A qué te dedicas?** is a very common expression that can mean *What do you do?*, *What's your occupation?*, *What do you spend your time doing?* or *What do you do for a living?*

⑥ Remember: **ser** *to be* is used to express unchanging, or at least long-term, characteristics. This includes nationalities and professions. Unless a particular job is considered very temporary, **ser** is always used: **Soy profesora.** *I'm a teacher* (f.). **Eres escritor.** *You're a writer* (m.). **Es panadera.** *She's a baker.* Note that in expressions like these the indefinite article *a/an* is omitted in Spanish.

Ejercicio 1: Traduzca

❶ Soy francés. ❷ Es extranjero. ❸ ¿En qué trabajas? ❹ ¿Cuál es tu número de teléfono? ❺ ¿Es tu amiga?

* * *

Ejercicio 2: Complete

❶ What's your *(informal)* job?
¿. . . . es . . . . ?

❷ I'm a teacher *(m.)*.
. . . profesor.

❸ Do you have a job?
¿Tienes . . . . ?

❹ I work in a bank.
. . . . un . . . . . .

❺ I have some free time *(a moment free)*.
. . . . rato . . . . . .

16 Lección dieciséis

Un buen amigo

1 – ¡**Hom**bre...! ① ¿**Có**mo es**tás**? ② ¡**Cuán**to **tiem**po!

Pronunciation
*oon bwayn ah-**mee**-go **1** ¡**om**-bray! ¿**ko**-mo es-**tahs**? ¡**kwahn**-to **tee-em**-po!*

Notes

① **¡Hombre!** (literally, 'Man!') is an exclamation widely used in everyday speech. It can take on quite different shades of meaning, depending on the context: *Hey!* (surprise), *Surely not!* (disbelief), *Go on!/No way!* (doubt), *Well!* (admiration), etc. ▸

Answers to Exercise 1
❶ I am French *(m.)*. ❷ He's a foreigner. ❸ What's your job? ❹ What's your telephone number? ❺ Is she your friend?

* * *

Answers to Exercise 2
❶ Cuál – tu profesión ❷ Soy – ❸ – trabajo ❹ Trabajo en – banco ❺ Tengo un – libre

Lesson sixteen 16

A good friend

1 – Hey *(Man)*! How are you *(informal)*? It's been ages *(How-much time)*!

It's used with men and women alike, but with the latter you can also use **¡Mujer!** ('Woman!').

② **¿Cómo estás?** *How are you* (informal)*?* Note the use of **estar** here, as the question is referring to a condition or physical state of the person. **Estar** is used to refer to things that are the result of something else as opposed to an unchanging characteristic. Other ways to ask how someone is include **¿Qué tal?** *How's it going?*, a less formal expression, and **¿Qué tal estás?**

2 – Sí, es ver**dad**. **Ha**ce ③ **a**ños…
3 – ¿Qué te pa**re**ce ④ si ce**na**mos **jun**tos **es**ta ⑤ **no**che y…
4 **lue**go **va**mos de **co**pas ⑥?
5 – ¿Por qué ⑦ no?
6 – ¡Estu**pen**do – invítame ⑧!

***2** see es bayr-**dad**. **ah**-thay **ah**-nyos **3** kay tay pah-**ray**-thay see thay-**nah**-mos **hoon**-tos **es**-tah **no**-chay ee **4** **lway**-go*

Notes

③ **hace** *he/she/it/you* (formal sing.) *do(es), make(s)* from **hacer** *to do* or *to make*. This important verb translates into English in a variety of ways, depending on the context: **¿Qué haces?** *What are you doing?* **Hace una diferencia.** *It makes a difference.* **Hace años.** *It's been years.*

In the lesson text, we have an example of **hace** to express time, for which English uses *to be* in the present perfect tense. Compare: **Hace una semana que**… *It's been a week since* ... ('It makes a week that …'). **Hace** can also mean *ago*, for example: **Hace dos mil años** *2,000 years ago*. See review lesson 21 for more information.

④ **¿Qué te parece?** ('How does it seem to you?') is a very common expression that usually means *What do you think (about this)? What's your opinion?* However, if reference is being made to a future event, then it is a suggestion best translated by *How about ...?* or *Why don't we ...?*
¿Has leído esta novela? ¿Qué te parece?
Have you read this novel? What do you think of it?
¿Qué te parece si vamos a la playa?
How about going to the beach?

Note that **parecer** conjugates in the same way as **gustar** (see lesson 9, note 6): that is, singular when referring to one thing, and plural when referring to more than one thing. **¿Qué te parecen estas novelas?** *What do you think of these novels?* ▸

2 – Yes, it has *(it's true)*. It's been *(It-makes)* years.
3 – How about having dinner *(How to-you it-seems if we-dine)* together tonight and …
4 then going *(we-go)* for a drink?
5 – Why not?
6 – Great – you're paying *(invite-me)*!

***bah**-mos day **ko**-pahs **5** por kay no **6** es-too-**pen**-do een-**bee**-tah-may*

⑤ The accent, both written and spoken, distinguishes the word **est<u>á</u>** *he/she/it is, you* (formal sing.) *are* from **<u>es</u>ta** *this* (line 3).

⑥ **copa** *cup, wine glass.* Just like the expression **ir de tapas** (lesson 1), the phrase **ir de copas** or **ir de vinos** refers to a similar Spanish custom of going from bar to bar with friends and having a drink in each establishment, with each person generally paying his or her round in turn. The difference between **ir de copas** and **ir de vinos** is that **copas** is late at night, after dinner, and could well involve spirits. **Vinos** will typically be before lunch or at the end of the afternoon before dinner, and usually consists of wine, beer or other light pre-dinner drink.

⑦ **¿Por qué?** *Why?* All question words and exclamations take a written accent. **¿Cómo?** *How?*, **¿Cuánto?** *How much?*, **¿Qué?** *What?*, **¿Cuál?** *Which?*, **¿Dónde?** *Where?* and **¿Adónde?** *(To) where?* (indicating movement towards something).

⑧ **invítame** *invite me* (informal singular command) – in Spanish, 'inviting' someone out means offering to pay for them, so you might want to keep this in mind! Also notice that with a positive command, the object pronoun is attached to the end of the verb, and is not two separate words as it is in English. Another example is **llámame** *call me*. As we've seen, this is also the case with an infinitive: **invitarnos** *to invite us*.

Ejercicio 1: Traduzca

❶ ¿Qué tal estás? ❷ Bien, ¿y tú? ❸ Tengo una amiga. ❹ ¿Qué te parece? ❺ ¿Por qué no?

* * *

Ejercicio 2: Complete

❶ He's a good friend.
.. un .... amigo.

❷ Yes, it's true.
Sí, ...

❸ We had dinner together.
..... cenado ....

17 Lección diecisiete

¿Qué hora es?

1 – ¿**Tie**nes **ho**ra, por fa**vor**?

Pronunciation
*kay **o**-rah es **1 tee-ay**-nays **o**-rah por fah-**bor***

Answers to Exercise 1
❶ How are you? ❷ Fine, and you? ❸ I have a friend *(f.)*. ❹ What do you think? ❺ Why not?

* * *

❹ Call me this evening.
Llámame ....

❺ How long has it been?
¿Cuánto .... ?

Answers to Exercise 2
❶ Es – buen – ❷ – es verdad ❸ Hemos – juntos ❹ – esta noche ❺ – tiempo hace

Everyone knows that the Spanish love **fiestas**, *and their* **afición** passion *for going out with a group of friends is legendary. Not surprisingly,* **trasnochar**, to go to bed very late *or* to stay out all night, *has almost become a national pastime, especially among young people. The time-honoured tradition of a night out in Spain is one of the country's defining features. It is said that Madrid is the city where people sleep least in the world – it's not uncommon to see traffic jams there in the middle of the night!*

Lesson seventeen 17

What time is it?

1 – Do you *(informal)* have [the] time *(hour)*, please?

2 – Sí. Es la ① **u**na y ② diez.
3 – En mi re**loj** son ③ las **cua**tro **me**nos **cuar**to.
4 – ¡Qué **ra**ro!
5 Es**pe**ra un mo**men**to; voy a ④ pregun**tar**.
6 Por fa**vor**, se**ño**ra ⑤, ¿qué ⑥ **ho**ra es?
7 – Las **cin**co y **me**dia.
8 – ¡Es**ta**mos apa**ña**dos! □

***2** see. es lah **oo**-nah ee dee-ayth **3** en mee rray-**lokH** son lahs **kwah**-tro **may**-nos **kwahr**-to **4** kay **rrah**-ro **5** es-**pay**-*

Notes

① When asking the time in Spanish, you ask for the *hour* **la hora**, without the definite article: **¿Qué hora es?** 'What hour is it?'. When giving someone the time, the definite article **la** or **las** is placed in front of the hour. The word **hora** or **horas** is understood. Note that in Spain the 24-hour clock is used for timetables, so you may see the hours indicated from 0 to 23.
Es la una. *It's one o'clock.* **Son las dos.** *It's two o'clock.*
El tren sale a las dieciséis horas.
The train leaves at 4:00 pm. (16:00)

Note that the Spanish word for *time* in general is **el tiempo**. It is not used for telling the time.
No tengo tiempo. *I don't have time.*

② **Los minutos** *minutes* (up to the half hour) are expressed by using the conjunction **y** *and*, plus the number of minutes. To say the minutes *to* the hour, use **menos** *minus*.
Es la una y cinco. *It's five past one.* ('one and five')
Son las ocho menos diez. *It's ten to eight.* ('eight minus ten') ▸

* * *

Ejercicio 1: Traduzca

❶ ¿Qué hora es? ❷ No tengo hora. ❸ Espera un momento. ❹ Voy a preguntar. ❺ Son las diez.

2 – Yes. It's ten past one *(It's the one and ten)*.
3 – By *(On)* my watch it's a quarter to four *(they-are the four minus quarter)*.
4 – How strange!
5 Wait a moment; I'll go *(to)* ask.
6 Excuse me, madam, what time is it?
7 – Half past five *(The five and half)*.
8 – We're in trouble *(We're fixed)*!

*rah oon mo-**men**-to boy ah pray-goon-**tahr** **6** por fah-**bor** say-**nyo**-rah ¿kay **o**-rah es? **7** lahs **theen**-ko ee **may**-dee-ah **8** es-**tah**-mos ah-pah-**nyah**-dos*

③ Except for **la una** *one o'clock*, Spanish uses the plural verb **son** *they are*, in reference to 'hours'. Quite logical really!
Son las once y veinticinco. *It's twenty-five past eleven.*

④ A verb that indicates 'movement towards' is always followed by the preposition **a** when it precedes an infinitive or a noun.
Voy a preguntar. *I'll go ask./I'm going to ask.*
El autobús va a salir. *The bus is going to leave.*
Vamos a la panadería. *We're going to the bakery.*

⑤ Although forms of address such as *madam* and *sir* are less and less frequent in English, in Spain, it is considered polite to use **señor** (for men), **señora** (for women) or **señorita** (for young women), when addressing a stranger.

⑥ The interrogative adjective *which* or *what* is **¿qué?**
¿Qué hora es? *What time is it?*
The interrogative pronoun *which?* (as in 'which one') is **¿cuál?**
¿Cuál quieres? *Which one do you want?*
See also lesson 21.

* * *

Answers to Exercise 1

❶ What time is it? ❷ I don't know what time it is. ❸ Wait a moment. ❹ I'll go ask. ❺ It's ten o'clock.

Ejercicio 2: Complete

❶ I've forgotten my watch.
.. olvidado el ....

❷ At what time does the bus leave?
¿. ... . sale .. autobús?

❸ At four twenty-five pm *(16:25)*.
.... dieciséis . veinticinco.

❹ I don't have [a] watch.
.. .. reloj.

❺ How strange!
¡... ....!

---

18 Lección dieciocho

A última hora

1 – El **avión sa**le a las **do**ce ① en **pun**to ②.
2 Hay que ③ es**tar** en el aero**puer**to dos **ho**ras **an**tes.

Pronunciation
ah ***ool****-tee-mah* ***o****-rah* ***1*** *el ah-****bee-on sah****-lay ah lahs* ***do****-thay en* ***poon****-to* ***2*** *a-ee kay es-****tahr*** *en el ah-ay-ro-****pwayr****-to dos* ***o****-rahs* ***ahn****-tays*

Notes

① **las doce** *noon* or *midnight.*
Son las doce./Son las doce de la mañana. *It's noon.*
Son las doce./Son las doce de la noche. *It's midnight.*
In general, common sense eliminates any doubt.

Answers to Exercise 2
❶ He – reloj ❷ A qué hora – el – ❸ A las – y – ❹ No tengo – ❺ Qué raro

The official time, **la hora**, *in Spain is that of the Central European Time zone, apart from one exception: the Canary Islands, which is one hour earlier. Canary Islands time is called* **la hora insular**. *When* **la hora** *is announced before a radio or television news bulletin, both times are given: for example, the nine o'clock news,* **las nueve**, *will begin like this:* **Son las nueve, las ocho en Canarias.** It's nine o'clock, eight o'clock in the Canary Islands.

¿Y AHORA? And now what?
Practice, practice and ... more practice!

Lesson eighteen 18

At the last minute *(hour)*

1 – The plane leaves at noon *(the twelve)* exactly *(on dot)*.
2 We must be at the airport two hours before.

② With regard to time, **en punto** means *exactly*, *on the dot*. **ser puntual** means *to be punctual*, *to be on time*.

③ As we mentioned in lesson 14, section 6, the expression **hay que** is always followed by an infinitive. This construction is used to express impersonal obligation and means *it is necessary to*. In colloquial English, we make the obligation personal with a subject pronoun and use *must* or *have to*. **Hay que ir.** *We must go.* **Hay que comer.** *You must eat.* **Hay que esperar.** *You have to wait*. etc. We will revisit this grammatical point in the review lesson.

3 Te**ne**mos que ④ co**ger** un **ta**xi.
4 – Sí, si no llega**re**mos con re**tra**so ⑤.
5 ¡Es**pe**ro que no **ha**ya ⑥ a**tas**cos!
6 – Son ya las **nue**ve y **cuar**to. ¿Es**táis lis**tos?
7 – Las ma**le**tas, los pasa**por**tes… sí, ¡**va**mos!
8 ¡**An**da! Mi pasa**por**te es**tá** cadu**ca**do. □

*3 tay-**nay**-mos kay ko-**hayr** oon **tah**-ksee 4 see see no yay-gah-**ray**-mos kon rray-**trah**-so 5 es-**pay**-ro kay no **ah**-yah ah-**tahs**-kos 6 son yah lahs **nway**-bay ee **kwahr**-to ¿es-**tah-ees lees**-tos? 7 lahs mah-**lay**-tahs los pah-sah-**por**-tays… see ¡**bah**-mos! 8 ¡**ahn**-dah! mee pah-sah-**por**-tay es-**tah** kah-doo-**kah**-do*

Notes

④ **tenemos que** *we have to.* Another way to express obligation is **tener que** + infinitive *to have to* + infinitive. However, in this construction, **tener** is conjugated to indicate the person who 'has to'. **Tengo que llamar.** *I have to call.* **Tienes que trabajar.** *You* (informal sing.) *have to work.* **No tenéis que ir.** *You* (informal plural) *don't have to go.* etc.

⑤ **llegar con retraso** *to arrive late, to be late.*
tener or **llevar retraso** *to be (running) late, behind schedule.*

⑥ For now, just note that in the phrase **que no haya**, translated above as *that there won't be ...*, **haya** is a present subjunctive form of **haber** *to have, to be* (to occur). We'll discuss the subjunctive mood in a later lesson.

* * *

Ejercicio 1: Traduzca

❶ Son las cinco y diez. ❷ Hay que coger la maleta. ❸ El avión tiene retraso. ❹ ¿Estás listo? ❺ ¡Vamos!

3 We have to take a taxi.
4 – Yes, otherwise *(if not)* we will arrive late *(with delay)*.
5 I hope that there won't be [any] traffic jams!
6 – It's already a quarter past nine. Are you *(informal plural)* ready?
7 – Suitcases, passports … yes, let's go *(we-go)*!
8 Good heavens *(Walk)*! My passport has *(is)* expired.

Pronunciation note

4 Remember: the Spanish **r** is heavily trilled when it begins a word or when it follows **l**, **n** or **s**. We transcribe it as *rr*.

* * *

Answers to Exercise 1

❶ It's ten past five. ❷ We must take the suitcase. ❸ The plane is late. ❹ Are you ready *(m.)*? ❺ Let's go!

Ejercicio 2: Complete

❶ It's eight o'clock on the dot.
. . . . . . ocho . . . .

❷ It is necessary to arrive on time.
. . . . . . llegar a . . . .

❸ You *(informal sing.)* have to catch the plane.
. . . . coger el avión.

❹ At the last moment!
¡. . . . . !

❺ Do you have your passport in your pocket?
¿Tienes el . . . . en el . . . . ?

---

19 Lección diecinueve

¡Taxi, por favor!

1 – Per**do**ne, ¿**dón**de hay ① **u**na pa**ra**da de…?
2 – Us**ted** no es de a**quí**, ¿ver**dad**?
3 – No, a**ca**bo de ② lle**gar** y…

Pronunciation
***tah**-ksee por fah-**bor** **1** payr-**do**-nay ¿**don**-day a-ee **oo**-nah pah-**rah**-dah day...? **2** oos-**ted** no es day ah-**kee** ¿bayr-**dad**? **3** no ah-**kah**-bo day yay-**gahr** ee*

Notes

① Don't forget the very useful word **hay** *there is/are* (used with both singular and plural). Here, **dónde hay** means *where is there a …* . Here are some other examples of **hay**:
Hay un avión a las cuatro de la tarde. *There is a plane at 4:00 pm.*
Hay atascos. *There are traffic jams.*

Answers to Exercise 2
❶ Son las – en punto ❷ Hay que – tiempo ❸ Tienes que – ❹ A última hora ❺ – pasaporte – bolsillo

Your knowledge of Spanish is now really beginning to take off! The last two lessons have placed particular emphasis on learning how to tell the time, **la hora**. *If you've been reading the names of the numbers that appear at the bottom of each page and at the start of each lesson, that will make telling the time in Spanish much easier. This will also have laid the groundwork for tackling the numerical adjectives, which we'll get to in the upcoming review lesson!*

Lesson nineteen 19

Taxi, please!

1 – Excuse me *(Pardon)*, where is the *(where is-there a)* stand for … ?
2 – You're not from here, are you *(true)*?
3 – No, I've just arrived *(I-finish from to-arrive)* and …

Pronunciation note
Title Before a vowel, the letter **x** is usually pronounced as it is in English, although it is sometimes pronounced like an **s**. We transcribe it as *ks*.

▸ ② Recent action is expressed in English with *to have just* + past participle. The equivalent in Spanish is **acabar de** *to finish from* + infinitive.
Acabo de llamar. *I've just called.*
Acabamos de llegar. *We've just arrived.*

4 – ¿De **dón**de es?
5 – Soy ita**lia**no, de Flo**ren**cia, **pe**ro…
6 – ¡Ah! ¡**Ita**lia! ¡Qué ③ mara**vi**lla!
7 – Sí, **pe**ro… qui**sie**ra ④ encon**trar** un **ta**xi.
8 – ¡Ha**bér**melo **di**cho ⑤! ¡Yo soy ta**xis**ta! □

***4** day **don**-day es **5** soy ee-tah-**lee-ah**-no day flo-**rayn**-thee-ah **pay**-ro **6** ¡ah! ¡ee-**tah**-lee-ah! ¡kay ma-rah-**bee**-ya! **7** see*

Notes

③ Exclamations such as *What a ...!* or *How ...!* are generally translated by **¡Qué ...!** + adjective or noun. Note that, in the case of a noun, the indefinite article is omitted in Spanish.
¡Qué bueno! *How great!*
¡Qué sorpresa! *What a surprise*!

④ To politely express a wish or desire in English we use *I'd like (I would like)*, which is the conditional. The Spanish equivalent is **quisiera**. We will see later that this is another example of the subjunctive, from **querer** *to want*, but for now there's no need to rush! (See also lesson 18, note 6.)

⑤ **¡Habérmelo dicho!** *Why didn't you say so!* For the moment, simply note that this exclamation contains **haber** *to have*, the pronouns **me** *me* and **lo** *it*, plus the past participle of **decir** *to say, to tell*: **dicho**. **¡Habérmelo dicho antes!** *You should have told me/said so before!*

* * *

Ejercicio 1: Traduzca

❶ Aquí hay una parada de taxis. ❷ Es verdad. ❸ ¿De dónde es usted? ❹ Soy español, de La Coruña. ❺ ¡Es una maravilla!

4 – Where are you from *(From where are-you[formal])*?
5 – I'm Italian *(m.)*, from Florence, but …
6 – Ah! Italy! How wonderful *(What marvel)*!
7 – Yes, but … I'd like to find a taxi.
8 – Why didn't you say so *(To-have-me-it said)*! I'm [a] taxi driver!

***pay**-ro... kee-**see-ay**-rah en-kon-**trahr** oon **tah**-ksee **8** ¡ah-**bayr**-may-lo **dee**-cho! ¡yo soy tah-**ksees**-tah!*

* * *

Answers to Exercise 1

❶ There's a taxi stand here. ❷ It's/That's true. ❸ Where are you from? ❹ I'm Spanish *(m.)*, from La Coruña. ❺ It's amazing/marvellous!

Ejercicio 2: Complete

❶ Taxi please!
¡Taxi, ... !

❷ I've just said so *(it)*.
. . . . decirlo.

❸ Right *(True)*?
¿ . . . . . . ?

❹ I'd like a tapa.
. . . . una tapa.

❺ Why didn't you say so before!
¡ . . . . antes!

---

20 Lección veinte

Sentido práctico

1 – **Tie**nes **ma**la **ca**ra. ¿Qué te **pa**sa? ①
2 – A**ca**bo de rom**per** con **Car**los.

Pronunciation

*sen-**tee**-do **prahk**-tee-ko **1** **tee**-**ay**-nays **mah**-lah **kah**-rah ¿kay tay **pah**-sah? **2** ah-**kah**-bo day rrom-**payr** kon **kahr**-los*

Notes

① **¿Qué te pasa?** *What's the matter with you? What's wrong?* The verb **pasar** *to happen*, *to pass* or *to spend* is a regular **-ar** verb that has many different meanings. Used impersonally, as ▸

Answers to Exercise 2
❶ – por favor ❷ Acabo de – ❸ Verdad ❹ Quisiera – ❺ Haberlo dicho –

Addressing people informally, speaking quickly, talkativeness, warmth and lots of hand gestures: these are some of the typical traits of the 'Spanish character', and they become increasingly pronounced the farther south you travel. A Mediterranean people, many Spaniards talk with their **manos** hands. *Indeed, when they are talking to you, they have no qualms about making* physical contact, **contacto físico**. *They'll show their friendliness by patting you on the back, taking you by the arm, hugging you affectionately or by putting their arm around your shoulder while you're walking along. Shaking hands, however, is mostly reserved for professional introductions, first meetings and other very specific, formal situations (when giving condolences, for example). Greeting with* cheek-kissing, **besos**, *is possible, but is not at all systematic. Often, people greet each other very simply without any kissing or handshaking, much as we do.*

Lesson twenty 20

Practicality *(Sense practical)*

1 – You don't look well *(You-have bad face)*. What's wrong *(What to-you happens)*?
2 – I've just broken up *(I-finish from to-break)* with Carlos.

▸ in the very common expression **¿Qué pasa?** it means *What's happening? What's going on? What's up?* To ask about an event that happened in the recent past you can say **¿Qué ha pasado?** *What has happened?*

3 – ¡No me **di**gas! ② ¿Por qué? ③
4 – ¡No es el **hom**bre de mi **vi**da!
5 – ¿Cuál es su **nú**mero de **mó**vil ④?
6 – ¿**Pa**ra qué? ⑤
7 – A mí, **Car**los **siem**pre ⑥ me ha gus**ta**do;
8 y… ¡**nun**ca se **sa**be! □

3 *¡no may* ***dee****-gahs! ¿por kay?* ***4*** *no es el* ***om****-bray day mee* ***bee****-dah* ***5*** *kwahl es soo* ***noo****-may-ro day* ***mo****-beel* ***6 pah****-rah kay* ***7*** *ah mee* ***kahr****-los* ***see-em****-pray may ah goos-****tah****-do* ***8*** *ee ¡****noon****-kah say* ***sah****-bay!*

Notes

② **¡No me diga(s)!** *You don't say! Really! Fancy that! Surely not!* etc.; literally, 'Don't tell me!'. This is an example of a negative command. Just memorize this as an expression for now.

③ A reminder: **¿por qué?** written as two words = *why?* **porque**, one word and no written accent = *because.* ▶

* * *

Ejercicio 1: Traduzca

❶ Acabo de llamar. ❷ ¿Por qué? ❸ Porque es el hombre de mi vida. ❹ ¿Qué ha pasado? ❺ ¡No me digas!

* * *

Ejercicio 2: Complete

❶ Carlos looks well.
Carlos . . . . . buena . . . . . .

❷ Where's your mobile?
¿ . . . . tu . . . . . ?

❸ What's going on?
¿ . . . . ?

3 – Really *(Not to-me tell)*! Why?
4 – He's not the man of my dreams *(of my life)*!
5 – What's his mobile number?
6 – Why *(For what)*?
7 – I've always liked Carlos *(To me Carlos always to-me has appealed)*;
8 and … you never know *(never one knows)*!

④ **teléfono móvil** or **móvil** *mobile phone*, *cell phone*. Otherwise, **móvil** simply means *mobile* (i.e. the adjective *movable*).
Note: **automóvil** *automobile*, *car*.

⑤ Spanish distinguishes between **¿por qué?**, which is used when enquiring about the underlying cause (see line 3), and **¿para qué?**, for enquiring about the future purpose or intent.

⑥ Unlike in English, in the present perfect tense, the auxiliary verb **haber** and the past participle cannot be separated. Any adverb or adverbial phrase must be placed either before or after the verb phrase.
Carlos ha trabajado siempre. *Carlos has always worked.*
Nunca he comido churros. *I have never eaten churros.*

* * *

Answers to Exercise 1

❶ I've just called. ❷ Why? ❸ Because he's the man of my dreams. ❹ What has happened? ❺ You don't say!

* * *

❹ What for?
¿. . . .   . . . ?

❺ Did you like it *(To-you it-has appealed)*?
¿Te . .   . . ?

Answers to Exercise 2

❶ – tiene – cara ❷ Dónde está – móvil ❸ Qué pasa ❹ Para qué ❺ – ha gustado

21 Lección veintiuna

Repaso

1 Numbers

1.1 Cardinal numbers

0 **cero**	10 **diez**	20 **veinte**	30 **treinta**
1 **uno**	11 **once**	21 **veintiuno**	40 **cuarenta**
2 **dos**	12 **doce**	22 **veintidós**	50 **cincuenta**
3 **tres**	13 **trece**	23 **veintitrés**	60 **sesenta**
4 **cuatro**	14 **catorce**	24 **veinticuatro**	70 **setenta**
5 **cinco**	15 **quince**	25 **veinticinco**	80 **ochenta**
6 **seis**	16 **dieciséis**	26 **veintiséis**	90 **noventa**
7 **siete**	17 **diecisiete**	27 **veintisiete**	100 **ciento, cien**
8 **ocho**	18 **dieciocho**	28 **veintiocho**	
9 **nueve**	19 **diecinueve**	29 **veintinueve**	

• **Use of the conjunction *y***
In Spanish, **y**, the equivalent of *and*, must be placed between tens and units. This rule is applied strictly and without exception starting from **treinta** *thirty.* With the lower numbers, from 16 to 29, instead of **diez y seis**, **diez y siete**, **veinte y uno**, etc., the preferred written forms are **dieciséis**, **diecisiete**, **veintiuno**, etc., as shown above.

So, you're almost at the end of your third week of learning Spanish! In order to reinforce the knowledge you've acquired so far, the next lesson provides a summary of the main grammatical points dealt with in the previous six lessons. With the exception of a few details, you'll find that it's merely a review of information that you've already seen: take the opportunity to test yourself!

¡Ánimo! You can do it!

Lesson twenty-one 21

• ***uno, un***

The numerical adjective **uno** loses the final **o** before a noun.
veintiún euros *twenty-one euros*
treinta y un niños *thirty-one children*

Before a feminine noun, **una** is used:
El avión sale a las veintiuna horas. *The plane leaves at nine pm.*

The numerical adjective is dropped for the numbers *one hundred* and *one thousand*:
one hundred = **cien** or **ciento**; *one thousand* = **mil**
But:
two hundred = **doscientos** or **doscientas**
two thousand = **dos mil** (no pluralization of the word **mil**).

Most of the hundreds are formed with the number + **cientos** (with a masculine noun) or **cientas** (with a feminine noun), but note the three irregular forms: *five hundred* = **quinientos** or **quinientas**, *seven hundred* = **setecientos** or **setecientas**, *nine hundred* = **novecientos** or **novecientas**.

• **Gender agreement**

From two hundred to nine hundred, the hundreds are always plural and must agree in gender with the accompanying noun:
seiscientas páginas *six hundred pages*
mil quinientas veinte personas *1520 people.*

21

1.2 Ordinal numbers

The following ordinal numbers are also used:

1st	**primero**	7th	**séptimo**	20th	**vigésimo**
2nd	**segundo**	8th	**octavo**	...	
3rd	**tercero**	9th	**noveno**	100th	**centésimo**
4th	**cuarto**	10th	**décimo**	...	
5th	**quinto**	11th	**undécimo**	1000th	**milésimo**
6th	**sexto**	12th	**duodécimo**		

• **Agreement and use**
Ordinal numbers always agree in both gender and number with the accompanying noun.
la tercera lección *the third lesson*
los primeros días *the first days*

Ordinal numbers are rarely used. In practice, Spanish uses only the first ten or twelve ordinals; beyond that, the cardinal numbers are used almost systematically.
Estamos en la tercera lección de repaso.
We are on the third review lesson.
Vivo en el cuarto piso. *I live on the fourth floor.*
But:
Estamos en el siglo XXI (veintiuno). *We are in the 21st century.*
Vivimos en el piso veinticuatro. *We live on the 24th floor.*
Notice that ordinal numbers come before the noun, and cardinal numbers come after the noun.

2 Telling the time

• The time is given by placing the definite article **la** or **las** in front of the number expressing the hour; the feminine word **la hora** *hour*, or **las horas** *hours*, is understood.
Es la una. *It's one o'clock.*
A las dos. *At two o'clock.*

The word for *time* in general, as opposed to time on the clock, is **el tiempo**.
El tiempo pasa rápido. *Time passes quickly.*
No tengo tiempo. *I don't have time.*
But: **No tengo hora.** *I don't know what time it is.*

• With the exception of **la una** *one o'clock*, the plural verb **son** *are* is used to agree with 'hours'.
Es la una. *It's one o'clock.*
Son las dos, las tres, las cuatro … *It's two, three, four... o'clock.*

• The number of **minutos** *minutes* (up to the half hour) is always preceded by the conjunction **y** *and*. The number of minutes *to* the hour is preceded by **menos** *minus*.
Es la una y cinco. *It's five past one.*
Son las ocho y veinticinco. *It's eight twenty-five.*
Son las siete menos cinco. *It's five to seven.*

• *a quarter past* = **y cuarto**; *a quarter to* = **menos cuarto**; *half past* = **y media**.
Son las siete y cuarto. *It's a quarter past seven.*
a las ocho menos cuarto *at a quarter to eight*
de las nueve y media a las diez y media
from half past nine until half past ten

• In everyday speech, the hours are usually given from 1 to 12, adding, if necessary, **de la mañana** *in the morning*, **de la tarde** *in the afternoon,* or **de la noche** *in the evening.*
at six o'clock am **a las seis** or **a las seis de la mañana**
at six o'clock pm **a las seis** or **a las seis de la tarde**
at eleven o'clock pm **a las once** or **a las once de la noche**

The 24-hour clock is used for official timetables at airports and bus or railway stations. Thus it might be announced that a particular train will depart at **las dieciséis treinta** *sixteen thirty (4:30 pm)* and will arrive at **las veintiuna cuarenta y cinco** *twenty-one forty-five (9:45 pm)*, for example.

• *Noon* and *midnight*:
Son las doce./Son las doce de la mañana. *It's noon.*
Son las doce./Son las doce de la noche. *It's midnight.*

3 Impersonal use of *haber*: 'there is'/'there are'

We've explained the chief role of **haber** as an auxiliary verb. However, **haber** may also be used in an impersonal way. It is then translated by *there* + a form of *to be*. We have seen this in the present tense in several lessons: **hay** *there is/are*.
Hay un tren en la estación. *There's a train at the station.*
Hay problemas. *There are problems.*

It can also be conjugated in other tenses. For example:

Imperfect tense:	**había** *there was/were*
Preterite tense:	**hubo** *there was/were*
Future tense:	**habrá** *there will be.*

4 Impersonal obligation with *hay que*

To express a general impersonal obligation, that is, 'it is necessary to', Spanish uses **hay que** + infinitive. The usual English equivalent is *one must/has to*, *you must/have to* or *we must/have to.*
Hay que preguntar. *You have to ask.*

This can also be conjugated in other tenses.

Imperfect tense:	**había que** *one had to* + infinitive
Preterite tense:	**hubo que** *one had to* + infinitive
Future tense:	**habrá que** *one will have to* + infinitive

5 Personal obligation with *tener que*

tener que + infinitive, *to have to*

Tener que is also always followed by an infinitive. The verb **tener** is conjugated according to the person who is obligated to do something.

Tengo que saber. *I have to know.*
Tienes que esperar. *You* (informal sing.) *have to wait.*

6 *Qué?* versus *¿Cuál?* or *¿Cuáles?*

• **¿Qué?** is always followed by a noun.
¿Qué hora es? *What time is it?*
¿Qué autobús es? *Which bus is it?*

• **¿Cuál?** (sing.) or **¿Cuáles?** (pl.) are NOT followed by a noun.
Aquí viene un tren, pero ¿cuál?
Here comes a train, but which one?
Aquí vienen los autobuses, pero ¿cuáles?
Here come the buses, but which ones?
¿Cuál es la capital de España?
What is the capital of Spain?

7 *Hace* in expressions of time

Hace has several meanings. It is the third-person singular form of the present tense of **hacer**, which is either *to do* or *to make*, depending on the context:
¿Qué hace? *What is he doing?*
Hace una diferencia. *It makes a difference.*

However, its use in idiomatic expressions of time is also very frequent, especially in the sense of 'ago':
hace tres semanas *three weeks ago*
no hace mucho *not long ago.*

It is also used to indicate that time has passed:
Hace tres semanas que estudio español. *I have been studying Spanish for three weeks.* ('It makes three weeks that I study ...')
Hace años que no nos vemos. *It has been years since we have seen each other.* ('It makes years that we do not see each other.')

Note that in these contexts English uses a perfect tense, while Spanish uses the simple present tense.

Here is a general overview of the present tense of regular **-ar** verbs. Read the conjugations aloud, but don't worry about trying to memorize them here.

Present tense of **cantar** *to sing*:

yo	**cant→**	o	*I sing*
tú	**cant→**	as	*you* (informal sing.) *sing*
él, ella, usted	**cant→**	a	*he/she/it/you* (formal sing.) *sing(s)*
nosotros, nosotras	**cant→**	amos	*we sing*
vosotros, vosotras	**cant→**	áis	*you* (informal plural) *sing* (m., f.)
ellos, ellas, ustedes	**cant→**	an	*they* (m., f.) / *you* (formal plural) *sing*

* * *

In Spain's large towns and cities, taxis can be recognized by the classic 'Taxi' sign on the roof and a plate bearing the letters **SP**, **servicio público** public service. *Taxis of the same town are identified by their colour, or sometimes by a horizontal, diagonal or vertical stripe on the side of the car. At night, a small green light signals that the vehicle is available to prospective customers, while during the daytime, look for a sign in the windscreen that says* **libre** free. *To find a taxi stand, look for a sign with a* **T** *or* **Taxis**.

La bajada de bandera the minimum fare *is not very expensive and the cost per ride is generally reasonable; nonetheless, be aware that there may be* **un suplemento** a surcharge *for any of several reasons: luggage, night surcharge (11:00 pm – 6:00 am), leaving*

1 – ¿Qué hora es, por favor?
2 – Son las ocho menos diez y …
3 ya llevamos retraso.
4 – ¡Oh, no!
5 – ¿Qué pasa?
6 – He olvidado el móvil en el banco.
7 – Hay que telefonear.
8 – Llegaremos con retraso al teatro.
9 – Tenemos que coger un taxi.
10 ¿Qué te parece?
11 – ¡Vamos!

Traducción

1 What time is it, please? **2** It's ten to eight and … **3** we are already late. **4** Oh no! **5** What's wrong? **6** I've left *(forgotten)* my mobile at the bank. **7** We'll have to phone. **8** We'll arrive late at the theatre. **9** We must take a taxi. **10** What do you think? **11** Let's go!

* * *

the city limits (including going to the airport), holidays, departure from a railway station, etc. The various rates are displayed inside the vehicle, and the taxi meter is visible to keep the passenger informed. Passengers may request **un recibo** a receipt. **La propina** the tip *is not obligatory, but very often the fare is rounded up.*

El taxista español, the Spanish taxi driver, *is a colourful character. He is generally affable, but he can also get angry, for example, if he gets stuck in an* **atasco** traffic jam. *If this occurs, however, he tactfully takes it out on those outside his taxi! Don't hesitate to ask him questions: he will be all too willing to give you detailed information. As far as language is concerned, he is equally engaging. Pay attention and you'll learn lots of expressions!*

¿Qué edad tienes?

1 – ¿Por qué has men**ti**do, Pa**bli**to ①?
2 – Yo no que**rí**a ②…
3 – ¿**Cuán**tos ③ años **tie**nes?
4 – **Cin**co **a**ños y **me**dio.
5 – Yo a tu e**dad** ④ no de**cí**a men**ti**ras.
6 – ¿Y a qué e**dad** empe**zas**te ⑤, ma**má**? □

Pronunciation
*kay ay-**dad** **tee-ay**-nays **1** por kay ahs men-**tee**-do pah-**blee**-to **2** yo no kay-**ree**-ah **3** **kwahn**-tos **ah**-nyos **tee-ay**-nays **4** **theen**-ko **ah**-nyos ee **may**-dee-o **5** yo ah too ay-**dad** no day-**thee**-ah men-**tee**-rahs **6** ee ah kay ay-**dad** em-pay-**thahs**-tay mah-**mah***

Notes

① **Pablo** *Paul*. The diminutive suffix **-ito** for masculine nouns and **-ita** for feminine nouns usually expresses 'smallness'.
un rato *a while*; **un ratito** *a little while*, *a moment*.
una muchacha *a girl*; **una muchachita** *a little girl*.
In colloquial language, the diminutives **-ito**, **-ita** used with names also convey affection. **Juan** *John*, **Juanito** *Johnny*.

② **Yo no quería** *I didn't want to*; **Yo no decía** (line 5) *I didn't tell/say*. This is a past tense called the imperfect. For **-er** and **-ir** verbs it is formed by adding **-ía**, **-ías**, **-ía**, etc. to the stem of the verb. There are only three irregular verbs in this tense – good news! The imperfect tense is used for regular, repeated actions in the past (often corresponding to the English *used to*), as in **No decía mentiras** *I didn't (use to) tell lies*. It is also used to describe a situation or feeling in the past: **yo no quería** *I didn't want to*. It has other uses, but for the moment simply compare and contrast it with note 5 on the use of the preterite (simple past) tense. ▸

How old are you *(What age have-you)*?

1 – Why did you lie, Pablito?
2 – I didn't want to …
3 – How old are you *(How-many years have-you)*?
4 – Five *(years)* and [a] half.
5 – When I was your age *(I at your age)* I didn't tell lies.
6 – And at what age did you start, Mum?

③ **¿Cuánto?** *How much?* When used with a noun, this word is an adjective with four possible forms, since it must agree with the noun in gender and number. **¿Cuántas lecciones has estudiado?** *How many lessons have you studied?*
However, **cuánto** doesn't change form when used with a verb. **¿Cuánto cuesta?** *How much does [it] cost?*

④ **la edad** *age* is feminine, as are all nouns ending in **-dad**. **la edad adulta** *adulthood*; **la verdad** *the truth.*

⑤ **tú empezaste** *you* (informal) *began* is the second-person singular of the preterite (simple past) tense of **empezar** *to begin, to start.* This tense is used for a one-time completed action in the past.

Ejercicio 1: Traduzca

❶ ¿Por qué llegas tarde? ❷ ¿Qué edad tiene? ❸ Tengo treinta y tres años. ❹ ¿Cuántos euros cuesta? ❺ Pablo quería venir.

* * *

Ejercicio 2: Complete

❶ I have a moment free.
. . . . libre.

❷ How old are you?
¿ . . . . tienes?

❸ At what age did you *(informal)* start to work?
¿A . . . . a trabajar?

❹ How many suitcases do you *(formal)* have?
¿ . . . . maletas tiene?

❺ Have you *(informal)* started?
¿ . . . . ?

23 Lección veintitrés

¡Feliz cumpleaños! ①

1 – ¿**Sa**bes? Hoy es mi cumple**a**ños.

Pronunciation
*fay-**leeth** koom-play-**ah**-nyos* **1** *¿**sah**-bays? oy es mee koom-play-**ah**-nyos*

Answers to Exercise 1

❶ Why are you arriving late? ❷ How old is he/are you *(formal)*? ❸ I am thirty-three. ❹ How many euros does it cost? ❺ Pablo wanted to come.

* * *

Answers to Exercise 2

❶ Tengo un ratito – ❷ Cuántos años – ❸ – qué edad empezaste – ❹ Cuántas – ❺ Has empezado

* * *

Most Spanish people are communicative and hospitable. They tend to put you at your ease immediately and have no hesitation in asking you all kinds of questions straight off (where you come from, your family, age, job, etc.) that may seem indiscreet to some cultural backgrounds. This apparent **curiosidad** curiosity *is actually a way to break the ice and allow you to join in. Once everyone knows who everyone else is, matters take their normal course and a curtain of* **reserva** reserve *falls again quite naturally. The initial curiosity often serves more as a rite of passage than true familiarity. Despite appearances, Spaniards are on the whole actually rather* **reservados** reserved.

Lesson twenty-three 23

Happy birthday!

1 – You *(informal)* know [what]? Today is my birthday.

Notes

① **¡Feliz cumpleaños!** *Happy Birthday!* The adjective **feliz** *happy* is used in many expressions: **¡Feliz Navidad!** *Merry Christmas!* **¡Feliz** (or **buen**) **viaje!** *Have a good trip!* **¡Feliz Año Nuevo!** *Happy New Year!* The plural form of **feliz** is **felices**: **¡Felices fiestas**! *Happy holidays!*

2 – ¡Felici**da**des! ②
3 – **Mu**chas **gra**cias ③.
4 – ¿Y **cuán**tos **a**ños **cum**ples ④?
5 – Cua**ren**ta.
6 – Se me ha olvi**da**do ⑤ el re**ga**lo.
7 Te lo trae**ré** ⑥ ma**ña**na.
8 – Más **va**le **tar**de que **nun**ca. □

2 *fay-lee-thee-**dah**-days* ***3*** ***moo**-chahs **grah**-thee-ahs* ***4*** *ee **kwahn**-tos **ah**-nyos **koom**-plays* ***5*** *kwah-**ren**-tah* ***6*** *say may ah ol-bee-**dah**-do el rray-**gah**-lo* ***7*** *tay lo trah-ay-**ray** mah-**nyah**-nah* ***8*** *mahs **bah**-lay **tahr**-day kay **noon**-kah*

Notes

② **la felicidad** *happiness, joy*. In the plural, **¡Felicidades!** (or **¡Muchas felicidades!**) is used to wish someone well. Here it means *Happy Birthday*; in other cases it can mean *My best wishes! All the best!* or *Congratulations!* Another expression for congratulating someone is **¡Enhorabuena!** *Congratulations!*

③ **mucho** *much*, *a lot [of]* has to agree in gender and number with the accompanying noun when used as an adjective: **muchos años** *many years*; **muchas personas** *many/a lot of people*. However, when used as an adverb it doesn't change: **Yo trabajo mucho.** *I work a lot.*

④ When talking about **años**, **cumplir** *to complete*, *to fulfill*, *to achieve* means 'to turn' or 'to be': **He cumplido treinta años.** *I turned thirty.* **Hoy cumple diez años.** *Today he/she is ten years old.* ▸

* * *

Ejercicio 1: Traduzca

❶ Mañana es mi cumpleaños. ❷ ¡Muchas felicidades! ❸ ¿Cuántos años tienes? ❹ Te lo traeré más tarde. ❺ ¿Qué te parece?

2 – Happy Birthday!
3 – Many thanks.
4 – And how old are you *(how-many years you-fulfill)*?
5 – Forty.
6 – I forgot your *(the)* present.
7 I'll bring it [to] you tomorrow.
8 – Better late *(More it-is-worth late)* than never.

The noun **cumpleaños** literally means 'completed years': **celebrar el cumpleaños de**… *to celebrate the birthday of …*

⑤ Here we have the reflexive verb **olvidarse**. The non-reflexive **olvidar** *to forget* would also be quite correct here: **He olvidado el regalo.** *I have forgotten the present*. However, the use of the reflexive form (the 'no-fault' **se**, as it is called) nuances the meaning: the subject is considered to be almost an innocent bystander – something has happened in spite of him or her. So **olvidarse** has the meaning of 'to slip one's mind'. Another example is **Se me cayó el libro.** *I dropped the book*, or literally, 'The book fell from me.' It didn't happen on purpose! In this example, you also see how the subject of the verb (here **el libro**) is often at the end of the sentence in Spanish.

⑥ **Te lo traeré** *I'll bring it to you* – literally, 'To you it I will bring'. As we've seen, in Spanish the direct object of the verb (here, *it*) is placed in front of the conjugated verb; the same is true of the indirect object (here, *you*). When used together, the indirect object pronoun (often referring to a person) always comes before the direct object pronoun.

* * *

Answers to Exercise 1

❶ Tomorrow is my birthday. ❷ Best wishes! ❸ How old are you? ❹ I'll bring it to you later. ❺ What do you think?

Ejercicio 2: Complete

❶ There aren't many taxis *(m.)*.
No . . . . taxis.

❷ He's over *(has more of)* thirty years [old].
Tiene . . . . . treinta . . . . .

❸ I'll bring it *(m.)* this evening.
. . traeré . . . .

* * *

El cumpleaños. *In Spain, birthdays are generally cause for a get-together with family and friends: for adults, a drink with colleagues from work and a meal at home or in a restaurant; for children, a birthday cake and candles with school friends; and for adolescents, a more festive night out. These are all common ways to* **celebrar** celebrate *the event. Note that if you celebrate your birthday by going out with friends, you are the one who offers to treat (***invitar***) and pays for the drinks!*

24 Lección veinticuatro

Delante del ① espejo ②

1 – ¿Por qué te has pin**ta**do ③ los **la**bios, a**bue**la?

Pronunciation
*day-**lahn**-tay del es-**pay**-ho **1** por kay tay ahs peen-**tah**-do los **lah**-bee-os ah-**bway**-lah*

Notes

① **delante** *in front*; **detrás** *behind*:
Alberto va delante. *Alberto goes in front.*
Inés está sentada detrás. *Inés is seated behind.*
In the examples above they are used as adverbs, but when they are prepositions they are followed by **de**: **delante de** and **detrás de** (remember that **de** + **el** contracts to **del**):
delante de la casa *in front of the house*
detrás del niño *behind the child.*

❹ I turned twenty-two.
He . . . . veintidós . . . . .

❺ Better late than never.
. . . vale . . . . . que . . . . . .

Answers to Exercise 2
❶ – hay muchos – ❷ – más de – años ❸ Lo – esta noche ❹ – cumplido – años ❺ Más – tarde – nunca

* * *

The tradition of giving a **regalo** present *remains very strong (even if it's just a* **regalito** *– because it's the thought that counts). As far as* **aniversarios** anniversaries *are concerned, just like anywhere else, there are all kinds, from the* **primer aniversario de boda** first wedding anniversary *to the* **setenta aniversario de la puesta en órbita de un satélite equis** 70th anniversary of the launch *(literally, 'putting into orbit')* of satellite 'x'.

Lesson twenty-four 24

In front of the mirror

1 – Why have you put on lipstick *(Why yourself you-have painted the lips)*, Grandma?

② **espejo** *mirror*: **mirarse en el espejo** *to look at oneself in the mirror.* **Los ojos son el espejo del alma.** *The eyes are the mirror of the soul.*

③ Here is another reflexive verb. Note how the reflexive pronoun can change the meaning of the verb. Whereas **pintar** means *to paint*, **pintarse** ('to paint oneself') means *to put on make-up*, as does **maquillarme**.
pintarse los labios *to put on lipstick*
pintarse los ojos *to put on eye make-up.*

2 – Me **gus**ta ④ maqui**llar**me.
3 – **Pe**ro… ¿**pa**ra qué?
4 – **Pa**ra es**tar** más **gua**pa ⑤.
5 – Y **e**so… ¿**cuán**to **tiem**po tarda**rá** ⑥ en ha**cer** e**fec**to? □

***2** may **goo**-stah mah-kee-**yar**-may **3 pay**-ro ¿**pah**-rah kay? **4 pah**-rah es-**tahr** mahs **gwah**-pah **5** ee **ay**-so ¿**kwahn**-to **tee-em**-po tahr-dah-**rah** en ah-**thayr** ay-**fek**-to?*

Notes

④ Remember: **me gusta** means *I like* or *it appeals to me*. When used with an action (something that you like doing), it is followed by an infinitive: **Me gusta ir al cine.** *I like to go to the cinema.*

⑤ **Ser** or **estar** for *to be*? Remember that **ser** expresses inherent essential characteristics that don't vary with the circumstances: **ser guapo/guapa** *to be handsome/beautiful* (to be that way naturally). **Estar** is used for conditions or states (lasting or not) resulting from the circumstances: **estar guapo/guapa** *to look good* (in a specific situation: if your clothes or hairstyle suit you particularly well). ▸

* * *

Ejercicio 1: Traduzca

❶ Hemos quedado delante del banco. ❷ No tengo tiempo de ir. ❸ Ella se pinta los labios. ❹ Me gusta la música. ❺ Acabo de llegar.

2 – I like to put on make-up *(To-me it-appeals to-make-up-myself)*.
3 – But … why *(for what)*?
4 – To be more beautiful.
5 – And *(that)*… how long *(how-much time)* will it take to have *(to make)* [an] effect?

⑥ **tardar** *to take time, to delay* is a widely used verb. **¿Cuánto tiempo tardarás?** *How long are you going to take?*
Note that the future tense is formed by adding the following endings to the infinitive: **-é**, **-ás**, **-á**, **-emos**, **-éis**, **-án**: **yo tardaré, tú tardarás, él/ella/usted tardará**, etc.

* * *

Answers to Exercise 1

❶ We've arranged to meet in front of the bank. ❷ I don't have time to go. ❸ She puts on lipstick. ❹ I like music. ❺ I just arrived.

Ejercicio 2: Complete

❶ I'm waiting for you in front of the cinema.
Te . . . . cine.

❷ I don't like to wear make-up.
. . . . maquillarme.

❸ You *(f.)* are very beautiful today. *(resulting condition)*
Estás . . . . hoy.

---

25 Lección veinticinco

Familia numerosa

1 – ¿Le ① **gu**sta el **pi**so?
2 – Me **gu**sta mu**chí**simo. Es muy tran**qui**lo.
3 – En**ton**ces, le ② pro**pon**go que va**ya**mos ③ a la a**gen**cia **pa**ra fir**mar**.
4 – **Ten**go que ④ ha**blar an**tes con mi ma**ri**do.

Pronunciation
*fah-**mee**-lee-ah noo-may-**ro**-sah **1** lay **goo**-stah el **pee**-so **2** me **goo**-stah moo-**chee**-see-mo. es moo-ee trahn-**kee**-lo **3** en-**ton**-thays lay pro-**pon**-go kay bah-**yah**-mos ah lah ah-**hen**-thee-ah **pah**-rah feer-**mahr** **4** **ten**-go kay ah-**blahr ahn**-tays kon mee mah-**ree**-do*

Notes

① **¿El piso le gusta?** *You* (formal) *like the flat/apartment?* ('The flat appeals to you?'). This formal situation requires the polite third-person – **te gusta** would be too familiar. So the third-person indirect object pronoun is used: **le**. We will return to this point in more detail later. Note that **piso** can also mean the *floor* or *storey* of a building. ▸

❹ You *(informal, m.)* are handsome. *(naturally)*

....

❺ How much time are you going to take?

¿...... ...... vas a ...... ?

Answers to Exercise 2

❶ – espero delante del – ❷ No me gusta – ❸ – muy guapa – ❹ Eres guapo ❺ Cuánto tiempo – tardar

Lesson twenty-five 25

Big *(Numerous)* family

1 – Do you *(formal)* like the flat?
2 – I like it very much. It's very quiet.
3 – Then *(to-you[formal])* I suggest that we go to the agency to sign [the contract].
4 – I have to speak *(before)* with my husband first.

② **le** *(to) you* (formal), but also *to him/her/it*, is a third-person indirect object pronoun (see note 1). As we've seen, Spanish object pronouns generally precede the conjugated verb. So **le propongo que** means *I suggest to you* (formal) *that*.

③ **que vayamos** *that we (should) go* → first-person plural of the present subjunctive of **ir** *to go*. So what is the subjunctive? This is a verb form called a 'mood' that is used to express possibility or something that is uncertain or subjective. Most of the verbs we've seen so far are in the indicative mood, which is used to present something as an objective fact. In Spanish, the subjunctive conjugates differently than the indicative (e.g. **vayamos** *we go* subjunctive; **vamos** *we go* indicative). You will often see the construction **que** + subjunctive, as in line 3. We'll come back to the subjunctive later.

④ Remember that **tengo que** + infinitive = *I have to* + infinitive.

5 – Per**do**ne, **pe**ro… ¿es**tá** ca**sa**da?
6 ¿Y… tam**bién tie**ne **hi**jos ⑤?
7 – ¡**Cla**ro! Seis **ni**ños pe**que**ños.
8 – ¡Ah!

*5 payr-**do**-nay **pay**-ro ¿es-**tah** kah-**sah**-dah? **6** ee tahm-**bee-en tee-ay**-nay **ee**-hos **7** ¡**klah**-ro! say-ees **nee**-nyos pay-**kay**-nyos **8** ah*

Notes

⑤ **hijo/hija** *son, child/daughter*; **niño/niña** *little boy/little girl*; **mi hijo** *my son/my child*; **mis hijos** *my children.*
Mi hijo es todavía un niño. *My son is still a child.*
The terms **niño(s)/niña(s)** are used for young children:
Los niños están en el colegio. *The children are in school.*
Voy a comprar golosinas para los niños. *I'm going to buy sweets for the children.*

* * *

Ejercicio 1: Traduzca

❶ Tengo un piso en Córdoba. ❷ ¿Te gusta? ❸ Voy a firmar. ❹ Vamos a la agencia. ❺ Estoy casado.

* * *

Ejercicio 2: Complete

❶ Very much!
¡ . . . . !

❷ Do you *(formal)* like the coffee?
¿ . . . . el café?

❸ I have to speak with my husband.
. . . . hablar con mi . . . .

5 – Excuse [me], but … you're married?
6 And … you also have children?
7 – Of course *(Clear)*! Six little children.
8 – Ah!

* * *

Answers to Exercise 1

❶ I have a flat/apartment in Cordoba. ❷ Do you like it? ❸ I'm going to sign. ❹ We're going to the agency. ❺ I'm *(m.)* married.

* * *

❹ I'm *(f.)* married and I have two children.
Estoy . . . . tengo dos . . . . . .

❺ How old is *(What age has)* the little girl?
¿. . . . . . . tiene la . . . . ?

Answers to Exercise 2

❶ Muchísimo ❷ Le gusta – ❸ Tengo que – marido ❹ – casada y – hijos ❺ Qué edad – niña

Despite the increasing individualism of Western societies, family solidarity **solidaridad familiar**, *continues to be an important characteristic of Spanish society. Family bonds remain strong on the whole. Once you have made the acquaintance of someone in Spain, they may well introduce you to members of their family.*

26 Lección veintiséis

Una ganga

1 – Me he com**pra**do ① un **co**che. ¿Te **gu**sta?
2 – ¿Es **nue**vo?
3 – No, es de se**gun**da **ma**no ②.
4 ¡He **he**cho un buen ne**go**cio ③!
5 – Pa**re**ce que ④ es**tá** bien…

Pronunciation

***oo**-nah **gahn**-gah **1** may ay kom-**prah**-do oon **ko**-chay ¿tay **goo**-stah? **2** es **nway**-bo **3** no es day say-**goon**-dah **mah**-no **4** ay **ay**-cho oon bwayn nay-**go**-thee-o **5** pah-**ray**-thay kay es-**tah** bee-en*

Notes

① **Me he comprado un coche.** *I've bought myself a car.* Or, alternatively, **He comprado un coche.** *I've bought a car.* Here, the pronoun **me** is equivalent to *myself.* Although it isn't necessary to the meaning, as in English, it reinforces the sense of possession and makes the sentence more familiar in tone. The use of the reflexive with certain verbs associated with possessing or acquiring is quite common in Spanish.
¿Cómo te ganas la vida? *How do you earn your(self a) living?*
Se aprovechó de las circunstancias.
He took advantage (for himself) of the circumstances.
Nos llevaremos todos los muebles.
We'll take (away with us) all the furniture. ▸

Nowadays, mainly because of the instability of the job market and high rent, many young people live with their parents longer. Another sign of the times is that **familias numerosas** big families *are much less common than in the past. Today Spain is among the countries in Europe with the lowest birth rates.*

Lesson twenty-six 26

A bargain

1 – I've bought myself a car. Do you like it?
2 – Is it new?
3 – No, it's *(of)* secondhand.
4 I got a bargain *(I've made a good deal)*!
5 – It seems *(that it's)* fine …

▸ (2) **de segunda mano** and **de ocasión** both mean *secondhand.*

(3) **un buen negocio** *a good deal.* In this context, **negocio** is a synonym of **ganga** or **chollo** *bargain.*

(4) **parecer** means *to look like, to appear, to seem.* You've already seen **¿Qué le parece?** *What do you think [of it]?*

6 – Con un arre**gli**llo ⑤…
7 – ¿Qué hay que ⑥ arre**glar**?
8 – **Na**da impor**tan**te. ⑦ **Só**lo le voy a cam**biar** el mo**tor**. □

*6 kon oon ah-rray-**glee**-yo **7** kay a-ee kay ah-rray-**glahr** **8** **nah**-dah eem-por-**tahn**-tay. **so**-lo lay boy ah kahm-**bee-ahr** el mo-**tor***

Notes

⑤ **arreglo** *repair, alteration*; **arreglillo** *minor repair*. We've already seen the diminutive **-ito**, **-ita**, which is by far the most frequent way to denote 'smallness'. The same idea can also be rendered by adding the suffix **-illo**, **-illa**. But be careful, ▸

* * *

Ejercicio 1: Traduzca

❶ ¿Tienes coche? ❷ He hecho un buen negocio. ❸ Es un coche de segunda mano. ❹ Ha sido una ganga. ❺ Me gustan los coches.

* * *

Ejercicio 2: Complete

❶ She has bought herself a new car.
Se . . comprado . . coche . . . . . .

❷ What do you *(informal)* think?
¿Qué . . . . ?

❸ I don't like her car.
Su coche . . . .

❹ What has to/must be done?
¿Qué . . . . . . hacer?

❺ Nothing much.
. . . .

6 – With a little repair …
7 – What has to be repaired?
8 – Nothing important. I'm only going to replace the engine *(Only to-it I'm going to change the motor).*

because using diminutives in certain contexts can be pejorative. For example, **un intelectualillo** is 'a petty intellectual.

⑥ **hay que + infinitivo** *one must/you have to* + infinitive, or alternatively, *it must/has to be* + past participle
Hay que repetir cada frase. *Each sentence must be repeated.*

⑦ **Nada importante** means *nothing important*, *nothing major*, *nothing much.* An expression that can come in handy in a variety of situations!

* * *

Answers to Exercise 1

❶ Do you have a car? ❷ I got a good deal. ❸ It's a secondhand car. ❹ It was a bargain. ❺ I like cars.

* * *

Answers to Exercise 2

❶ – ha – un – nuevo ❷ – te parece ❸ – no me gusta ❹ – hay que – ❺ Nada importante

El automóvil the car *continues to be the preferred mode of transport in Spain. Even if you can get around easily using public transport, most people feel that having your own* **vehículo** vehicle *gives you more freedom. Nonetheless,* **el alquiler de vehículos** vehicle rental *is becoming increasingly common. As a tourist, you'll find that* **alquilar un coche** renting a car *is cheaper than in many places in Europe, and you can find rental companies in all large towns.*

De tal palo, tal astilla ①

1 – ¡No a**guan**to ② más!
2 – ¿Qué **pa**sa?
3 – ¡No te so**por**to!
4 Me voy ③ a ④ **ca**sa de mi **ma**dre.
5 – Me **te**mo que no la vas a encon**trar**.
6 – ¿Qué **di**ces?

Pronunciation
*day tahl **pah**-lo tahl ah-**stee**-yah **1** no ah-**gwahn**-to mahs **2** kay **pah**-sah **3** no tay so-**por**-to **4** may boy ah **kah**-sah day mee **mah**-dray **5** may **tay**-mo kay no lah bahs ah en-kon-**trahr** **6** kay **dee**-thays*

Notes

① The expression **De tal palo, tal astilla** (literally, 'From such wood, such splinter') conveys the same idea as the expression 'A chip off the old block' or 'Like father, like son' – in this context, 'Like mother, like daughter'. **un palo** *stick, wooden pole, tree*; **una astilla** *splinter, wood fragment.*

② **aguantar** *to bear, to tolerate, to endure* as well as *to hold (something).* As you can imagine, this expression is as common as its English equivalent 'I can't take it anymore!'. This verb can also be used in the sense of line 3: **No te aguanto** is synonymous with **No te soporto.** *I can't stand you.*

③ **ir** *to go*; **irse** *to go away, to be off* or *to leave.* In Spain, the reflexive verb **irse** is more frequently used than **partir** *to leave*, which can have the same meaning. **Me voy** *I'm off, I'm leaving*; **¿Te vas?** *Are you off? Are you leaving?*

④ Remember, after a verb that indicates movement towards a particular destination, the preposition **a** is used: ▶

Like mother, like daughter

1 – I've had enough *(I don't tolerate more)*!
2 – What's the matter *(What's happening)*?
3 – I can't *(don't)* stand you!
4 I'm off *(I'm going away)* to my mother's *(to house of my mother)*.
5 – I'm afraid that you won't find her [there].
6 – What are you saying?

Voy a la piscina. *I'm going to the swimming pool.*
Cristina se ha ido al Tíbet. *Cristina has left for Tibet.*
Los niños han bajado a la calle. *The children have gone down to the street.*
Vamos a aterrizar. *We're going to land.* (i.e. in an airplane)
Note that the idea of going inside a place is expressed with the preposition **en**: **entrar en el banco** *to go into the bank.*

In this dialogue we see **a casa**, which conveys the idea of going to a house, whereas **en casa** connotes being at a house:
Voy a su casa. *I'm going to her house.*
Estoy en su casa. *I'm at her house.*

(**la casa** *house*; **el hogar** *home.* **Esta casa es mi hogar.** *This house is my home.*)

7 – Sí, a**ca**ba de lla**mar pa**ra de**cir**me que ha discu**ti**do ⑤ con tu **pa**dre…

8 … y que se ha **i**do a **ca**sa de tu a**bue**la. □

*7 see ah-**kah**-bah day yah-**mahr pah**-rah day-**theer**-may kay ah dee-skoo-**tee**-do kon too **pah**-dray **8** ee kay say ah **ee**-do ah **kah**-sah day too ah-**bway**-lah*

* * *

Ejercicio 1: Traduzca

❶ ¿Qué dices? ❷ ¡No aguanto más! ❸ Me voy. ❹ ¿Adónde vas? ❺ Voy a casa de mi padre.

* * *

Ejercicio 2: Complete

❶ What's the matter?
¿. . . . . . . ?

❷ She can't take it anymore.
No . . . .

❸ She has just left.
. . . . . de . . . . .

❹ She had an argument and she left.
. . . . se ha ido.

❺ She's gone off to her son's.
Se ha ido . . . . su . . . . .

7 – Yes, she just called to tell me that she's had an argument *(has argued)* with your father …
8 ... and that she's gone to your grandmother's *(to house of your grandmother)*.

Notes

⑤ The main meaning of **discutir** is *to discuss* or *to debate*. But in colloquial speech, when followed by the preposition **con**, it often means *to argue, to quarrel*; to have a heated discussion.

* * *

Answers to Exercise 1

❶ What are you saying? ❷ I've had enough! ❸ I'm off./I'm leaving. ❹ Where are you going? ❺ I'm going to my father's.

* * *

Answers to Exercise 2

❶ Qué pasa ❷ – aguanta más ❸ Acaba – irse ❹ Ha discutido y – ❺ – a casa de – hijo

The next lesson is a review of the most important points raised in the last six, bringing to an end this set of lessons. Think about how much progress you've already made. You'll no longer need many of the reminders that we've been giving you so far, as your level is improving all the time!

28 Lección veintiocho

Repaso

1 Suffixes

In Spanish, new words can be formed by adding a suffix to a noun or an adjective, especially in colloquial language. However, as suffixes can have different interpretations, the meaning can vary depending on the context and the tone. Be aware that suffixes can lend the word an affectionate, scornful or ironic touch, depending on the situation. Use them with great care in order to avoid misunderstandings!

1.1 The diminutive suffix *-ito*, *-ita*

The diminutive suffix **-ito**, **-ita** is by far the most frequently used. It is also the only one that is unambiguous in meaning; it always expresses the idea of 'smallness'.
un rato *a while*; **un ratito** *a little while*, *a moment*

Often it expresses the idea of affection, attachment, tenderness, etc. In certain situations, this additional shade of meaning may have to be translated into English by using a second adjective.
un piso *a flat*, *an apartment*; **un pisito** *a nice little flat*

1.2 Formation

• For polysyllabic words ending in **-o** or **-a**, you simply replace the ending with **-ito** or **-ita**, respectively.
un trabajo *a job*; **un trabajito** *a little job*
una muchacha *a girl*; **una muchachita** *a little girl*

• For polysyllabic words ending in a consonant other than **-n** or **-r**, you just add **-ito**, **-ita** to the end of the word.
un árbol *a tree*; **un arbolito** *a little tree*

• For polysyllabic words that end in **-e**, **-n** or **-r**, you add **-cito**, **-cita** at the end of the word.
un café *a coffee*; **un cafecito** *a small coffee*
una lección *a lesson*; **una leccioncita** *a little lesson*

• For monosyllabic words and also for polysyllabic words where the spoken accent falls on a diphthong, you add **-ecito**, **-ecita**.
una flor *a flower*; **una florecita** *a little flower*
una siesta *a nap*; **una siestecita** *a little nap*

1.3 The diminutive suffix *-illo*, *-illa*

The suffix **-illo**, **-illa** is also common. Primarily, it stresses the idea of smallness. The rules for forming words with this suffix are the same as the rules for the diminutive suffix **-ito**, **-ita**.
un pan *a loaf of bread*; **un panecillo** *a small loaf of bread*

However, this suffix must be used with great care as it can imply the pejorative meaning 'insignificant'. In addition, it is used in certain words that have acquired a specific meaning. So, for example, **ventanilla** (from **ventana** *window*) does not mean 'small window', but *counter window* (in a bank, post office, railway station or other public place) or *car window*. So for the time being, make the suffix **-ito**, **-ita** your first choice.

2 Pronouns

Direct and indirect object pronouns (*me, you, him, her, it, us, them*) are used to replace nouns in sentences to avoid repetition. So far in the lessons, we've seen that in Spanish these pronouns go in front of conjugated verbs (though they are placed at the end of infinitives) and, when used together, the indirect object comes first. We've also seen reflexive pronouns (the equivalent of *myself, yourself, oneself*, etc.), which are an integral part of reflexive verbs. In Spanish, there is also a special set of pronouns used after prepositions (e.g. *at, to, with*, etc.). See the grammatical appendix for the full list of Spanish personal pronouns.

Here is a review of the object and reflexive pronouns you've seen so far, in their context. Don't try to learn them by heart, just relax and read each one aloud. The number in parentheses indicates the lesson where the phrase appeared, so you can refer back if you want to get more detail regarding context and exact meaning. **¡Adelante!** *Carry on!*

¿Cómo **te** llamas?	(lesson 2)
Me llamo …	(" 2)
Podemos ir**nos** al cine	(" 4)
¿a qué **te** dedicas?	(" 15)
¿Qué **te** parece …?	(" 16)
¡…, invíta**me**!	(" 16)
¡Habér**melo** dicho!	(" 19)
¡No **me** digas!	(" 20)
Se me ha olvidado …	(" 23)
Te lo traeré mañana	(" 23)
¿Por qué **te** has pintado …?	(" 24)
Me gusta maquillar**me**	(" 24)
¿**Le** gusta el piso?	(" 25)
Me gusta …	(" 25)
… **le** propongo…	(" 25)
Me he comprado …	(" 26)
¿**Te** gusta?	(" 26)
¡No **te** soporto!	(" 27)
Me voy a casa …	(" 27)
… para decir**me** que …	(" 27)
… **se** ha ido a …	(" 27)

¿Qué tal?
Don't worry if you hesitated a bit here and there; the point of the exercise is to get used to the pronouns, not to remember each and every one of these phrases. We'll be finding out more about pronouns in lessons to come!

3 The past tense: preterite vs. imperfect

We've now seen several different types of past tense in Spanish. The present perfect (**haber** + past participle) is used for a recent completed action that may continue into the present. The preterite (or simple past) is used for a one-off completed action in the past.

Here are a couple of examples to refresh your memory:
Mi hermano ya ha comido tres tapas. *My brother has already eaten three tapas.* (Present perfect: recent completed action, with the possibility of more tapas!)
Yo comí tres tapas anoche. *I ate three tapas last night.* (Preterite: one-time completed action.)

In this set of lessons, you've seen another past tense, the imperfect. The imperfect is used to express regular, repeated actions in the past, corresponding to the English 'used to':
No decía mentiras. *I didn't [use to] tell lies.*

It is also used for continuous actions in the past, or to describe the background to or feelings about something that happened in the past. For example: **Yo no quería …** *I didn't want to …*

Note that the imperfect tense of **-er** and **-ir** verbs is formed by adding **-ía**, **-ías**, **-ía**, etc. to the stem of the verb. In later lessons, we'll find out how to form the imperfect of **-ar** verbs and the three irregular verbs in this tense (**ser** *to be*, **ir** *to go* and **ver** *to see*).

4 *mi*, *tu*, *su*… possessive adjectives

There are two kinds of possessive adjectives in Spanish, those that come before the noun and those that follow it (emphatic possessives). For the moment, let's look only at those that come before the noun.

• When the possessor is singular, and what is possessed is singular:

mi hermano/hermana	*my brother/sister*
tu hijo/hija	*your* (informal sing.) *son/daughter*
su abuelo/abuela	*his/her/your* (formal sing.) *grandfather/grandmother*

• When the possessor is singular, and what is possessed is plural, you just add an **-s** to the possessive adjective:

mis hermanos/hermanas	*my brothers/sisters*
tus hijos/hijas	*your* (informal sing.) *sons, children/daughters*
sus ...	*his/her/its/your* (formal sing.) ...

• When the possessor is plural, and what is possessed is singular:

nuestro coche	*our car* (masc. noun)
nuestra calle	*our street* (fem. noun)
vuestro piso	*your* (informal plural) *flat* (masc. noun)
vuestra maleta	*your* (informal plural) *suitcase* (fem. noun)
su casa	*their/your* (formal plural) *house*

Notice that **nuestro, nuestra** and **vuestro, vuestra** need to agree with the gender of the noun they describe.

* * *

Diálogo recapitulativo

1 – Para su cumpleaños …
2 … mi abuela se ha comprado un coche.
3 – ¿A su edad?
4 ¿Y para qué?
5 – Para ir al cine.
6 – ¿Y el coche te gusta?
7 – Me gusta mucho.
8 Te propongo …
9 … que vayamos a su casa.
10 – ¡Estupendo! ¡Puede invitarnos al cine!

• When the possessor is plural and what is possessed is plural, simply add an **-s** to the possessive adjective:

nuestros coches	*our cars*
nuestras calles	*our streets*
vuestros pisos	*your* (informal plural) *flats*
vuestras maletas	*your* (informal plural) *suitcases*
sus casas	*their/your* (formal plural) *houses*

Note that **su, sus** can mean *his*, *her*, *its*, *their* or *your* (formal):
su pelo: *his/her hair*
su pelo: *its hair*
su pelo: *their hair*
su pelo: *your* (formal) *hair*

See lesson 63, section 4 for the so-called emphatic possessives, which follow the noun.

* * *

Traducción

1 For her birthday … **2** … my grandmother has bought herself a car. **3** At her age? **4** And what for? **5** To go to the cinema. **6** And do you like the car? **7** I like it a lot. **8** I suggest … **9** … that we go to her house. **10** Great! She can treat us to a film!

29 Lección veintinueve

En el médico ①

1 – Me **due**le ② **to**do el **cuer**po.
2 **Cre**o que es muy **gra**ve.
3 – **Dí**game lo que ③ le **pa**sa.
4 – **Cuan**do me **to**co la ca**be**za ④, me **due**le.
5 – ¿**O**tros do**lo**res ⑤?
6 – Si me a**prie**to un **po**co el cora**zón**, me **due**le mu**chí**simo.
7 – Curi**o**so.

Pronunciation
From now on, we'll only indicate the pronunciation of words that appear for the first time or that merit a little reminder ...

Notes

① *At the doctor's* is **en el médico**. But *I'm going to the doctor's* is **Voy al medico.** (Note that it is 'to the doctor', not 'doctor's'.) In Spain, **médico** *doctor, physician* is preferred to **doctor** *doctor*, which can also refer to the holder of a university doctorate. To refer to the doctor's office itself: **en la consulta** *at the office/surgery*, i.e. where you go to consult the doctor.

② **doler** *to hurt*; **me duele** *it hurts me.*
Me duele la cabeza. *My head hurts.* ('It hurts me the head.')
Me duelen los pies. *My feet hurt.* ('They hurt me the feet.')
Notice that in the Spanish construction, the subject (the body part) is at the end of the sentence. The verb is used in the third-person and conjugates to agree with the singular or plural subject in the same way as **gustar** (lesson 9, note 6).

The verb **doler** is a stem-changing verb. The vowel **o** changes to **ue** when the verb is conjugated (in all persons apart from **nosotros** and **vosotros**). There are also stem-changing verbs in which the **e** changes to **ie**. Stem-changing verbs we've seen ▸

At the doctor's

1 – My whole body hurts *(Me it-hurts all the body).*
2 I think *(that)* it's very serious.
3 – Tell me what's wrong with you *(Tell[formal]-me that which to-you[formal] happens).*
4 – When I touch my *(the)* head, it hurts.
5 – [Any] other pain*(s)*?
6 – If I press a bit on my chest *(the heart)*, it hurts a lot.
7 – Strange.

*... **may**-dee-ko **1** ... **dway**-lay ... **kwayr**-po **2** ... **grah**-bay **3** **dee**-gah-may ... **4** ... kah-**bay**-thah ... **5** ... do-**lo**-res **6** ... ah-**pree-ay**-to ... ko-rah-**thon** ... moo-**chee**-see-mo **7** koo-ree-**o**-so*

so far are: **tener** *to have* → **tiene**; **dormir** *to sleep* → **duerme**; **poder** *to be able to* → **puede**; **querer** *to want* → **quiere**; and **volver** *to return* → **vuelve**. For now, just note this – the grammatical appendix also has information on these verbs.

(3) **lo que** translates to *what* in the sense of *that which*:
Lo que dices es verdad. *What you say is true.*
¡Eso es lo que cuenta! *That's what counts!*

(4) As you can see throughout this conversation, in Spanish, body parts are referred to by the definite article (**el**, **la**, **los** or **las**), rather than a possessive adjective (e.g. *my*, *your*). To make it clear who the body part belongs to, a pronoun is used with the verb: for example, **me toco la cabeza** *I touch my head* or literally, 'I touch me the head'.

(5) **el dolor** *pain*; **los dolores** *pains*. (Yes, like the name Dolores!) Another way to say something hurts is **tener dolor de**:
Me duele el vientre. *My stomach hurts.*
Tengo dolor de vientre. *I have a stomach ache.*

8 – **Cuan**do me **to**co el **vien**tre, me **due**le.
9 – ¡Qué ex**tra**ño!
10 – Me **to**co la **pier**na, y tam**bién** me **due**le.
11 – Voy a exami**nar**la.
12 Res**pi**re **hon**do… Muy bien… **De**se ⑥ la **vuel**ta…
13 ¡Se**ño**ra! Us**ted** no **tie**ne **na**da en nin**gún** **si**tio ⑦.
14 ¡**Só**lo **tie**ne la **ma**no **ro**ta!

8 *…* ***bee-en****-tray …* ***9*** *…eks-****trah****-nyo* ***10*** *…* ***pee-ayr****-nah …* ***11*** *… eks-ah-mee-****nahr****-lah* ***12*** *rres-****pee****-ray* ***on****-do …* ***day****-say …* ***bwayl****-tah* ***13*** *… neen-****goon see****-tee-o* ***14*** *…* ***rro****-tah*

Notes

⑥ **Dese la vuelta.** *Turn around.* ('Give-yourself the turn.') The command **dese** is the formal imperative of the reflexive verb **darse** *to give oneself.* Review lesson 35 has more information on forming the imperative. The verb **dar** *to give* pops up in many common expressions, for example:
darse la vuelta *to turn around* (not to be confused with **dar una vuelta** *to take a turn*, i.e. take a walk or a ride in a vehicle)
darse la mano *to shake hands.*

* * *

Ejercicio 1: Traduzca

❶ ¿Dónde te duele? ❷ No me parece muy grave. ❸ Tienes que ir a ver al médico. ❹ El niño dice que tiene dolor de vientre. ❺ Es muy curioso.

8 – When I touch my stomach, it hurts.
9 – How odd!
10 – I touch my leg, and it hurts as well.
11 – I'm going to examine you *(formal, fem.)*.
12 Breathe *(formal)* deep[ly] … Very good … Turn around *(Give-yourself[formal] the turn)*…
13 Madam! There's nothing wrong with you anywhere *(You not have nothing in no place)*.
14 All you have is a broken hand *(Only you-have the hand broken)*!

▸ ⑦ Compare:
nowhere **en ningún sitio** or **en ninguna parte** ('in no site' or 'in no part')
everywhere **en todos los sitios** or **en todas partes** ('in all the sites' or 'in all parts').

* * *

Answers to Exercise 1

❶ Where does it hurt *(you)*? ❷ That doesn't seem very serious to me. ❸ You must go to see the doctor. ❹ The boy says that he has a stomach ache. ❺ It's very strange.

Ejercicio 2: Complete

❶ Does your *(informal)* head hurt?
¿.. ..... la ...... ?

❷ I don't know what is wrong.
No sé .. ... pasa.

❸ Tell *(formal)* me what you think.
.... piensa.

❹ What is the doctor's address?
¿.... .. .. dirección del ...... ?

❺ I like him/her/it very much.
.. gusta ....

---

30 Lección treinta

Políticamente correcto

1 Dos cre**ti**nos di**ná**micos, emple**a**dos de **u**na em**pre**sa multinacio**nal**,
2 **char**lan por la ma**ña**na ① **jun**to a la **má**quina de ② ca**fé**:

Pronunciation
*po-**lee**-tee-kah-men-tay ko-**rrek**-to **1** ... kray-**tee**-nos dee-**nah**-mee-kos em-play-**ah**-dos ... em-**pray**-sah mool-tee-*

Notes

① **por la mañana** *in the morning.* **Iré al banco por la mañana.** *I will go to the bank in the morning.*
mañana (noun) *morning*, e.g. **esta mañana** *this morning*
mañana (adverb) *tomorrow*, e.g. **te veré mañana** *I'll see you tomorrow.*

▸

Answers to Exercise 2

❶ Te duele – cabeza ❷ – lo que – ❸ Dígame lo que – ❹ Cuál es la – médico ❺ Me – muchísimo

Ir al médico going to the doctor's *in Spain is a comparable experience to that of most countries in the European Union. The Spanish National Health System is public, and its citizens have universal coverage for free or low-cost health care. European nationals can receive free medical care in the* **hospitales de la Seguridad Social** Social Security hospitals *if they have a* **Tarjeta Sanitaria Europea** European Health Insurance Card.

If you're visiting Spain, an important word to know is **farmacia** drugstore, pharmacy, chemist's *(to find one, just look for the green cross). A useful telephone number to know is* **112** *(the number for* **urgencias** emergencies *everywhere in Spain).*

Lesson thirty 30

Politically correct

1 Two enterprising idiots, employees of a multinational company,

2 are chatting one morning *(in the morning)* next to the coffee machine:

*nah-thee-o-**nahl** 2 **chahr**-lahn … mah-**nyah**-nah **hoon**-to … **mah**-kee-nah …*

So … **mañana por la mañana** *tomorrow morning.* (See also lesson 10, note 5.)

② **la máquina de café** *the coffee machine.* Remember, where English uses a noun (here, *coffee*) to describe another (e.g. *machine*), Spanish uses a prepositional phrase with **de**: **la máquina de coser** *the sewing machine.*

3 – Y tú, ¿cuántos **hi**jos **tie**nes?
4 – **Cin**co.
5 – ¿Y **có**mo se **lla**man?
6 – Ma**rí**a, Ale**jan**dro, **San**dra, **Li**sa y Cheng Hui Kang.
7 – ¡Ca**ram**ba! ¡Y el **úl**timo **nom**bre… ③ **có**mo a**sí**?
8 – ¿Qué **pa**sa? ④
9 ¿Toda**ví**a no **sa**bes que **u**no de **ca**da ⑤ **cin**co **ni**ños que **na**cen ⑥ en el **mun**do es **chi**no? □

***4 theen**-ko **5** … **yah**-mahn **6** … ah-lay-**hahn**-dro **sahn**-drah **lee**-sah … **7** ¡kah-**rahm**-bah! … **ool**-tee-mo **nom**-bray … **9** … **nah**-then … **moon**-do … **chee**-no*

Notes

③ **nombre** *first name*; **apellido** *last name, surname.* In Spain, to request someone's full name in official situations, **nombre** is generally used: **¿Cuál es su nombre?** *What is your* (formal) *name?* In the reply, you give your first name and then your last name. But don't forget the more conversational way to ask someone's name: **¿Cómo se llama?** *What's your name?* (formal) and **¿Cómo te llamas?** (informal). ▸

* * *

Ejercicio 1: Traduzca

❶ ¿Dónde trabajas? ❷ Soy empleado en un banco. ❸ Me voy mañana por la mañana. ❹ ¿Cómo se llama tu hija? ❺ ¿Dónde has nacido?

3 – And you, how many children do you have?
4 – Five.
5 – And what are their names?
6 – María, Alejandro, Sandra, Lisa and Cheng Hui Kang.
7 – Good heavens! And the last name … how come *(how so)*?
8 – What's the problem?
9 Didn't you know *(Still you don't know)* that one of every five children that [is] born in the world is Chinese?

④ We've already seen the expression **¿Qué pasa?** with the meanings *What's happening? What's the matter?* or *What's new?* in different contexts. As we see here, **¿Qué pasa?** can also mean *So what's the problem? What of it?*, expressing a note of defiance.

⑤ **uno de cada** *one of every/each* followed by a number and a noun means *one out of/one in ...*: **una de cada diez personas** *one out of ten people*, *one person in ten.*

⑥ **nacen**, from **nacer** *to be born*. Notice that this verb is active in Spanish (the baby does it, sort of like hatching!), but passive in English, where the mother, although unmentioned, at least gets some credit! You might hear either of the past tense forms, although the preterite is more common:
Yo nací en Inglaterra. / He nacido en Inglaterra.
I was born in England.

* * *

Answers to Exercise 1

❶ Where do you work? ❷ I'm a bank employee *(m.)*. ❸ I leave tomorrow morning. ❹ What's your daughter's name? ❺ Where were you born?

Ejercicio 2: Complete

❶ I don't have money for the coffee machine.
No tengo . . . . . . para la . . . .

❷ We chatted for a bit.
Hemos . . . . ratito.

❸ Do you *(informal)* want to come by tomorrow?
¿. . . . . . . pasar . . . . . . ?

---

31 Lección treinta y una

'Enganchados' ① a la tele

1 **Sue**na ② el te**lé**fono:
2 – Emer**gen**cias. ¡**Di**ga! ③
3 – ¿Ser**vi**cio de ur**gen**cias, **cien**to **do**ce?

Pronunciation
***1 sway**-nah ... **2** em-ayr-**hen**-thee-ahs ¡**dee**-gah! **3** sayr-**bee**-thee-o day oor-**hen**-thee-ahs **thee-en**-to...*

Notes

① **enganchar** *to hook*; **enganchado** *hooked.* Like in English, apart from its literal meaning, this word has the figurative meaning of *addicted.* Here it is used in the sense of **fanático** *a fanatic, fan, devotee.* But it can also mean physically addicted: **estar enganchado a la droga, al alcohol** *to be hooked on drugs, alcohol.*

② **suena** is the third-person singular present tense of **sonar** *to ring*, a stem-changing verb. In the present tense, stem changes occur in all persons except **nosotros** and **vosotros**. In line 9, **suelta** is the third-person singular present tense of the stem-changing verb **soltar** *to release, let go, let out.* ▶

❹ What's his/her/your *(formal)* [full] name?
¿ . . . . es su . . . . . . ?

❺ He still hasn't arrived.
. . . . no ha . . . .

Answers to Exercise 2
❶ – dinero – máquina de café ❷ – charlado un – ❸ Quieres – mañana ❹ Cuál – nombre ❺ Todavía – llegado

Lesson thirty-one 31

'Hooked' on TV

1 The telephone rings:
2 – Emergency. Hello *(Tell[formal])*!
3 – Emergency Services, 112?

③ **¡Diga!** ('Tell!') and **¡Dígame!** ('Tell me!'), the formal singular command of **decir**, is traditionally how people in Spain answer the telephone, rather than saying the equivalent of 'Hello'. However, these days, many young people use **Hola**, especially at home. In much of Latin America, people answer the phone with **¡Aló!**

4 – Sí, **dí**game.

5 – Por fa**vor**, **ven**gan ④ de**pri**sa, mi **hi**jo
se ha tra**ga**do ⑤ la **pi**la del **man**do de la
televi**sión**.

6 – ¡Tranqui**lí**cese! ⑥ ¡No se preo**cu**pe! ⑦

7 **Aho**ra **mis**mo ⑧ le en**via**mos un **mé**dico y
una ambu**lan**cia.

8 **Cuan**do la ambu**lan**cia se dispo**ní**a ⑨ a
sa**lir** ⑩…

9 **vuel**ve ⑪ a so**nar** el te**lé**fono y la **mis**ma
voz **suel**ta:

10 – ¡**Dé**jelo, seño**ri**ta, ya **he**mos encon**tra**do
otra! ☐

5 … **ben**-gahn … trah-**gah**-do … **pee**-lah … **mahn**-do …
tay-lay-bee-**see-on** **6** ¡trahn-kee-**lee**-thay-say! … pray-o-
koo-pay **7** … en-**bee**-ah-mos … ahm-boo-**lahn**-thee-ah **8** …
dees-po-**nee**-ah … **9** bwayl-bay … so-**nahr** … both **swayl**-
tah **10** **day**-hay-lo sen-yo-**ree**-tah … en-kon-**trah**-do **o**-trah

Notes

④ **vengan** is the formal plural command of **venir**. Like **diga**, it
is in the subjunctive mood, which is used for all commands
apart from positive (affirmative) informal commands.
First-person present tense of **venir** → **vengo** *I come*
Third-person present subjunctive of **venir** → **venga**
Imperative: formal singular → **venga**
Imperative: formal plural → **vengan**
You'll find out more about the imperative in lesson 35.

⑤ **tragar** *to swallow* is often used reflexively, **tragarse**.

⑥ **tranquilizarse**, literally, 'to tranquilize oneself', means *to
keep calm, to take it easy* when used in the imperative. The
noun **un tranquilizante** is *a tranquilizer*.

⑦ **preocuparse** *to worry*. Some common expressions:
No se preocupe. *Don't worry.* (formal singular)
No te preocupes. *Don't worry.* (informal singular) ▶

4 – Yes, hello *(tell[formal]-me)*.
5 – Please come *(formal)* quickly, my son has swallowed *(himself has swallowed)* the battery from the TV remote control.
6 – Stay calm *(Calm-yourself[formal])*! Don't worry *(Don't worry yourself[formal])*!
7 *(Now even to-you[formal])* We are sending a doctor and an ambulance right now.
8 As *(When)* the ambulance is *(was)* preparing *(itself)* to leave
9 the telephone rings again and the same voice blurts out *(lets-loose)*:
10 – Never mind *(Leave[formal]-it)*, miss, *(already)* we've found another [one]!

⑧ **ahora mismo** generally corresponds to *right now* or *immediately* (**inmediatamente**).
Hay que encontrar una farmacia ahora mismo.
We have to find a pharmacy right away.
Hay que llevarle ahora mismo a urgencias.
We have to take him to the emergency room immediately.

⑨ **se disponía a** *he/she/it/you* (formal) *was preparing to*, *getting ready to*. Remember that the imperfect tense of **-er** and **-ir** verbs is formed by adding **-ía**, **-ías**, **-ía**, **-íamos**, **-íais**, **-ían** to the stem. Here, we again have a reflexive use of the verb.

⑩ A reminder: **salir** can mean either *to leave* or *to go/come out*.
El tren sale a las ocho de la mañana.
The train leaves at eight o'clock in the morning.
Juan ha salido a dar una vuelta. *Juan has gone out for a walk.*

⑪ The idea of a repeated action – something happening again – is often expressed by **volver a** followed by an infinitive (**volver** *to turn*, *to return*, *to come/go back*):
volver a hacer *to do again*, *to redo*
volver a sonar *to ring again*
volver a leer *to read again.*

We'll come back (**Volveremos**) to expressing repetition and to the verb **volver** itself.

Ejercicio 1: Traduzca

❶ ¿Ha sonado el teléfono? ❷ Voy a telefonear al ciento doce. ❸ ¡No te preocupes! ❹ ¿A qué hora sale el tren? ❺ ¡Diga!/¡Dígame!

* * *

Ejercicio 2: Complete

❶ The doctor is getting ready to leave.
El . . . . salir.

❷ Do you *(informal)* want anything else?
¿ . . . . algo más?

❸ I'm going to redo *(return to do)* the exercise.
Voy a . . . . el ejercicio.

❹ We're going right away.
Vamos . . . .

❺ Never mind *(Leave[formal]-it)*, it's not a good idea!
¡ . . . . . . , no es una . . . . !

---

32 Lección treinta y dos

En la sección de caballeros

1 – ¡**Ho**la, **bue**nas! ① ¿Le a**tien**den? ②

Pronunciation
*... sek-**thee-on** ... kah-bah-**yay**-ros **1** ... ah-**tee-en**-den*

Notes

① **¡Hola, buenas!**, **¡Muy buenas!** or just **¡Buenas!** are common greetings that are a bit less formal in tone than the standard ▸

Answers to Exercise 1

❶ Has the telephone rung? ❷ I'm going to call 112. ❸ Don't worry! ❹ What time does the train leave? ❺ Hello! *(when answering the telephone)*

* * *

Answers to Exercise 2

❶ – médico se dispone a – ❷ Quieres – ❸ – volver a hacer – ❹ – ahora mismo ❺ Déjelo – buena idea

* * *

Inside the European Union, a common **número de urgencia** emergency number *was introduced in the 1990s. To reach any emergency service in any EU country, just call* **el ciento doce** 112 *from any phone, free of charge, and you will be put through to the appropriate service. In Spain, the call is received by the* **Servicio de Emergencias** Emergency Services, *a central switchboard that dispatches calls depending on the service required, for example, to a hospital, the police, the fire brigade, etc., each of which also has its own number.*

Lesson thirty-two 32

In the men's department

1 – Good afternoon! Is someone helping you *(You[formal] they-serve)*?

▸ **¡Buenos días!** You can use them at any time of day, in any situation.

② **atender** *to attend to*, *to serve*, *to help*. This is another stem-changing verb. **¿Le atienden?** *Are you being helped?*

Simply learn this as a set phrase.

2 – ¡Muy **bue**nas! Me gusta**rí**a ③ pro**bar**me esos ④ za**pa**tos ⑤.

3 – ¿**És**tos?¿Los a**zu**les?

4 En **es**te ⑥ mo**de**lo los te**ne**mos tam**bién** a **ra**yas **ver**des y ama**ri**llas…

5 – No, **é**sos ⑦ no; los a**zu**les no.

6 **Quie**ro los que es**tán jus**to al **la**do. Los de ⑧ co**lor li**la.

7 – **Pe**ro… caba**lle**ro, ¡**é**sos no son de co**lor li**la! ¡Son **blan**cos!

8 – ¿Y… us**ted nun**ca ⑨ ha **vis**to **li**las **blan**cas?

***2** … goo-stah-**ree**-ah pro-**bahr**-may **ay**-sos thah-**pah**-tos*
***4** … **es**-tay mo-**day**-lo … **rrah**-yahs **bayr**-days … ah-mah-*

Notes

③ **me gustaría** *I would like*. Remember **me gusta**? This is the conditional mood, which we'll find out more about later. **Me gustaría** is also a handy expression to learn, as it is a polite way to order or ask for something.

④ **esos zapatos** *those shoes*; **estos zapatos** *these shoes*. The demonstrative adjectives **esos** and **estos** are used with masculine plural nouns.

⑤ **Me gustaría un par de zapatos.** *I would like a pair of shoes*. In a shoe store, you might also see the term **el calzado** *footwear*. When referring to shoe size, the Spanish verb is **calzar**: **Calzo el cuarenta.** *I take/wear shoe size 40*. This is not the place to go into the different shoe sizes in different countries – Spain of course uses European sizes.

⑥ **este modelo** *this style*, *model*; **ese modelo** *that style*, *model*. The demonstrative adjectives **este** and **ese** are used with masculine singular nouns.

⑦ **éstos** (line 3) *these (ones)*; **ésos** (line 5) *those (ones)*. When written with an accent, **éstos** and **ésos** are demonstrative pronouns that replace masculine plural nouns. Ditto for **éste** ▸

2 – Good afternoon! I would like to try on *(myself)* those shoes.
3 – These? The blue [ones]?
4 In this style they also come *(them we-have also)* with green and yellow stripes …
5 – No, not those; not the blue [ones].
6 I want those that are right next *(just at-the side)* [to them]. Those lilac-coloured [ones].
7 – But … sir, those aren't *(of colour)* lilac! They're white!
8 – And … you've never seen white lilacs?

***ree**-yahs* **6** ***kee-ay**-ro … **hoos**-to ahl **lah**-do … ko-**lor** **lee**-lah* **7** *… **blahn**-kos* **8** *… oos-**ted** **noon**-kah … **bees**-to **lee**-lahs **blan**-kahs*

and **ése**, with a written accent: *this (one)* and *that (one)*. (Note that in English, we often need to add 'one' or 'ones', effectively changing the demonstrative pronoun back into an adjective.)

⑧ **los que están …** *the ones that are*; *those that are …*

los de color … *the ones/those that are coloured …*

In this construction, rather than **ésos** etc., the corresponding definite article (**el, la, los, las**) is used as the pronoun, followed by **que** or **de**.

el que quieres *the [one(m.)] that you want*

los que están a la izquierda *the [ones(m.)] that are on the left*

la de mi madre *the [one(f.)] that belongs to my mother.*

⑨ **usted <u>nunca</u> ha visto** or **usted no ha visto <u>nunca</u>** *you have never seen*; both constructions are correct. But remember that no word can be placed between the auxiliary verb (**haber**) and its past participle. So where in English we can say *I haven't yet eaten*, in Spanish it must be **<u>todavía</u> no he comido** or **no he comido <u>todavía</u>**. The adverb can go in front or behind, but never in the middle!

Ejercicio 1: Traduzca

❶ ¿De qué color es tu coche? ❷ Me gustaría ver otro modelo. ❸ Ese piso no me gusta. ❹ ¿Le atienden, caballero? ❺ Los taxis de Barcelona son negros y amarillos.

* * *

Ejercicio 2: Complete

❶ I don't like this style.
. . . . modelo no . . . .

❷ I want those shoes.
. . . . zapatos.

❸ I live next to the pharmacy.
Vivo . . . . . . de la . . . .

❹ That suitcase is the [one that belongs to] *(of)* my mother.
Esta maleta . . . .

❺ Have you seen my mobile [phone]?
¿Has . . . . . mi . . . . . ?

ME GUSTARÍA VER OTRO MODELO.

Answers to Exercise 1

❶ What colour is your car? ❷ I'd like to see another style. ❸ I don't like that apartment. ❹ Are you being helped, sir? ❺ Barcelona taxis are black and yellow.

* * *

Answers to Exercise 2

❶ Este – me gusta ❷ Quiero esos – ❸ – al lado – farmacia ❹ – es la de mi madre ❺ – visto – móvil

* * *

Caballero, *derived from* **caballo** horse, *historically referred to a* knight *(literally, 'cavalier'). It is one of those words that has managed to survive through the centuries to become part of everyday vocabulary. One of its oldest connotations is that of* gentleman. *Cervantes, in his novel* Don Quixote, *immortalized the figure of the* **caballero andante** knight errant *par excellence.*

While retaining its original meaning, **caballero** *has evolved over time; today, it is used in numerous ways. One is as the title for a man who behaves with loyalty, distinction and courtesy; that is, as a synonym for* **señor** sir. *However, its use varies from one region to another: for example, it is used much more extensively in Castilla than in the Basque Country. Its use is also related to one's social background –* **caballero** *lays claim to a certain distinction.*

Men may also be referred to as **caballero** *in a restaurant or shop, in a queue, at a ticket counter, or in other public places, as a gesture of politeness. Very often you will also find* **caballeros**, *in the plural, competing with* **hombres** men *or* **señores** gentlemen *written on certain doors you may find yourself in need of when you're out and about in town.*

Just remember that it never hurts to behave like a gentleman: **comportarse como un caballero**.

En el terminal de llegada

1 – **Va**mos, la **cin**ta ① ya se ha **pues**to ② en **mar**cha.
2 – ¡Mi**rad**, a**hí** ③ **vie**ne **par**te de **nues**tro equi**pa**je!
3 – Co**ged** ④ **ca**da **u**no **u**na **co**sa.
4 – **Es**ta ma**le**ta **pe**sa **mu**cho.

Pronunciation
*... tayr-mee-**nahl** ... yay-**gah**-dah* **1** *... **theen**-tah ... **pways**-to ... **mahr**-chah* **2** *mee-**rad** ... **nways**-tro ay-kee-**pah**-hay* **3** *ko-**hay**d ... **ko**-sah* **4** *... **pay**-sah ...*

Notes

① **la cinta** *belt*, *ribbon*, *strap*, *tape* here refers to **la cinta transportadora** *conveyor belt*, which can be a moving walkway or, as here, a baggage carousel. Other ways **cinta** is commonly used are **cinta adhesiva** *sticky tape*, *adhesive tape* and **una cinta de vídeo** *a videotape*.

② **ya se ha puesto en marcha** or **se ha puesto ya en marcha**: both constructions are possible, but remember, the adverb always goes in front or behind the auxiliary verb and past participle, never between them!

③ **ahí** *there*; **aquí** *here*. But, **ahí** sometimes has the meaning of *here*: **está ahí** *it's there*, but **ahí tiene** *here you are* (i.e. when someone gives you something). ▸

At the arrivals terminal

1 – Come on *(Let's go)*, the carousel has already started up *(already itself has put in operation)*.
2 – Look *(informal plural)*, here *(there)* comes part of our luggage!
3 – Everybody grab one *(Grab[informal plural] each one one thing)*.
4 – This suitcase is very heavy *(weighs a lot)*.

▸ ④ To form the second-person plural (informal) imperative, just replace the final **-r** of the infinitive with a **-d**. There are no exceptions.

coger → coged *Take! Pick up! Grab!*

mirar → mirad *Look! Watch!* (line 2)

Don't forget that the second-person plural is used when addressing more than one person you know well.

5 – **Bue**no, **dá**mela ⑤ y **to**ma ⑥ **es**ta **o**tra que es más pe**que**ña ⑦.
6 – **És**ta ⑧ tam**bién pe**sa dema**sia**do **pa**ra mí.
7 – **Co**ge ⑨ lo que ⑩ **quie**ras.

*5 ... **dah**-may-lah ... 6 ... day-mah-**see-ah**-do ... 7 **ko**-hay ... **kee-ay**-rahs*

Notes

⑤ **dámela** *give it* (f.) *to me*. **Da** is the second-person singular (informal) imperative of **dar** *to give*. In lesson 16, we saw that if an object pronoun is used with the imperative, it is attached to the end of the verb. If there are two pronouns, both of them are attached to the verb, one after the other. The indirect object pronoun (usually a person) always comes first, so **dámela** is literally 'give me it'. The direct object pronoun here is feminine because it refers to **la maleta** *the suitcase*. Here is another (irregular) example with the singular informal imperative of **decir → di**:
Dime *Tell me!* **Dilo** *Say it!* **Dímelo** *Tell it to me!*
(The written accent shows which syllable is stressed.)

⑥ **toma** is the second-person singular (informal) imperative of **tomar** *to take*. You'll hear this verb in many contexts in Spanish. For example, it is used in reference to eating and drinking the way we use 'to have' in English: **tomar un café** *to have a coffee*, **tomar el desayuno** *to have breakfast*.

In Spain, **coger** (lines 3, 7 and 8) is used to express the idea *to take hold of, to grab, to pick up*: **coger el pasaporte** *to take the passport*. But remember that **coger** has a lewd meaning in most of Latin America and is to be avoided there.

⑦ **más pequeña** *smaller* ('more small'). In Spanish, comparatives (formed in English with *more* or *-er*) are always rendered by using **más** plus the adjective or adverb. To form the superlative (formed in English with *most* or *-est*), add the article: **es <u>la</u> más pequeña** 'it *(f.)* is the most small' *it is the smallest*.

5 – Well, give it to me *(give[informal sing.]-me-it[f.])* and take this other [one] which is smaller *(more small)*.
6 – This [one is] also too heavy *(weighs too-much)* for me.
7 – Pick up *(informal sing.)* whichever *(that which)* you want.

▸ ⑧ **ésta** *this (one)*; **ésa** *that (one)* (with a written accent) are demonstrative pronouns that replace feminine singular nouns. All these thises and thats – are you still with us? **No te preocupes**, we'll go over all the variations in lesson 35!

⑨ **Coge** *Take!* This is the singular informal imperative. You may have already spotted the pattern for forming this. You just drop the final **-r** of the infinitive.
coger → **coge** *Take!*
mirar → **mira** *Look! Watch!*

There are some exceptions, as we saw with **decir** → **di**. We'll learn these gradually. We'll also see how to form a negative imperative (*Don't look! Don't tell me!* etc.).

⑩ **lo que** *what, that which, whichever.* **Coge lo que quieras.** *Take what/whichever you want*. Note here that **quieras** is a present subjunctive form. The use of the equivalent of *-ever*, or of the modal *may* or *might*, often signals the subjunctive mood in Spanish. We'll be finding out more about the subjunctive later, but if you'd like a preview of its uses you can look in the grammatical appendix. In constructions such as 'whatever will be will be', the *what(ever)*, *which(ever)*, *who(ever)*, etc. is conveyed by using the present subjunctive (in whatever person) on either side of **lo que**.
haga lo que haga *whatever I (may) do*
digas lo que digas *whatever you (may) say*
comamos lo que comamos *whatever we (may) eat*
cueste lo que cueste *whatever it may cost.*

8 – ¡Vale! Cogeré esa mochila o esa bolsa de viaje.

9 – Pero, Isabel, ¡eso ⑪ no es nuestro! □

8 ¡**bah**-lay! ko-hay-**ray** … mo-**chee**-lah … **bol**-sah … **bee**-**ah**-hay 9 … ee-sah-**bel** …

* * *

Ejercicio 1: Traduzca

❶ Mirad, ahí hay una parada de taxis. ❷ Coge la maleta. ❸ Esta bolsa pesa demasiado. ❹ Ésta es más pequeña. ❺ ¡Vale!

* * *

Ejercicio 2: Complete

❶ Where have you *(informal)* put the passports?
¿Dónde … …… los ………?

❷ Our luggage hasn't come out yet.
……. ……… todavía no ha salido.

❸ I don't like that.
… no .. …… .

❹ Give *(informal sing.)* me your hand!
¡ …. la …. !

❺ Whose is that backpack/rucksack?
¿De ….. es … ……. ?

8 – Okay! I'll take that backpack or that travel bag.
9 – But, Isabel, that's not ours!

Notes

⑪ **eso** *that*: **¡Eso es!** *That's it!*
esto *this*: **¡Mira esto!** *Look at this!*
esto and **eso** are neuter forms of the demonstrative pronoun. Notice that they do not have a written accent. See review lesson 35 for a full explanation.

* * *

Answers to Exercise 1

❶ Look *(informal plural)*, there's a taxi stand. ❷ Take *(informal sing.)* the suitcase. ❸ This bag is too heavy. ❹ This one is smaller. ❺ Okay!

* * *

Answers to Exercise 2

❶ – has puesto – pasaportes ❷ Nuestro equipaje – ❸ Eso – me gusta ❹ Dame – mano ❺ – quién – esa mochila

¡Vale! *Things are coming along nicely. Just take the lessons at your own pace and don't worry about the things that are difficult to keep straight at the moment. We'll be summarizing all the main points in the review lesson.*

En ① la aduana

1 – ¿**Al**go que decla**rar**?
2 – **Na**da.
3 – ¿Qué **lle**va en **e**sas ma**le**tas?
4 – Co**mi**da ② **pa**ra mi **pe**rro y mi **ga**to.
5 – **Á**bralas ③, por fa**vor**.
6 A**quí**… yo **ve**o re**lo**jes, pa**ñue**los ④ de imita**ción** fraudu**len**ta, anfeta**mi**nas…
7 **Con**que… co**mi**da **pa**ra sus anima**li**llos do**més**ticos, ¿eh?

Pronunciation
*… ah-**dwah**-nah* ***1 ahl**-go … day-klah-**rahr** **3** … **yay**-bah … **4** ko-**mee**-dah … **pay**-rro … **gah**-to **5 ah**-brah-lahs ... **6** ... **bay**-o rray-**lo**-hays pah-**nway**-los … ee-mee-tah-**thee-on** frah-oo-doo-**len**-tah ahn-fay-tah-**mee**-nahs **7 kon**-kay … soos ah-nee-mah-**lee**-yos do-**mays**-tee-kos …*

Notes

① More on prepositions… Generally where English uses *in* or *at* to refer to a place, Spanish uses **en**. The Spanish preposition **a** usually translates as *to*, but sometimes as *at*.
Mi amiga trabaja en un banco. *My friend works in a bank.*
Estoy en la frontera. *I am at the border.*
Vamos al restaurante. *We're going to the restaurant.*
Te veo a las cinco. *I'll see you at five.*

② **comida**, here meaning *food*, can also mean *meal*:
comprar comida *to buy food*
la hora de la comida *mealtime*
comer tres comidas al día *to eat three meals a day.*

③ **abrir** *to open*; **abra** *Open!* (formal sing.); **ábralas** *Open them* (f.)*!* Here we see another imperative, but this time it is formal. ▸

In customs

1 – Anything to declare?
2 – Nothing.
3 – What are you carrying in those suitcases?
4 – Food for my dog and my cat.
5 – Open *(formal sing.)* them, please.
6 Here … I see watches, fake scarves *(scarves of imitation fraudulent)*, amphetamines …
7 So … food for your little pets, eh?

▸ We'll be looking at the imperative in detail, but here is a quick review: **abre** (informal sing.), **abrid** (informal plural), **abra** (formal sing.) and **abran** (formal plural). Apart from the two informal forms, all other imperatives, including negative commands (prohibitions), use the present subjunctive. For example, remember **¡Diga!** (lesson 31, note 3) for answering the phone? This is the formal singular imperative (and the third-person subjunctive) of **decir**. It's formal because you never know who will be at the other end of the phone!

④ **pañuelo** *scarf, shawl*, but also *handkerchief.*
¿Tienes un pañuelo de papel? *Do you have a tissue/Kleenex?*

8 – Sí, se**ñor**. Yo se lo ⑤ **e**cho ⑥, y si no lo **co**men, **lue**go lo **ven**do. □

*8 ... say-**nyor** ... **ay**-cho ... **ko**-men **lway**-go ... **ben**-do*

Notes

⑤ **yo se lo echo** *I give it to them*; 'I them it *(m.)* give'. (Make sure to pronounce the 'ch' as in *chew* and not as a 'k' – it's not the English word 'echo'!) Here is a statement with both a direct and an indirect object pronoun. Yes, the word order no doubt seems strange! You'll soon get used to this construction, but if you want to review pronoun use, go to lesson 49! ▸

* * *

Ejercicio 1: Traduzca

❶ ¿Tienes algo que decir? ❷ No, nada. ❸ ¿Qué hay en la mochila? ❹ Vivo en Valencia. ❺ ¡Abre el coche!

* * *

Ejercicio 2: Complete

❶ Do you have a tissue *(scarf of paper)*?
¿Tienes .. ..?

❷ The children want a dog or a cat.
... . quieren .. ..

❸ She doesn't know where she has left her watch.
.. .. ha dejado el ..... .

❹ It's mealtime.
.. ..

❺ Can you pour me [some] water?
¿Puedes ....?

8 – Yes, sir. I give it to them, and if they don't eat it, then I sell it.

▸ ⑥ The main meaning of **echar** is *to throw*, but it has lots of uses and is employed in many different expressions.
echar un hueso al perro *to give the dog a bone*
echar de comer al gato (al caballo, a los pájaros, etc.) *to feed the cat (the horse, the birds,* etc.*)*
But: **dar de comer al niño** *to feed the child.*
Another use is in the sense of *to pour*: **echar agua en un vaso** *to pour water into a glass.* Another common expression is **echar de menos** *to miss (something)*:
Echo de menos a mi familia. *I miss my family.*

* * *

Answers to Exercise 1
❶ Do you have something to say? ❷ No, nothing. ❸ What is there in the backpack? ❹ I live in Valencia. ❺ Open *(informal sing.)* the car!

* * *

Answers to Exercise 2
❶ – un pañuelo de papel ❷ Los niños – un perro o un gato ❸ No sabe dónde – reloj ❹ Es la hora de la comida ❺ – echarme agua

You're now already a third of the way through this book! Allow yourself a moment to appreciate how much progress you've made. Your vocabulary is growing apace, and you're recognizing more and more words as you come across them again. Not only that, but among other things, you can introduce yourself, ask for information, understand directions and signs and use some common expressions.
¡Continúe así! Keep it up!

35 Lección treinta y cinco

Repaso

1 The imperative

The imperative (the command form of the verb) conjugates differently depending on who you are talking to: one person or more than one person, in an informal or formal context. Let's look at the different types of affirmative command we've seen so far.

• When speaking to one person informally (second-person singular), replace the infinitive ending with **-a** or **-e**.

Verbs ending in **-ar**	stem + **-a**	**llamar**	→	**llama**	*Call!*
Verbs ending in **-er**	stem + **-e**	**comer**	→	**come**	*Eat!*
Verbs ending in **-ir**	stem + **-e**	**abrir**	→	**abre**	*Open!*

There are some Spanish verbs that are irregular; we'll look at these as they come up. However, if you wish to know more about them right now, you can go directly to the section of the grammatical appendix that deals with conjugations.

• When speaking to more than one person informally (second-person plural), replace the final **-r** of the infinitive with **-d**.

Verbs ending in **-ar**	**cambiar**	→	**cambiad**	*Change!*
Verbs ending in **-er**	**beber**	→	**bebed**	*Drink!*
Verbs ending in **-ir**	**salir**	→	**salid**	*Leave!*

Don't forget that this form is used only when speaking informally to two or more people, say a group of friends. There are no irregular forms.

In all other cases, for example, formal and negative commands, the imperative is the same form as the corresponding person in the present subjunctive. So far we have seen several examples of this (some of which are irregular verbs).

• When speaking to one person formally:

dar	→	**dé**	*Give!*
respirar	→	**respire**	*Breathe!*
abrir	→	**abra**	*Open!*
decir	→	**diga**	*Tell!*

• When speaking to more than one person formally:

venir	→	**vengan**	*Come!*

We will look more closely at the imperative, as well as explain how to form the subjunctive, in the upcoming lessons.

Remember:
• In the affirmative imperative, any object pronouns come after the verb, just as in English, but in Spanish they are attached to the verb.
Dame el pañuelo. *Give me the scarf.* (informal sing.)
Dejadme pasar, por favor. *Let me pass, please.* (informal plural)

• If there are two pronouns, both are attached to the verb, one after the other. The indirect object pronoun (usually a person) always comes first.
Dámelo. *Give it to me.* ('Give-me-it') (informal sing.)
Dejádmelo. *Leave it to me.* ('Leave-me-it') (informal plural)

One thing to note: when the second-person plural is followed by the second-person plural object pronoun **os** *you*, the verb loses its final **d**: **Daos la mano.** *Shake hands.* ('Give-yourselves [informal plural] the hand.')

2 Colours

el color *colour* is a masculine noun. In Spanish, nouns ending in **-or** are typically masculine: **el calor** *heat*; **el humor** *humour, mood*; **el sabor** *taste*; **el valor** *value*, etc.

There are some rare exceptions, the most noteworthy being **la flor** *the flower*.

35 As for the colours themselves, note that **azul** *blue*, **gris** *grey*, **verde** *green* and **marrón** *brown*, among others, do not vary with gender: **una casa azul** *a blue house*; **una gata gris** *a grey cat (f.)*; **una pradera verde** *a green meadow.*

But **blanco** *white*; **negro** *black*; **amarillo** *yellow* and **rojo** *red* agree in both gender and number:
la camisa blanca y los zapatos negros
the white shirt and the black shoes
la falda de rayas rojas y amarillas
the skirt with red and yellow stripes.

3 Demonstratives

3.1 Demonstrative adjectives

Demonstrative adjectives (e.g. *this*, *that*, *these*, *those*) help to indicate the distance (in space or time) of something from the speaker or the person spoken to. In Spanish, there are three demonstrative adjectives: **este**, **ese** and **aquel**, which have different forms depending on whether the noun to which they refer is feminine or masculine, singular or plural.

- **este** refers to what is close to the person who is speaking (*this*)
- **ese** refers to what is close to the person being spoken to (*that*)
- **aquel** refers to what is distant from both the speaker and the person spoken to (*that over there*).

	Masculine	Feminine
sing.	**este** *this*	**esta** *this*
plur.	**estos** *these*	**estas** *these*
sing.	**ese** *that*	**esa** *that*
plur.	**esos** *those*	**esas** *those*
sing.	**aquel** *that (over there)*	**aquella** *that (over there)*
plur.	**aquellos** *those (over there)*	**aquellas** *those (over there)*

3.2 Demonstrative pronouns

Demonstrative pronouns stand on their own, replacing rather than modifying a noun (e.g. *This is fascinating.*). In Spanish, they are identical to the demonstrative adjectives, except for a written accent on the stressed syllable. The accent is not only a written marker that distinguishes these pronouns from the adjectives, it also indicates a spoken emphasis. (However, it is now common to see all demonstrative pronouns without a written accent.)

If the pronoun replaces a specific noun, it must agree with its gender and number. However, there are also neuter demonstrative pronouns (**esto** *this*, **eso** *that* and **aquello** *that*), which are used to refer to an unknown object, or an idea, concept or situation that isn't specifically named. These are invariable (they do not change for gender or number) and do not take a written accent.

(Note that in English we sometimes add the word 'one' or 'ones' to indicate the object – Spanish does not.)

	Masculine	Feminine	Neuter
sing. plur.	**éste** *this (one)* **éstos** *these*	**ésta** *this (one)* **éstas** *these*	**esto** *this*
sing. plur.	**ése** *that (one)* **ésos** *those*	**ésa** *that (one)* **ésas** *those*	**eso** *that*
sing. plur.	**aquél** *that (one over there)* **aquéllos** *those*	**aquélla** *that (one over there)* **aquéllas** *those*	**aquello** *that over there*

¿ DÓNDE TRABAJA ?
SOY EMPLEADO EN UN BANCO.

35 Translate the following phrases using the correct demonstrative adjective and then the corresponding demonstrative pronoun. The gender of each noun is indicated in parentheses. There are no neuter pronouns, because each example refers to a specific noun.

Example:
1 *this model* (m.): **este modelo** *this (one)*: **éste**

Over to you:

2 *this leg* (f.): *this (one):*
3 *these shoes* (m.): *these (ones):*
4 *these backpacks/rucksacks* (f.): *these (ones):*
5 *that employee* (m.): *that (one):*

* * *

Diálogo recapitulativo

1 – Vamos a ver al médico.
2 – ¿Cómo así?
3 – El niño no está bien.
4 – ¿Qué le pasa?
5 – No sé, pero le duele el vientre.
6 – ¡Tranquilízate!
7 – Llama al médico.
8 … ¡Diga! …
9 – Dice que podemos ir ahora mismo.
10 – ¡Vamos! ¡Deprisa! ¡Ese taxi está libre!
11 En la consulta:
12 – ¡Hola, buenas!
13 Voy a examinarle.
14 No tiene nada.
15 Le duele el vientre porque ha comido demasiado chocolate.
16 Cincuenta euros y … ¡menos chocolate, por favor!

6 *that machine* (f.):	*that (one):*
7 *those scarves* (m.):	*those (ones):*
8 *those bags* (f.):	*those (ones):*
9 *that dog over there* (m.):	*that (one) over there:*
10 *that flower over there* (f.):	*that (one) over there:*
11 *those colours over there* (m.):	*those (ones) over there:*
12 *those suitcases over there* (f.):	*those (ones) over there:*

Answers
2 esta pierna / ésta **3** estos zapatos / éstos **4** estas mochilas / éstas **5** ese empleado / ése **6** esa máquina / ésa **7** esos pañuelos / ésos **8** esas bolsas / ésas **9** aquel perro / aquél **10** aquella flor / aquélla **11** aquellos colores / aquéllos **12** aquellas maletas / aquéllas

* * *

Traducción
1 We're going to see the doctor. **2** How come? **3** The little boy isn't well. **4** What's the matter with him? **5** I don't know, but his stomach hurts. **6** Calm down! **7** Call the doctor. **8** Hello! *(on the phone)* **9** He says that we can go right now. **10** Come on! Quick! That taxi is free! **11** At the doctor's office/surgery: **12** Hello! **13** I'm going to examine him. **14** He has nothing [wrong with him]. **15** His stomach hurts because he has eaten too much chocolate. **16** Fifty euros and … less chocolate, please!

36 Lección treinta y seis

Locura de amor

1 – **Qui**que ①, ¿ver**dad** que soy un en**can**to ②?
2 – Sí.
3 – ¿A que ③ ha**rí**as ④ cual**quier** ⑤ **co**sa por mí?
4 – Sí.

Pronunciation

*lo-**koo**-rah ... **1** ... en-**kahn**-to **3** ... kwal-**kee-ayr** ...*

Notes

① Diminutives of first names (e.g. in English, Bob from Robert or Jim from James) are rather common in Spanish, and are often very different from the original name. So, for example, **Enrique** *Henry* changes to **Quique**; **José** *Joseph* to **Pepe**; **Concepción** *Conception* to **Concha** or **Conchita**, etc.

② **Ser un encanto** *to be a delight, to be adorable*; **el encanto** *enchantment, charm, fascination.*
Es una persona con mucho encanto or **encantadora.**
He/she is a very charming person.

encantar *to enchant, delight.* **Encantado/-a de conocerle.** *Delighted to meet you.* (This last expression includes the useful verb **conocer** *to know, to meet.* It is used in the sense of 'to be familiar with'; not to be confused with another verb we've already learned for *to know*, **saber**, which is used in the sense of 'to know a fact' or 'to know how'. More on this in lesson 42!)

③ **¿A que ...?** when starting a question can have two meanings:
• It can correspond, as in this dialogue, to what in English is called a question tag, which is an affirmative or negative statement that has been turned into a question and occurs at the end of a sentence (e.g. '... don't you?', '... are they?', '... ▸

Madly in love *(Madness of love)*

1 – Quique, aren't I adorable *(true that I'm a darling)*?
2 – Yes.
3 – You'd do anything for me, wouldn't you?
4 – Yes.

isn't it?', etc.). It is used when the expected reply is simply a confirmation of the question. It is an alternative to the construction **¿Verdad que ...?** (lines 1, 5 and 9) or simply **¿verdad?** or **¿no?** at the end of the sentence.
¿Verdad que harías cualquier cosa por mí?
Harías cualquier cosa por mí, ¿verdad? or **¿no?**
You'd do anything for me, wouldn't you?
Pretty simple, **¿verdad?**
• In other contexts, **A que ...** can correspond to the English *I bet* ... with the verb **apuesto** *I bet* (from **apostar** *to bet*) left out, as it is understood. **(Apuesto) a que llego antes que él.** *I bet [that] I arrive before him.*

④ **harías** *you* (informal sing.) *would do*, from **hacer** *to do*, *to make*, is the conditional mood. The conditional is formed in English with the auxiliary *would* + infinitive, but in Spanish it is formed by adding an ending to the infinitive (**hacer** is an irregular verb). There is another example in line 7: **no sabrías** *you* (informal sing.) *wouldn't know.* We also saw **gustaría** in lesson 32, which is a regular example of the conditional. We'll discover more about how to form the conditional in lesson 39.

⑤ In this context, **cualquier** is an adjective meaning *any*; **cualquier cosa** means *anything*.

5 – ¿Ver**dad** que mis **o**jos te **vuel**ven ⑥ **lo**co?
6 – Sí.
7 – ¿A que es **cier**to que no sa**brí**as vi**vir** sin mí?
8 – Sí.
9 – ¿Ver**dad** que me **quie**res con lo**cu**ra?
10 – Sí.
11 – ¿A que no hay **o**tra mu**jer** tan maravi**llo**sa **co**mo ⑦ yo?
12 – No.
13 – ¡Dios de mi **vi**da! ⑧ **¡Qui**que, a**mor mí**o ⑨!
14 **Pa**sa el **tiem**po y **ca**da **dí**a te **quie**ro más ⑩…
15 ¡por las **co**sas tan ⑪ bo**ni**tas que me **di**ces! □

***7** … **thee-ayr**-to ... **11** ... moo-**hayr** … mah-rah-bee-**yo**-sah … **13** dee-os …*

Notes

⑥ The verb **volver**, which we saw in lesson 31, has many meanings. Here's a new one: **volver loco** *to drive mad/crazy.* **Me vuelve loca.** *He/she/it drives me crazy.* or *You* (formal) *drive me crazy.*

⑦ The comparative of equality, expressed in English by *as...as*, is formed in Spanish using **tan … como**.
Clara es tan encantadora como su madre.
Clara is as charming as her mother.

⑧ **¡Dios de mi vida!** or, more commonly, **¡Dios mío!** The latter is not as strong as its literal translation *My God!* and is closer to *Goodness gracious!*

⑨ **¡Mi amor!** or **¡Amor mío!** *My love!* The **mío** here and in note 8 is the masculine possessive adjective *my* or *mine.* Spanish has two forms of possessive adjectives, a short form used before ▶

5 – My eyes *(True that my eyes)* drive *(turn)* you crazy, don't they?
6 – Yes.
7 – Isn't it true *(certain)* that you wouldn't be able *(not would-know-how)* to live without me?
8 – Yes.
9 – You love me madly *(with madness)*, don't you?
10 – Yes.
11 – There's no other woman as wonderful as me, is there?
12 – No.
13 – Oh my God *(God of my life)*! Quique, my love *(love of-mine)*!
14 Time goes by and every day I love you more …
15 for the beautiful things *(things so pretty)* that you say to me!

nouns, and a longer form used after nouns. The possessive adjective has to agree in number and gender with the noun it modifies – here, **mío** is used because **amor** is a masculine noun. When used with a definite article, the long form becomes a pronoun: **el mío** *mine.*

(10) **cada vez más** 'each time more' or **cada día más** 'each day more' basically means *more and more*. The same construction can be used with an adjective to provide more detail – in English we sometimes use the comparative to express this:
Los días son cada vez más largos.
The days are longer and longer.

(11) When **tan** is not used to introduce a comparison (**tan … como**), it means *so* or *such*.
¡Estas cosas son tan bonitas! *These things are so pretty!*

Ejercicio 1: Traduzca

❶ ¿Verdad que es maravillosa? ❷ Tiene unas manos muy bonitas. ❸ Su casa me parece cada vez más bonita. ❹ ¿Sabrías decirlo? ❺ ¡Tienen unos hijos tan encantadores!

* * *

Ejercicio 2: Complete

❶ I bet he arrives late.
. . . . llega con . . . .

❷ Don't buy *(informal sing.)* [just] anything!
¡No compres . . . . !

❸ That doctor is as good as mine.
Ese . . . . bueno . . . . el mío.

❹ Delighted *(f.)* to meet you *(formal)*!
. . . . de . . . .

❺ I love you *(informal)*.
. . . .

---

37 Lección treinta y siete

En una piscina municipal

1 El soco**rris**ta, emple**a**do del Ayunta**mien**to ①,

Pronunciation
*1 … ah-yoon-tah-**mee-en**-to*

Answers to Exercise 1

❶ She's wonderful, isn't she? ❷ She has very pretty hands. ❸ His/her/your *(formal)* house seems prettier and prettier [each time I see it]. ❹ Would you know how to say it? ❺ They have such delightful children!

* * *

Answers to Exercise 2

❶ A que – retraso ❷ – cualquier cosa ❸ – médico es tan – como – ❹ Encantada – conocerle ❺ Te quiero

In the next lesson, we're going to look at the subjunctive mood in more detail. As usual, we'll take things gradually, so don't worry! Just pay attention to the constructions in the lessons to start getting used to them. The review lesson will provide more information, which will be filled in as we go along. As you work through the lessons and exercises, you'll find yourself picking up the rules intuitively.

Lesson thirty-seven 37

At a public swimming pool

1 The lifeguard, [an] employee of the town hall,

Notes

① Nowadays, the word **ayuntamiento** applies both to the city government and the actual town hall building. Another less common term is **alcaldía** (from **alcalde** *mayor*).

2 se a**cer**ca a ② un ba**ñis**ta y le **dice**:

3 – Caba**lle**ro, le **rue**go **sal**ga ③ del **a**gua,

4 se **vis**ta y aban**do**ne ④ el re**cin**to.

5 – ¿Qué **pa**sa? ¿Qué he **he**cho?

6 – ¿No **sa**be que está prohi**bi**do me**ar** en la pis**ci**na ⑤?

7 – ¿No me va a de**cir** a**ho**ra que soy el **ú**nico que **ha**ce pis en la pis**ci**na?

8 – Sí se**ñor**, **des**de el trampo**lín**, us**ted** es el **ú**nico. ☐

3 *kah-bah-**yay**-ro* … ***rrway**-go* … **4** … *rray-**theen**-to* **6** … *pro-ee-**bee**-do* … **8** … *trahm-po-**leen*** …

Notes

② **acercarse a** *to approach, to draw near, to come closer* (from the preposition **cerca** *near, close*).
Acércate a la mesa. *Approach/Come up to the table.*

③ **Le ruego salga** or **le ruego que salga** *I must ask that you* (formal) *leave*. In this phrase, **ruego** is the present tense of the stem-changing verb **rogar** *to request, to beg* and **salga** is the subjunctive of **salir** *to leave, to get out*. In Spanish, after verbs that express an order, a request, a wish or advice, the subjunctive is used. The word **que**, which frequently introduces a subjunctive clause, is often omitted in very formal contexts. The extremely formal language in this dialogue is amusingly incongruous to the situation. The lifeguard would have been much more likely to say **¡Oiga, haga el favor de salir del agua!** *Hey, you, get out of the water, please!* – with a much less polite tone!

④ The verbs in the continuation of the lifeguard's request are also in the subjunctive: **(que) se vista** *that you get dressed* and **(que) abandone** *that you quit*. These are respectively the ▸

2 approaches *(nears himself to)* a swimmer *(bather)* and says to him:
3 – Sir, I must ask you to *(I beg [that] you)* leave *(from)* the water,
4 get dressed *(dress yourself)* and quit *(abandon)* the premises.
5 – What's the matter? What have I done?
6 – Don't you know that it is forbidden to urinate *(to pee)* in the swimming pool?
7 – Now you're not going to tell me that I'm the only one who pees in the pool?
8 – Yes, sir, from the diving board, you're the only one.

▸ third-person singular (formal) forms of the present subjunctive of **vestirse** *to get dressed* and **abandonar** *to leave, to abandon.*

⑤ **la piscina** *the swimming pool, the swimming baths.* Both **mear** and **hacer pis** are used colloquially, with the former somewhat stronger, as in *to have a piss.* In normal circumstances if the urge arises, the most polite thing to say is **ir al baño** or **ir al servicio** *to go to the bathroom.*

Ejercicio 1: Traduzca

❶ Le ruego que salga del coche. ❷ ¿Qué pasa? ❸ Tienes que vestirte enseguida. ❹ El niño quiere hacer pis. ❺ Aquí, está prohibido.

* * *

Ejercicio 2: Complete

❶ We have spoken with a town hall employee *(f.)*.
. . . . . hablado . . . una . . . .
. . . .

❷ There he is, on the diving board.
. . . . allí, en . . . .

❸ At this table, I'm *(m.)* the only one who's drinking water.
En esta . . . . , soy . . . . que bebe . . . . .

❹ Come *(informal sing.)* closer.
. . . .

❺ What is prohibited?
¿. . . . .?

38 Lección treinta y ocho

Taxista precavido

1 – ¡**Pón**gase el cintu**rón** ① de seguri**dad**, se**ño**ra!

Notes

① **Póngase** or **Abróchese** or **Átese el cinturón.** *Put on* or *Buckle up* or *Attach your seatbelt.* (formal) ▸

Answers to Exercise 1

❶ I must ask you to get out of the car. ❷ What's the matter? ❸ You have to get dressed immediately. ❹ The little boy wants to pee. ❺ It's not allowed here.

* * *

Answers to Exercise 2

❶ Hemos – con – empleada del Ayuntamiento ❷ Está – el trampolín ❸ – mesa – el único – agua ❹ Acércate ❺ Qué está prohibido

* * *

In Spain's administrative structure, **el municipio** the municipality *or* town *is the smallest territorial unit. Each* **municipio** *has an* **ayuntamiento** town hall. **El concejo** the town council *is elected in* **elecciones municipales** municipal elections, *which in Spain take place every four years. The council is headed by* **el alcalde** the mayor *and deals with governing the municipality.*

The verb **ayuntar** *means* to unite, to assemble, *originally from* **la yunta**, *the yoke used to harness oxen, a meaning that has fallen out of use in modern times. Hence, an* **ayuntamiento** *is literally an* assembly.

Lesson thirty-eight 38

Prudent taxi driver

1 – Fasten *(Put-on-yourself)* your seat belt *(the belt of safety)*, ma'am!

▸ **abrocharse** has the colloquial meaning of *to button up.* **Abróchate la chaqueta.** *Button up your jacket.* (informal)

2 – ¡**Cla**ro que sí! Y us**ted**, ¡**ten**ga cui**da**do! ②
3 Soy muy ma**yor** ③ **pe**ro…
4 ¡**quie**ro ver cre**cer** ④ a mis **nie**tos!
5 ¡No **co**rra ⑤, no **ten**go **pri**sa ⑥!
6 Res**pe**te ⑦ las se**ña**les de **trá**fico ⑧.
7 Si **o**tro **co**che **quie**re adelan**tar**le,
8 **pé**guese a la de**re**cha.
9 Re**duz**ca la veloci**dad** en los **cru**ces.

Pronunciation
***3** … mah-**yor** … **4** … kray-**thayr** … **8 pay**-gay-say … **9** rray-**dooth**-kah … bay-lo-thee-**dad** …*

Notes

② **tener cuidado** *to take care, to pay attention.*
¡Tenga cuidado! *Watch out!* (formal)
¡Ten cuidado! *Watch out!* (informal)
¡Cuidado! *Careful!*
And also **¡Atención! ¡Peligro!** *Warning! Danger!*

③ **una persona mayor** *an elderly person.*
Mis padres son ya mayores. *My parents are already elderly.*
Later we will see that the irregular comparative **mayor** *bigger, older* can mean various things.

④ **crecer** *to grow up* also means simply *to grow* (unless you're talking about growing something, which is **cultivar**).
Las plantas crecen. *The plants grow.*
Mi padre cultiva plantas en su jardín.
My father grows plants in his garden.
La ciudad crece. *The city is growing.*

⑤ **correr** *to run.* **¡No corras, tenemos tiempo!** *Don't run, we have time!* (informal). In the context of driving, **no corra** means *Don't go so fast!* (formal). Other words used for *to drive* are **conducir** in Spain, and **manejar** in Latin America. ▶

2 – Of course *(Clear that yes)*! And you, be careful *(have care)*!
3 I'm very old but …
4 I want to see my grandchildren grow up!
5 Don't drive [too fast] *(Don't run)*, I'm not in a hurry *(I don't have haste)*!
6 Obey *(Respect)* the road signs *(signals of traffic)*.
7 If [an]other car wants to overtake you,
8 keep *(stick-yourself)* to the right.
9 Slow down *(Reduce the velocity)* at the crossroads.

⑥ **la prisa** *haste*: **tener prisa** *to be in a hurry, to be rushed.* **Tengo prisa.** *I'm in a hurry.*
Note also: **¡Deprisa!** or **¡De prisa!** *Quick! Hurry up!*

⑦ **Respete** *Respect!* is the imperative of **respetar** *to respect, to honour, to obey* when addressing one person formally. This form of the imperative is the third-person singular of the present subjunctive. Reminder: all imperatives use the present subjunctive, with the exception of affirmative informal commands (singular and plural). Check lesson 35 if you need to refresh your memory, or jump forward to lesson 42.

⑧ **tráfico** *traffic, trafficking.*
accidente de tráfico *traffic accident*; **tráfico de drogas** *drug trafficking*; **policía de tráfico** *traffic police* (Note: **la policía** *the police* or *policewoman*, but **el policía** *policeman*).

38 **10** No se **sal**te ⑨ nin**gún** se**má**foro.
11 Cir**cu**le des**pa**cio, la cal**za**da es**tá** mo**ja**da…
12 – Sí, se**ño**ra. **Pe**ro si a pe**sar** de **to**do ⑩ te**ne**mos un acci**den**te…
13 ¿**tie**ne us**ted** prefe**ren**cia por un hospi**tal** en particu**lar**? □

Notes

⑨ **saltar** *to jump.* **saltarse un semáforo** *to run a red light.*

⑩ Note this useful phrase: **a pesar de** *in spite of, despite.* **a pesar de todo** *in spite of everything.*

* * *

Ejercicio 1: Traduzca

❶ Hay que ponerse el cinturón de seguridad. ❷ ¡Ten mucho cuidado! ❸ ¿Tus padres son muy mayores? ❹ ¿Tienes prisa? ❺ ¡Cuidado, hay un cruce!

* * *

Ejercicio 2: Complete

❶ Today there is too much traffic.
. . . . . . demasiado . . . .

❷ There's a car that wants to overtake.
. . . . que quiere . . . .

❸ The traffic sign is on your left.
. . . . está a tu . . . .

❹ Quick, it's time!
¡ . . . . , . . la . . . . !

❺ Drive *(formal)* on the right.
. . . . por la . . . .

10 Don't run *(Don't yourself jump)* any traffic light[s].
11 Drive *(Circulate)* slowly, the road surface is wet …
12 – Yes, ma'am. But if in spite of everything we have an accident …
13 is there any particular hospital you prefer *(have you preference for a hospital in particular)*?

***12** … ahk-thee-**den**-tay*

* * *

Answers to Exercise 1

❶ One must put on one's seatbelt. ❷ Be *(informal sing.)* very careful! ❸ Are your parents very elderly? ❹ Are you in a hurry? ❺ Watch out, there's a crossroads/intersection!

* * *

Answers to Exercise 2

❶ Hoy hay – tráfico ❷ Hay un coche – adelantar ❸ La señal de tráfico – izquierda ❹ Deprisa, es – hora ❺ Circule – derecha

La red de carreteras españolas the network of Spanish roads *is fairly dense. The biggest cities are connected by* **autopistas de peaje** toll motorways/expressways, *or by* **autovías** dual carriageways/divided highways. *Speed is limited to 120 kph (75 mph) on motorways and highways, 90 kph (57 mph) on* **rutas nacionales** *(single carriageways/state roads) and 50 kph (31 mph) in towns and built-up areas.* **Las multas** fines *are frequently given for* **exceso de velocidad** exceeding the speed limit – *immediate payment can be demanded, especially when the vehicle is from outside of Spain. When parking, make sure you pay the* **precio de la consumición** *('price of consumption') by buying a ticket at one of the numerous* **parquímetros** parking meters, *which are sprinkled liberally throughout cities. Most have* **zonas azules** *('blue zones'),* limited-time paid-parking zones *where* **grúas municipales** municipal tow trucks *prowl for infractions.*

Lección treinta y nueve

¡De película! ①

1 – Ayer **fui**mos ② a ver '¡Que te den mor**ci**lla!' ③
2 – ¿Ha**bía** ④ **mu**cha **gen**te ⑤ en el **ci**ne?
3 – ¡No me **ha**bles ⑥, ha**bía** **u**na **co**la e**nor**me!
4 – Yo fui a **ver**la la se**ma**na pa**sa**da.
5 – ¿Y qué te pare**ció**?

Pronunciation
*1 ah-**yayr** ... mor-**thee**-yah* **2** *... **hen**-tay ...*

Notes

① **una película** or, less frequently, **un filme** *a film/movie.*

¡De película! is here an ironic play on words, as the expression is normally used to refer to something amazing or incredible. It describes an extraordinary situation, in the sense of 'just like in a film'. **¡De película!** or **¡De cine!** *Fantastic!* – which was apparently far from the case for this particular film!

② **fuimos** *we went* is the preterite tense. The preterite is used here because the action is a single, completed action in the past. See note 8 for a reminder of the contrast in use between preterite and imperfect tenses.

③ **¡Que te den morcilla!** This expression literally means 'May they give you black pudding!' and translates to *Go take a hike! Get lost!*

④ **había** *there was*, *there were* is the imperfect tense of **haber**; like its equivalent in the present tense, **hay** *there is*, *there are*, it stays singular in form, even when the English is plural (lesson 14). See also note 8.

⑤ **la gente** *people* is a feminine singular noun.

Fantastic! *(Of film!)*

1 – Yesterday we went to see 'You Have It Coming!'.
2 – Were there a lot of people in the cinema?
3 – Don't even ask *(Don't speak to me)*, there was a huge queue!
4 – I went to see it last week *(the week past)*.
5 – And what did you think of it *(how to-you it-seemed)*?

⑥ **¡No me hables!** (informal sing.) is used in the sense of 'Tell me about it!' Negative commands (prohibitions) use the present subjunctive, which involves a change in the final vowel. If the infinitive ends in **-ar**, the vowel changes from **a** to **e**; if the infinitive ends in **-er** or **-ir**, it changes from **e** to **a**. For example, **¡No vengas!** *Don't come!* (informal sing.) from **venir** (an irregular verb). The corresponding affirmative <u>informal</u> commands do NOT take the subjunctive endings, however. Most simply drop the **s**: **¡Habla!** *Speak!*, but a few are irregular, for example, **¡Ven!** *Come!*

6 – ¡Me**nu**do **ro**llo! ⑦
7 **Hu**bo ⑧ **mu**chos que no aguan**ta**ron **has**ta el fi**nal**.
8 Y a ti, ¿te gus**tó** ⑨?
9 – **Na**da! ¡**Na**da de **na**da! ⑩
10 Y el desen**la**ce… ¡ni ⑪ te **cuen**to! ¡Un de**sas**tre!
11 El protago**nis**ta no ten**drí**a que ⑫ mo**rir** le**yen**do el pe**rió**dico.
12 Ten**drí**a que pe**gar**se un **ti**ro.
13 – ¿Por qué?
14 – ¡**Por**que a**sí** los especta**do**res se desperta**rí**an!

*6 … **rro**-yo **10** … des-en-**lah**-thay … **11** … lay-**yen**-do …*

Notes

⑦ In this context, the expression **¡Menudo rollo!** means *What a boring film!* The primary meaning of **rollo** is *roll*, but it also means *reel* or *spool*. You could also say **¡Menudo tostón!** or **¡Qué tostón!** *How boring!* Before a noun, **menudo** *slight*, *small* is used in various expressions: **¡Menudo jaleo!** *What a racket!*; **¡Menudo lío!** *What a mess!*

⑧ **hubo** *there was*, *there were* is the preterite tense of **haber**. The preterite is used to refer to a specific action in the past (here, people leaving the cinema), while the imperfect **había** is used to describe the context, or what something was like in the past.

Ayer hubo una buena película en la televisión.
Yesterday there was a good film on television.
(One-time action in the past = preterite)

En aquel entonces había películas, pero no había televisión.
At that time there were films, but there was no television.
(Description in the past = imperfect)

6 – Boring rubbish!
7 There were a lot [of people] who couldn't stick it out *(that they didn't endure)* to *(until)* the end.
8 And *(to)* you, did you like [it]?
9 – Not at all! Absolutely not! *(Nothing of nothing!)*
10 And the ending … I can't even tell you *(neither to-you I-tell)*! A disaster!
11 The main character *(protagonist)* shouldn't have died [while] reading the paper.
12 He should have shot himself *(hit-himself a shot)*!
13 – Why?
14 – Because that would have woken up the audience *(that-way the spectators would-have-awakened)*!

▸ (9) **gustó** is the preterite of **gustar** *to please, to like* when referring to something singular (here, a film). Note the similarity to **pareció** (line 5). Both these verbs are the same in all persons (**me**, **te**, **le**, **nos**, **os**, **les**) when speaking about one thing.

(10) **nada** *nothing* means *not at all* when used as an adverb. **¡Nada de nada!** means *No way!* or *Absolutely not!*

(11) **¡Ni te cuento!** *I can't even tell you!* Although **ni** means *neither, nor*, it can translate the idea of *not even*, which is **ni/no … siquiera** or **ni siquiera**. So **Ni ha telefoneado** means the same as **Ni siquiera ha telefoneado.** *He hasn't even phoned.*

(12) **tener que** *to have to*; **tendría que** *I, he/she, you* (formal sing.) *should have to*. Here we have the conditional again. For regular verbs, it is formed by adding the imperfect tense endings of **-er** and **-ir** verbs (**-ía**, **-ías**, **-ía**, **-íamos**, **-íais**, **-ían**) to the infinitive.

Ejercicio 1: Traduzca

❶ Ayer fui al cine. ❷ Vamos a hacer la cola. ❸ En esta calle, la semana pasada hubo un accidente. ❹ ¿Qué te parece? ❺ Quiero ver esa película.

* * *

Ejercicio 2: Complete

❶ Many people drive too fast *(rapidly)*.
.... circula demasiado ....

❷ What a traffic jam!
¡...... ......!

❸ I would like to read the paper.
.... leer el ....

❹ He hasn't even come *(Not even he-has come)*.
.. .. ha venido.

40 Lección cuarenta

¡Seguro de sí mismo!

1 – ¿Me ha lla**ma**do?
2 – Sí, **pa**se. **Sién**tese. **Pón**gase **có**modo.
3 – Sí, **gra**cias.
4 – Bien. **Pron**to negocia**re**mos ① un impor**tan**te con**tra**to

Notes

① **negociaremos** *we will negotiate.* You may remember that future tense endings are added to the infinitive. Perhaps you also noticed that the future tense takes the same endings in ▸

Answers to Exercise 1

❶ Yesterday I went to the cinema. ❷ We are going to queue/line up. ❸ In this street there was an accident last week. ❹ What do you think of it? ❺ I want to see that film.

* * *

❺ Was there much of an audience *(Were-there many spectators)*?
¿. . . . . muchos . . . . ?

Answers to Exercise 2

❶ Mucha gente – deprisa ❷ Menudo atasco ❸ Quisiera – periódico ❹ Ni siquiera – ❺ Había – espectadores

---

Lesson forty 40

Sure of himself!

1 – Did you call me?
2 – Yes, come in *(pass)*. Sit down *(Seat-yourself)*. Make *(Put)* yourself comfortable.
3 – Yes, thank you.
4 – Good. Soon we will negotiate an important contract

▸ all three conjugations (**-ar**, **-er** and **-ir**). These endings are identical to those of the present tense of **haber** *to have*.

5 con **u**na **fir**ma ② estadouni**den**se ③ y…
6 he pen**sa**do en us**ted pa**ra diri**gir** las nego**cia**cio**nes**.
7 – Es un ho**nor pa**ra mí. Se lo agra**dez**co ④ **mu**cho, **pe**ro…
8 mi in**glés** es bas**tan**te defi**cien**te.
9 A de**cir** ver**dad**… ¡in**clu**so di**rí**a que es **fran**camente **ma**lo!
10 – No se preo**cu**pe ⑤. Ha**rá** un **cur**so inten**si**vo de in**glés**.

Pronunciation
5 *… es-tah-do-oo-nee-**den**-say …* ***6*** *… dee-ree-**heer** …*
7 *… ah-grah-**deth**-ko …* ***8*** *… day-fee-**thee-en**-tay*

Notes

② **firma** *firm*, *business*; you can also say **sociedad** ('society'), **compañía** *company* or **empresa** *enterprise*. The more common meaning of **firma** is *signature*: **Todo está listo para la firma.** *Everything is ready for signature.*
And **firmar** is *to sign*:
Tiene que firmar aquí. *You* (formal sing.) *must sign here.*

③ You may hear **norteamericanos** or **americanos** (line 18) used to refer to nationals of the United States. However, this is actually a misuse since **los canadienses** *Canadians* also live in **América del Norte** *North America*, as do, technically speaking, most **mexicanos** *Mexicans*. Not to mention that **los brasileños** *Brazilians* or **los chilenos** *Chileans*, for example, are also **americanos**, generally known as **latinoamericanos** *Latin Americans* or **sudamericanos** *South Americans*. So **estadounidense** *American* (from the United States) is the best term to use.

④ **se lo agradezco** *I thank you for it* or *I'm grateful to you for it* (formal) is a common expression you'll hear; the adverb **mucho** is added if the speaker is very grateful. Note the ▸

5 with a company *(firm)* [in the] United States and …
6 I thought of *(in)* you for directing *(to direct)* the negotiations.
7 – It is an honour for me. I'm very grateful to you for it, but …
8 my English is rather inadequate *(deficient)*.
9 To tell [the] truth … I would even say *(including I-would-say)* that frankly it is bad!
10 – Don't worry. You will take *(do)* an intensive English course.

▸ similarity of **agradecer** *to thank*, *to be grateful* to **gracias** *thanks*. **Agradecer** adds a **z** before the **c** in the first-person present tense, as does **conocer** *to know*, *to meet*, *to be familiar with*. All other persons and tenses of these verbs are regular.
Te agrade<u>c</u>e el regalo. *He/she thanks you for the present.*
Te cono<u>c</u>e bien. *He/she knows you well.*
But: **Le agrade<u>zc</u>o su llamada.** *I thank you for your call.*
Cono<u>zc</u>o esa ciudad. *I know that city.*

⑤ Remember that the formal imperative (lesson 38) and negative commands (lesson 39) require the subjunctive. This involves a change in the final vowel: **preocup<u>e</u>** from **preocup<u>ar</u>**, or in line 2, **pas<u>e</u>** from **pas<u>ar</u>**, **siént<u>e</u>se** from **sent<u>ar</u>se** (a stem-changing verb), **póng<u>a</u>se** from **pon<u>er</u>se** (an irregular verb), etc. Notice also that in negative commands, the object pronoun goes before the verb and not after it as in affirmative commands.
Siéntese. *Sit down.* **No se siente.** *Don't sit down.*
Póngase ahí. *Stand there.* ('Put yourself there.')
No se ponga ahí. *Don't stand there.*

11 Le he bus**ca**do ⑥ un profe**sor** particu**lar**.
12 – **Pe**ro…
13 – ¡No hay **pe**ro que **val**ga! ⑦
14 ¡Con**fí**e en sí ⑧ **mis**mo!
15 De re**gre**so a Es**pa**ña, el subordi**na**do es convo**ca**do por el direc**tor**:
16 – ¿Y qué? ¿Ha te**ni**do dificul**ta**des con el in**glés**?
17 – ¿Yo? ¡En abso**lu**to! ⑨ ¡Nin**gu**na!
18 **Quie**nes ⑩ han te**ni**do dificul**ta**des han **si**do los ameri**ca**nos.

*15 … rray-**gray**-so …*

Notes

⑥ Normally, **buscar** means *to seek, to look for*; **encontrar** is *to find*. But in the phrase **le he buscado un profesor**, it is understood that the teacher has been found, so 'I've looked for a teacher for you' actually means 'I've found you a teacher'.

⑦ **¡No hay pero que valga!** (literally, 'There is no but that has value!') includes the present subjunctive **valga** from **valer** *to be worth, to have value*. The very common expression **¡Vale!** *OK!* (lesson 10) also comes from this verb.

⑧ We've seen **sí** *yes*, but here it is a pronoun: **sí mismo** *yourself* (in reference to a man). Compare this with the title of the lesson, where **sí mismo** is *himself* or *oneself* (m.). The **mismo** reinforces the pronoun – in some contexts it can be dropped: **entre sí** *between themselves*. If it is used, it needs to agree in gender and number: **sí misma** *herself*; **sí mismos** *themselves*. ▸

* * *

Ejercicio 1: Traduzca

❶ ¡Siéntese, por favor! ❷ Llegaremos pronto. ❸ Tienes que firmar aquí. ❹ Pablo ha ido a buscar a su hijo a casa de sus amigos. ❺ Tu español es francamente bueno.

11 I have found *(sought)* you a private teacher.
12 – But …
13 – There are no ifs, ands or buts about it *(There is no but that's valid)*!
14 Have confidence in yourself *(Trust in yourself)*!
15 Back in *(Of return to)* Spain, the subordinate is called in *(convoked)* by the director:
16 – Well? Did you have difficulties with your *(the)* English?
17 – Me? Not at all *(In absolute)*! None!
18 It was the Americans who had trouble *(Who they-have had difficulties have been the Americans)*!

⑨ **En absoluto** *not at all*, *absolutely not*. Not to be confused with **absolutamente** *absolutely*!

⑩ **Quienes han tenido dificultades** or **Los que han tenido dificultades** *the ones/those who had difficulties*. Remember that when referring to people, **quien** or **quienes** can be used to mean **el que** *the one* (masc. sing.) *who*; **la que** *the one* (fem. sing.) *who*; **los que** *those* (masc. plural) *who*, etc.

* * *

Answers to Exercise 1

❶ Sit down, please! ❷ We will soon arrive. ❸ You must sign here. ❹ Pablo went to look for his son at his friends' house. ❺ Frankly, your Spanish is good.

Ejercicio 2: Complete

❶ I thank you very much for it *(m.)*.
Te .. ..

❷ Stand *(Put-yourself[formal])* to the side, you'll be more comfortable *(m.)*.
.... al ...., ... más ....

❸ Do you *(formal)* want to take *(do)* an intensive course?
¿...... ..... un ....?

* * *

There are many options for studying Spanish in Spain. These range from weekly or monthly language stays to full-year university exchange programmes or **los cursos de verano** summer courses *organized by various Spanish universities. You can get information about the possibilities from Spanish tourist offices, consulates and embassies or, of course, online. Many cities in Spain also have* **escuelas de idiomas** language schools *that offer courses – some intensive, some less so – at all levels throughout the year.*

41 Lección cuarenta y una

Con mucha cara ①

1 – ¿Qué es**tás** ha**cien**do ②?

Notes

① **cara** *face*. **tener cara de niño** *to have a baby face*; **lavarse la cara** *to wash one's face*; **echar a cara o cruz** *to toss for heads or tails* ('face or cross'); **tener buena cara** *to look well*. In colloquial language, **tener mucha cara** means *to be gutsy* or *to have a lot of cheek/nerve*. **¡Qué cara dura!** *What cheek! What a nerve!* (**duro** *hard, difficult*) ▸

❹ Have you *(informal)* had difficulties in finding a teacher?
¿… …… ………… para ……… un profesor?

❺ No, none!
¡…, …….!

Answers to Exercise 2

❶ – lo agradezco mucho ❷ Póngase – lado, estará – cómodo ❸ Quiere hacer – curso intensivo ❹ Has tenido dificultades – encontrar – ❺ No, ninguna

* * *

In addition there are **los cursos particulares** private courses, *which you can easily find by checking classified ads, noticeboards or through chance meetings. Language exchanges – an hour of English in exchange for an hour of Spanish – are also popular. Whatever you choose, remember that the best way to learn is to practice as much as possible: listen, read, take notes, speak and* **¡Confíe en sí mismo/misma!** Have confidence in yourself!

Lesson forty-one 41

What a nerve!

1 – What are you doing?

② Like in English, a continuous or progressive action can be expressed in Spanish using the equivalent of *to be* + present participle (an *-ing* verb). The Spanish construction is **estar** + present participle (e.g. in line 1, **haciendo** *doing*):
¿Qué estás leyendo? *What are you reading?* (**leer** *to read*)
Estamos jugando. *We are playing.* (**jugar** *to play*)

2 – **Si**go ③ en **pa**ro y… es**toy** le**yen**do los a**nun**cios.
3 **Ten**go que encon**trar** tra**ba**jo.
4 – ¡**Mi**ra, a**quí** hay **u**no intere**san**te!
5 'Se ④ nece**si**ta leña**dor**. **Trein**ta **a**ños de expe**rien**cia.'
6 – **Pe**ro… ¡Yo **nun**ca he cor**ta**do un **ár**bol!
7 – ¿Qué más da? ⑤ ¡A lo me**jor** ⑥ fun**cio**na!
8 Tú, pre**sén**tate. **Lue**go… ¡ya ve**rás**!
9 En la ofi**ci**na del Insti**tu**to Nacio**nal** de Em**ple**o (INEM):
10 – Bien, se**ñor**; ¿y **cuán**tos **a**ños me **di**ce que ha es**ta**do cor**tan**do **ár**boles?
11 – Pues… **ca**si cua**ren**ta **a**ños.
12 – Muy bien; ¿y **dón**de principal**men**te?
13 Sorpren**di**do, tras un ins**tan**te de indeci**sión**,
14 el candi**da**to al **pues**to **suel**ta lo pri**me**ro ⑦ que le **vie**ne a la ca**be**za:

Pronunciation
*5 … lay-nyah-**dor** … ex-pay-**ree-en**-thee-ah **12** … preen-thee-pahl-**men**-tay **13** … een-day-thee-**see-on***

Notes

③ **seguir** *to follow, to continue* is a stem-changing verb (**e → i**). In the present tense, stem changes occur in all persons except **nosotros** and **vosotros**. When this verb is used to express a continuing condition, it has the sense of *still*.
Sigo en el paro. *I am still out of work.*
El cielo sigue cubierto. *The sky is still overcast* ('covered').

④ This use of the reflexive verb best translates into the passive voice in English (*to be* + past participle): **necesitar** *to need*, **necesitarse** *to be needed*: ▸

2 – I'm still out of work *(I-continue on stop)* and … I'm reading the classifieds.
3 I have to find work.
4 – Look, here's *(here there-is)* an interesting one!
5 'Woodcutter needed. Thirty years of experience.'
6 – But … I've never cut [down] a [single] tree!
7 – So what *(What more gives)*? It might work *(At the best it-works)*!
8 *(You)* [Just] apply. Then … *(already)* you'll see!
9 At the National Employment Agency:
10 – Well, sir, so *(and)* tell me, how many years have you been cutting trees?
11 – Uhh … nearly forty years.
12 – Very good; and where mostly?
13 Surprised, after a moment's hesitation *(an instant of indecision)*,
14 the job applicant *(candidate to-the post)* blurts out *(releases)* the first thing that comes into his head:

▸ **Necesitamos camarero.** *We need a waiter*. (Active: the subject, *we*, performs the action.)
Se necesita camarero. *A waiter is needed.* (Passive: the subject is not expressed, making the action impersonal.)

⑤ **¿Qué más da?** ('What more gives?') is a useful expression that means *What does it matter? So what?*

⑥ **a lo mejor** ('at the best') is a very common expression meaning *possibly, perhaps*:
A lo mejor viene. *He might come.*

⑦ **lo primero** *the first thing.* **Lo primero que haremos será …** *The first thing that we will do will be...*
Not to be confused with **el primero** *the first (one)* (m.).

15 – En el **Sá**hara.
16 – ¿En el **Sá**hara? ¡**Pe**ro si ⑧ **allí** no hay **ár**boles!
17 – ¡A**ho**ra! ¡A**ho**ra! □

Notes

⑧ It would also be possible to leave out the **si** here: **¿En el Sáhara? ¡Pero allí no hay árboles!** *In the Sahara? But there are no trees there!* The **si** is quite common in colloquial language and has the sense of *but I'm telling you that there aren't any trees there!*

* * *

Ejercicio 1: Traduzca

❶ ¡Acércate! ❷ ¿Estás estudiando? ❸ Leo los anuncios del periódico. ❹ Estoy buscando trabajo. ❺ ¡Mira, éste parece interesante!

* * *

Ejercicio 2: Complete

❶ Have you *(informal)* found a job?
¿. . . . . un empleo?

❷ You have a lot of experience.
Tú . . . .

❸ 'Spanish [is] spoken.'
'. . . . .'

❹ I'm still out of work.
. . . . trabajo.

15 – In the Sahara!
16 – In the Sahara? But *(if)* there aren't [any] trees there!
17 – Not anymore *(Now)*! Not anymore *(Now)*!

* * *

Answers to Exercise 1
❶ Come closer! ❷ Are you studying? ❸ I read the classified ads in the newspaper. ❹ I'm looking for work. ❺ Look, this seems interesting!

* * *

❺ It's the first thing that one has to do/that must be done.
Es .. .. hay ... hacer.

Answers to Exercise 2
❶ Has encontrado – ❷ – tienes mucha experiencia ❸ Se habla español ❹ Sigo sin – ❺ – lo primero que – que –

42 Lección cuarenta y dos

Repaso

1 Imperative / Present subjunctive

1.1 Reminder

Spanish imperatives are identical to the forms of the present subjunctive, with the sole exception of affirmative informal commands. Remember these from lesson 35? The second-person singular (**tú**) command is formed simply by dropping the **s**:
Tú pasas. *You come in.* → **¡Pasa!** *Come in!*
Tú corres. *You run.* → **¡Corre!** *Run!*

The second-person plural (**vosotros**, **vosotras**) informal command is formed by dropping the final **r** of the infinitive and substituting the letter **d**:
Vosotros abrís la puerta. *You open the door.* →
¡Abrid la puerta! *Open the door!*

With affirmative commands, any object pronouns follow the verb, as in English. However, in Spanish they are attached to the verb:
¡Invítame! *Invite me!*
¡Escribidnos! *Write [to] us!*
¡Decidlo! *Say it!*

When there are two object pronouns, the indirect object pronoun (usually a person) comes first:
¡Déjamelo! *Leave it [to] me!*
¡Léemelo! *Read it [to] me!*
¡Abrídmelo! *Open it [for] me!*

When the second-person plural command is followed by the pronoun **os** *you* (plural) (for example, in situations where you command two or more people to do something to/with each other), it loses the final **d**:
¡Daos la mano! *Shake (each other's) hand[s]!*
¡Escribíos! *Write [to] each other!*

1.2 Other imperative forms

These are (almost) all identical to the present subjunctive.

• First-person plural (in English, *Let's …*):
¡Hablemos! *Let's talk!*
¡Comamos! *Let's eat!*
¡Abramos la ventana! *Let's open the window!*

• Formal commands:
¡Circule por la derecha! *Drive on the right!* (singular)
¡Circulen! *Drive!* (plural)
¡Póngase cómodo! *Make yourself comfortable!*
¡Pónganse cómodos! *Make yourselves comfortable!*

1.3 Negative commands (prohibitions)

All negative imperatives, which prohibit someone from doing something, use the present subjunctive. This is the case for <u>all persons</u>, including the informal second person (**tú** and **vosotros**). Compare:
¡Llama! *Call!* **¡No llames!** *Don't call!* (singular)
¡Corred! *Run!* **¡No corráis!** *Don't run!* (plural)

In negative commands, the object pronouns come <u>before</u> the verb:
¡Cómpralo! *Buy it!* **¡No lo compres!** *Don't buy it!*
¡Siéntate! *Sit [yourself] down!* **¡No te sientes!** *Don't sit down!*
¡Póngase ahí! *Stand there!* **¡No se ponga ahí!** *Don't stand there!*

2 Comparative adjectives

2.1 Comparative of equality

The English comparative of equality *as ... as* is formed in Spanish using **tan ... como**:
Mi maleta es <u>tan</u> grande <u>como</u> la tuya.
My suitcase is <u>as</u> big <u>as</u> yours.

2.2 Comparatives of superiority and inferiority

English can show comparisons of superiority using an *-er* ending on an adjective and then placing the word *than* in front of the second term in the comparison:
She is prettier than you. **Ella es más bonita que tú.**

But some adjectives and adverbs require using *more/than* (superiority), *less/than* (inferiority), which is similar to the Spanish construction (in Spanish, **más** *more* or **menos** *less* + adjective, followed by **que** *than*):
She is more beautiful than you. **Ella es más hermosa que tú.**
She is less attractive than you. **Ella es menos atractiva que tú.**

In Spanish, the same construction is always used, whereas the English construction can vary:
Mi coche es más pequeño que el tuyo.
My car is smaller than yours.
Pablo es menos inteligente que Juan.
Pablo is less intelligent than Juan.

Summary:

más ... que	→	*more ... than* or *(-er... than)*
menos ... que	→	*less ... than*
tan ... como	→	*as ... as*

2.3 The superlative

The superlative (in English, *the most* or *-est*, *the least*) is formed in Spanish by using the appropriate definite article (**el**, **la**, **los** or **las**) before **más/menos**.

Ella es la chica más bonita del mundo.
She is the prettiest girl in the world.

Pablo es el hombre menos inteligente de la ciudad.
Pablo is the least intelligent man in the city.

3 Future tense

In English, the future tense is formed using *will* (or *shall*) + the infinitive of the verb. Spanish, however, conjugates the verb by adding endings to the infinitive. These are the same as the present tense endings of **haber** *to have*. Note that all forms, with the exception of the first-person plural, take a written accent on the final syllable. This indicates that the final syllable is stressed.

hablar	→	é	*I will speak*
comer	→	ás	*you* (informal sing.) *will eat*
buscar	→	á	*he/she/it/you* (formal sing.) *will look for*
dejar	→	emos	*we will leave*
llamar	→	éis	*you* (informal pl.) *will call*
acabar	→	án	*they/you* (formal pl.) *will finish*

In this tense, there are only 12 common irregular verbs. One we've seen is **habrá** (from **haber**), lesson 21. The others are **caber** *to fit*, **poder** *to be able to*, **querer** *to want*, **saber** *to know*, **poner** *to put*, **salir** *to leave*, **tener** *to have*, **valer** *to be worth*, **venir** *to come*, **decir** *to say*, *to tell* and **hacer** *to do*, *to make*. You can check the verb tables in the grammatical appendix to see the irregular forms.

4 Conditional

The conditional mood (in English, *would/should* + the infinitive of the verb) is also formed in Spanish by adding endings to the infinitive. The endings of the conditional are those of the imperfect tense of **-er** and **-ir** verbs.

hablar	→	ía	*I would speak*
comer	→	ías	*you* (informal sing.) *would eat*
buscar	→	ía	*he/she/it/you* (formal sing.) *would look for*
dejar	→	íamos	*we would leave*
llamar	→	íais	*you* (informal pl.) *would call*
acabar	→	ían	*they/you* (formal pl.) *would finish*

The same 12 common verbs that are irregular in the future tense are also irregular in the conditional. We have already seen **harías** (from **hacer**), lesson 36, and **tendría** (from **tener**), lesson 39.

5 Preterite tense (simple past)

In Spanish, when an action took place in a period of time that is viewed as completely elapsed at the moment of speaking, the preterite tense is used.
Ayer fuimos al cine. *Yesterday we went to the cinema.*
El martes comí en un restaurante.
On Tuesday, I ate at a restaurant.
Trabajé para ellos el año pasado. *I worked for them last year.*

The preterite tense has many irregular verbs, so it requires a certain amount of practice. We'll be including it frequently in the coming lessons so that you can start to recognize its characteristic forms. We'll discuss this tense in more detail later.

In the meantime, here are some examples using the three main past tenses: preterite, imperfect and present perfect.
Ayer yo leí los anuncios. *Yesterday I read the classifieds.*
Ayer yo leía los anuncios mientras comía.
Yesterday I was reading the classifieds while I was eating.
Yo he leído los anuncios. *I read/have read the classifieds.*

6 Present continuous (present progressive)

The English present continuous is formed using the verb *to be* + the present participle, which ends in *-ing*. The Spanish equivalent is very similar, using **estar** (but never **ser**) + the present participle, which ends in **-ando** (for **-ar** verbs) and **-iendo** (for **-er** and **-ir** verbs) added to the stem of the infinitive. This tense is used almost exactly like its English counterpart to express a continuous or progressive action in the present.
Yo estoy hablando. *I am speaking.*
Ella está comiendo. *She is eating.*

In Spanish, there are two distinct verbs for *to know* that are used in specific contexts.

• **saber** means *to know a fact*, *to know how* or *to possess knowledge about something*. (Note the highly irregular first-person present tense form, **yo sé**. It takes a written accent to distinguish it from the otherwise identical personal pronoun **se**.)
No sé cuántos años tiene. *I don't know how old she is.*
Sabe nadar. *He knows how to swim.*

• **conocer** means *to know someone or something*, *to be familiar with* or *to recognize*. Because of spelling rules, it too has an irregular first-person present tense form, **yo conozco**.
Conozco a Roberto. *I know Roberto.*
Conoce bien la zona. *She knows the area well.*

conocer is also used for *to meet someone*:
Fui a conocer a sus padres. *I went to meet his parents.*

There are occasionally cases where either **saber** or **conocer** can be used interchangeably, as there can be some crossover between possessing knowledge about something and being familiar with something, but generally speaking only one or the other is appropriate in a given context.

1 – ¡Deprisa! ¡Ponte el cinturón de seguridad!
2 – ¡Ten cuidado! ¡No corras!
3 – ¡A que llegamos tarde!
4 – No es tan tarde como crees.
5 La película comienza* a las ocho y media y…
6 ni siquiera son las siete.
7 – ¡Cada vez hay más tráfico!
8 – ¡Bueno, tranquilízate!
9 Pronto estaremos bien sentados y cómodos.
10 Y luego… ¿quién sabe? ¡A lo mejor es un rollo!

* From the stem-changing verb **comenzar** *to start, begin.*

---

43 Lección cuarenta y tres

A la llegada ① del tren

1 – **Pe**ro… ¿qué te **pa**sa?
2 Es**tás pá**lido.
3 ¿Te ha sen**ta**do mal ② el **via**je?
4 – Me he mare**a**do ③.

Notes

① **la llegada** *arrival* and **la salida** *departure* are words that are particularly useful when travelling. Note that **salida** also means *exit, way out*: **salida de socorro** *emergency exit*; **Te espero a la salida del cine.** *I'll wait for you outside* ('at the exit of') *the cinema.*

② **sentarse** *to sit down, be seated*; **Siéntese, por favor.** *Please be seated.* However, **sentar bien/mal** has quite a different meaning. Depending on the context it can mean *to agree with/ not agree with*; *to suit/not suit*; *to do good/to do harm*. It is ▸

Traducción
(All in informal sing.)
1 Quick! Put on your seatbelt! **2** Be careful! Don't speed! **3** I bet we'll arrive late! **4** It's not as late as you think. **5** The film begins at eight-thirty and ... **6** it's not even seven o'clock. **7** There is more and more traffic! **8** OK, calm down! **9** Soon we'll be sitting comfortably *(well seated and comfortable)*. **10** And then... who knows? It might be a real bore!

Lesson forty-three 43

At the train's arrival

1 – But ... what's the matter with you?
2 You're pale.
3 The journey didn't agree with you?
4 – I felt queasy.

▸ chiefly used like **gustar**, i.e. the noun following the verb (**el viaje** in line 3) is the subject of the sentence.
Note also that the stem changes (**e** → **ie**) in the present tense.
El café me ha sentado mal. *The coffee didn't agree with me.*
Una infusión te sentará bien. *An herbal tea will do you good.*
Esos zapatos te sientan muy bien. *Those shoes suit you very well.*

③ **marearse** *to feel nauseous, dizzy.* **Me mareo.** *I'm feeling queasy.* The origin of the word **marearse** is **el mar** *the sea.* This will help you remember that on a boat, **marearse** means *to be seasick.*

5 Me **pon**go mal**í**simo ④
6 **cuan**do **via**jo de es**pal**das ⑤ al sen**ti**do de la **mar**cha.
7 – ¿Y por qué no has pe**di**do a la per**so**na que **i**ba ⑥ sen**ta**da en**fren**te
8 que te cam**bia**se ⑦ el **si**tio?
9 La **gen**te ⑧ com**pren**de **es**te **ti**po de situa**cio**nes,
10 y **sue**le ⑨ ser a**ma**ble.
11 – Ya lo he pen**sa**do, **pe**ro no he po**di**do;
12 no ha**bí**a **na**die, es que el a**sien**to **i**ba va**cí**o. □

Pronunciation
9 *... see-too-ah-**thee-o**-nays* ***10*** *... **sway**-lay ...*

Notes

④ **ponerse enfermo** (or **malo**) *to get sick, to fall ill*. The verb **ponerse** followed by an adjective often expresses a temporary change of state; that is 'becoming' or 'turning':
¡Cuidado, el semáforo se ha puesto rojo!
Look out, the traffic light is turning red!

poner enfermo (or **malo**) is also commonly used in the figurative sense of *to make one sick*: **El ruido y los gritos me ponen malo.** *The noise and the shouting make me sick.*

⑤ **la espalda** and **las espaldas** *the back*. The singular is used strictly in an anatomical sense, denoting the part of the body from **el hombro** *the shoulder* to **la cintura** *the waist*.
Me duele la espalda. *My back hurts.*
dar la espalda *to turn one's back.*

After **de**, the plural is generally used: **de espaldas** *from behind, facing backwards*; **de espaldas a** *with one's back to.*

⑥ **iba** *went, was going* is the first- and third-person singular imperfect of **ir** *to go*, an irregular verb. Note that in contexts that ▸

5 I get very sick
6 when I travel facing backwards *(of back to-the direction of the motion)*.
7 – And why didn't you ask the person who was sitting *(went seated)* opposite
8 to change places with you *(that with-you he/ she-changed the place)*?
9 People understand *('The people' understands)* this type of situation*(s)*
10 and are usually *(is-accustomed-to being)* kind.
11 – I thought about it *(Already it I-have thought)*, but I couldn't;
12 there was nobody [there], the seat was *(went)* empty.

▸ imply movement (here, a train), **ir** can be used interchangeably with **estar**.

⑦ **¿Has pedido a la persona que te cambiase de sitio?** *Did you ask the person that he/she change places with you?* Remember that after a verb that expresses a command, request or wish, the subjunctive is used, introduced by **que**. The form **cambiase** is an imperfect subjunctive (referring to the past), rather than the present subjunctive, but don't worry about that now – we'll deal with it later! The **-se** is an imperfect subjunctive ending, not to be confused with the personal pronoun **se**.
Me pide que le cambie (present subjunctive) **el sitio.**
He/she is asking that I change places with him/her.

⑧ **la gente** *people*. This feminine noun is accompanied by the definite article **la** and is always singular (unlike its English equivalent *people*, which is plural). So the verb used with it takes the third-person singular form!

⑨ **soler** + infinitive, *to be used to*, *to be accustomed to* + present participle (e.g. **soler ser** *to be used to being*), most naturally translates into English with a verb accompanied by the adverb *usually*: **Suelo tomar el tren.** *I usually take the train.* It is a stem-changing verb, conjugating like **volver: suelo**, **sueles**, **suele**, **solemos**, **soléis**, **suelen** *I usually …*, *you usually…*, etc.

Ejercicio 1: Traduzca

❶ El tren ha llegado con retraso. ❷ Estás muy pálida, ¿qué te pasa? ❸ Los viajes en barco no me sientan bien. ❹ Siempre me mareo. ❺ Tomaremos una infusión.

* * *

Ejercicio 2: Complete

❶ Do you *(informal)* know what time the train leaves *(which is the hour of departure of-the train)*?
¿. . . . . cuál . . . . de . . . . ?

❷ I request that you exit on that side.
Le . . . . por . . . lado.

❸ My back hurts.
. . . . la . . . .

❹ I usually phone him every week.
. . . . todas las . . . .

❺ I thought about it *(Already it I-have thought)*.
Ya . . . .

44 Lección cuarenta y cuatro

Lógica descarada

1 Un se**ñor en**tra en un restau**ran**te con un ci**ga**rro encen**di**do en la **ma**no.

Pronunciation
*1 … thee-**gah**-rro en-then-**dee**-do …*

Answers to Exercise 1

❶ The train has arrived late. ❷ You're very pale, what's happened to you? ❸ Boat trips don't agree with me. ❹ I always get seasick. ❺ We'll drink an herbal tea.

* * *

Answers to Exercise 2

❶ Sabes – es la hora – salida del tren ❷ – ruego que salga – ese – ❸ Me duele – espalda ❹ Suelo telefonearle – semanas ❺ – lo he pensado

Until recently, travellers crossing into Spain from France by train, **tren**, *were likely to travel on the* **Talgo**, *a special train conceived by* **Red Nacional de Ferrocarriles Españoles** National Network of Spanish Railways *or* **RENFE** *to cope with the difference in track gauge (1.44 metres in most European countries, but 1.6 metres in the Iberian peninsula), which meant that French trains could not cross into Spanish territory on the old tracks. How did the Talgo get around this difficulty? With adjustable axles! This is a trick that Spanish engineers came up with to change the distance between the wheels.*

Today, there is a high-speed train in Spain, the **AVE** *(***Alta Velocidad Española***), which now links Madrid to cities including Seville, Cordoba, Malaga, Valencia, Barcelona – and on to Paris!*

Lesson forty-four 44

Brazen logic

1 A gentleman enters *(into)* a restaurant with a lighted cigarette in his *(the)* hand.

2 **Na**da más ① sen**tar**se, el cama**re**ro se di**ri**ge a él y le **di**ce:

3 – Caba**ll**ero, a**quí** es**tá** prohi**bi**do fu**mar** ②.

4 ¿No ha **vis**to el le**tre**ro?

5 **Es**ta **zo**na es**tá** reser**va**da a los no fuma**do**res.

6 – Ya ③ lo sé, con**tes**ta el re**cién** lle**ga**do.

7 – Dis**cul**pe ④, **pe**ro **tie**ne us**ted** un ci**ga**rro en la **ma**no, in**sis**te el cama**re**ro.

8 – ¡Y **da**le… ⑤!

9 ¡Tam**bién lle**vo ⑥ za**pa**tos en los pies y no **an**do! □

6 … *rray-***thee-en** …

Notes

① **nada más** *nothing more*, *nothing else* followed by an infinitive usually means *barely*, *scarcely*, *as soon as*, etc.
Nada más llegar, telefoneó. *As soon as he arrived, he phoned.*
Se ha ido nada más comer. *She left as soon as she had eaten.*

You're already familiar with **más** *more*. Don't forget **además** *moreover, in addition to* – however, if you want to say 'in addition' in the negative sense of *to top it all off*, you would say **encima** (literally, 'on top'). **¡Fuma mucho y encima se queja!** *He smokes a lot, and on top of that he complains!*

② **Está prohibido fumar.** *Smoking is forbidden.*
Aquí, está prohibido aparcar. *It is forbidden to park here.*
Prohibido fumar/aparcar *No smoking/parking.*

③ When used at the beginning of a sentence, **ya** *already* reinforces the following statement, implying that it is obvious. So **Ya lo sé** is more like *I know it* or *Yes, I know* than simply *I know*. **¡Ya lo sabía!** *I knew it!* Another example: **Ya te lo he dicho.** *I told you so.* Note also the highly irregular – and very frequently used – first-person present form of **saber**: **sé**, which is distinguished from the pronoun **se** by its written accent.

④ **disculpar** *to excuse*, *pardon* is very commonly used to beg someone's pardon in formal settings. ▸

2 As soon as [he is] seated, the waiter heads over *(directs himself)* to him and says *(to him)*:
3 – Sir, it is forbidden to smoke here.
4 Did you not see *(You haven't seen)* the sign?
5 This area is reserved for *(the)* non-smokers.
6 – [Yes,] I know *(Already it I-know)*, replies the newcomer *(recently arrived)*.
7 – Excuse me, but you have a cigarette in your hand, the waiter insists.
8 – Here we go again!
9 I'm also wearing shoes on my feet, but *(and)* I'm not walking!

▸ **Disculpe** or **Discúlpeme** *Excuse me./I'm sorry.* (formal)
pedir disculpas a *to apologize to* ('to ask pardon from')
Le ruego que me disculpe. *Please excuse me.* ('I request that you excuse me.')

⑤ **¡Y dale!** (literally, 'And give him!'), when spoken in an annoyed tone, expresses aggravation with someone's stubborn insistence, e.g. *There you go again! Stop going on about it!* In a weary tone, **¡Y dale que dale!** is roughly the equivalent of *the same old song* or *over and over again*, whereas an energetic **¡Dale!** is used informally as encouragement: *Come on!*

⑥ **llevar** *to take*, *to carry* can also mean *to wear* in the sense of *to have on*, referring to clothes, jewellery, make-up, etc. The verb **tener** can also be used in this way.
Mira, Lidia lleva/tiene unos pendientes muy bonitos.
Look, Lidia is wearing/has on very pretty earrings.

Ejercicio 1: Traduzca

❶ ¿Cómo se llama el restaurante? ❷ Se ha dirigido a mí para pedirme un cigarro. ❸ ¿Esta mesa está reservada? ❹ Preguntaré al camarero. ❺ Disculpe, esta sala es para no fumadores.

* * *

Ejercicio 2: Complete

❶ As soon as he ate breakfast, he left for work.
. . . . desayunar, ... a trabajar.

❷ I know it.
. . . .

❸ It's a newly opened restaurant.
. . . . abierto.

❹ No entry.
. . . .

45 Lección cuarenta y cinco

Distraída

1 – ¿Comisa**rí**a de poli**cí**a?
2 – Sí, **dí**game.
3 – **Ven**gan **rá**pido, por fa**vor**. ¡Me han ro**ba**do ①!

Pronunciation
1 *ko-mee-sah-**ree**-ah …*

Notes

① In English, we would be more likely to say 'I've been robbed!' (passive voice: *to be* + past participle) than 'They've robbed me!' (active voice, here with the impersonal subject *they*), but ▸

Answers to Exercise 1
❶ What's the name of the restaurant? ❷ He/she came over to me to ask me for a cigarette. ❸ Is this table reserved? ❹ I'll ask the waiter. ❺ Excuse me, this room is for non-smokers.

* * *

❺ She was wearing black shoes.

....

Answers to Exercise 2
❶ Nada más – se ha ido – ❷ Ya lo sé ❸ Es un restaurante recién – ❹ Prohibido entrar ❺ Llevaba zapatos negros.

Lesson forty-five 45

Absent-minded *(Distracted[f.])*

1 – Police station?
2 – Yes, hello *(tell[formal]-me)*.
3 – Come quickly, please. I've been robbed *(Me they-have robbed)*!

▸ the passive voice is mostly avoided in Spanish. So although here the person who committed the act is unknown, it is still expressed in the active voice.
Me han robado el dinero. *My money has been stolen.* ('They have stolen my money.')
Me lo han quitado todo. *Everything has been taken.* ('They have taken everything from me.')

4 – ¡Tran**qui**la ②, se**ño**ra!
5 ¿Qué ha pa**sa**do?
6 ¡Ex**plí**quese ③!
7 – Es**toy** en mi **co**che… Me lo ④ han qui**ta**do **to**do:
8 el vo**lan**te, el acelera**dor**, los pe**da**les del **fre**no y del em**bra**gue,
9 la **ra**dio ⑤, la pa**lan**ca de **cam**bio, el salpica**de**ro…
10 ¡Impo**si**ble arran**car**!
11 – ¿Y **dón**de es**tá** us**ted** a**ho**ra?
12 – Pues… **bue**no… a**ho**ra es**toy** a**quí**… en el **co**che… sen**ta**da…

*8 … ah-thay-lay-rah-**dor** … em-**brah**-gay*

Notes

② **tranquila** *calm* (f.) is used as an adjective here, not a verb. **¡Tranquilo/a!** *Don't worry about it! Take it easy! Stay calm!*

③ Don't forget:
• formal commands use the third-person (singular or plural)
• **se** is the third-person reflexive pronoun (singular or plural)
• all formal commands (both affirmative and negative) use the present subjunctive endings, so the verb ends with the letter opposite to the one normally expected. Here, the infinitive is **explicar** (**-ar** verb), but the command ends in **-e**: **explique**. (Because of Spanish spelling rules, the **c** of **explicar** changes to **qu** before the letter **e**.)
• in affirmative commands, any pronouns (here, **se**) are attached to the verb, forming a single word.

④ The inclusion of the pronoun **lo** *it* simply reinforces the object **todo** *all*. In Spanish, when **todo** is used in a sentence, **lo** is ▸

4 – Calm [down], madam!
5 What happened?
6 Explain *(yourself)*!
7 – I'm in my car … They have taken everything *(Me it they-have removed everything)*:
8 the steering wheel, the accelerator, the pedals for *(of)* the brake and clutch,
9 the radio, the gear stick *(the lever of change)*, the dashboard …
10 Impossible to start!
11 – And where are you now?
12 – Well … er … now I'm here … in the car … sitting …

▸ also included, whereas in English the object pronoun can be omitted: **Tú lo sabes todo.** *You know everything.* ('You know it all.'). Compare also: **Yo lo sé.** *I know.* ('I know it.')

⑤ Be careful with the gender of this word: **la radio** (f.) *the radio*, but **el radio** (m.) *the radius*. So it's **encender <u>la</u> radio** *to switch on* ('to light') *the radio.*

13 ¡**Cuer**nos ⑥! ¡Per**do**ne…!
14 ¡No se mo**les**te… ⑦! ¡Lo he encon**tra**do **to**do!
15 ¡Es que me ha**bí**a sen**ta**do en el a**sien**to tra**se**ro!

Notes

⑥ **¡Cuernos!** *Oh dear! Gosh!* literally means 'horns' and comes from the expression **ponerle cuernos** *to put horns on him*, referring to the belief in the Middle Ages that if a wife was unfaithful to her husband, horns would grow on his head: hence, **el cornudo** *cuckold.* **Cuernos** is nowadays simply a fairly mild expression of annoyance.

* * *

Ejercicio 1: Traduzca

❶ Le pediré una explicación. ❷ Explícate, ¿qué ha pasado? ❸ Ha sido un verdadero desastre. ❹ Le han robado el coche. ❺ Ha ido a la comisaría.

* * *

Ejercicio 2: Complete

❶ He/she is a very absent-minded person.
.. ..

❷ They have phoned you *(informal)* from work.
.. ... telefoneado del ....

❸ No, you aren't disturbing me.
.., usted .. ..

❹ I was listening to the radio.
.... la radio.

13 Oh dear *(Horns)*! I'm sorry *(Pardon)*... !
14 Never mind *(Don't bother yourself)*…!
I've found everything!
15 *(It's that)* I was sitting *(myself I-had seated)* in the back seat *(seat rear)*!

⑦ **molestar** is not to be confused with *to molest*! It means *to bother* or *disturb*, and it's very commonly used:
¿Le molesta si fumo? *Does it bother you if I smoke?/Do you mind if I smoke?*
No molesten *Do not disturb* (in a hotel, for example).
Or the reflexive form **molestarse**:
No se moleste. *Don't trouble yourself.*

* * *

Answers to Exercise 1

❶ I'll ask him/her for an explanation. ❷ Explain yourself; what has happened? ❸ It's been a real disaster. ❹ His/her car has been stolen. ❺ He/she has gone to the police station.

* * *

❺ She was sitting in front.
Estaba ....

Answers to Exercise 2

❶ Es una persona muy distraída ❷ Te han – trabajo ❸ No – no me molesta ❹ Estaba escuchando – ❺ – sentada delante

46 Lección cuarenta y seis

Coto de pesca

1 – ¡Eh, **chi**co ①! ¿No has **vis**to el le**tre**ro?
2 ¡A**quí** es**tá** prohi**bi**do pes**car**!
3 **Ten**go que po**ner**te **u**na **mul**ta.
4 – **Pe**ro, **oi**ga… ② ¡yo no es**toy** pes**can**do!
5 – ¿Y la **ca**ña, y el ca**rre**te ③, y el an**zue**lo, y esa lom**briz**?
6 – ¡Ah, sí, es ver**dad**! Es que es**toy** ense**ñan**do ④ a na**dar** al gu**sa**no.
7 – Pues… ⑤ ¡vas a pa**gar u**na **mul**ta de **to**das **for**mas!

Pronunciation
*5 … an-**thway**-lo … lom-**breeth***

Notes

① **chico/chica** is often used in colloquial speech to refer to or to address young people.
Llevar a los chicos al cine. *Take the kids to the cinema.*
Es una chica muy seria. *She's a very serious young lady.*

As an adjective, **chico** can mean *small.* **Estos guantes son chicos para mí.** *These gloves are [too] small for me.*

② **oiga** is the third-person present subjunctive of **oír** *to hear*, *listen*, and like the informal command **¡Oye!** is used colloquially to attract someone's attention:
¡Oye, Pedro, di a Carmen que voy enseguida!
Hey, Pedro, tell Carmen that I'm going right away!
¡Oiga (señora), se olvida el paraguas!
Excuse me (ma'am), you're forgetting your umbrella!

No fishing *(Fishing preserve)*

1 – Hey, young man! Haven't you seen the sign?
2 It is forbidden to fish here!
3 I'll have to fine you *(put-you a fine)*.
4 – But, listen … I'm not fishing!
5 – And the rod, and the reel, and the hook, and that worm?
6 – Ah, yes, that's true! [The thing] is that I'm teaching the worm to swim *(teaching to swim the worm)*.
7 – Well … you're going to pay a fine anyway!

This use is extremely common, but as it's considered familiar, it's best to avoid when speaking to people you don't know.

③ **el carrete** *reel*; but outside the context of fishing, the more usual meaning is *spool*, *roll of film*.

④ **enseñar** *to teach*, *to instruct*, *to show*.
Me enseñó a nadar. *He/she taught me to swim.*
Enseña en la universidad. *He/she teaches at the university.*
Ven, voy a enseñarte algo. *Come [here], I'm going to show you something.*

⑤ **Pues…** has various meanings, but at the start of a sentence, it reinforces the idea that follows and is often equivalent to *Well* ...
Pues haremos como estaba previsto.
Well, we'll do [it] as it was planned.

8 – **Pe**ro… no hay mo**ti**vo… ¿Por qué?
9 – **Por**que tu gu**sa**no se es**tá** ba**ñan**do ⑥ des**nu**do ⑦.

Notes

⑥ **bañarse** can mean *to have a bath*, but it also means *to have a swim, to take a dip.* **Se está bañando.** *He/she is taking a dip.* Remember that **estar** + present participle = *to be* + present participle. **¡Yo no estoy pescando!** *I'm not fishing!* **Estoy enseñando.** *I'm teaching.*

* * *

Ejercicio 1: Traduzca

❶ ¿Has visto que está prohibido aparcar aquí? ❷ Hay un letrero en su puerta. ❸ Había más chicas que chicos. ❹ Sí, soy yo quien pagará el carrete. ❺ Vamos a bañarnos en la piscina.

* * *

Ejercicio 2: Complete

❶ I like to go fishing.
. . . .

❷ You're going to get a fine *(To-you they're going to put a fine).*
Te . . . .

❸ I told you so.
. . te lo . . . .

❹ Are you *(informal)* coming for a dip?
¿. . . . . ?

❺ Her parents have taught her to swim.
. . . . le han . . . .

8 – But … there's no reason *(motive)*… Why?
9 – Because your worm is swimming [in the] nude.

⑦ **desnudo/a** *nude, naked.* So, **bañarse desnudo** *to skinny-dip.* **desnudarse** *to get undressed*, **desvestirse** *to take one's clothes off.* Note that in Spanish, many daily routines are expressed with reflexive verbs:
Me levanto, me ducho, me lavo los dientes y me peino. *I get up, I shower, I brush* ('wash') *my teeth and I comb my hair.*

* * *

Answers to Exercise 1

❶ Did you see that it's forbidden to park here? ❷ There's a sign on his/her door. ❸ There were more girls than boys. ❹ Yes, it's me who will pay for the roll of film. ❺ We're going to take a dip in the swimming pool.

* * *

Answers to Exercise 2

❶ Me gusta ir a pescar ❷ – van a poner una multa ❸ Ya – había dicho ❹ Vienes a bañarte ❺ Sus padres – enseñado a nadar

La pesca fishing *has long been an important industry in Spain. The Spanish fishing fleet is one of the world's largest. Although Spanish waters are still relatively abundant in fish, awareness is growing regarding the potential danger of overfishing.*

Along with the Portuguese, the Spanish are the greatest consumers of **pescado** fish *and* **mariscos** seafood *in Europe. Wherever you go to eat* **tapas**, *you will have a choice of delicious seafood, especially if you find yourself in Galicia.*

47 Lección cuarenta y siete

Mal negocio

1 – Me han **di**cho ① que has a**bier**to ② **u**na **tien**da de **dis**cos y **ví**deos.
2 ¿**Có**mo van los ne**go**cios ③?
3 – ¡No me **ha**bles! ¡Ma**lí**simamente ④!

Notes

① **me han dicho que** *they've told me that* or *I've been told that.* As we've seen, in English we often use the passive voice in impersonal contexts (see lesson 45, note 1).

② **abierto** *opened*, the irregular past participle of **abrir** *to open.*

③ **los negocios**, although usually plural in Spanish, is best translated as *business*: **Mi hermano es un hombre de negocios.** *My brother is a businessman.* **Es un buen/un mal negocio.** *It's a good/bad business.*

Or in the singular: **Tengo un negocio en el centro de la ciudad.** *I have a shop* ('a business') *in the town centre.*

However, in the sense of *business* meaning *matter* or *affair*, the word is **el asunto**: **Tengo que atender a un asunto personal.** *I have to attend to personal business.*

④ **malísimo** *very bad* (**muy malo**). Remember that adding the suffix **-ísimo, -ísima** to an adjective intensifies or emphasizes it. ▸

Fishing with rod and reel, either in fresh water or the sea, is also a popular **afición** pastime. *If you want to go on a fishing expedition or cast a line in one of the many rivers where fish abound, you'll have to obtain* **una licencia de pesca** a fishing licence, *issued depending on the season by each* **Comunidad Autónoma**. *If you book in advance, many hotels and travel agents can handle all the procedures for you. You can also obtain information from the* **Federación Española de Pesca**, *which will give you details regarding the fishing season.*

Lesson forty-seven 47

Bad business

1 – They tell *(have told)* me that you've opened a record and video shop.
2 How's business going?
3 – Don't ask *(talk to me)*! Very, very badly!

Este café está malísimo. *This coffee is very bad.* (Note that **estar** is used to describe the speaker's perception of things, including the way things taste, sound or look.)

Buenísimo *very good* (**muy bueno**) is the opposite of **malísimo**: both are used frequently. The corresponding adverbs are **malísimamente** *very badly* (**muy mal**) and **estupendamente** *very well, marvellously, great.*

4 ¡**Ca**da vez pe**or** ⑤!
5 **Pa**ra que te **ha**gas ⑥ **u**na i**de**a: el **o**tro día ven**dí** **só**lo un **CD** ⑦,
6 a**yer** **na**da y hoy… ¡toda**ví**a ha **si**do pe**or** ⑧!
7 – ¡No es po**si**ble!
8 ¿**Có**mo te **pue**de ha**ber** **i**do ⑨ pe**or** que a**yer**?
9 – Hoy ha ve**ni**do el **clien**te del **o**tro **dí**a a devol**ver**me ⑩ el **CD** y…
10 yo he te**ni**do que devol**ver**le el di**ne**ro. □

Pronunciation
5 *… thay-**day*** ***9*** *… day-bol-**bayr**-may …*

Notes

⑤ **cada vez** *each/every time*; **cada día** *each/every day*; **cada año** *each/every year*; **cada uno** *each/every one*, etc. However, **cada vez peor** *from bad to worse* or *worse and worse*; **cada vez mejor** *better and better*; **cada vez más** *more and more*; **cada vez menos** *less and less*. Note that the adjective **cada** does not change to agree with the noun's gender.

⑥ **para que te hagas una idea** *so that you [may] get an idea*: **hagas** is the second-person singular present subjunctive of **hacer**. It is formed in a regular way – present subjunctives are formed from the stem of the first-person present tense (in this case, **yo hago**). The use of **para que** to introduce a clause requires the use of the subjunctive.

⑦ **un CD** *[thay-**day**]*; **un disco compacto** *a compact disc*. The word **compact** is also used, while calling it simply **un disco** *disc* is also heard more and more (**cada vez más**).

⑧ **peor** *worse* is the irregular comparative of **malo** *bad*. There are three more irregular comparatives: **mayor** *greater*, *older* (the comparative of **grande** with regard to age); **menor** *lesser*, ▸

4 From bad to worse!
5 [Just] to give you *(So that you form)* an idea: the other day, I sold only one CD,
6 yesterday nothing and today … it's been even worse!
7 – It's not possible!
8 How can it have been *(gone)* worse for you than yesterday?
9 – Today the customer from the other day came to return *(to-me)* the CD and …
10 I had to give him his money back *(I have had to-return-to-him the money)*.

younger (the comparative of **pequeño** with regard to age) and **mejor** *better*. Try not to confuse **mayor** and **mejor**!
Yo soy mayor que tú, pero no soy mejor que tú.
I am older than you, but I'm not better than you.

⑨ **Irle bien o mal a alguien** *to go well or badly for someone* is a very common expression. Note the pronoun **le** attached to the infinitive **ir**, which is here used in the third-person like **gustar**. Other ways of asking how things are going are **¿Qué tal?** *How's it going?* **¿Cómo estás?** *How are you?* or **¿Cómo te va?** *How is it going for you?* In the past, this becomes **¿Cómo te ha ido?** *How have you been?*

⑩ **devolver** conjugates in the same way as **volver**, which we'll look at in more detail in the upcoming review lesson. In the meantime, note **devolver** *to return something*: **devolver un artículo (en una tienda)** *to return an article (in a shop)*; **devolver un libro prestado** *to return/give back a borrowed book*; **devolver** *to refund, reimburse*.
He anulado el viaje y me han devuelto el importe del billete.
I cancelled the trip and they refunded me the cost of the ticket.

Ejercicio 1: Traduzca

❶ Es un buen negocio. ❷ Ni ha telefoneado. ❸ Es una película buenísima. ❹ Ese disco me gusta muchísimo. ❺ ¿Cómo te va?

* * *

Ejercicio 2: Complete

❶ They've opened a new restaurant.
... . un ..... restaurante.

❷ There are more and more cars.
.... hay ... coches.

❸ I'll give you *(informal)* the book back this week.
.. .. el libro esta ....

❹ I don't know if you'll be reimbursed *(if to-you[formal] they-will-reimburse)* the money.
.. .. .. le .... el ....

48 Lección cuarenta y ocho

Advertencia ①

1 En un ho**tel** de **cua**tro es**tre**llas,
2 el direc**tor** se di**ri**ge a un **clien**te que atra**vie**sa el ves**tí**bulo ② en pi**ja**ma:

Pronunciation
*ad-bayr-**ten**-thee-ah* **1** *... es-**tray**-yahs* **2** *... bes-**tee**-boo-lo ... pee-**hah**-mah*

Notes

① **una advertencia** *a warning, a caution*, from the stem-changing (**e** → **ie**) verb **advertir** (line 7) *to warn, to let know, to inform, to admonish*, etc.

Answers to Exercise 1
❶ It's a good business. ❷ He/she hasn't even phoned. ❸ It's a very good film. ❹ I absolutely love this disc. ❺ How is it going (for you)?

* * *

❺ He is a good customer.

. . . .

Answers to Exercise 2
❶ Han abierto – nuevo – ❷ Cada vez – más – ❸ Te devolveré – semana ❹ No sé si – devolverán – dinero ❺ Es un buen cliente

Lesson forty-eight 48

Warning

1 In a four-star hotel,
2 the manager addresses a guest *(client)* who is crossing the lobby in pyjama[s]:

Te advierto que eso no se puede hacer.
I'm warning you that that can't be done.
Te advertiré (or **te avisaré) antes de irme.**
I'll let you know before I go.
In the context of sports, *a caution* or *warning* is **una amonestación**.

② In public places, the word **hall**, pronounced *[hol]*, is used interchangeably with **vestíbulo** to refer to a lobby or foyer.
Tenemos cita en el hall de su hotel.
We are meeting in the lobby of her hotel.

3 – ¡**Oi**ga, se**ñor**! ¿**Pe**ro... **dón**de se **cre**e que es**tá**?
4 ¡**Pe**ro… **va**mos! ¿En qué ③ es**tá** pen**san**do?
5 – ¡Oh, lo **sien**to ④ mu**chí**simo! Es que soy so**nám**bulo.
6 – Pues **se**pa ⑤ que no es**tá** permi**ti**do pase**ar**se en pi**ja**ma por ⑥ el ho**tel**.
7 Y… se lo ⑦ ad**vier**to:
8 ¡eso cual**quie**ra ⑧ que **se**a su reli**gión**! □

*8 … rray-lee-**hee-on***

Notes

③ Careful: **pensar en …** *to ponder, consider, think about* and **pensar de …** *to have an opinion* are quite different:
¿Piensas en ella? *Are you thinking about her?* (pondering)
¿Qué piensas de ella? *What do you think of her?* (opinion)

④ **lo siento (mucho)** *I'm (very) sorry*, literally, 'it I feel (much)', from the stem-changing verb **sentir** *to feel*. (Not to be confused with **sentar** *to sit*!) In some situations, **lo siento** can mean *I beg your pardon, excuse me.*

You'll also see the reflexive verb **sentirse** used in many expressions to do with how one feels, for example: **Me siento bien/mal.** *I feel well./I don't feel well.*

⑤ **sepa** is the highly irregular first- and third-person singular present subjunctive of **saber**. Here, the latter is used because this is a formal command: 'Know that …' or *Be aware that …*

⑥ To indicate movement inside a place, Spanish uses **por** where English generally uses *in*, *through* or *around*. *Around* in line 6 means inside the hotel, not *around* it outside!
Los niños corrían por el bosque. *The children ran through (around in) the forest.* Note also:
caminando por la calle *walking down* (or *up*) *the street.* ▸

3 – Hey *(Listen)*, sir! But … where do you think *(believe yourself that)* you are?
4 For goodness sake … come now *(But ... let's go)*! What are you thinking of *(On what are-you thinking)*?
5 – Oh, I'm very, very sorry *(it I-feel very-much)*! [The thing] is that I'm [a] sleepwalker.
6 – Well, be aware *(know)* that it is not allowed to walk around the hotel in pyjamas.
7 And … I warn you *(advise you of it)*:
8 *(that [pertains])* whatever your religion may be!

⑦ When there are two consecutive third-person object pronouns, the indirect object (**le** or **les** – almost always referring to a person, as the direct object generally refers to a thing) becomes **se** (not to be confused with **se** the reflexive pronoun).
Se lo **daré.** *I will give it to him/her.*
Se lo **daré.** *I will give it to them.*
Se lo **daré.** *I will give it to you* (formal).
Context will often indicate exactly who is involved. Don't worry! We'll go over all this in the review lesson.

⑧ We've seen **cualquier** *any* used before a noun as an adjective: **cualquier cosa** *anything* (lesson 36). Here we see it used on its own as a pronoun: **cualquiera** *whichever, whatever.* Note that **cualquiera** + **que** is followed by a verb in the subjunctive. In line 8, **sea** is the third-person present subjunctive of **ser** *to be.* **Cualquiera que sea su decisión ...** *Whatever your decision may be ...* (*may* often indicates a subjunctive in English).

Ejercicio 1: Traduzca

❶ Quisiera hablar con el director. ❷ ¿Hay piscina en el hotel? ❸ Pienso en la cita de esta tarde. ❹ ¿Tienes cita? ❺ A las seis, en la entrada del cine.

* * *

Ejercicio 2: Complete

❶ It's a three-star hotel.
Es .. ..

❷ I'm sorry, the train has arrived late *(with delay)*.
.. .., ... ha llegado ... .

❸ Be aware *(Know[formal])* that it is forbidden to smoke here.
.... aquí ....

❹ It's for you; I'm giving it to you.
.. para usted, ...

❺ At any time!
¡ . ... hora!

49 Lección cuarenta y nueve

Repaso

1 Impersonal statements

1.1 The impersonal plural 'they'

In this set of lessons, we've seen that in impersonal statements (where the action is emphasized rather than the person who performs it), Spanish often uses the active voice where English would use the passive voice: **Me han robado**, 'They robbed me' (active), would be in English *I've been robbed* (passive: *to be* + past participle).

Answers to Exercise 1

❶ I'd like to speak to the manager. ❷ Is there a swimming pool at the hotel? ❸ I'm thinking about my *(the)* date this afternoon. ❹ You have a date? ❺ At six o'clock, at the entrance to the cinema.

* * *

Answers to Exercise 2

❶ – un hotel de tres estrellas ❷ Lo siento, el tren – con retraso ❸ Sepa que – está prohibido fumar ❹ Es – se lo doy ❺ A cualquier –

QUISIERA HABLAR
CON EL DIRECTOR.

Lesson forty-nine 49

Although the passive voice does exist in Spanish (**ser** + past participle), it is mostly avoided. The use of the active but impersonal subject **ellos** *they* is far more common (though the pronoun **ellos** remains unexpressed):

Me lo han quitado todo. 'They've taken everything from me.' or *I've had everything stolen.*

Le han llamado del trabajo. 'They've called him from work.' or *He's been called from work.*

Dicen que … 'They say that ...' or *It is said that ...*

Llaman (a la puerta). 'They're knocking (at the door).' or *Someone is knocking (at the door).*

1.2 The passive *se*

Spanish also has another way of making impersonal statements: using the reflexive pronoun **se**. This has the effect of making the verb passive. Let's take the example of **necesitar** *to need*, **necesitarse** *to be needed*:
Necesitamos camarero. *We need a waiter.*
Se necesita camarero. *Waiter needed.* (e.g. in a job ad)

With **se**, the third-person singular is used if the noun is singular, and the third-person plural is used if the noun is plural:
Necesitamos voluntarios. *We need volunteers.*
Se necesitan voluntarios. *Volunteers needed.*

The passive **se** is also used to translate the concept of 'one', 'you' or 'people' when talking about something generally:
Se vive bien en España. 'One lives well in Spain.' or
People live well in Spain.
En ese restaurante se come de maravilla.
In this restaurant, one eats wonderfully.

2 *Volver*

2.1 Conjugation

In the present tense (both indicative and subjunctive), the stem of **volver** *to return, to go/come back, to turn* changes from **o** to **ue** in all three singular persons and in the third-person plural, as well as in the singular informal imperative. (In the other tenses, the stem of **volver** does not change when conjugated.)

Present indicative	Present subjunctive	Informal imperative
vuelvo	**vuelva**	
vuelves	**vuelvas**	**vuelve**
vuelve	**vuelva**	
volvemos	**volvamos**	
volvéis	**volváis**	**volved**
vuelven	**vuelvan**	

Don't worry about memorizing all these forms now. We'll be looking in more detail at stem-changing and other irregular verbs later on. If you need to, you can always check the verb tables in the grammatical appendix.

2.2 Expressing repetition

The idea of a repeated action can be expressed in Spanish by using **volver a** followed by an infinitive:
¡Vuelve a empezar! *Begin again!*
Volveremos a vernos. *We'll see each other again.*
Vuelva a leer los ejemplos. *Reread the examples.*

Note that this idea can also be expressed using the adverbs **otra vez** 'another time' or **de nuevo** 'of new/anew':
Me lo pidió de nuevo / otra vez. *He asked me for it again.*

Sometimes, both can be found in one statement:
Me lo ha vuelto a pedir otra vez. *He has asked me for it again.*

2.3 Past participle

The irregular past participle of **volver** is **vuelto**:
¿Cuándo has vuelto? *When did you return?*
Alicia no ha vuelto todavía. *Alicia has not yet come back.*

2.4 Common uses

To return: **Volveremos el verano próximo.**
We'll return next summer.
To get back: **Volvamos a nuestros asuntos.**
Let's get back to our business.
To turn: **Volver la cabeza** *To turn one's head.*
To come back: **He vuelto muy tarde.** *I came back very late.*

Note that **regresar** *to return, to come back* can be used interchangeably with **volver** in the sense of returning somewhere.

2.5 Volverse

To go back, to return: **Me vuelvo a casa.** *I'm going back home.*
To turn, to change: **El tiempo se vuelve lluvioso.** *The weather is turning to rain.* (**el tiempo** means *weather* as well as *time*)
To become (often to express a change considered to be relatively permanent): **Volverse rico** *To become rich.*

3 A review of personal pronouns

There are different forms of pronouns, depending on whether they are subject, object or reflexive pronouns or whether or not they are preceded by a preposition. In the table below, we've listed the subject pronouns and their equivalent object pronouns when used without a preposition. (There is a complete table of pronouns in the grammatical appendix.)

	Person	Subject pronoun	Direct object	Indirect object
Sing.	1st	**yo** *I*	**me** *me*	**me** *(to) me*
	2nd	**tú** *you* (inf.)	**te** *you*	**te** *(to) you*
	3rd	**él** *he/it* **ella** *she/it* **usted** *you* (form.)	**lo (le)*** *him/it* **la** *her/it* **lo (le)*** *you*	**le (se)** *(to) him/her/it* *(to) you* (form.)
Plural	1st	**nostotros/as** *we* (m./f.)	**nos** *us*	**nos** *(to) us*
	2nd	**vosotros/as** *you* (inf.) (m./f.)	**os** *you*	**os** *(to) you*
	3rd	**ellos** *them* (m.) **ellas** *them* (f.) **ustedes** *you* (form.)	**los (les)*** *them* **las** *them* (f.) **los (les)*** *you*	**les (se)** *(to) them* *(to) you* (form.)

3.1 Two remarks

• The direct and indirect pronouns are identical except in the third-person singular and plural.
• Only the third-person direct object pronouns have a masculine and feminine form.

3.2 Four reminders

• Object pronouns come before the conjugated verb (**Te compro un helado.** *I buy you an ice cream.*) except in the case of an affirmative command (imperative), where placement after the conjugated verb is obligatory: **Háblenme.** *Speak to me.* The object must also be placed after an infinitive or a present participle used on its own: **Hacerlo de aquella manera…** *To do it in this way …* **Haciéndolo.** *By doing it.* However, the placement is optional if two verbs are used together: **Quieren hablarme.** or **Me quieren hablar.** *They want to speak to me.* **Están hablándome.** or **Me están hablando.** *They are speaking to me.* If placed after the infinitive or present participle, the pronoun is attached to the verb.

• When the verb is accompanied by two object pronouns, the indirect pronoun (usually a person) comes first:
Voy a comprártelo. *I'm going to buy it for you.*
Cómpramelo. *Buy it for me.*

• When there are two consecutive third-person pronouns, the indirect pronoun (**le** or **les**) always changes to **se**:
Se lo digo. *I say it to him/her/you/them.*
Decírselo. *To tell it to him/her/you/them.*

• The formal third-person pronouns **usted** and **ustedes** are replaced by the corresponding third-person pronouns **le** or **les**:
Quiero pedirle un favor. *I want to ask you* (sing.) *a favour.*
Les ruego … *I request you* (plural) …

* The use of **le** instead of **lo** as a direct object pronoun is quite common; there exists a certain amount of confusion in this regard. Without getting into the debate or going into regional details, we will just say that the **Real Academia Española** authorizes the use of the pronoun **le** instead of **lo** as a direct object when it refers to a person, so we can say **No lo conozco** or **No le conozco.** *I don't know him/you.* (For the feminine, the use of **la** is obligatory: **No la conozco.** *I don't know her.*).

4 Returning to *volver*

Let's see some of the uses of **volver**'s past participle, **vuelta** (note that **regreso** can also be used in the sense of *return*).

La Vuelta a España *The Tour of Spain* (i.e. the bicycle race)
ir a dar una vuelta *to go for a walk/spin*
estar de vuelta (regreso) *to be back*

49 **a la vuelta del trabajo** *back from work*
un billete de ida y vuelta *a return ticket.*

* * *

Diálogo recapitulativo

1 – Esa señora está fumando y...
2 lo hace bien;
3 se ve que tiene experiencia.
4 Pero yo me estoy poniendo malo.
5 Y además, en este tren no está permitido fumar.
6 Voy a decírselo.
7 Disculpe, señora, aquí está prohibido fumar.
8 – Lo siento mucho; le ruego que me disculpe.
9 – ¿No ha visto el letrero?
10 – Sí, pero…
11 – Soy de la policía;
12 le voy a poner una multa.
13 – ¡Cada vez peor!
14 ¡No sólo no se puede fumar,
15 encima te ponen una multa!

If all this coming and going is making your head spin (**hace que la cabeza le dé vueltas**), then **vaya a dar una vuelta** *go take a walk*. But then **¡Vuelva**! *Come back!* to finish the last exercise in this set of lessons.

* * *

Traducción

1 This lady is smoking and ... **2** she does it well; **3** one sees *(it is seen)* that she has experience. **4** But it makes me sick. **5** And moreover, in this train smoking is not allowed. **6** I'm going to tell her. **7** Excuse me, madam, it is forbidden to smoke here. **8** I'm very sorry; *(I ask that you)* please excuse me. **9** Didn't you see the sign? **10** Yes, but … **11** I am from the police; **12** I'm going to give you a fine. **13** From bad to worse! **14** Not only can one not smoke, **15** to top it off they give you a fine!

* * *

La segunda ola *The second wave*

In the next lesson, you will begin what we call the 'second wave', or the more active phase of your learning. You've already made considerable progress: you have a good grammatical base, your vocabulary is developing rapidly, you know a number of common expressions, your understanding is improving, and you can construct relatively simple sentences. The **segunda ola** *will allow you to see for yourself the progress you've made, while helping you consolidate and build on what you know. We'll explain what it involves at the beginning of the next lesson.*

¡Enhorabuena! Congratulations! *for what you've accomplished so far, and* **¡Ánimo!** Go for it! *for what's yet to come!*

50 Lección cincuenta

At first glance, this dialogue may seem rather long and to contain some tricky turns of phrase. But in fact, it simply brings together a number of things that we've already seen – in particular, some commonly used expressions. Now that you've started the second

En correos ①

1 – Por fa**vor**, ¿**pa**ra en**viar u**na **car**ta certifi**ca**da y com**prar se**llos ②?
2 – **Co**ja un **nú**mero y es**pe**re su **tur**no;
3 **mien**tras ③, re**lle**ne **es**te im**pre**so y
4 pre**sén**telo en venta**ni**lla **cuan**do le **to**que ④
5 Un **po**co más **tar**de:

Notes

① **correo** *post* or *mail.*
correo electrónico *electronic mail (e-mail).*
echar una carta al correo *to post/mail a letter.*
The plural **correos** is an abbreviation for **oficina de correos** *post office*: **ir a correos** *to go to the post office.*

② Like in English, the plural indefinite article **algunos/algunas** *some* can often be left out: **comprar sellos** *to buy stamps*, **vender libros** *to buy books*, **comer cerezas** *to eat cherries.* If **algunos/algunas** is used, it tends to translate to *a few.* **Voy a comprar algunos sellos.** *I'm going to buy a few stamps.*

Note that there is no negative plural indefinite article in Spanish, so where English requires *any* in negative sentences or questions, Spanish has no article: **No tenemos sellos.** *We don't have [any] stamps.*

③ **mientras**, **mientras tanto** or **entretanto**, *meanwhile* or *in the meantime*, expresses the idea of two actions occurring at ▸

wave, you'll need to search your memory to recall what you already know. Don't worry if it doesn't all come back to you immediately: we'll be returning to it again.

At the post office

1 – [Is it possible] to send a registered letter and buy [some] stamps, please?
2 – Take a number and wait your turn;
3 meanwhile, fill in this form and
4 present it at the window when it's your turn *(when you it-touches).*
5 A little later:

the same time: **Voy a hacer la cola; mientras, puedes ir a comprar el periódico.** *I'll queue/line up; meanwhile, you can go buy the newspaper.*

Mientras can also be used as the conjunction *while*: **Por favor, niños, no hagáis ruido mientras estoy al teléfono.** *Please, kids, don't make [any] noise while I'm on the phone.*

④ **cuando le toque (a usted)** *when it's your turn*. Note that **toque** is the present subjunctive of **tocar** (there is a spelling change from **c** to **qu**), whose main meaning is *to touch*; so literally this expression means 'when it may touch you'. In a subordinate clause introduced by **cuando**, the subjunctive is required if the situation is viewed as hypothetical or anticipated. Another example (**sepa** is the irregular present subjunctive of **saber**): **Te llamaré cuando lo sepa.** *I'll call you when I know.*

Another way to say that it's someone's turn is:
Me toca a mí. *It's my turn.*
Te toca a ti. *It's your turn.* (informal sing.)

6 – ¡**Ho**la, **bue**nas! ¿Qué de**se**a?
7 – En**viar** **es**ta **car**ta, por co**rre**o ur**gen**te.
8 – Ha olvi**da**do us**ted** ⑤ indi**car** el **có**digo pos**tal**.
9 ¡**To**me, a**quí** **tie**ne un bo**lí**grafo!
10 – ¡Ah, sí! ¡Per**do**ne!
11 – ¿**Al**go más? ⑥
12 – No, **na**da más ⑦. **Gra**cias.
13 ¡Ay, sí! ¡Se me olvi**da**ban ⑧ los **se**llos!
14 ¡Qué me**mo**ria que **ten**go!
15 – ¡Ah, la e**dad**, se**ño**ra, la e**dad**! □

Notes

⑤ Here the pronoun **usted** is included as a sign of respect towards the customer. In such cases, the pronoun frequently comes after the verb.

⑥ **¿Algo más?** *Anything else?* **Nada más.** *Nothing else.*
In both cases, **más** *more* translates as *else.*

⑦ **nada** *nothing*, a word you already know, is the opposite of **algo** *something/anything.* **¿Quieres tomar algo?** *Do you want something/anything to drink?* **No, gracias, no quiero nada.** *No thank you, I don't want anything.* (Note that English uses *not ... anything*, whereas Spanish uses a double negative: 'I don't want nothing.')

⑧ The verb **olvidar** *to forget* can be used with or without a reflexive pronoun, so there are various possible constructions:
• **olvidar** without a reflexive pronoun requires a direct object:
He olvidado que tenía una cita. *I forgot that I had a date.*
• **olvidarse** with a reflexive pronoun does not require a direct object. If it has one, the object comes directly after the verb or after **de** (optional). However, if what has been forgotten is an action rather than an object, **de** is required:
<u>Me</u> he olvidado (d)el móvil. *I've forgotten my mobile.*
<u>Me</u> he olvidado <u>de</u> llamar a casa. *I forgot to call home.*
<u>Me</u> he olvidado <u>de</u> que tenía una cita. ▸

6 – Hello, good [afternoon]! How can I help you *(What you-desire)*?
7 – [I'd like] to send this letter by express mail.
8 – You've forgotten to indicate the post code.
9 Here *(Take)*, here's a pen!
10 – Ah, yes! Sorry!
11 – Anything else *(more)*?
12 – No, that's it *(nothing more)*. Thanks.
13 Oh, yes! I was forgetting the stamps!
14 What [a] memory *(that)* I have!
15 – Ah, age, ma'am, age!

• **olvidarse** plus an indirect object **(olvidársele)** is never followed by **de: <u>Se me</u> ha olvidado que tenía una cita.**

This last construction is an example of the 'no fault **se**', which is used for actions that were not intended to happen. The subject becomes the indirect object – the inadvertent receiver of the action. This is the use we see in the lesson text, with the verb (which works like **gustar**) in the imperfect tense:
¡Se me olvidaban los sellos! *I forgot the stamps!* (Passive voice: 'The stamps were forgotten by me!')

¡No lo olvide! *Don't forget it!*

Ejercicio 1: Traduzca

❶ ¿Cuándo me toca a mí? ❷ Ahora mismo, en la ventanilla dos. ❸ Tengo que comprar sellos. ❹ ¿Desea algo más? ❺ No, no quiero nada más.

* * *

Ejercicio 2: Complete

❶ That's all.
. . . es . . . . .

❷ I've sent you *(formal sing.)* a registered letter.
Le . . . . una . . . .

❸ While I wait for you *(informal sing.)*, I'll read the newspaper.
. . . . espero, leeré . . . .

❹ Whose turn is it *(To whom him it-touches)*?
¿A . . . . ?

❺ It seems to me that it's your turn *(yours)*, sir.
Me . . . . le toca . . . . . . , señor.

Spanish post offices, **las oficinas de correos**, *are signposted* **'Correos'**. *In Spain,* a public letterbox/mailbox, **un buzón de correos**, *is yellow and usually cylindrical, so can be easily spotted on the street. In villages, letterboxes are usually smaller and built into a wall.* Stamps, **los sellos**, *are also sold at* **estancos** *or* **tabacos**, tobacconist's *(which also often serve as newsagent's), recognizable by their yellow logo on a brown background.*

Travellers can receive mail in Spain by having it sent to the poste restante *or* general delivery service, **lista de correos**, *in the town where they are staying. To get your mail, all you have to do is show some form of identification. The service is free. And if you don't receive anything, you can always tell yourself:* **¡Sin noticias, buenas noticias!** No news is good news!

Answers to Exercise 1

❶ When is it my turn? ❷ Right now, at window two. ❸ I have to buy [some] stamps. ❹ Would you like anything else? ❺ No, I don't want anything else.

* * *

Answers to Exercise 2

❶ Eso – todo ❷ – he enviado – carta certificada ❸ Mientras te – el periódico ❹ – quién le toca ❺ – parece que – a usted –

This lesson is the first in the **segunda ola** second wave *of your learning; that is, the more active phase. What does it involve? It's quite simple: from now on, after having studied a new lesson, you'll go back to an earlier lesson starting from the beginning of the book (we'll tell you which one to go back to). But this time, after reviewing the lesson, you'll translate the English into Spanish instead of the other way around. Then read your Spanish translation out loud – don't be shy, speak loudly and articulate clearly. Go over the pronunciation as many times as you need to. The 'second wave' will allow you to reinforce what you've already learned, consolidating your knowledge while continuing to build on it.*

¡Adelante! Onwards!

¡Animo! Go for it!

Second wave: 1st lesson

51 Lección cincuenta y una

Ganas ① de amargarse ② la vida

1 – ¿Por qué **llo**ras?
2 – ¡Es muy ③ **du**ro!
3 **Pien**so en mi ma**ri**do.
4 – ¿Qué **pa**sa?
5 – ¡No sé qué va a ser de ④ mí!
6 – ¡Qué me **di**ces? ⑤
7 ¿**Tie**nes pro**ble**mas con An**drés**?
8 – ¡No, no es **e**so!
9 Nos que**re**mos ⑥ mu**chí**simo.
10 – ¿Le **pa**sa **al**go? ¿Es**tá** en**fer**mo?
11 – ¡No, en abso**lu**to! ⑦

Notes

① **gana** *desire, wish* is most often used in the plural: **ganas**. For example, in the expression **tener ganas** *to feel like (doing something), to have the urge (to do something).*
Tengo ganas de ir a la playa. *I feel like going to the beach.*
It is a feminine noun; adjectives need to agree with it:
Tengo muchas ganas de verte. *I really want to see you.*
Of course, you can also say **No tengo ganas.** *I don't feel like it.*

② **amargar** *to make bitter, to spoil, to sour.*
Este café es amargo. *This coffee is bitter.*
amargarse *to become embittered, to get upset*:
No te amargues la vida por eso. *Don't get upset about it.* (The **u** is added to retain the sound of the hard **g**.)
So **ganas de amargarse la vida** literally means 'the desire to embitter your life'!

③ **muy** *very*; **demasiado** *too much.* In everyday speech, **muy** often has the sense of *too much.* ▸

Worrying about nothing

1 – Why are you crying?
2 – It's too difficult *(very hard)*!
3 I'm thinking about my husband.
4 – What's the matter?
5 – I don't know what is going to become *(to be)* of me!
6 – What are you saying *(to me)*?
7 Are you having problems with Andrés?
8 – No, that's not it!
9 We love each other very much!
10 – Has something happened *(happens)* to him? Is he ill?
11 – No, absolutely not *(in absolute)*!

④ **¿Qué va a ser de mí?** ('What is going to be of me?') *What will become of me?* Another useful expression: **¿Qué es de ti?** *How are things with you?*

⑤ **¡Qué me dices?** is midway between an exclamation and a question and indicates a mixture of disbelief and curiosity: *What are you telling me? What do you mean?* or *Surely not!* Note that when a sentence is both an exclamation and a question, it is introduced by an exclamation mark and ends with a question mark, or vice versa.

⑥ **querer** *to want* also means *to love* (**amar**).
Te quiero./Te amo. *I love you.*

⑦ **¡En absoluto!** *Absolutely not!* seems to have the opposite meaning, but in Spanish, it means 'not at all'. **¿Te molesta si…?** *Does it bother you if …?* **En absoluto.** *Not at all.*

51 **12** **Tie**ne **u**na sa**lud** de **hier**ro.
 13 – Y en**ton**ces… ¿qué es?
 14 – ¡No sé lo que ⑧ voy a ha**cer cuan**do se
 muera ⑨! □

Notes

⑧ Remember: **lo que** means *what* in the sense of 'that which'.

⑨ Here is another example of the subjunctive following **cuando**.
Don't forget: *when* + a hypothetical or anticipated action =
cuando + **presente de subjuntivo**.
Venid cuando queráis. *Come whenever you want to.*
('Come when you may want.' [informal plural])

* * *

Ejercicio 1: Traduzca

❶ Es un niño que no llora mucho. ❷ ¿De qué
tienes ganas? ❸ Pienso en lo que haremos mañana.
❹ ¿Estás enfermo? ❺ No, me siento bien.

* * *

Ejercicio 2: Complete

❶ How are things with you *(What is of you)*?

¿ · · · · · · · ti?

❷ Are you *(informal)* having problems at *(in the)* work?

¿ · · · · · · · · · · · · · · · · · el trabajo?

❸ No, absolutely not.

· · , · · · · · · · · · · •

❹ What's the matter with Andrés?

¿ · · · · · · · · · · Andrés?

12 He has an iron constitution *(a health of iron)*.
13 – Well *(And)* then … what is it?
14 – I don't know what *(that which)* I'm going to do when he dies!

* * *

Answers to Exercise 1
❶ He's a child who doesn't cry much. ❷ What do you feel like doing? ❸ I'm thinking about what we will do tomorrow. ❹ Are you ill? ❺ No, I feel fine.

* * *

❺ We love each other very much.
Nos ....

Answers to Exercise 2
❶ Qué es de – ❷ Tienes problemas en – ❸ No, en absoluto ❹ Qué pasa con – ❺ – queremos mucho

Second wave: 2nd lesson

52 Lección cincuenta y dos

En la charcutería

1 – **Pón**game **cua**tro **lon**chas ① de ja**món** york.
2 – ¿**Al**go más?
3 – Sí, tres**cien**tos **gra**mos de ja**món** se**rra**no ②.
4 – Hay un **po**co más, ¿se lo re**ti**ro ③?
5 – No, **dé**jelo; ¡no im**por**ta ④!
6 **De**me tam**bién u**na **sar**ta ⑤ de cho**ri**zo, y…
7 **dí**game, ¿a **có**mo es**tán** ⑥ los **hue**vos?
8 – A**quí** los **tie**ne. ¡Son bio**ló**gicos! ¡A **vein**te **eu**ros la do**ce**na!

Notes

① **unas lonchas** (or **lonjas**; sometimes, **rajas**) **de jamón** *a few slices of ham*. **loncha** and **lonja** are used especially when referring to a thin slice, particularly of cured ham or deli meat (charcuterie). The word **raja** has a wider sense: **una raja de melón**, **de sandía** *a slice of melon*, *of watermelon*; or you might also hear **una rodaja de chorizo**, **de salchichón** *a slice of chorizo*, *of sausage* (i.e. dry, cured sausage like salami), or **de pan** *of bread*, **de limón** *of lemon*, or **una rebanada de pan con mantequilla** *a slice of bread with butter*.

② The name **jamón serrano** *mountain ham* refers to the fact that this cured ham is dried in **la sierra** *the mountains*. The word **sierra** means both *saw* (the carpenter's tool) and *mountain range*: **pasar las vacaciones en la sierra** *to spend the holidays in the mountains*.

③ **¿se lo retiro?** Remember the rule about two consecutive third-person pronouns (lesson 48, note 7). Note also that the English *shall I*, used for asking permission or making a suggestion, is ▸

At the deli

1 – Give *(Put)* me four slices of York ham.
2 – Anything else?
3 – Yes, 300 grams of Serrano ham.
4 – It's a little over *(There's a bit more)*, [shall] I remove some for you *(for-you it I-withdraw)*?
5 – No, leave it; it doesn't matter *(it's not important)*!
6 Give me a string of chorizo as well, and …
7 tell me, how much are the eggs?
8 – Here they are *(Here them you-have)*. They are organic *(biological)*! 20 euros a dozen!

the simple present tense in Spanish: **¿Le doy una docena de huevos?** *[Shall] I give you a dozen eggs?*

④ The frequently heard **¡No importa!** means *It doesn't matter! It's OK! It's not important!* The expression **¡No pasa nada!** has the same meaning.

⑤ **sarta** *string* refers to a succession of identical things. **Chorizo** [*cho-**ree**-tho*] is often sold in strings; however, in many regions the word **sarta** can refer to just one sausage. A figurative usage is **una sarta de mentiras** *a pack of lies*. **ristra** is a synonym of **sarta**: **una ristra de cebollas** *a string of onions.*

And while we're on the subject of food: **el ajo** *garlic*; **una cabeza de ajo** *a head of garlic*; **un diente de ajo** *a clove* ('a tooth') *of garlic.*

⑥ **¿<u>A</u> <u>cómo</u> <u>están</u> los huevos?** *How much are the eggs?* **<u>A</u> 20 euros.** *20 euros.* Note this common way of asking the price of something when shopping. The verb **estar** is used, not **ser**.

9 – ¡Ni bio**ló**gicos, ni **na**da! ¡Es**tán** ca**rí**simos ⑦!
10 ¡**Pron**to no se po**drá** ⑧ co**mer** ni tor**ti**lla! ¡Qué barbari**dad**! ⑨
11 – ¡Tam**po**co es **pa**ra **tan**to ⑩, se**ño**ra!
12 **Ten**ga en **cuen**ta ⑪ que un **hue**vo su**po**ne **pa**ra **u**na ga**lli**na
13 ¡alrede**dor** de un día de tra**ba**jo! □

Notes

⑦ **caro** *dear, expensive*; **carísimo** *very dear, expensive.* **barato** *cheap*; **baratísimo** *very cheap.*

⑧ **no se podrá comer** *one won't be able to eat* is another use of the passive **se** (see lesson 49, section 1).

⑨ **barbaridad** *barbarity, cruelty, atrocity* comes from **bárbaro** *barbaric* (but informally, *fantastic, great*). When preceded by **que**, it has a wide range of meanings depending on the context, from horror to astonishment to outright admiration: *How awful! Good Lord!* or *Incredible!* In everyday speech, **barbaridad** can also have the sense of *outrageous* or *excessive*: **decir barbaridades** *to say outrageous things*; **comer una barbaridad** *to eat a huge amount.*

⑩ **¡Tampoco es para tanto!**, **¡No hay que exagerar!** *There's no need to exaggerate!* **Tampoco** *neither, not ... either* is the negative equivalent of **también** *also*, just as **nada** *nothing* or *not anything* is the opposite of **algo** *something.* ▸

* * *

Ejercicio 1: Traduzca

❶ El jamón es más caro que el salchichón. ❷ Póngame cinco o seis lonchas de jamón serrano. ❸ Tomaré una tortilla de chorizo. ❹ ¿Quiere algo más? ❺ No, nada más. Gracias.

9 – Organic, never mind organic *(Neither biological, nor nothing)*! They're very expensive!
10 Soon one won't be able to eat even [an] omelette! It's outrageous!
11 – No need to exaggerate *(Neither is-it for so-much)*, ma'am!
12 Keep in mind *(Take into account)* that an egg involves *(supposes)* for a hen
13 around *(of)* a [full] day's work!

EL JAMÓN ES MÁS CARO QUE EL SALCHICHÓN.

▸ ⑪ **tenga en cuenta que** *take into account that, don't forget that, keep in mind that.*
Tenga en cuenta que mañana es domingo y cerramos. *Don't forget that tomorrow is Sunday and we are closed.*
Lo tendré en cuenta. *I'll bear it in mind.*

* * *

Answers to Exercise 1

❶ The ham is more expensive than the cured sausage (i.e. salami). ❷ Give me five or six thin slices of Serrano ham. ❸ I'll have a chorizo omelette. ❹ Do you want anything else? ❺ No, nothing else. Thank you.

Ejercicio 2: Complete

❶ How much is the melon?
¿. .... está .. .. ?

❷ That seems very expensive to me.
Me .... caro.

❸ It doesn't matter!
¡No .... !

❹ There's no need to exaggerate!
¡No ... ... !

❺ These trousers cost around 100 euros.
..... pantalones cuestan .... cien euros.

Second wave: 3rd lesson

53 Lección cincuenta y tres

En la consulta ① del psicoanalista

1 – Doc**tor**, **ven**go **pa**ra que me a**yu**de ②.
2 Me **sien**to **fran**camente mal.

Notes

① **la consulta** can refer both to the act of consulting, *the consultation*, and *the office*, *consultation room* where this takes place. Sometimes it simply means *the appointment*. Some uses include: **horas de consulta** *office hours*, **consulta previa petición de hora** *consultation by appointment*, **tener consulta con un especialista** *to have an appointment with* or *to consult a specialist*, **consulta a domicilio** *house call (medical)*. And don't forget that sometimes when one has a ▸

Answers to Exercise 2
❶ A cómo – el melón ❷ – parece muy – ❸ – importa ❹ – hay que exagerar ❺ Estos – alrededor de –

In Spain, **charcutería** cured meats, cold cuts *are sold in the delicatessen section of* **supermercados** supermarkets, *in many* **carnicerías** butcher's shops, *in most* **tiendas de comestibles** *or* **tiendas de ultramarinos** grocery stores *or* corner shops, *as well as, of course, in* **charcuterías**, *which you can find in many markets.*

There is a great range of Spanish **charcutería**, *and if you enjoy discovering new foods, it's a good idea to get information on the speciality of the region where you are staying and make sure you try foods that you may not find elsewhere. Here we shall mention only* **jamón ibérico** Iberian ham, *the most famous kind of* **jamón serrano** mountain ham. **Jamón ibérico** *comes from black Iberian pigs, called* **pata negra** *'black legged', which are raised free-range and feed on acorns. Today this cured ham, produced in the* **Salamanca** *region (in* **Castilla y León**), *in* **Trevélez** *(in the province of* **Granada**) *and in the* **Jabugo** *region (in the province of* **Huelva**, *in Andalusia), is considered among the finest in the world.*

Lesson fifty-three 53

At the psychoanalyst's office

1 – Doctor, I've come for your help *(I come so that you may help me)*.
2 I feel really *(frankly)* bad.

problem, **hay que consultar con la almohada** *one needs to sleep on it* ('it's necessary to consult with the pillow')!

② **para que me ayude** *so that you may help me*: **ayude** is the third-person present subjunctive of **ayudar** *to help, to aid* (**la ayuda** is the noun *aid, assistance*). The subjunctive is obligatory after **para que** because it points towards a hypothetical situation in the future. Here's a tip: the subjunctive is often used after the marker **que** when it introduces a change of subject: **vengo para que me ayude** 'I come **so that** you might help me'.

3 – ¡**Cuén**teme! ③
4 – **Ten**go **u**na i**de**a **fi**ja que me obse**sio**na.
5 – Sí.
6 – Me **ve**o **co**mo **u**na mu**jer** muy acomple**ja**da.
7 – ¿Y qué le **ha**ce pen**sar** **e**so?
8 – **Cuan**do me com**pa**ro con **o**tras mu**je**res,
9 **siem**pre **cre**o que soy más **fe**a que **e**llas.
10 – ¡Ah, no, se**ño**ra! ¡Al con**tra**rio!
11 El **ú**nico pro**ble**ma que us**ted tie**ne es su extraordi**na**ria luci**dez**. □

Notes

③ **Cuénteme** *Tell me*, from **contar** *to tell, to count*. Note the stem change from **o** to **ue**. The verb **contar** takes the same stem change as **volver** (see lesson 49): **el cuento** *story*.

* * *

Ejercicio 1: Traduzca

❶ ¿Qué te pasa? ❷ No me siento muy bien. ❸ Me duele mucho el vientre. ❹ Tengo consulta con el médico. ❺ ¿Dónde tiene la consulta?

* * *

Ejercicio 2: Complete

❶ On the contrary, that has no importance!
¡. . . . ., eso no . . . . . importancia!

❷ I need assistance.
. . . .

❸ Do you want to help me?
¿Quieres . . . . ?

❹ Do you want me to tell the kids a story? *(You-want that I-tell a story to the children?)*
¿Quieres que . . . . . . un . . . . . . a los . . . . . ?

3 – Go on *(Tell me).*
4 – I have an obsession *(a fixed idea that obsesses me).*
5 – Yes.
6 – I see myself as a woman with a mass of complexes *(a woman very complexed).*
7 – And what makes you think that?
8 – When I compare myself with other women,
9 I always believe that I am uglier than them.
10 – Oh, no, madam! You're quite wrong *(On the contrary)*!
11 The only problem that you have is your extraordinary perceptiveness *(lucidity).*

* * *

Answers to Exercise 1

❶ What's the matter with you? ❷ I don't feel very well. ❸ My stomach hurts a lot. ❹ I have an appointment with the doctor. ❺ Where is his/her *(does he/she have the)* office/surgery?

* * *

❺ The only specialist that I know doesn't work on *(the)* Mondays.
.. .. especialista ... . no trabaja ... .

Answers to Exercise 2

❶ Al contrario – tiene – ❷ Necesito ayuda ❸ – ayudarme ❹ – cuente – cuento – niños ❺ El único – que conozco – los lunes

Second wave: 4th lesson

Un telefonazo ①

1 – ¡A**hí** va! ¡Te**ní**a ② que ha**ber** lla**ma**do a Con**chi**ta!

2 – Yo tam**bién** me he de**ja**do ③ el **mó**vil en **ca**sa.

3 ¡No te preo**cu**pes; encontra**re**mos **u**na ca**bi**na por a**quí cer**ca ④!

4 – **Pe**ro… no **ten**go ni tar**je**ta ni di**ne**ro **suel**to.

5 – No **pa**sa **na**da; po**de**mos en**trar** en un bar.

6 **Mi**ra, en la a**ce**ra de en**fren**te hay un locu**to**rio ⑤.

7 – ¡Estu**pen**do, **va**mos a**llá**!

8 ¡**Ho**la, **bue**nas! Qui**sié**ramos ⑥ ha**cer u**na lla**ma**da. Lo**cal**.

Notes

① **dar un telefonazo** is a colloquial expression meaning *to give (someone) a ring/buzz*. Adding the suffix **-azo** or **-ada**, known as augmentative suffixes, often expresses the idea of force, as in a blow or strike. Here are some other examples where the link may be more obvious than for a telephone call:
un martillo *a hammer* → **un martillazo** *a hammer blow*
una puerta *a door* → **un portazo** *a door slam*
una pata *a leg (of an animal)* → **una patada** *a kick*.

② **Tenía que haber llamado** *I was supposed to have called*; note that **tenía** is in the imperfect ('I was having to have called'). In spoken Spanish, the imperfect tense of **tener**, **deber**, **poder** and **querer** is sometimes used instead of the conditional to mean *should have*.

③ The use of **dejar** *to let, to leave* in the reflexive form (**dejarse**) often expresses the idea of 'leaving (something) behind accidentally, forgetting'.

A phone call

1 – Oh, no! I was supposed to have called Conchita!
2 – I've left my mobile at home too.
3 Don't worry; we'll find a [phone] booth *(cabin)* around here *(by here near)*!
4 – But … I don't have a *(neither)* card, nor [any] change *(money loose)*.
5 – It doesn't matter *(happens nothing)*; we can go into *(enter)* a bar.
6 Look, on the other side of the street *(on the sidewalk of opposite)* there's a 'locutorio'.
7 – Great, let's go *(there)*!
8 Hello, good [morning]! We'd like to make a call. Local.

▸ **He dejado el reloj sobre la mesa.** *I left my watch on the table.* But: **Me he dejado el reloj sobre la mesa.** *I've left my watch* (by accident) *on the table./I forgot my watch on the table.*

④ The adverb **cerca** *near, nearby* could be omitted here, but it is often used after **por aquí** to stress the proximity of something.
Por aquí [cerca] hay muchos bares y cafeterias.
Around here there are many bars and cafés.
cerca de aquí *near here.*

⑤ **locutorios** are call shops, a bit like internet cafés, that have several telephone booths from which customers can make low-priced calls. They can be found in most Spanish towns.

⑥ **quisiéramos** *we would like.* This is the imperfect subjunctive, which can be used to politely express a wish or desire. The example here is from **querer** *to want* (see lesson 19, note 4). But it would not be impolite to use the present tense **queremos**, or even better, the imperfect **queríamos**.

9 – Sí. A**llí**, la ca**bi**na tres es**tá li**bre.
10 **Mar**quen ⑦ pri**me**ro el **ce**ro **pa**ra te**ner lí**nea.
11 – Sí, sí, **dí**game, ¿es**tá** Con**chi**ta?
12 – **Pe**ro… ¿por qué **cuel**gas?
13 – He de**bi**do de ⑧ confun**dir**me ⑨ de **nú**mero y he caído con un bro**mis**ta;
14 **cuan**do he pregun**ta**do '¿Es**tá** Con**chi**ta?'
15 me ha contes**ta**do ⑩ 'No, es**tá** con Tar**zán**' ⑪.

Notes

⑦ **marcar** *to mark* also means *to dial* (note the spelling change from **c** to **qu**).
Para telefonear al Reino Unido tienes que marcar el cuarenta y cuatro. *To phone the UK, you must dial 44.*

⑧ **deber** + infinitive means *must/ought to*, i.e. **tener que**. But **deber <u>de</u>** + infinitive expresses probability.
Tienes que comer./Debes comer. *You must eat.* (obligation)
Deben <u>de</u> ser las diez y cuarto. *It must be a quarter past ten.* (probability)

⑨ **confundir** *to confuse, mix up*. **confundirse de número** *to get the number wrong, to misdial*. Both **confundirse** and **equivocarse** mean *to make a mistake*:
Te equivocas. *You are mistaken.*

⑩ **contestar** *to reply, answer*. Beware of false cognates (words that look similar in two languages but have different meanings)! ▶

* * *

Ejercicio 1: Traduzca

❶ No sé dónde he dejado el móvil. ❷ Buscaré una cabina. ❸ No tenía dinero y no he podido comprar una tarjeta de teléfono. ❹ ¡No te preocupes, no pasa nada! ❺ ¿Te has equivocado?

9 – Yes. [Over] there, booth three is free.
10 Dial zero first to get *(have)* [a] line.
11 – Yes, yes, hello, is this *(it)* Conchita?
12 – But … why are you hanging up?
13 – I must have misdialled the number and I got *(have fallen with)* some joker;
14 when I asked 'Is that Conchita?'
15 he replied *(to me)*, 'No, she's with Tarzan.'

NO SÉ DÓNDE HE DEJADO EL MÓVIL.

▸ **contestar al teléfono** *to answer the phone*; **contestar una pregunta/una carta** *to reply to a question/a letter.*

⑪ To understand this punchline, you have to know that the 'joker' is breaking down **Conchita** into **con** (*with*) and **Chita** (Spanish form of *Cheeta*, the name of Tarzan's chimp). That makes his answer a pretty logical one!

* * *

Answers to Exercise 1

❶ I don't know where I left my mobile. ❷ I'll look for a [telephone] booth/box. ❸ I didn't have any money and I couldn't buy a phone card. ❹ Don't worry, it doesn't matter! ❺ Did you make a mistake?/ Did you misdial?

Ejercicio 2: Complete

❶ We should have come earlier *(We-were-having to have come before).*

. . . . venido antes.

❷ Who answered?

¿. . . . . ?

❸ I got the number wrong.

. . . . número.

❹ What number did you *(informal)* dial?

¿Qué número . . . . ?

❺ I've forgotten my wallet at home.

. . . . el monedero . . . .

Second wave: 5th lesson

---

55 Lección cincuenta y cinco

Bronca ①

1 – **Pero… ¿qué significa esto ②, señor Merino?**

Notes

① **bronca** *quarrel, row* or *reprimand, dressing down.*
El jefe me ha echado una bronca.
The boss gave me a dressing down.
llevarse una bronca *to get a telling-off.* ▸

Answers to Exercise 2

❶ Teníamos que haber – ❷ Quién ha contestado ❸ Me he confundido de – ❹ – has marcado ❺ Me he olvidado – en casa

Las cabinas de teléfonos telephone booths/boxes *are rarer with the advent of mobile phones, but you can still find them fairly easily in Spain. If you have to make* **una llamada internacional** an international call, *it's best to get* **una tarjeta** a card*; you can buy them at* **los estancos** tobacco shops, newsagents *and at* **los quioscos** kiosks, newspaper stands.

You can also often phone from bars, which usually have a phone that takes coins or has a counter. Another good solution is to go to a **locutorio**, *a call shop with private telephone booths. These are more comfortable, the calls are generally cheaper, and they usually have* **guías** telephone directories. *They also allow you to make* **unas llamadas a cobro revertido** reverse charge calls. *Some useful vocabulary:*
¡No cuelgue! Don't hang up! (*from the stem-changing verb* **colgar** to hang)
Está comunicando. The line is engaged/busy.

Lesson fifty-five 55

A telling-off

1 – But … what is the meaning of this *(what does this mean)*, Mr Merino?

▸ In other contexts, **bronca** means *uproar*, *fuss*, *trouble*. **El partido terminó con una bronca.** *The match ended in uproar.*

② **¿Qué significa eso?** *What does that mean?* is an expression that might come in handy when you're in Spain! Another more common way of saying this is **¿Qué quiere decir eso?** or **¿Qué quieres decir?** *What do you mean?*

2 ¿Se da us**ted cuen**ta ③ de que **lle**ga al tra**ba**jo con **ca**si tres **ho**ras de re**tra**so?
3 – Lo **sien**to. Le **rue**go que me dis**cul**pe ④;
4 **pe**ro me ha ocu**rri**do ⑤ **al**go…
5 – ¿Qué le ha ocu**rri**do?
6 – Es**ta**ba ten**dien**do la **ro**pa ⑥ y…
7 me he ca**í**do ⑦ por la ven**ta**na.
8 – ¡Ah, se ha ca**í**do por la ven**ta**na!
9 Y, ¿en qué **pi**so ⑧ **vi**ve?
10 – En el **quin**to.
11 – ¿En el **quin**to, eh?

Notes

③ **darse cuenta de** *to realize*, *to understand* + something. **¿Te das cuenta de la hora que es?** *Do you realize what time it is?*

④ **Le ruego (que) me disculpe.** *Please excuse me.* 'I beg you (that) you excuse me.' Remember that after verbs that express wishes, orders, requests or advice, Spanish uses **que** + subjunctive, where English usually avoids the subordinate clause by using an infinitive.
Quiero que vengas. *I want you to come.* 'I want that you come.'
Te aconsejo que vayas. *I advise you to go.* 'I advise that you go.'

As already mentioned, **que** + subjunctive is used only if the subject in the main clause changes in the subordinate clause, as in the examples above. If there is no change, the infinitive is used, as in English: **Quiero venir.** *I want to come.*

⑤ **ocurrir** *to occur, to happen* is a common synonym of **pasar**:
¿Qué ocurre? *What's happening?* (**¿Qué pasa?**)
¿Qué ha ocurrido? *What's happened?* (**¿Qué ha pasado?**)
¿Qué te ocurrió? *What happened to you?*

⑥ **ropa** here *laundry*, but also *clothing*, *clothes* (plural in English, but singular in Spanish); **ropa interior** *underwear*; **quitarse la ropa** *to take off one's clothes*, *to undress*. And an idiomatic ▸

2 Do you realize *(Do you give yourself account of)* that you're arriving at work *(with)* almost three hours late *(of delay)*?
3 – I'm sorry. Please *(I ask that you)* excuse me;
4 but something happened to me …
5 – What happened to you?
6 – I was hanging out the laundry *(clothes)* and …
7 I fell out of *(through)* the window.
8 – Ah, you fell out of the window!
9 And on what floor do you live?
10 – On the fifth.
11 – On the fifth, eh?

HE LLEGADO CON CASÍ UNA HORA DE RETRASO.

▸ expression: **saber nadar y guardar la ropa** ('to know how to swim and keep your clothes on') *to sit on the fence*; *to tread the middle ground*; *to proceed with caution.*

⑦ **caer** *to fall* is often used reflexively, making the action sudden or involuntary: **caerse de espaldas** *to fall [flat] on one's back*, *to be bowled over*; **caerse de sueño** *to be falling asleep.*

⑧ **piso** *flat*, *apartment*, which you already know, can also mean *floor*, *storey*. **Mi amiga se ha comprado un piso.** *My friend has bought an apartment.* **Vivo en el tercer piso.** *I live on the third floor.*

12 ¡**Pe**ro, se**ñor** Me**ri**no, por quién me **to**ma us**ted**?

13 ¿Us**ted quie**re que yo me **cre**a que ca**er des**de el **quin**to **pi**so le ha lle**va**do ⑨ **ca**si tres **ho**ras? □

Notes

⑨ **llevar** *to carry*, *to wear*, but also *to bring*, *to lead*; **llevarse** *to carry off*, *to take away*, *to get*; **llevarse bien/mal** *to get on well/badly with someone* … these verbs have various meanings. In the context of time, **llevar** means *to take*.

* * *

Ejercicio 1: Traduzca

❶ ¿Qué significa eso? ❷ He llegado con casi una hora de retraso. ❸ ¿Qué te ha ocurrido? ❹ Me he caído en la calle. ❺ ¿En qué piso vives?

* * *

Ejercicio 2: Complete

❶ Do you realize what that means?
Te . . . . quiere decir?

❷ Please excuse me *(I beg that you[formal] excuse me)*.
Le . . . .

❸ I'm going to go buy myself [some] underwear.
Voy . . . .

❹ How much time will it take you *(informal)* to prepare the meal?
¿Cuánto tiempo . . . . preparar . . . . ?

12 But, Mr Merino, what *(for whom)* do you take me [for]?
13 You want me to believe *(You want that I myself believe)* that falling from the fifth floor has taken you almost three hours?

▸ **Redactar esta carta me ha llevado una hora.**
To write this letter has taken me an hour.
¿Cuánto tiempo le llevará lavar la ropa?
How long will it take you to wash the clothes?

* * *

Answers to Exercise 1

❶ What does that mean? ❷ I arrived almost an hour late. ❸ What's happened to you? ❹ I fell [down] in the street. ❺ What floor do you live on?

* * *

❺ I have to tell you *(informal)* something.
Tengo … ……. …. .

Answers to Exercise 2

❶ – das cuenta de lo que eso – ❷ – ruego que me disculpe ❸ – a ir a comprarme ropa interior ❹ – te llevará – la comida ❺ – que decirte algo

Second wave: 6th lesson

56 Lección cincuenta y seis

Repaso

1 The present subjunctive: formation

The endings for the present subjunctive are as follows:
-e, **-es**, **-e**, **-emos**, **-éis**, **-en**: for first conjugation verbs (**-ar**)
-a, **-as**, **-a**, **-amos**, **-áis**, **-an**: for second and third conjugation verbs (**-er** and **-ir**).

Note that, in general, the vowel of the subjunctive ending is the opposite of that of the indicative and the infinitive (**-ar** verbs take the vowel **e**, while **-er** and **-ir** verbs take the vowel **a**).

The endings are added to the stem of the infinitive; so for **-ar** verbs, such as **hablar** *to speak*, *to talk*:

habl → e	*that I speak*
habl → es	*that you* (informal sing.) *speak*
habl → e	*that he/she/it speaks, that you* (formal sing.) *speak*
habl → emos	*that we speak*
habl → éis	*that you* (informal plural) *speak*
habl → en	*that they speak, that you* (formal plural) *speak*

For **-er** and **-ir** verbs, such as **comer** *to eat* and **escribir** *to write*:

com → a *(that I eat)*	**escrib** → a *(that I write)*
com → as	**escrib** → as
com → a	**escrib** → a
com → amos	**escrib** → amos
com → áis	**escrib** → áis
com → an	**escrib** → an

Careful! When a verb is irregular in the first-person present indicative, this irregularity is found in the present subjunctive (apart from a few exceptions). For example, **hacer** *to do*, *to make*:
present indicative: **hago, haces, hace, hacemos, hacéis, hacen**
I do, you do, etc.

present subjunctive: **haga, hagas, haga, hagamos, hagáis, hagan** *that I do, that you do*, etc.

The endings are regular, but the stem retains the irregularity of the first-person present indicative.

The English translations above are preceded by the word *that* (**que**). This is because in most circumstances a subjunctive clause is introduced by **que**.

Be aware that this is a very general overview of the subjunctive; we'll go into more detail as necessary when exceptions come up. The first exceptions to the rules about forming the subjunctive are six verbs that are so highly irregular in the first-person indicative that their corresponding subjunctive forms must be dealt with separately:

Infinitive	First-person sing. present indicative	First-person sing. present subjunctive
haber *to have*	**he** *I have*	**que haya** *that I have*
saber *to know*	**sé** *I know*	**que sepa** *that I know*
dar *to give*	**doy** *I give*	**que dé** *that I give*
estar *to be*	**estoy** *I am*	**que esté** *that I be**
ser *to be*	**soy** *I am*	**que sea** *that I be**
ir *to go*	**voy** *I go*	**que vaya** *that I go*

* The English subjunctive here is *be*, rather than *am*.

2 Use of the subjunctive

• The subjunctive is often used in a subordinate clause introduced by **que** *that*. However, only if there is a change in the subject of the sentence:
Quiero que vengas. *I want you to come.*

If there is no change in subject, the infinitive is used:
Quiero venir. *I want to come.*

• The subjunctive is used (following **que**) in subordinate clauses after verbs expressing commands, wishes, advice, etc.
Dile que me llame. *Tell him to call me.*
Me aconseja que lea este libro.
She recommends that I read this book.
Le ruego que venga. *Please come.*

• As detailed in review lesson 42, the subjunctive is used to form all commands <u>except</u> affirmative informal commands.

• The subjunctive is used in subordinate clauses following **cuando** *when* (or a number of other conjunctions or relative pronouns that introduce a subordinate clause expressing the hypothetical future):
Te lo enseñaré cuando vengas. *I'll show it to you when you come.*
Haz como quieras. *Do as you wish.*

* * *

Diálogo recapitulativo

1 – ¿Qué pasa? ¿Adónde vas?
2 – Voy a correos a retirar una carta certificada.
3 Creo que es una carta de mi ex marido.
4 ¡No sé qué va ser de mí! Me vuelve loca.
5 – ¡Mujer, tampoco es para tanto!
6 A lo mejor quiere que le des un consejo.
7 – El único consejo que puedo darle es que se olvide de mí.
8 ¿Te das cuenta de que me escribe dos cartas por semana?
9 – Dale un telefonazo y habla con él.
10 – ¡No sé por quién me toma!
11 – ¡El amor, amiga, el amor!

Haremos lo que tú digas. *We'll do whatever you say.*
Para que lo sepas… *So that you know…*

• A form of the subjunctive, **quisiera** *I/he/she/you* (formal) *would like*, is used for polite requests (this is the imperfect subjunctive and merely replaces the conditional).
Quisiera hablar con el señor Martínez.
I would like to speak with Mr Martínez.

> *That's it for our first detailed look at the Spanish subjunctive.* **Un consejo** A piece of advice: *don't worry about learning everything by heart. You'll pick things up gradually as we return to them.*

* * *

Traducción

1 What's the matter? Where are you going? **2** I'm going to the post office to pick up a registered letter. **3** I think it's a letter from my ex-husband. **4** I don't know what's going to become of me! He's driving me crazy. **5** Hey, there's no need to exaggerate! **6** Perhaps he wants you to give him some advice. **7** The only advice that I can give him is to forget me. **8** Do you realize that he writes me two letters a week? **9** Give him a ring/call and talk to him. **10** I don't know who he takes me for! **11** Love, my friend, love!

Second wave: 7th lesson

Sospechas

1 Un hon**ra**do ① **pa**dre de fa**mi**lia que sa**lí**a a traba**jar**
2 acu**dió** al lo**cal** de bici**cle**tas de su **ca**sa ②.
3 Y no dio con ③ la **su**ya ④.
4 En el por**tal** ⑤ de la **ca**sa, se cru**zó** con el **hi**jo de la por**te**ra.
5 Y sospe**chó** de él ⑥.

Notes

① **honrado/a** *honourable, honest, upstanding, respectable.*

② **acudir** means 'to go somewhere with a specific purpose'. The word **casa** means *house, home* and is also used generally to refer to where one lives, or *residence*. Here it refers to a block of flats/apartment building **(inmueble)**, a living situation that is common for urban families in Spain. Line 4 mentions the **portero/a** *caretaker, superintendent*, who looks after the building and grounds, and sometimes lives on the premises.

③ **dar con** (literally, 'to give with') is synonymous with **encontrar** or **hallar** *to find*. (**dio** is the irregular third-person singular preterite of **dar** *to give*.) Although in English the negative of 'to find' tends to be formed with 'couldn't' or 'can't', in Spanish it isn't necessary to include this.
No doy con su dirección. *I can't* (don't) *find his/her address.*

④ **su** (line 2) and **suya** (line 3) are both forms of the third-person possessive (here, *his*). The former is used before a noun, and the latter after a noun or, as here, with a definite article to refer to a previously mentioned object. The **-a** ending indicates that the object possessed is feminine (**la bicicleta**): **la suya** *his* ▸

Suspicions

1 An upstanding family man *(honourable father of family)* who was leaving for work
2 went to the bicycle stand *(premises of bicycles)* in his apartment building *(house)*.
3 And couldn't find his [bike] *(And not gave with the his)*.
4 In the entranceway of the building, he crossed [paths] with the son of the caretaker.
5 And he [began to] suspect him *(And suspected of him)*.

(referring to the bicycle). Another word for **la bicicleta** is the abbreviation **la bici** *the bike [**bee**-thee]*.

⑤ **el portal** *the entrance, doorway*. One can often find there **un ascensor** *a lift, elevator* and **los buzones** *mailboxes*.

⑥ **sospechar de alguien** *to suspect someone*. Note the use of the preposition **de**.

6 Le salu**dó**.

7 Y que**dó** persua**di**do de que su ma**ne**ra de respon**der e**ra la de un la**drón** de bici**cle**tas.

8 Al cami**nar** ⑦ ⑧ tras ⑨ él,

9 esti**mó** que su **for**ma de an**dar e**ra sin **du**da al**gu**na ⑩ la de un la**drón** de bici**cle**tas.

10 El **jo**ven se encon**tró** ⑪ en la pa**ra**da del auto**bús** con al**gu**nos de sus compa**ñe**ros.

11 Y el hon**ra**do **pa**dre de fa**mi**lia juz**gó** ⑫ que su ma**ne**ra de ha**blar**les **e**ra la de un la**drón** de bici**cle**tas.

12 No ca**bía** ⑬ la me**nor du**da;

Notes

⑦ **al** + infinitive indicates an action that is happening at the same time or just before the action of the main verb.
Al subir al autobús, resbaló.
While getting on the bus, he/she slipped.
Al salir del museo, cogí un taxi.
On leaving the museum, I took a taxi.

⑧ **caminar** (and **andar**, line 9) *to walk*.
Alberto camina (or **anda**) **despacio.** *Alberto walks slowly.*
el camino *the road*, *the way*; **el sendero** and **la senda** *the path*.
El Camino de Santiago *The Way of Saint James* (the famous pilgrimage route to Santiago de Compostela).

⑨ **tras** *after*, *behind* is mostly used in a figurative sense. To refer to a physical location, it is more common to use **detrás de**, e.g. **detrás de la silla** *behind the chair*. When used as an adverb, it can also be translated by **atrás**: **ir atrás** (or **detrás**) *to walk* or *to go behind*; **echar marcha atrás** *to go back on*, *reconsider* or, in a vehicle, *to put into reverse gear*; **quedarse atrás** *to lag behind*, *to trail*.

⑩ **sin ninguna duda** or **sin duda alguna** *without any doubt*.
alguno/a *any* when placed after the noun becomes negative: ▶

6 He greeted him.
7 And he was convinced *(remained persuaded of)* that the way he answered *(his manner of responding)* was that of a bicycle thief.
8 Walking behind him,
9 he deemed that his gait *(his form of walking)* was without any doubt that of a bicycle thief.
10 The young [man] came across some friends at the bus stop *(found himself at the stop of the bus with some of his companions)*.
11 And the upstanding family man judged that his way of speaking to them was that of a bicycle thief.
12 There was no doubt about it *(It did not fit the least doubt)*;

▸ **No tengo ninguna duda** or **No tengo duda alguna.**
I have no doubt. I don't have any doubt.
No doubt (**sin duda**) you won't fail to notice the use of **algunos** as a pronoun in line 10: **algunos/as** *some, a few.*

⑪ **encontrar** *to find* or *to meet, encounter*; **encontrarse** *to be located* or *to come across, run into, bump into each other.*
Se encontró con sus amigos. *He bumped into his friends.*
El estanco se encuentra en la próxima calle.
The tobacconist's is located in the next street.
Compare also a different meaning of this stem-changing verb (lesson 60): **No me encuentro bien.** *I don't feel well.*

⑫ **juzgó** *judged*, from **juzgar**. This is the last preterite verb form in this lesson. Did you spot them all? There are nine in total, and only one is irregular. We'll look more at the preterite tense in review lesson 63.

⑬ **caber** *to fit into, to hold*, as in 'to have enough room'.
La maleta no cabe en el maletero.
The suitcase doesn't fit in the boot/trunk.
No cabe duda. *There is no (room for) doubt.*

13 si se le mi**ra**ba bien…

14 ¡**to**do en su acti**tud** lo dela**ta**ba **co**mo un la**drón** de bici**cle**tas!

(continua**rá**) □

* * *

Ejercicio 1: Traduzca

❶ Alberto es una persona muy honrada. ❷ La portera está hablando con él en el portal. ❸ Tengo una bici nueva. ❹ ¿Es la suya? ❺ No doy con su número de teléfono.

* * *

Ejercicio 2: Complete

❶ On returning from work, he ran into *(with)* his daughter.
. . volver de trabajar . . . . su hija.

❷ She is very old; she walks slowly.
Es . . . . , ...

❸ Get *(Put yourself)* behind *(of)* me.
Ponte . . . .

❹ Do any of you know where my bike is?
¿ . . . . . . de vosotros sabe . . . . ?

❺ I still have doubts.
Yo . . . .

13 if you took a good look at him *(if one was watching him well)* …
14 everything in his manner *(attitude)* betrayed him as a bicycle thief!
[to be continued *(it will continue)*]

* * *

Answers to Exercise 1

❶ Alberto is a very honest person. ❷ The caretaker is talking with him in the doorway. ❸ I have a new bike. ❹ Is it *(f.)* his/hers/yours *(formal)*? ❺ I [can]not find his/her telephone number.

* * *

Answers to Exercise 2

❶ Al – se encontró con – ❷ – muy mayor, anda despacio ❸ – detrás de mí ❹ Alguno – dónde está mi bici ❺ – todavía tengo dudas

Although this lesson was fairly dense, with the exception of a couple of new points, you've already seen most of the information. Hopefully, you're finding that new things fall easily into place given what you've already learned. Take your time and read the lesson texts as many times as necessary. If you want, you can also refer back to review lessons or check in the grammatical appendix for additional information. Alternatively, you can just let yourself be guided along without trying to grasp every little thing! Bear in mind that the dialogue of the next lesson is a continuation of this one, so be patient – it may answer certain questions you might have.
¡Adelante, caminante! Keep going, traveller!

As the poet Antonio Machado said:
¡Se hace camino al andar! The road is made by walking!

Second wave: 8th lesson

58 Lección cincuenta y ocho

Sospechas (continuación)

1 **Cuan**do el hon**ra**do **pa**dre de fa**mi**lia vol**ví**a ① de traba**jar**,
2 vio ② extra**ña**do que su **hi**jo vol**ví**a del co**le**gio en su **bi**ci ③.
3 Al **dí**a si**guien**te,
4 se cru**zó** ④ de **nue**vo con el **hi**jo de la por**te**ra.
5 La ma**ne**ra de respon**der** a su sa**lu**do,

Notes

① **cuando... volvía...** *when/as ... was returning ...* This construction is an alternative to **al** + infinitive, which we saw in the previous lesson. You could just as easily say **al volver del trabajo** *on returning from work.*

② **vio** *he/she saw* (or *you saw*, formal) is the third-person singular preterite of **ver** *to see*. The preterite is used here because the action is considered completely elapsed. Compare with the use of the imperfect in line 1 (**volvía** *was returning*), which describes an action not yet completed.

③ It can be a bit tricky to know who **su** refers to since it can mean *his, her, its, your* (formal) or *their* (lesson 28). If you need to clarify, you can add **de** + the relevant personal pronoun:
su bici (de él): *his bike*
su bici (de ella): *her bike*
su bici (de usted/ustedes): *your bike* (formal sing./plural)
su bici (de ellos/ellas) *their bike* (m./f.)
Here, **en su bici** *on his bike*, refers to the father's bicycle (hence his surprise).

Lesson fifty-eight 58

Suspicions (continued)

1 When the upstanding family man was returning from work,
2 he saw to his surprise *(surprised)* that his son was coming back from school on <u>his</u> bike!
3 The next day *(On-the day following)*,
4 he again crossed [paths] with the son of the caretaker.
5 His *(The)* way of answering when greeted *(to his greeting)*,

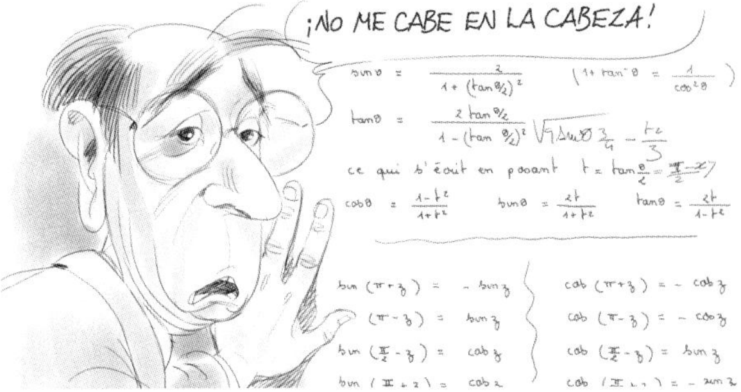

④ **se cruzó** *he/she/you* (formal sing.) *bumped into*, *came across*, *crossed paths with*. Here's another example of the preterite. You've no doubt noticed the written accent on the last syllable: the first- and third-person singular forms of <u>regular</u> preterites always have one. However, many <u>irregular</u> preterites do not. Such irregulars are verbs that occur in daily use with very high frequency, so it's best simply to memorize their forms. You've already seen several of them: **fui** *I was* or *I went* and **fue** *he/she/it/you* (formal sing.) *was/were* or *went*; **di** *I gave* and **dio** *he/she/it/you* (formal sing.) *gave*; **vi** *I saw* and **vio** *he/she/it/you* (formal sing.) *saw*.

6 su **for**ma de an**dar**,
7 la ma**ne**ra de ha**blar** a sus compa**ñe**ros,
8 su acti**tud** ⑤…
9 ya no ⑥ **eran** las de un la**drón** de bici**cle**tas. □

Notes

⑤ **la actitud** *attitude, bearing.*

⑥ **ya no** before a verb, or **no** + verb + **ya** = *no longer, no more, not ... any longer, not ... anymore.*
Ya no llueve. *It's no longer raining.*
Ahora no tengo ganas ya de salir.
Now I don't feel like going out anymore.

* * *

Ejercicio 1: Traduzca

❶ Al ir a trabajar se encontró con Luis. ❷ Le vio en el portal. ❸ Ya no volverá. ❹ Al día siguiente fui a su casa. ❺ ¿Cuál era su actitud?

* * *

Ejercicio 2: Complete

Instead of the usual fill-in-the-blank exercise, here is a review activity based mainly on the two lessons that you've just completed. You'll see how much you've picked up without even realizing it!

The exercise consists of several lines of verse by the poet Antonio Machado, who died in exile in the south of France at the end of the Spanish Civil War (1936–39). We've provided translations only of words or expressions that you've not seen before. You'll find the poem in Spanish at the end of the lesson. Over to you!

6 his gait,
7 his *(the)* way of speaking to his friends,
8 his [whole] bearing *(his attitude)*...
9 were no longer *(already were not)* those of a bicycle thief.

▸ Note that **no** may be replaced by another negative word: **Nadie cogía ya la antigua carretera** or **Ya nadie cogía la antigua carretera.** *Nobody took the old road anymore.*

* * *

Answers to Exercise 1

❶ On going to work, he/she ran into Luis. ❷ He/she saw him at the entrance [to the building]. ❸ He/she won't come back anymore. ❹ The next day I went to his/her place. ❺ How was his attitude?

* * *

❶ Traveller, your tracks are *(are your tracks...)* the road
. . . . , . . . tus huellas . . . .

❷ And nothing else;
. . . . . más;

❸ Traveller, there is no road,
. . . . , ... ,

❹ One makes [the] road by walking.
. . . .

⑤ By walking one makes [the] road,

.. ..,

⑥ And on looking *(returning the view)* behind

. .. volver la vista .....

⑦ One sees the path that never

.. ..

⑧ Again one will tread.

Se ha de volver a pisar.

⑨ Traveller, there is no road,

........., ...,

⑩ But wakes in the sea.

Sino estelas en la mar.

59 Lección cincuenta y nueve

Hacer una reserva en un parador

1 – ¡Ya es**tá**! ¡Me he arre**gla**do en la ofi**ci**na ①!
2 **Den**tro de un mes nos **va**mos de vaca**cio**nes.
3 He pe**di**do **u**na se**ma**na de per**mi**so y me la han conce**di**do.
4 ¡Nos **va**mos de **gi**ra por Extrema**du**ra!
5 ¡En fa**mi**lia!

Notes

① **la oficina** *the office*. **ir a la oficina** *to go to the office* is another way of saying **ir a trabajar** or **ir al trabajo**. Another word for ▸

Traducción

❶ "Caminante, son tus huellas el camino
❷ Y nada más;
❸ Caminante, no hay camino,
❹ Se hace camino al andar.
❺ Al andar se hace camino,
❻ Y al volver la vista atrás
❼ Se ve la senda que nunca
❽ Se ha de volver a pisar.
❾ Caminante, no hay camino,
❿ Sino estelas en la mar."

(Antonio Machado, 1875–1939)

You are indeed making your own path. And with each step, you're advancing.

Second wave: 9th lesson

Lesson fifty-nine 59

Making a reservation at a parador

1 – That's it! I've arranged [everything] at work!
2 In *(Inside of)* a month we're going on holiday.
3 I asked for a week off *(of permission)* and they have given *(granted)* it to me.
4 We're going on [a] tour of Extremadura!
5 A family trip *(In family)*!

▸ *office* is **el despacho**, referring to the room that serves as an office or study.

6 – ¡Estu**pen**do, **ha**ce **a**ños que ② te**ní**a **ga**nas de ir!
7 ¿**Cre**es que ha**brá si**tio en al**gún** ③ para**dor**?
8 – Sí, **pe**ro te**ne**mos que reser**var cuan**to **an**tes ④.
9 Voy a en**viar** a**ho**ra **mis**mo un 'e**mi**lio' ⑤ a Jaran**di**lla de la **Ve**ra ⑥.
10 Si **tie**nen habita**cio**nes, confirma**ré** por fax.
11 – **U**na con **ca**ma de matri**mo**nio ⑦ y…
12 **o**tra con tres **ca**mas **pa**ra los **ni**ños.
13 – Pa**pá**, ¿qué te pa**re**ce si in**vi**to a mi a**mi**ga **Nie**ves? □

Notes

② **Hace años que tenía ganas de ir** *I've been wanting to go for years* ('It makes years that I've had desire to go'). **Hace**, from **hacer**, is frequently used in time expressions. If it is followed by **que** + clause, it corresponds to the English *for* + the period of time: **Hace diez minutos que espero.** *I've been waiting for ten minutes.* Notice that where English uses a perfect tense (*I've been ...-ing*), Spanish is much simpler and uses either the imperfect or the present tense: **¿Cuánto tiempo hace que estudias español?** *How long have you been studying Spanish?* **hace** can also mean *ago*, especially if <u>not</u> followed by **que**: **hace tres meses** *three months ago.*

③ In lesson 57, we saw **alguno/a** *any* (plural, **algunos/as** *some, a few*). The masculine singular **alguno** shortens to **algún** if used before a masculine noun. Compare with the negative form **ningún** in lesson 29.
Su vecino me dio algunos consejos.
Her neighbour gave me some advice.
Su vecino no me dio ningún consejo.
His neighbour didn't give me any advice.

6 – Fantastic, I've wanted to go for years *(it makes years that I was wanting to go)*!
7 Do you think there will be room at a *(in any)* parador?
8 – Yes, but we have to reserve as soon as possible *(how much before)*.
9 I'm going to send an e-mail to Jarandilla de la Vera right now.
10 If they have rooms, I'll confirm by fax.
11 – One with [a] double bed *(of matrimony)* and …
12 another with three beds for the kids.
13 – Dad, how about *(what do you think)* if I invite *(to)* my friend Nieves?

▸ **Ningún problema.** *No problem.*
Algún día te acordarás. *Someday you'll remember.*

④ **cuanto antes** *as soon as possible.*
Telefonéeme cuanto antes. *Phone me as soon as you can.*

⑤ In colloquial language, you might hear **emilio** (from the name **Emilio**) for *e-mail* (**correo electrónico** *electronic mail* or **e-mail** *[ee-**may**-eel]*).

⑥ Jarandilla de la Vera is a town in Extremadura that is home to the **'Carlos V' parador**, a castle where the Holy Roman Emperor Charles V (1500–58) stayed towards the end of his life, before retiring to the nearby Monastery of Yuste. Find out more about **paradores** at the end of the lesson.

⑦ **una cama de matrimonio** *a double bed.*
Queremos una habitación con cama de matrimonio y baño.
We want a room with a double bed and bathroom.
un matrimonio *a married couple*; **un matrimonio joven** *a young married couple*; **el matrimonio** *marriage.*

Ejercicio 1: Traduzca

❶ Se ha arreglado con sus amigos. ❷ ¿Has reservado ya? ❸ Voy a pedir unos días de permiso. ❹ No sé si habrá sitio. ❺ El tren sale dentro de cinco minutos.

* * *

Ejercicio 2: Complete

❶ They have given *(granted)* me three days off from the office.
Me han . . . . tres días . . . .
. . . .

❷ Come as soon as possible.
Ven . . . .

❸ Do you *(informal)* have her e-mail address?
¿. . . . . dirección de correo . . . . ?

❹ We don't have any more rooms with [a] double bed.
. . . . nos quedan habitaciones . . . .
. . . .

❺ To confirm, send *(formal)* me an e-mail.
. . . . , ...

EL TREN SALE DENTRO DE CINCO MINUTOS.
TAXI

Answers to Exercise 1

❶ He/she has arranged [everything] with his/her friends. ❷ Have you already reserved/booked? ❸ I'm going to ask for some days off. ❹ I don't know if there will be room. ❺ The train leaves in five minutes.

* * *

Answers to Exercise 2

❶ – concedido – de permiso en la oficina ❷ – cuanto antes ❸ Tienes su – electrónico ❹ Ya no – con cama de matrimonio ❺ Para confirmar, envíeme un e-mail

Los Paradores Nacionales de Turismo *are grand state-owned hotels run by* **el Ministerio de Turismo** the Ministry of Tourism. *The word* **parador** *is first mentioned in Spanish classical literature, referring to establishments of a higher category than the ordinary inns where most travellers stayed with their horses and carriages – they were reserved for distinguished guests. Following that tradition, in 1926 the Marquis of Vega-Inclán, the Royal Commissioner for Tourism under King Alfonso XIII, proposed the creation of a chain of state-run* **paradores** *to promote tourism. The first opened in 1928 in Gredos, Ávila, and today almost 100* **paradores** *are found throughout Spain.*

The basic concept remains the same as at the beginning of the 20th century: the government funds the creation of hotels, mainly at historic sites, which private investors consider not profitable enough to finance. Priority is given to the restoration of ancient monuments, palaces, monasteries, castles, and other sites of cultural or historical interest. Staying in a **parador** *allows the traveller to take a trip back in time through the history of Spain.*

Like hotels, **los paradores** *are rated depending on the level of accommodation they offer. Some are grander and more luxurious than others. The price of the rooms varies according to the number of stars,* **estrellas**. *Many also have restaurants that serve excellent regional specialities. Any* Tourist Office, **Oficina de Turismo**, *can give you information about the* **Red Nacional de Paradores** National Paradores Network.

Second wave: 10th lesson

Excelente consejo

1 – Doc**tor**, **ven**go a pe**dir**le con**se**jo.
2 **Lle**vo ① **u**na tempo**ra**da ② con la ten**sión** **al**ta ③.
3 – ¿**Tie**ne **mu**cho es**trés**?
4 – No, en abso**lu**to. **Lle**vo **u**na **vi**da muy tran**qui**la.
5 Por las ma**ña**nas me le**van**to con el **can**to del **ga**llo.
6 Reco**noz**co, **e**so sí, que tra**ba**jo **co**mo **u**na **mu**la; **pe**ro…
7 lo com**pen**so **por**que **co**mo **co**mo **u**na **fie**ra ④.

Notes

① To express a continuous action, **llevar** is often used with a time phrase. **Llevar** has numerous meanings depending on the context (*to carry*, *to lead*, *to take*, *to wear*, etc.), but this construction generally translates as 'to have been …-ing/to have had for [period of time]'. So **hace** + amount of time + **que** + present/imperfect tense (lesson 59) means the same thing as **llevar** + amount of time + present participle (*-ing* form).
Llevo una hora esperando. or **Hace una hora que espero.** *I've been waiting for an hour.*
Lleva diez días enfermo. *He's been ill for ten days.*

② The primary meaning of **temporada** is *season*: **temporada de lluvias** *rainy season*; **temporada de verano** *summer season (summertime)*; **temporada alta/baja** *high/low season*; **fuera de temporada** *out of season*, *off-season*. But it can also mean ▸

Excellent advice

1 – Doctor, I['ve] come to ask you [for your] advice.
2 For some time I've had high blood pressure *(I carry a period with the pressure high).*
3 – Do you have a lot of stress?
4 – No, absolutely not. I lead a very quiet life.
5 In the mornings I get up when the rooster crows *(with the song of the rooster).*
6 I admit *(recognize)*, however *(that yes)*, that I work like a mule, but …
7 I make up *(compensate)* for it because I eat like a horse *(beast).*

▸ *period*, *spell*, referring to a length of time between a week and several months.
David atraviesa una mala temporada.
David is going through (traversing) *a bad spell.*

③ **tener la tensión alta**; **tener mucha tension**; **tener hipertensión** *to have high blood pressure*; *to be very tense*; *to have hypertension.*

④ **comer como una fiera** or **como un león** ('to eat like a wild animal' or 'like a lion') means *to eat like a horse*. In line 8, **acostarse con las gallinas** 'to go to bed with the chickens' means *to go to bed early.* And after a big meal and an early night, in Spain you sleep like **una marmota** *a marmot* (an animal that hibernates) rather than like a log or a baby!

8 Me a**cues**to ⑤ con las ga**lli**nas.
9 Y **duer**mo **co**mo **u**na mar**mo**ta.
10 **Pe**ro… a pe**sar** de **to**do, **co**mo le de**cí**a, no me en**cuen**tro bien.
11 ¡No sé qué me **pa**sa!
12 – Pues… ¡no sé qué de**cir**le!
13 Yo, en su lu**gar** ⑥, consulta**rí**a a un veteri**na**rio. □

Notes

⑤ **acostarse** *to go to bed, to lie down*, like **volver** and **contar** (lesson 53), has a stem change (**o** to **ue**) in the present tense. Remember that the stem changes for all persons except **nosotros/vosotros**. So: **acostarse** *to go to bed* → **me acuesto** *I go to bed.* Other examples of verbs with this stem change are **dormir** ▸

* * *

Ejercicio 1: Traduzca

❶ María encontró trabajo hace tres días. ❷ Quiero pedirte un consejo. ❸ ¿Te sientes mal? ❹ Tengo mucho estrés en el trabajo. ❺ ¿A qué hora te acuestas?

* * *

Ejercicio 2: Complete

❶ How long have you *(informal)* been waiting?
¿. . . . . . tiempo . . . . . . esperando?

❷ In the mornings I leave for work *(to work)* at eight o'clock.
. . . . salgo . . . .
. . . . .

❸ I admit that I was mistaken.
. . . . que me he . . . .

8 I go to bed with the chickens *(hens)*.
9 And I sleep like a lamb *(marmot)*.
10 But … in spite of everything, as I was telling you, I don't feel *(find myself)* well.
11 I don't know what's wrong with me *(is happening to me)*!
12 – Well … I don't know what to tell you!
13 If I were you *(Me, in your place)*, I would consult *(to)* a vet.

▸ (line 9) *to sleep* → **duermo** *I sleep* and **encontrarse** (line 10) *to find oneself, to feel, to be located* → **me encuentro** *I feel.* (Note that **encontrarse** is a synonym of **sentirse** *to feel* → **me siento** I feel.)

⑥ **en tu lugar, yo…** *if I were you/in your position, I …*
el lugar *place*; **el lugar ideal** *the ideal place.*

* * *

Answers to Exercise 1

❶ María found work three days ago. ❷ I want to ask your advice. ❸ Do you feel bad ? ❹ I have a lot of stress at work. ❺ At what time do you go to bed?

* * *

❹ In spite of everything, he sleeps like a baby *(a marmot).*
. . . . como una marmota.

❺ If I were him *(I in his place)*, I would eat right now.
Yo . . . . , ... mismo.

Answers to Exercise 2

❶ Cuánto – llevas – ❷ Por las mañanas – a trabajar a las ocho ❸ Reconozco – equivocado ❹ A pesar de todo duerme – ❺ – en su lugar, comería – ahora –

61 Lección sesenta y una

En el supermercado

1 – Ten, a**quí tie**nes **u**na **fi**cha, ve a co**ger** un **ca**rro;
2 yo voy a co**ger** un **nú**mero en la pescade**rí**a ①.
3 Nos encon**tra**mos en la sec**ción** de pro**duc**tos conge**la**dos ②.
4 – De a**cuer**do. No **tar**des ③.
5 – Hay **u**na **co**la e**nor**me.

Notes

① **el pescado** *fish* (the food); **el pescadero** *the fish seller, fishmonger*; **la pescadería** *the fish market, fish section* (in a supermarket). **Voy a la pescadería.** *I'm going to the fish shop/ counter.* Note that **el pez** (plural **los peces**) refers to a live fish. Once it has been caught it is called **el pescado** (literally, 'the fished', from the verb **pescar**). ▸

As you're doing the exercises at the end of each lesson, it's quite possible that you'll come up with answers that are different from the ones we suggest. This is a very good sign. It means your knowledge of the language is expanding considerably and that you're able to come up with alternative ways of expressing things. Even if your answer is a valid alternative, try to complete Exercise 2 the way we're looking for anyway, as this is good practice. The exercises concentrate on colloquial expressions and everyday language and provide an additional review of what you've learned in the lesson.

Second wave: 11th lesson

Lesson sixty-one 61

At the supermarket

1 – Here, take *(Have, here you have)* a token, go [and] get a cart;
2 I'm going to take a number at the seafood counter *(fish shop)*.
3 We['ll] meet up in the frozen foods section.
4 – OK. Don't take too long *(Don't delay)*.
5 – There's a huge queue.

② **los productos congelados** *frozen foods*; **congelar** *to freeze*; **el congelador** *the freezer*.

③ **tardar** *to delay, to take [a long] time.*
No tardaré mucho. *I won't take/be long.*
¿Cuánto tarda el tren de Madrid a Lisboa?
How long does the train from Madrid to Lisbon take?
Sólo tardaré una hora. *I'll only be an hour.*

6 Nos da**rá tiem**po ④ a lle**nar** el **ca**rro
7 **an**tes de que ⑤ nos **to**que ⑥ a no**so**tros.
8 – **Va**mos, yo ya he co**gi**do los pro**duc**tos de lim**pie**za ⑦, la be**bi**da, el to**ma**te concen**tra**do ⑧ y la **car**ne pi**ca**da;
9 **pe**ro… **sa**ca la **lis**ta.
10 – ¡Cre**í**a que la te**ní**as tú!
11 – **Bue**no, **va**mos por ⑨ el pan de **mol**de, los cere**a**les, la mante**qui**lla, los yo**gu**res y…
12 ¡ha**brá** que vol**ver** más **tar**de si nos **fal**ta **al**go ⑩!
13 La ca**je**ra: '¿Van a pa**gar** en me**tá**lico o con tar**je**ta ⑪?'

Notes

④ **me (te, le, nos,** etc.) **da tiempo** *I (you, he/she/you, we,* etc.*) have time* ('it gives me time'); **no me da tiempo** *I don't have time.* This expression can be used in any tense: **No me dará tiempo.** *I won't have time. That won't give me time.* Here **dar** is used in the third-person, much the same way as **gustar**.

⑤ The conjunction **antes de que** *before* is always followed by a verb in the subjunctive:
antes de que te vayas *before you leave*
antes de que anochezca *before it gets dark.*

⑥ **tocar** (lesson 50) and **sacar** (line 9) are regular verbs, but in order to maintain the same sound, the **c** of the stem becomes **qu** when the verb ending starts with **e**. This occurs in all forms of the present subjunctive and in the first-person singular preterite tense.

tocar, present indicative	→	**toco, tocas, toca,** etc.
present subjunctive	→	**toque, toques, toque,** etc.
preterite	→	**toqué, tocaste, tocó,** etc.

There is nothing irregular about this spelling change. On the contrary, it allows the verb to stay regular.

6 It will give us time to fill the cart
7 before it's our turn *(before that it may touch to us)*.
8 – Let's go, I've already picked up the cleaning products, the drink[s], the tomato paste and the ground beef;
9 but … get out the list.
10 – I thought *(that)* you had it!
11 – All right, let's go find *(go for)* a loaf of bread *(the bread of baking-pan)*, the cereal*(s)*, the butter, the yoghurt*(s)* and …
12 we'll have to come back later if we're missing anything *(if to-us is-lacking something)*!
13 The cashier: 'Are you going to pay in cash or with a credit card?'

▸ ⑦ **los productos de limpieza** *cleaning products*; **limpiar** *to clean*; **la limpieza** *cleanliness, cleaning*; **limpieza en seco** *dry cleaning.*

⑧ **el tomate** *tomato*; **el tomate concentrado** *tomato paste/ tomato concentrate*; **concentrarse** *to concentrate, to focus on*.

⑨ **ir por** ('to go for') *to go and get, to fetch.* **Voy por el pan.** *I'm going to get the bread.* (or **Voy a buscar el pan.**)

por *for* can also be used in the same way after verbs such as **venir** *to come*; **bajar** *to go down (to the street)*; **salir** *to go out*; **enviar (por)** *to send (for)*; etc.
Vengo por el periódico. *I've come for the newspaper.*

⑩ **si nos falta algo** *if we're missing something.* The verb **faltar** *to be lacking, to be missing* works like **gustar** and **tocar**. The subject comes after the verb, which conjugates only in the third-person (singular or plural): here it literally translates to 'if to us is lacking something'.

⑪ **en metálico** ('in metallic') *in cash*; **pagar con tarjeta** *to pay with a card*; **tarjeta de crédito** *credit card*; **tarjeta de visita** *business card*; **tarjeta telefónica** *telephone card*; **postal** or **tarjeta postal** *postcard.*

14 – ¡No sé **dón**de **ten**go la ca**be**za!
15 ¡Me he de**ja**do tam**bién** la car**te**ra! □

* * *

Ejercicio 1: Traduzca

❶ ¿Tienes una moneda para coger un carro? ❷ ¿Qué número tenemos nosotros? ❸ No tardaré mucho. ❹ ¿Crees que nos falta algo? ❺ Delante del cine hay una cola muy grande.

* * *

Ejercicio 2: Complete

❶ I'll leave before it gets too hot.
Saldré . . . . haga . . . .

❷ I won't have time to go to the fish shop.
No . . . . a pasar por la . . . .

❸ It's your turn.
. . . . usted.

❹ We'll *(One will)* have to go out for the bread.
. . . . salir . . . . . pan.

❺ I prefer to pay in cash.
Prefiero . . . .

* * *

It's not easy to be specific about **los horarios de apertura** opening times *for businesses in Spain because these can vary between northern and southern Spain and are often not the same in winter as in summer. It also depends on the type of business. In general, in towns,* **los supermercados** supermarkets *as well as other* **tiendas** shops, stores *are open from 9:30 or 10:00 a.m. to 1:30 or 2:00 p.m.* **por la mañana** in the mornings, *and from 4:30 or 5:00 to 7:30 or 8:00 p.m.* **por la tarde** in the afternoons.

14 – I don't know where my head is *(where I have the head)*!

15 I've forgotten my *(the)* wallet as well!

* * *

Answers to Exercise 1

❶ Do you have a coin to get a cart/trolley? ❷ What number do we have? ❸ I won't be long. ❹ Do you think that we're missing anything? ❺ In front of the cinema there's a very long queue/line.

* * *

Answers to Exercise 2

❶ – antes de que – demasiado calor ❷ – me dará tiempo – pescadería ❸ Le toca a – ❹ Habrá que – por el – ❺ – pagar en metálico

Los hipermercados hypermarkets *and* **centros comerciales** shopping centres, malls, *mostly located on the outskirts of big cities, don't close for lunch. Many* **comercios** businesses *in town also tend to stay open in the middle of the day.* **El cierre** closing *on Saturday afternoons, which used to be the rule everywhere, is also on the decline. Big stores now very often open on Sunday mornings as well. This is also true of many* **comercios** *located in tourist areas, which can stay open as late as 10:00 or 11:00 p.m.*

Second wave: 12th lesson

Lección sesenta y dos

Ociosas en la playa ①

1 – ¿Qué te **pa**re**ce** si exten**de**mos a**quí** las to**a**llas ②?
2 – Muy bien, **hace una bri**sa ③ muy agra**da**ble.
3 – ¿**Quie**res que te **pon**ga un **po**co de **cre**ma ④ protec**to**ra
4 **pa**ra que no te **que**me el sol ⑤?
5 – Sí, ¡a ver si ⑥ me **pon**go mo**re**na ⑦ ense**gui**da!

Notes

① **ocioso** *idle* **(desocupado)**, *doing nothing*. **El ocio** *idleness* is also, more positively, *leisure*, so **los momentos** or **ratos de ocio** are *moments of free time*. In Madrid, every week you can buy **la guía del ocio** ('the guide to leisure') where you can find out what's happening in the city: listings for cinemas, theatres, museums, music events, current exhibitions and other activities for passing the time.

② **toalla** *bath towel*; **toalla de papel, papel absorbente** *paper towel* (a *table napkin* is **servilleta**).

③ Note that **hacer** is used in several impersonal expressions (i.e. in which the subject is not clearly defined) that have to do with the weather, whereas in English we use *to be*:
hace frío, calor, bueno, malo, fresco *it's cold, hot, nice, horrible, cool.* Also: **hace una pequeña brisa** *there's a little breeze*; **hace mucho viento** *it's very windy.*

④ **ponerse** or **echarse una crema** or **una pomada** *to put on, to apply, to rub in a cream/lotion* or *an ointment.* ▸

Lounging *(Idle[fem. pl.])* on the beach

1 – How about *(What do you think)* if we spread out the towels here?
2 – Very well, there's *(it makes)* a very pleasant breeze.
3 – Do you want me to put *(that on you I put)* a bit of sunscreen on you
4 so that you don't get sunburned *(you it doesn't burn the sun)*?
5 – Yes, let's see *(to see)* if I get a tan *(myself put brown)* quickly!

⑤ **quemar** *to burn*; **quemarse** *to burn oneself* and also *to get sunburned.*
Me he dormido en la playa y me he quemado la espalda.
I fell asleep on the beach and my back got sunburned.

⑥ The expression **a ver si …** *Let's see if …* can mean different things depending on context. Very often, as here, it expresses a wish for something. **¡Ojalá!** *Hopefully! Let's hope so!* has a similar meaning. When followed by what one hopes for, the subjunctive is used (**que** is optional): **¡Ojalá (que) se ponga moreno!** *Hopefully he'll get a tan!*

⑦ The main meaning of **moreno/a** is *brown, dark, dark-haired.* **Es rubio pero de piel morena.** *He's blond, but dark-skinned* (**la piel** *skin*).

In many popular songs, '**morena**' means a young woman. Also, **moreno/a** can mean *suntanned. To tan* (**broncear** 'to bronze') is usually expressed by **ponerse moreno** *to get a tan.*

6 – Por **cier**to ⑧, **A**sun ⑨, ¿qué fue de a**quel** e**mir,** rey del pe**tró**leo,
7 con quien li**gas**te ⑩ el ve**ra**no pa**sa**do?
8 – ¡**Chi**ca ⑪, no me **ha**bles! ¿Qué **quie**res que te **di**ga?
9 Lo encon**tré** **me**ses des**pués** en la **ca**lle;
10 por casuali**dad**, ¡a la en**tra**da del Li**ce**o ⑫!
11 – ¿Y qué ha**cí**a a**llí**?
12 – Ven**dí**a cas**ta**ñas a**sa**das ⑬ y palo**mi**tas de ma**íz**.

Notes

⑧ The adjective **cierto/a** means *certain*: **ciertas personas** *certain people*. The adverb **cierto** means *certainly*, *true*, but the set phrase **por cierto** means *by the way*.

⑨ **Asun** is short for **Asunción** *Assumption*, a first name that has no English equivalent. Find out more about names at the end of the lesson.

⑩ **ligar** *to tie, join, connect*. **ligar con alguien** is a colloquialism meaning *to pick up someone, to get off with someone*.

⑪ This exclamation is used among young women, and takes on different shades of meaning, either positive or negative, depending on the context and the tone of voice. Like **¡Hombre!** or **¡Mujer!** (lesson 16), it can express surprise, delight, exasperation, etc.

* * *

Ejercicio 1: Traduzca

❶ ¿Has cogido una toalla para la piscina? ❷ ¿Puedes poner las servilletas en la mesa? ❸ Hoy no hace demasiado viento. ❹ Ha vuelto muy morena de vacaciones. ❺ ¡Qué quiere que le diga?

6 – By the way, Asun, what happened with *(what was of)* that emir, the oil king,
7 that you picked up *(with whom you connected)* last summer?
8 – Oh, don't [even] talk to me [about it]! What do you want me to *(that I)* tell you?
9 I bumped into him months later *(afterwards)* in the street;
10 by chance, at the entrance to the Liceo!
11 – And what was he doing there?
12 – He was selling roasted chestnuts and popcorn.

⑫ **El Gran Teatro del Liceo** (**Gran Téatre del Liceu** in Catalan) is the Barcelona opera house, located on the famous Las Ramblas. It is one of the most renowned operas in Europe.

⑬ **castaña** *chestnut*; **castañas asadas** *roasted chestnuts*.
asar *to roast*, *grill*; **carne asada** *grilled meat* (usually beef).
asar a la plancha *to grill*, *barbecue*, *roast* (meat, fish, etc.).

Answers to Exercise 1

❶ Have you brought *(taken)* a towel for the pool? ❷ Can you put the napkins/serviettes on the table? ❸ Today it's not too windy. ❹ She has come back from [her] holidays very tanned. ❺ What do you want me to tell you?

Ejercicio 2: Complete

❶ He wasn't careful, and his back has been sunburned *(he has burned the back).*

No ha tenido . . . . se ha . . . .

❷ By the way, I haven't seen your brother for awhile *(it makes a period that I not see to your[informal] brother).*

. . . ., ... una temporada . . . . hermano.

❸ Three months ago.

. . . .

❹ This ointment is very good, you *(informal)* can put it on her.

. . . . muy buena, ... ponérsela.

❺ It's nice [weather], but it's windy.

. . . ., ... hace . . . .

63 Lección sesenta y tres

Repaso

1 The preterite

1.1 Usage

In Spanish, when the action takes place within a period of time that has fully elapsed at the time of speaking, the preterite tense is used:
El martes fui al museo. *On Tuesday I went to the museum.*

But when referring to an action that took place within a time period that includes the moment of speaking, the present perfect is used:
Esta semana he ido al museo. *This week I went to the museum.*

Answers to Exercise 2
❶ – cuidado y – quemado la espalda ❷ Por cierto, hace – que no veo a tu – ❸ Hace tres meses ❹ Esta pomada es – puedes – ❺ Hace bueno, pero – viento

Until fairly recently, first names given to children were often of religious origin because of Spain's strong Catholic tradition. Biblical or saints' names were typical, and girls were often named after virgins revered by the Catholic Church. Thus you find some women's names that are rather surprising if you think about their literal meaning. For example: **Dolores** *(pains),* **Natividad** *(nativity),* **Inmaculada** *(immaculate),* **Remedios** *(remedies),* **Angustias** *(anguish),* **Amparo** *(protection),* **Pilar** *(pillar) and* **Soledad** *(solitude), whose radiant diminutive is* **Sol** *(sun)! These first names were often used in some combination with* **María** *(Mary), but are far less frequent now than they used to be.*

Second wave: 13th lesson

Lesson sixty-three 63

1.2 Formation

The preterite tense of regular verbs is formed by adding the following endings to the stem of the infinitive:

• **-ar** verbs, such as **hablar** *to speak*:

habl → é	*I spoke*
habl → aste	*you* (informal sing.) *spoke*
habl → ó	*he/she/you* (formal sing.) *spoke*
habl → amos	*we spoke*
habl → asteis	*you* (informal pl.) *spoke*
habl → aron	*they/you* (formal pl.) *spoke*

63 • **-er** and **-ir** verbs, such as **comer** *to eat*, and **vivir** *to live*:

com → í *(I ate)*	**viv → í** *(I lived)*
com → iste	**viv → iste**
com → ió	**viv → ió**
com → imos	**viv → imos**
com → isteis	**viv → isteis**
com → ieron	**viv → ieron**

The written accent is important, and when speaking be sure to stress the syllable that bears it or you will be misunderstood:
Hablo bien. *I speak well.*
Habló bien. *He/she/you* (formal) *spoke well.*

Note: In parts of Spain, and in many Latin American countries, the preterite is generally used rather than the present perfect.

2 Irregular preterite forms

There are a lot of these, but you'll only need to use about 20 of them frequently. It's a good idea to note them down and memorize them whenever they appear in the lessons. We'll point them out so you don't miss them.

A helpful hint: even for irregular forms, it is usually easy to recognize a preterite because the endings never vary (apart from the fact that the first- and third-person singular endings of irregular preterites do not take a written accent).

Here are some irregular preterites that we've seen already:
Ayer tuve (tener) una reunión. *Yesterday I had a meeting.*
La semana pasada fui (ir) al cine. *Last week I went to the cinema.*
En julio hizo (hacer) muy bueno. *In July it was very nice.*
Sintió (sentir) no haber podido venir.
He/she was sorry not to have been able to come.
Le di (dar) las gracias por su ayuda.
I thanked him/her for his/her help.
Mi hermano me dijo (decir) que le gustaría ir de acampada.
My brother told me that he would like to go camping.

3 'Only' and 'not anymore'

• The concept of *only* can be expressed in different ways:

sólo … → **Sólo tengo una hora.** *I have only an hour.*
no … más que → **No tengo más que una hora.** *I have no more than an hour.*
no … sino → **No tengo sino una hora.** *I have but an hour.*

ya (*already*) is often added to such constructions:
ya sólo …
ya no … más que
ya no … sino

For example, all of the below mean:
There are only ten minutes left before the arrival of the train.
Ya sólo quedan diez minutos para la llegada del tren.
Ya no quedan más que diez minutos para la llegada del tren.
Ya no quedan sino diez minutos para la llegada del tren.

• The concept of *not anymore* is also constructed with **ya**, which in some contexts translates better in English as *now*, although the meaning is the same as *anymore*:
ya no … (before the verb)
no … ya (verb in the middle)
ya no … más (**más** after verb)

Examples:
Ya no vendrá./No vendrá ya. → *He/she won't come now.* or *He/she won't come anymore.*
Ya no fumaré más. → *I won't smoke anymore.*

4 Possessives

4.1 Adjectives

• **Possessive adjectives that precede the noun**
These were introduced in detail in lesson 28. Here's a recap: **mi** *my*; **tu** *your* (informal sing.); **su** *his/her/its/your* (formal)/*their*; **nuestro** *our*; **vuestro** *your* (informal pl.).

63 These forms always come before a singular noun:
mi hijo *my son*; **tu cuñada** *your sister-in-law*; **nuestro barrio** *our neighbourhood*, etc.

If the object possessed is plural, an **s** is added: **mis hijos** *my children.* And **nuestro** and **vuestro** also show the gender of the object possessed: **nuestra casa** *our house*, **nuestras casas** *our houses.*

Remember too that **su(s)** can be tricky because it can mean *his, her, its, their* or *your* (formal):
su pelo *his/her/its/their/your* (formal) *hair.*

You can add the preposition **de** + personal pronoun to clarify if the context is not clear:
su pelo de él *his hair*
su pelo de ella *her hair*, etc.

• **Possessive adjectives, emphatic form**

mío, -a, -os, -as: *of mine*
tuyo, -a, -os, -as: *of yours* (informal sing.)
nuestro, -a, -os, -as: *of ours*
vuestro, -a, -os, -as: *of yours* (informal pl.)
suyo, -a, -os, -as: *of his, hers, yours* (formal), *theirs*

These are always placed after the noun and are used less frequently.
• they can express affection: **hija mía** *my daughter*
• they can be used to clarify: **el hijo mío** *my son* (as opposed to someone else's)
• they can begin a formal letter: **Muy señor mío / Muy señores míos** *Dear Sir(s)*
• they can translate the English constructions *of mine*, etc.: **un amigo mío** *a friend of mine.*

Often it's more natural in English to use the possessive adjectives *my, your, his, her*, etc.
¿Te acuerdas de Cristina? Pues la niña que está junto al tobogán es hermana suya. *Do you remember Cristina? Well, the girl next to the slide is her sister* (a sister of hers).

The possessive pronoun takes exactly the same form as the emphatic possessive adjective (**mío, tuyo, suyo,** etc.), but is preceded by the definite article:
el mío, la mía, los míos, las mías: *mine*
el tuyo, la tuya, etc.: *yours* (informal sing.)
el suyo, la suya, etc.: *his*, *hers*, *yours* (formal), *theirs*
el nuestro, la nuestra, etc.: *ours*
el vuestro, la vuestra, etc.: *yours* (informal plural)
¡Estupendo, aquí están los billetes! Éste es el mío, está a mi nombre; y este otro es el tuyo. *Great, here are the tickets! This is mine, it's in my name; and this other [one] is yours.*

5 Irregular verbs

Rather than going into detail about irregular verbs here, we suggest that you consult the conjugation tables in the grammatical appendix when you come across new verbs that don't seem to follow the regular pattern. As you've progressed, you've been assimilating the regular verb forms for a number of tenses and persons – and you'll be surprised how many irregular forms you've also picked up. But when in doubt, just check out the tables at the back of the book. The more you start to recognize patterns, the easier it will be to spot and get used to the exceptions!

The tables in the appendix list the verbs in different categories:
• the 3 regular conjugations: **-ar**, **-er** and **-ir**
• the key irregular verbs **haber**, **tener**, **ser** and **estar**
• 12 irregular verb groups
• 20 or so common verbs that are uniquely irregular and cannot be neatly categorized.

¡Caminante! You've come a long way!

1 – Ayer me encontré con Daniel en la playa.
2 Me dijo que llevaba tres meses sin trabajo.
3 – ¿Y que hacía en la playa?
4 Además… ¡con el frío que hacía ayer!
5 – Buscar trabajo.
6 – ¡No me digas! ¿En la playa?
7 – Él dice que es el lugar ideal para concentrarse.
8 – No cabe duda, ¡cada uno a su manera!
9 Y… ¿qué le gustaría hacer?
10 – Ser director de una gran empresa.

64 Lección sesenta y cuatro

Una buena acción

1 – Con **e**sa **ca**ra que **po**nes ①…

Notes

① **poner cara de** *to make/pull a face*, *to look like.*
poner cara de entierro *to look gloomy* (literally, 'to put on face of funeral').

Traducción

1 Yesterday I bumped into Daniel at the beach. **2** He told me that he had been without a job for three months. **3** And what was he doing at the beach? **4** Particularly *(Moreover)* since it was so cold yesterday! **5** Looking for work. **6** Really! At the beach? **7** He says that it's the ideal place for concentrating. **8** No doubt about it, to each his own *(each one in their way)*! **9** And what would he like to do? **10** Be [the] managing director of a big company.

Second wave: 14th lesson

Lesson sixty-four 64

A good deed

1 – By your face *(With that face that you put)*…

2 me da que ② **vie**nes a pe**dir**me ③ **al**go; ¿a que sí?

3 – Sí, ma**má**, ¿po**drí**as ④ **dar**me dos **eu**ros?

4 – ¿Y qué has **he**cho con los que te di a**yer**?

5 – Se los di a un **po**bre **hom**bre.

6 – Es**tá** bien, **hi**jo. **Tie**nes buen cora**zón**.

7 **To**ma, a**quí tie**nes tres **eu**ros.

8 ¿Y qué te empu**jó** ⑤ a ser tan gene**ro**so?

9 – Fue, ma**má**, **co**mo **u**na atrac**ción** ⑥ a la que no **pu**de resis**tir**;

10 **co**mo **u**na es**pe**cie de fle**cha**zo ⑦.

Notes

② **me da que** is a colloquial expression that introduces a supposition, hunch, etc. Depending on the context, it can be translated as *I feel that* (**siento que**), *I have the impression that* (**tengo la impresión de que**), *I believe/think that* (**creo que**) or *it seems to me that* (**me parece que**). It is used in the third-person in the same way as **gustar**.

Me da que estás cansado. *You seem tired to me.*
Me da que va a llover. *I believe it's going to rain.*

③ **pedir** *to request, ask for, order* (in a restaurant) is not to be confused with **preguntar** *to ask* in the sense of *to ask a question*. **pedir** is a stem-changing verb (**e** → **i**). The stem vowel changes in the present tense in all persons except **nosotros** and **vosotros**, and it also takes the same stem change in the preterite (third-person only). So: **pedir** → **pido** *I request, ask for, order*; **pidió** *he/she requested*; **pidieron** *they requested*.

④ **poder** *to be able to* ('can') is an irregular verb whose forms you'll quickly learn because of its frequent use. **podrías** *you could, you would be able to* (informal sing.) is the conditional. In line 9, we see the irregular first-person preterite form of ▸

2 I can tell that you['ve] come to ask me for something, right?
3 – Yes, Mummy, could you give me two euros?
4 – And what have you done with what *(those that)* I gave you yesterday?
5 – I gave it *(To-him them I gave)* to a poor man.
6 – That's good, son. You have a good heart.
7 Take [this], here's three euros.
8 And what prompted you to be so generous?
9 – It was *(Mummy)* like an attraction *(to the which)* I couldn't resist;
10 like a sort of thunderbolt *(arrow-strike)*.

▸ **poder**, which is **pude** *I was able to*, *I could.* As with all the most commonly used irregular preterites, stress falls on the next-to-last syllable and there is no written accent.

It is important to bear in mind that irregular verbs are not necessarily irregular in all tenses. This is good news! Many irregular verbs are used frequently in daily conversation, so you'll soon pick them up.

⑤ **empujó** *it propelled*, *it pushed*, from **empujar** *to push*, *to shove.* Another preterite! The accent on the last syllable is typical of all regular preterites in the first- and third-person singular forms.

⑥ **atracción** *attraction*, from **atraer** *to attract*, *to be appealing*: **sentir atracción por alguien** *to feel attracted to someone.* It is also used in **parque de atracciones** *amusement park.*

⑦ In lesson 54, we noted that the augmentative suffix **-azo** often expresses the idea of force or a blow. Here is a rather special case: **flechazo** *a strike from an arrow* (**una flecha**) can also mean *thunderbolt* or *lightning strike*! The phrase **como un flechazo** might suggest the English *smitten*, as in by Cupid's arrow: **Fue un flechazo.** *It was love at first sight.*

11 – ¡**Hi**jo! ¿Y **dón**de encon**tras**te a **e**se **po**bre **hom**bre?

12 – En la **ca**lle, ven**dí**a cara**me**los ⑧. □

Notes

⑧ False cognate warning! **Los caramelos** are *sweets*, *candies*; the word for *caramel* is **caramelo** (singular). Note that **un** ▸

* * *

Ejercicio 1: Traduzca

❶ ¿Has visto qué cara ha puesto su padre? ❷ ¿Qué te ha preguntado? ❸ ¿Podrías darme su dirección de correo electrónico? ❹ ¿Qué has hecho esta tarde? ❺ Tiene muy buen corazón, es muy generosa.

* * *

Ejercicio 2: Complete

❶ I believe it's going to be cold.
. . . . va a hacer . . . . .

❷ Your plan appeals to me greatly.
Tu . . . . mucho.

❸ By the way, what was he selling?
. . . . , ¿qué . . . . . . ?

❹ I couldn't resist.
. . . .

❺ I'm asking you for a favour.
Te . . . . un . . . . . .

11 – Son! And where did you find this poor man?

12 – In the street – he was selling sweets!

▸ **bombón** is *a chocolate* (plural, **bombones**), while the generic word for *chocolate* is **chocolate** *[cho-ko-**lah**-tay]*: **chocolate caliente** *cocoa* (the drink), *hot chocolate*.

* * *

Answers to Exercise 1

❶ Did you see the face his/her father pulled? ❷ What did he/she ask you? ❸ Could you give me his/her e-mail address? ❹ What did you do this afternoon? ❺ She has a big *(very good)* heart; she's very generous.

* * *

Answers to Exercise 2

❶ Me da que – frío ❷ – proyecto me atrae – ❸ Por cierto – vendía ❹ No pude resistir ❺ – pido – favor

Second wave: 15th lesson

65 Lección sesenta y cinco

El chico del chiringuito

1 En la **a**re**na** ya no **que**da **hue**lla ① al**gu**na
2 del a**le**gre corre**te**ar ② de los **ni**ños,
3 ni de las **i**das y ve**ni**das
4 de **to**dos a**que**llos que a**yer** pa**sa**ron un **dí**a de **pla**ya.
5 De madru**ga**da ③, los **hom**bres y las **má**quinas del ayunta**mien**to
6 han cum**pli**do su come**ti**do.
7 Las tum**bo**nas, a**zu**les y ama**ri**llas,
8 tam**bién** des**can**san api**la**das por pe**que**ños **gru**pos a**quí** y a**llá**.

Notes

① **huella** *trace, track, imprint.*
En la nieve se veían las huellas de los esquís. *In the snow, the tracks of the skis could be seen.* ('In the snow were seen the tracks of the skis.') Remember that Spanish often uses a reflexive verb where the passive voice would be used in English: **ver** *to see*, **verse** *to be seen.*
las huellas digitales or **dactilares** *fingerprints.*

② **corretear** (from **correr**) is a colloquial verb that means *to run around, to scamper to and fro*, like children playing.

③ **de madrugada** *at daybreak, at dawn* (**al alba**).
Tenemos que hacer muchos kilómetros, saldremos de madrugada (or **temprano/pronto**). *We have to cover a lot of kilometers; we'll leave at daybreak* (or *early*).

Lesson sixty-five 65

The boy at the 'chiringuito'

1 In the sand no trace remains
2 of where happy children ran *(of the happy scampering of the children)*,
3 nor of the comings and goings *(goings and comings)*
4 of all those who yesterday spent a day at the beach.
5 At daybreak, the men and machines from the town council
6 completed their mission.
7 The deck chairs, blue and yellow,
8 are also resting, stacked up in little piles *(groups)* here and there.

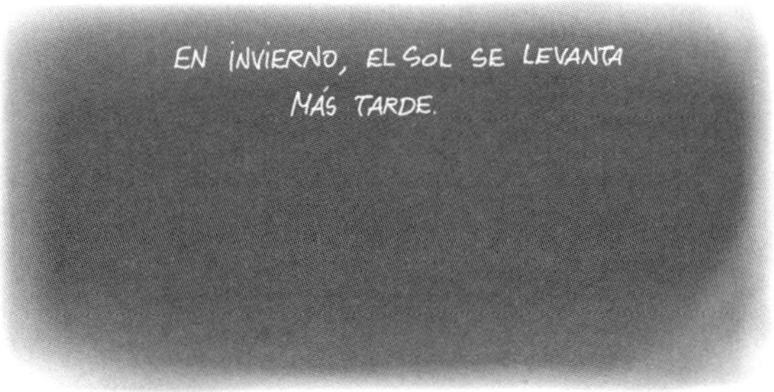
EN INVIERNO, EL SOL SE LEVANTA
MÁS TARDE.

▸ **Me he levantado temprano.** *I got up early.*
Note also the (regular!) verb **madrugar** *to get up early.*
Hoy he madrugado. *Today I got up early.*

9 El sol se le**van**ta y, en ④ la **pun**ta ex**tre**ma del male**cón**,

10 un viejecito con vi**se**ra

11 **so**bre el que revolo**te**a un pu**ña**do de gav**io**tas,

12 **lan**za a lo **le**jos el se**dal**.

13 El **rui**do de las **o**las pa**re**ce acer**car**se: la ma**re**a es**tá** su**bien**do.

14 Y no **le**jos del **ban**co en el que ⑤ me he sen**ta**do a le**er** el pe**rió**dico,

15 **mien**tras dis**po**ne dos me**si**tas y **cua**tro **si**llas bambole**an**tes,

16 silbo**te**a a**ho**ra el **chi**co ⑥ del chirin**gui**to. ⑦ □

Notes

④ Preposition reminder: if the verb describes where something or someone is or what is happening there, **en** is often used:
Estamos en la playa. *We are at the beach.*
Mi hijo está en su habitación. *My son is in his room.*
Está jugando en el suelo. *He/she is playing on the floor.*

⑤ When *where* simply expresses the idea of place without indicating movement, it can be translated as **en donde**, **donde**, **en que** or **en el que**, **en la que**, etc. Thus, *not far from the bench where I sat down* could be: **no lejos del banco en donde me he sentado / donde me he sentado / en que me he sentado** or **en el que me he sentado.** ▸

* * *

Ejercicio 1: Traduzca

❶ Los niños han ido a jugar con la arena. ❷ Ponte la visera, hace demasiado sol. ❸ Hoy hay muchas olas. ❹ En invierno, el sol se levanta más tarde. ❺ El viejecito descansa en una tumbona.

9 The sun rises and, at the furthest end *(point extreme)* of the jetty,
10 a little old man with [a] peaked cap,
11 above whom *(over the which)* flutters a handful of seagulls,
12 casts afar his *(the)* fishing line.
13 The sound of the waves seems to draw near *(approach)*: the tide is rising.
14 And not far from the bench where *(on the which)* I have sat down to read the newspaper,
15 while setting up *(while he sets up)* two small tables and four rickety chairs,
16 the boy at the 'chiringuito' whistles [without a care] *(whistles now the boy of the chiringuito)*.

⑥ **chico**, as we saw in lesson 46, can be used for someone who is not necessarily a child. For example, a young man who is a *messenger* is a **chico (de los recados)**.

⑦ Here the rather unusual word order is a stylistic choice for this lyrical text. In ordinary speech it would be more common to say: **y no lejos del banco en el que me he sentado a leer el periódico, el chico del chiringuito silbotea mientras dispone dos mesitas …**

* * *

Answers to Exercise 1

❶ The children went to play in *(with)* the sand. ❷ Put on your cap, there's too much sun. ❸ Today there are a lot of waves. ❹ In winter, the sun rises later. ❺ The little old man is resting in a deck chair.

Ejercicio 2: Complete

❶ Tomorrow I have to get up early.

. . . . . . tengo que . . . .

❷ In the city where *(in that)* I was born, there is a big beach.

. . . . nací, ...
. . . . . .

❸ I have the impression that the tide is beginning to come in *(to rise)*.

. . da . . . . empieza . . . .

❹ I [can]not hear you *(informal)*, there's too much noise.

. . . ., ...

❺ We sat down on a bench and rested.

. . . hemos . . . . y . . . . .
. . . .

---

66 Lección sesenta y seis

Petición de mano ①

1 – ¡Pa**pá**, ma**má**! ¡No os po**déis** imagi**nar** lo fe**liz** que soy ②!

2 Fer**nan**do me ha pe**di**do que me **ca**se ③ con él.

Notes

① **petición de mano** ('request of hand') *asking for someone's hand in marriage.* **petición** *petition, request*; **a petición de** *at the request of*; **a petición del interesado** *at the request of the interested party.*

② Reminder: **lo que** usually translates as *what*, in the sense of *that which.* **Mira lo que he comprado.** *Look what I have bought.* But: **lo … que** with an adjective or adverb in between is ▸

Answers to Exercise 2

❶ Mañana – madrugar ❷ En la ciudad en que – hay una gran playa ❸ Me – que la marea – a subir ❹ No te oigo, hay demasiado ruido ❺ Nos – sentado en un banco – hemos descansado

Un chiringuito *is a kind of open-air refreshment stand, especially at the beach. Usually it is operated seasonally. There are all kinds of* **chiringuitos**, *from very basic to quite sophisticated. Some sell only* **helados** ice creams, **golosinas** sweets *and a few* **refrescos** cold drinks, *while others offer a few tapas,* **bebidas alcohólicas** alcoholic beverages *and more substantial meals. If you spend a few days at the beach in Spain, sit down at a* **chiringuito** *and enjoy an al fresco platter of fried fish washed down with* **una bebida fresca**!

Second wave: 16th lesson

Lesson sixty-six 66

A marriage proposal

1 – Dad, Mum! You can't imagine how happy I am *(the happy that I am)*!

2 Fernando has asked me to marry him *(that I marry with him)*.

translated by *how*. **¡No sabes lo contento que estoy!** *You don't know how happy I am!*

③ Reminder: in Spanish, a request is followed by a separate clause, if there is a change of subject, introduced by **que** + subjunctive. In English, there is usually just one clause in this context, with the second verb an infinitive.
Me pide <u>que</u> (me) <u>vaya</u> con él. ('He is asking me that I go with him.') *He is asking me to go with him.*

3 – **Bue**no, **bue**no… De **mo**do que ④ Fer**nan**do **quie**re ca**sar**se con**ti**go ⑤, ¿eh?
4 – Sí, a**sí** es, pa**pá**; me **quie**re.
5 – Es**tá** bien; **pe**ro me ima**gi**no ⑥ que **an**tes ha**brá** pen**sa**do en la responsabili**dad** que **e**so con**lle**va;
6 y, por su**pues**to, su**pon**go ⑦ que **go**za de **u**na **bue**na situa**ción**
7 y dis**po**ne de los **me**dios sufi**cien**tes **pa**ra mante**ner** ⑧ a **u**na fa**mi**lia.
8 – ¡Pues **cla**ro! Lo pri**me**ro ⑨ que me ha pregun**ta**do es **cuán**to ga**na**bas. □

Notes

④ The expression **de modo que** *so, so that* can be replaced by **de manera que, así pues, así que** or **conque**:
Esta tarde cerramos, de modo que no venga.
This afternoon we're closed, so don't come. (present subj.)
Te he avisado, así que ahora no te quejes.
I warned you, so now don't complain. (present subj.)

⑤ When they follow the preposition **con** *with*, the prepositional pronouns **mí** *me*, **ti** *you* (informal sing.), **sí** *himself, herself, itself, oneself, yourself* (formal sing.), *themselves, yourselves* become **conmigo** *with me*, **contigo** *with you* and **consigo** *with himself, herself*, etc.
¿Quieres venir conmigo? *Do you want to come with me?*
¿Está contigo? *Is he/she with you?*

⑥ **me imagino que**, with the pronoun **me**, is more colloquial than **imagino que** *I imagine that*. Apart from making the tone more familiar, **me** makes the phrase more emphatic.

⑦ Composite verbs (that is, verbs composed of a stem plus a prepositional prefix that modifies the meaning), apart from one or two very specific exceptions, conjugate like the stem verb. In this lesson: **con<u>llevar</u>** (line 5), **su<u>poner</u>** (line 6), **dis<u>poner</u>** and **man<u>tener</u>** (line 7). ▸

3 – Well, well … So Fernando wants to marry *(with)* you, huh?
4 – Yes, that's right *(so it is)*, Dad; he loves me.
5 – That's fine, but I imagine that first *(before)* he will have thought about the responsibility which that involves;
6 and, of course, I suppose that he has *(enjoys of)* a good [financial] situation
7 and has *(has-at-his-disposal)* sufficient means to support a family.
8 – Well, of course! The first thing he asked me is how much you earn *(earned)*.

⑧ **mantener** *to maintain*, *to support*, *to keep*, but also *to hold*: **mantener una opinión** *to hold an opinion*; **mantener una conversación** *to hold a conversation*. And an expression: **mantenerse en sus trece** (literally, 'to maintain oneself in one's thirteen') *to stick to one's guns*, *to dig in one's heels*, *to stand one's ground*, etc.

⑨ Don't confuse **lo primero** *the first thing* and **el primer(o)/la primera/los primeros/las primeras** *the first one(s)*.
lo primero que hay que hacer *the first thing there is to do*
el primero en llegar *the first (one) to arrive* (m.)
los primeros días del mes *the first days of the month*.
Note that **el/los, la/las** must agree with the gender and number of the noun they refer to, whereas **lo** is neuter.
La primera clase es a las nueve. La segunda es a las diez. *The first class is at nine o'clock. The second is at ten.*

Ejercicio 1: Traduzca

❶ Se casarán dentro de tres meses. ❷ ¡No sabes lo contentos que están! ❸ Me pide que vaya a su despacho cuanto antes. ❹ ¿De qué medios dispones? ❺ Trabaja con niños, tiene muchas responsabilidades.

* * *

Ejercicio 2: Complete

❶ The parents met at [the] request of the headmaster/principal *(director of the school).*

. . . . se reunieron* . . . . del . . . . del colegio.

❷ We have *(enjoy)* a good [financial] situation.

. . . . de una . . . .

❸ I imagine that he will come to see us today.

. . . . que pasará . . . .

* **reunirse** *to meet, gather*

67 Lección sesenta y siete

La víspera del día de Reyes

1 **Hace** un **frí**o que **pe**la ①, **pe**ro no im**por**ta ②;

Notes

① **hace un frío que pela** (literally, 'it makes a cold that peels', as in the skin!): *It's absolutely freezing.*

② **no importa** (lesson 52) is a very common expression that can be used to play something down, excuse someone from ▸

Answers to Exercise 1
❶ They will get married in three months. ❷ You don't know how happy they are! ❸ He/she's asking me to go to his/her office as soon as possible. ❹ What means do you have available? ❺ He/she works with children [and] has a lot of responsibilities.

* * *

❹ It's raining and it's very windy, so I won't take the car.
Llueve . ..., ... no cogeré el coche.

❺ He's sticking to his guns!
Se ....

Answers to Exercise 2
❶ Los padres – a petición – director – ❷ Gozamos – buena situación ❸ Me imagino – a vernos hoy ❹ – y hace mucho viento, así que – ❺ – mantiene en sus trece

Second wave: 17th lesson

Lesson sixty-seven 67

The eve of Epiphany *(day of Kings)*

1 It's bitterly cold, but no matter;

▸ responsibility or express indifference when faced with a choice. So it can mean: *It doesn't matter*, *It's not important*, *Never mind*, or even *So what? Who cares?* You can also say: **No me importa.** *I don't care. It doesn't matter to me.*

2 **u**nos y **o**tros se **po**nen ③ el a**bri**go y la bu**fan**da;
3 y… ¡**rá**pido, **to**do el **mun**do a la **ca**lle!
4 Los **ni**ños los pri**me**ros.
5 **Des**de que ④ se han levan**ta**do, no **pa**ran **quie**tos ⑤:
6 ma**ña**na **lle**gan los **Re**yes **Ma**gos.
7 – ¡**Va**mos, pa**pá**! ¡**A**le, ma**má**, que ⑥ no **va**mos a lle**gar**!
8 En la **Pla**za Ma**yor** ⑦, **tér**mino del reco**rri**do de la cabal**ga**ta ⑧
9 **to**do es agita**ción**, alga**za**ra, febrili**dad**.

Notes

③ **poner** *to put*, *to place*; **ponerse** (reflexive) *to put on* (clothes). **Me pongo el abrigo/la chaqueta.** *I put on my coat/jacket.* Note that Spanish uses a definite article rather than a possessive adjective in this context.

④ **desde** *from*, *since* is a preposition used in reference to time: **desde entonces** *since then.* In the construction **desde que**, it must be followed by a verb: **desde que se casó** *[ever] since he got married.*

⑤ **parar** *to stop*, *stay*; **no parar quieto** *to not stay still*, *to fidget.* **¡Párate quieto!** *Stay still! Don't move!* (Or more commonly, **¡No te muevas!** from the reflexive verb **moverse** *to move.*)

⑥ After a command, the conjunction **que** is often used to introduce an explanation. This **que** has the meaning of **porque** *because.* In English, this is usually understood rather than explicitly expressed. **Vamos, niños, que se hace tarde.** *Come on, kids – it's getting late.*

⑦ Almost every town and village has its **Plaza Mayor** *main square*, the hub around which the rest of the town developed over the centuries. Formerly (and often still today), the life of the town centred on the **Plaza Mayor**, where the town hall, church, shops and cafés were located, and the daily market was ▸

2 all don *(put on)* a *(the)* coat and scarf;
3 and … in a flash *(rapidly)*, everyone [goes out] into the street!
4 The children *(the)* first.
5 Since getting out of bed *(From that they got up)*, they [can]not stay still:
6 tomorrow the Three Wise Men *(Kings Magi)* [will] arrive.
7 – Let's go, Dad! Come on, Mum – *(that)* we're not going to arrive [on time]!
8 On the Plaza Mayor, [the] end of the parade route,
9 all is excitement, hullabaloo, feverish anticipation *(feverishness)*.

held. In big cities, **las plazas mayores** today are surrounded by a maze of narrow streets that make up the old quarter, or historic district.

⑧ **una cabalgata** is a *parade* or *cavalcade* (from **cabalgar** *to ride on horseback*), complete with floats, dancers, music and a festive atmosphere. In Spain, most towns celebrate Epiphany with **la cabalgata de los Reyes Magos** on the evening of 5 January (see the note at the end of the lesson). The word **desfile** *march, procession*, is used for more solemn occasions, such as **un desfile militar** *a military parade*.

10 La llegada de los camellos cargados de regalos
11 y los saludos de Melchor, Gaspar y Baltasar desde sus carrozas
12 desatan el entusiasmo de grandes y pequeños.
13 – ¿Crees que me traerán todo lo que les he pedido ⑨?
14 No sé, hijo; pero… no se olvidarán de ti.
15 Unos fuegos artificiales cierran la fiesta en las calles
16 y abren un paréntesis de larga espera.
17 Es hora de volver a casa e ⑩ ir a dormir …
18 ¡los Reyes nos harán madrugar! □

Notes

⑨ In Spain, children write to **los Reyes Magos** at Epiphany, rather than (or as well as) to *Father Christmas* **Papá Noel** (these days, they often get presents from both!). In **la carta** *the letter*, they **piden regalos** *ask for presents*, and then the Three Wise Men (Magi) **los traen** *bring them* – or not! ▸

* * *

Ejercicio 1: Traduzca

❶ Ponte el abrigo, nos vamos. ❷ No he comido nada desde que me he levantado. ❸ Esta noche iremos a ver los fuegos artificiales. ❹ ¿Mañana vas a madrugar? ❺ No creo que lleguemos a tiempo.

10 The arrival of the camels loaded with gifts
11 and the greetings of Melchior, Gaspar and Balthazar from their floats
12 unleash the enthusiasm of old and young [alike].
13 – Do you think *(that)* they'll bring me everything *(that)* I asked *(them)* for?
14 I don't know, son; but … they won't forget about *(of)* you.
15 Fireworks bring to an end *(Some fires artificial close)* the fiesta in the streets
16 and mark the beginning of a *(and open an interval of)* long wait.
17 It's time *(hour)* to return home and go to sleep
18 … the Kings will make us get up early!

▸ ⑩ **y** *and* becomes **e** before a word beginning with **i** or **hi** (unless **hi** is followed by a vowel):
bueno e inteligente *good and intelligent*
dátiles e higos *dates and figs*
But: **nieve y hielo** *snow and ice.*

* * *

Answers to Exercise 1

❶ Put on your coat, we're going. ❷ I haven't eaten anything since I got up. ❸ This evening we'll go to see the fireworks. ❹ Tomorrow are you going to get up early? ❺ I don't think that we'll arrive in time.

Ejercicio 2: Complete

❶ Pedro and Isabel will return in a few days.
Pedro . Isabel . . . .

❷ I will never forget you *(informal)*.
. . . .

❸ Don't worry, it doesn't matter.
. . . . preocupes, ...

❹ You can't imagine everything *(all that which)* the kids have asked for.
. . te . . . . los niños
. . . .

❺ We're meeting *(We have date)* at the main square.
. . . . la . . . . . Mayor.

Second wave: 18th lesson

68 Lección sesenta y ocho

Tres cubiertos ①

1 – ¿Han ele**gi**do ya?
2 – Sí, la **ni**ña toma**rá** un **pla**to combi**na**do, el **nú**mero **cin**co;

Notes

① **cubierto** is the irregular past participle of **cubrir** *to cover*, as in **La montaña se ha cubierto de nieve.** *The mountain has become covered in snow.* But **cubierto** has a number of other meanings. As an adjective, it can mean *cloudy*: **un cielo cubierto** *an overcast sky*. As a noun, it can refer to a *place* ▸

Answers to Exercise 2

❶ – e – volverán dentro de unos días ❷ No te olvidaré nunca ❸ No te – no importa ❹ No – puedes imaginar todo lo que – han pedido ❺ Tenemos cita en – Plaza –

January 6, Epiphany, is also known in Spain as **el día de los Reyes (Magos)** *'the Day of the Magi', who we know better as the Three Kings or Wise Men. This day commemorates the visit of the Magi to Baby Jesus, to whom they gave offerings of gold, frankincense and myrrh.*

Over the course of time, it became traditional in Spain to offer **regalos** gifts *to loved ones on this day; in particular to children. Thus, the eve of Epiphany has become fixed in Spanish children's imaginations as a magical night, when* **Melchor, Gaspar** *and* **Baltasar** *steal into each house to leave the long-awaited presents to be discovered early in the morning of January 6. A special ring-shaped cake,* **el roscón de Reyes**, *made from sweet bread dough and candied fruit, is baked during this period.*

Epiphany is also a public holiday, and marks the end of the Christmas *(***Navidad***) holidays; children normally have to go back to school between 7–10 January.*

Lesson sixty-eight 68

A table of three
(Three covers)

1 – Have you already chosen?
2 – Yes, she *(the girl)* will have *(take)* a combination plate, number 5;

setting (**el plato** *plate*; **el vaso** *glass*; **la servilleta** *serviette, napkin*; **la cuchara** *the spoon*; **la cucharilla** *the coffee spoon*; etc.), or, in the plural, **los cubiertos** *cutlery*. By extension, it can also refer to the price per person or a fixed-price meal at a restaurant. Note that *to lay/set the table* is **poner la mesa** (see line 12).

3 y **trái**gale tam**bién** una bote**lli**ta de **a**gua ② mine**ral** ③, por fa**vor**.
4 **Pa**ra mi **hi**jo, el me**nú** del **día** ④.
5 Yo toma**ré** una ensa**la**da y un fi**le**te ⑤ con pa**ta**tas **fri**tas.
6 – Los hay de ⑥ diez y de **tre**ce **eu**ros.
7 – ¿Y cuál me reco**mien**da ⑦ us**ted**?
8 – ¡Por su**pues**to, el de **tre**ce **eu**ros, se**ñor**!
9 – ¿Es más **gran**de?¿O qui**zá** de me**jor** cali**dad**?
10 – No, en abso**lu**to; son e**xac**tamente i**gua**les.
11 – Y en**ton**ces… ¿por qué **e**sa dife**ren**cia de **pre**cio?
12 – Es que con el de **tre**ce **eu**ros po**ne**mos …
13 un tene**dor** en condi**cio**nes ⑧ y un cu**chi**llo me**jor** afi**la**do.

Notes

② **el agua** *water* – however, **agua** is in fact feminine. Feminine nouns that begin with a stressed **a** (or **ha**) take the masculine article **el** (or **un**, **algún**, etc.) for pronunciation reasons. Other feminine nouns that follow the same rule are **el alma** *soul* and **el hacha** *axe*. If the article is contracted, the same rule applies: **tirarse al agua** *to throw oneself into the water*. **El mango del hacha es de madera.** *The handle of the axe is made of wood.* But be careful, because any adjectives accompanying the noun remain feminine: **el agua fría** *cold water*.

If the **a** (or **ha**) is not stressed, the normal article **la** is used: **la abeja** *bee*.

③ Tap water is safe to drink in Spain, but in restaurants, many prefer a bottle of **el agua mineral sin gas** *still water*, or **con gas** *fizzy*, *sparkling*. Of course, you can always just ask for **una jarra** *a jug* of tap water.

3 and also bring her a small bottle of *(mineral)* water, please.
4 For my son, today's set menu.
5 I'll have a salad and a steak with fries.
6 – There is one at *(of)* ten or at *(of)* thirteen euros.
7 – And which do you recommend *(to me)*?
8 – Naturally, the one at thirteen euros, sir!
9 – Is it bigger? Or perhaps of better quality?
10 – No, not at all; they are exactly [the] same *(equal)*.
11 – *(And)* so … why this difference in price?
12 – *(It's that)* with the one for thirteen euros we provide *(put)* …
13 a fork in [good] condition and a sharper knife *(better sharpened)*.

④ **el menú del día** *the daily special* or *set menu* generally consists of three courses: **un primero** *a first course*; **un segundo**, or **plato fuerte** *main course*, and **un postre** *a dessert*. A useful question: **¿En qué consiste el menú del día?** *What is today's set menu?*

⑤ **un filete** *fillet*: when referring to **la carne de vaca** 'meat from a cow' or *beef*, this means *steak*, whereas **filete de ternera** is *veal cutlet*.

⑥ **los hay de** *there are [x] of them* ('them there are of') is another way of saying **hay** when speaking about more than one thing.

⑦ **recomendar** *to recommend* conjugates like **pensar** *to think*, with a present-tense stem change from **e** → **ie** (see lesson 70).

⑧ **en (buenas) condiciones** *in good condition*, *proper*;
en condiciones de + infinitive *in a position to.*
Este niño tiene fiebre, no está en condiciones de ir a la escuela. *This child has a fever; he is in no condition to go to school.*

Ejercicio 1: Traduzca

❶ ¿Qué van a tomar? ❷ Perdone, todavía no hemos elegido. ❸ ¿Quieren beber algo mientras tanto? ❹ Les recomiendo la especialidad de la casa. ❺ ¡Buen provecho!

* * *

Ejercicio 2: Complete

❶ Have you *(informal sing.)* chosen already?
¿. . .   . . ?

❷ Are you *(informal sing.)* going to have wine?
¿ . . .   . ?

❸ No, not today; I have to drive *(take the car).*
. . , ... ;   . . . .

❹ What is today's set menu *(the menu of the day)*?
¿. . . .   . ?

❺ The price of the meal seems right.
. .   . . correcto.

* * *

El plato combinado combination plate *is mainly served in cafeteria-style or fast food restaurants, which are increasingly replacing* **las casas de comidas** *and other* **pequeños restaurantes***: small, usually family-owned, restaurants.*

Apart from tapas, **el plato combinado** *is often the best buy. It includes a main course and various side dishes, all on one plate. Bread, and often a beverage, is included in the price. As generally*

Answers to Exercise 1

❶ What will you have? ❷ Excuse us, we haven't chosen yet. ❸ Do you want to drink something in the meantime? ❹ I recommend *(to you[pl.])* the house speciality. ❺ Enjoy your meal!

* * *

Answers to Exercise 2

❶ Has elegido ya ❷ Vas a tomar vino ❸ No, hoy no; tengo que coger el coche ❹ Cuál es el menú del día ❺ El precio de la comida me parece –

* * *

several **platos combinados** *are offered, the name usually relates to its main ingredient (meat, eggs, fries, sausage, salad, fish or squid, for example), and each has a number to make it easier to order.*

Although **el plato combinado** *has no claim to being a gourmet dish, it's good value for money and a good option for children.*

Second wave: 19th lesson

Lección sesenta y nueve

Gusto por la fiesta

1 **Des**de la más pe**que**ña al**de**a,
2 pa**san**do ① por **ca**da **pue**blo
3 **has**ta las **gran**des capi**ta**les,
4 **to**da aglomera**ción** fes**te**ja en Es**pa**ña su **san**to pa**trón**.
5 Rome**rí**as ②, proce**sio**nes, **fe**rias,
6 reconstitu**cio**nes his**tó**ricas y **to**do **ti**po de manifesta**cio**nes fes**ti**vas
7 se orga**ni**zan ③ en **to**das **par**tes en **tor**no al **dí**a del **san**to.
8 A esas **fe**chas de **fies**tas,
9 espe**cí**ficas de **u**na locali**dad** o re**gión**,
10 se a**ña**den los pe**rí**odos o **dí**as de **fies**ta de ca**rác**ter nacio**nal**;
11 ya **se**a ④ de o**ri**gen reli**gio**so:
12 Navi**dad**, Se**ma**na **San**ta, **To**dos los **San**tos, etc.;

Notes

① **pasando** *passing*. More about the present participle (or *-ing* form) in lesson 70.
Llegaremos a tiempo cogiendo un taxi.
We will arrive on time [by] taking a taxi.

② Nowadays, **una romería** (from **romero**, the name given to pilgrims who in former times went to Rome) is *a procession* or *pilgrimage* (**una peregrinación**) to a shrine, generally followed by festivities.

A taste for fiestas

1 From the smallest village,
2 *(passing)* through each town
3 to *(until)* the major capital cities,
4 every urban area in Spain celebrates its patron saint.
5 'Romerías', processions, festivals,
6 historical reenactments and all kinds *(all type)* of festive events
7 are organized everywhere *(in all parts)* around the saint's day.
8 To these holiday dates,
9 specific to a locality or region,
10 are added the national holiday periods or days *(holidays of national character)*;
11 whether *(it be)* of religious origin:
12 Christmas, Holy Week, All Saints' Day, etc.

▸ ③ Note the use of the reflexive here and in line 10, which translates to the passive voice in English.

④ **ya sea … ya sea** (lines 11 and 13); **ya … ya**; **sea … (o) sea**; **bien … (o) bien**, etc., are translated by *whether ... or*; *on the one hand ... on the other*; or even by *either... or* **(o … o)**.
Vendrá sea* sólo, (o) sea acompañado. *He will come, whether alone or accompanied.*
* **sea** is the first- and third-person present subjunctive of **ser** *to be*, as in the more formal English 'He will come, be it alone or be it accompanied'.

13 ya **se**a en conmemora**ción** de **o**tro **ti**po de aconteci**mien**tos:

14 **Fies**ta del Tra**ba**jo, **Dí**a de la Constitu**ción**, etc.

15 Es**tán** ⑤, ade**más**, el carna**val**,

16 las celebra**cio**nes dedi**ca**das a la prima**ve**ra, al sols**ti**cio de ve**ra**no, a la co**se**cha y…

17 **to**do un sin**fín** ⑥ de conmemora**cio**nes que,

18 cual**quie**ra que ⑦ **se**a su o**ri**gen

19 – pues cual**quier** ex**cu**sa **va**le –,

20 dan i**de**a del ca**rác**ter fes**ti**vo ⑧ de los espa**ño**les. □

Notes

⑤ **estar**, in agreement with its subject, is used in the sense of *there is/there are* (**hay**) if the subject is introduced by a definite article or a possessive adjective.
Y además, están <u>las</u> fiestas patronales.
And in addition, there are the festivals of the patron saints.
Y además, hay fiestas patronales.
And in addition, there are festivals of the patron saints.

⑥ **un sinfín** (from **sin fin** *without end*) or **un sinnúmero** (from **sin número** *without number*) are translated by *a myriad* **(una infinidad)**, *an endless amount, a great number.*
Se registraron un sinfín (un sinnúmero) de llamadas.
A huge number of calls were recorded. (See note 3.) ▸

* * *

Ejercicio 1: Traduzca

❶ ¿Hasta cuándo te vas a quedar? ❷ Hasta el domingo que viene. ❸ El Primero de Mayo es la Fiesta del Trabajo. ❹ En ese bar hay todo tipo de tapas. ❺ El Día de Navidad es un día festivo.

13 [or] whether *(it be)* in commemoration of other kind[s] of occasions:
14 Labour Day, Constitution Day, etc.
15 There is *(They are)*, in addition, Mardi Gras *(carnival)*,
16 the celebrations dedicated to spring, to the summer solstice, to the harvest and
17 a whole myriad of commemorations that,
18 whatever their origin may be –
19 because any excuse is valid –
20 give an idea of the festive nature of the Spanish.

⑦ Compare: **cualquiera + que** (introducing a subordinate clause containing the subjunctive) → *whatever may ...*, and the adjectival use, **cualquier** + noun → *any, whichever.*
cualquiera que sea tu elección *whatever your choice may be*
cualquier marca de café *any brand of coffee.*

⑧ The verb **festejar** (line 4), from **fiesta** *festival*, means **celebrar** *to celebrate.* **festivo** means *festive*, and is also used in the expression **día festivo** *holiday* or *day off.*
El Primero de Mayo es (un) día festivo.
The 1st of May is a holiday.

* * *

Answers to Exercise 1

❶ Until when are you going to stay? ❷ Until next Sunday. ❸ The first of May is Labour Day. ❹ In this bar, there are all kinds of tapas. ❺ Christmas Day is a holiday.

Ejercicio 2: Complete

❶ You *(informal)* will learn Spanish [by] studying it.
Aprenderás español . . . .

❷ We will arrive either at one o'clock or at two.
. . . . a la una . . . . . a las dos.

❸ Whatever your decision may be, we will respect it.
. . . . tu decisión la
. . . .

❹ Next Thursday *(The Thursday that comes)* is [a] holiday.
. . . . que viene . . . .

❺ You *(informal)* can come any day.
. . . .

El calendario oficial the official calendar *of Spanish holidays is:*

Año Nuevo	**1 de Enero**	*New Year's Day*
Epifanía, Reyes	**6 de Enero**	*Epiphany, Three Kings' Day*
Viernes Santo		*Good Friday*
Fiesta del Trabajo	**1 de Mayo**	*Labour Day*
Asunción	**15 de Agosto**	*Feast of the Assumption of Mary*
Día de la Hispanidad	**12 de Octubre**	*National Day*
Todos los Santos	**1 de Noviembre**	*All Saints' Day*
Día de la Constitución	**6 de Diciembre**	*Day of the Constitution*
Inmaculada Concepción	**8 de Diciembre**	*Feast of the Immaculate Conception*
Navidad	**25 de Diciembre**	*Christmas Day*

Answers to Exercise 2

❶ – estudiándolo ❷ Llegaremos ya sea – ya sea – ❸ Cualquiera que sea – respetaremos ❹ El jueves – es festivo ❺ Puedes venir cualquier día

If you're planning a trip to Spain, try to find out ahead of time if it coincides with a holiday – either a national holiday or one of the many other local fiesta days – to make sure you don't get caught out if you need a bank or other service. It should also be noted that if the official holiday falls on a Thursday or Tuesday, the Spanish don't hesitate to take the intervening day(s) off to build so-called **puentes** *(literally, 'bridges'); that is,* long weekends*!*

Second wave: 20th lesson

70 Lección setenta

Repaso

1 Saying 'where'

• *where*, as an adverb of place, is normally **donde** (or sometimes **en donde**). When *where* implies movement towards (*to where*), it is **adonde** or **a donde**; **de donde** is *from where*, and **por donde** is *through/along/by where, which way.* When used in a direct or indirect question, **dónde** takes a written accent.
Vamos adonde quieras. *We'll go where you want.*
¿Adónde vamos? *Where are we going?*
el país de donde procede *the country it comes from* ('the country from where it comes')
¿De dónde es? *Where is he/she from?*

• *where*, as a relative pronoun, can also be expressed (in addition to **donde**, **en donde**, **de donde,** etc.) by *on/in which* – **en el que (del que, por el que,** etc.) **en el cual (del cual, por el cual,** etc.) – or, if there is movement towards something, *to which* **adonde, al que, al cual**, etc.
La playa donde (en la que, etc.**) nos bañábamos.**
The beach where (on which) we swam.
El hotel en el que nos paramos.
The hotel where (in which) we stayed.
La playa adonde (a la que, etc.**) solíamos ir a bañarnos.**
The beach where (to which) we used to go to swim.
El parque adonde me gusta ir a pasear.
The park where (to which) I like to go for a walk.

2 The present participle (the '-ing' form)

To form the present participle (the '-ing' form of the verb), a suffix is added to the stem of the infinitive: **-ando** for **-ar** verbs, and **-iendo** for **-er** and **-ir** verbs. (There are a few **-ir** verbs that take a stem change in the third-person preterite and therefore also in the present participle, for example: **p<u>e</u>dir → p<u>i</u>diendo**.)

In Spanish, the present participle can express various concepts:

• <u>How something is done</u>, usually expressed in English with *by* + present participle, to answer the question **¿Cómo?** *How?* (Note that in Spanish, the 'by' is not needed.)
Me gano la vida trabajando. *I earn my living [by] working.*

• <u>Simultaneity</u>, which can also be expressed by **al** + infinitive.
Viendo/Al ver que no llegábamos a tiempo, decidimos volver. *Seeing that we were not going to arrive on time, we decided to turn back.*

• <u>An action in progress, continuity or progression</u> is expressed using an auxiliary verb + present participle.
→ an action in progress: **estar** + present participle (*to be* + present participle):
Estoy comiendo. *I am eating.*
→ continuity: **seguir** + present participle (*to continue, to keep* + present participle)
Seguí escribiendo. *I continued/kept writing.*
→ progression or a series of actions: **ir** + present participle (this construction implies *little by little*, *one after the other*, *progressively*, *successively*, etc.).
Los invitados iban llegando. *The guests arrived gradually.*

The present participle is used frequently in Spanish. This is just a summary of the uses we've already encountered, but we'll call your attention to it in future lessons as necessary.

A final point: as with the infinitive and the affirmative command, the object pronoun is attached to the end of the present participle.
Una lengua se aprende estudiándola y practicándola.
A language is learned by studying it and practicing it.

70 3 Saying ‘whether’, ‘either … or’, etc.

There are several ways to express a parallel supposition such as *whether ... or; on the one hand ... on the other; either... or* (**o… o**).
ya … ya
ya sea … o ya sea
sea … o sea
bien sea … o bien sea
bien … o bien

sea is the first- and third-person singular present subjunctive of **ser** *to be*:
Vendrá sea sólo, (o) sea acompañado. *He’ll come, either* (‘be it’) *alone or* (‘be it’) *accompanied.*

Note:
→ The **o** preceding the second term is often omitted.
→ Except in the first case (**ya … ya**), the second part of each term can be expressed simply by **o**.
Ya por esto, ya por aquello, siempre se encuentra una excusa or **Ya sea por esto, o por aquello, siempre se encuentra una excusa.** *Whether for this or for that, an excuse is always found.*

4 Stem-changing verbs in the present tense

There are three basic types of stem changes:
e → ie; o → ue; e → i.

4.1 Group 1: *e → ie*

pensar *to think*

Present indicative	Present subjunctive	Imperative
pienso *(I think)*	**piense** *(that I think)*	
piensas	**pienses**	**piensa** *(Think!)*
piensa	**piense**	
pensamos	**pensemos**	**pensemos** *(Let’s think!)*
pensáis	**penséis**	**pensad**
piensan	**piensen**	**piensen**

The stem change does not occur in the **nosotros** and **vosotros** indicative forms. But, in the present subjunctive of the **-ir** verbs in this group, the **nosotros** and **vosotros** forms take the same stem change as that of the preterite. We'll look at the stem changes in the preterite and present participle later (lesson 84).

Here are a few more examples of this type of verb:
recomendar → Te recomiendo este vino. *I recommend this wine to you.*
cerrar → ¿A qué hora cierran? *At what time do they/you close?*
sentarse → Siéntate. *Sit down.*

4.2 Group 2: *o → ue*

volver *to return*

Present indicative	Present subjunctive	Imperative
vuelvo *(I return)*	**vuelva** *(that I return)*	
vuelves	**vuelvas**	**vuelve** *(Come back!)*
vuelve	**vuelva**	
volvemos	**volvamos**	**volvamos** *(Let's go back!)*
volvéis	**volváis**	**volved**
vuelven	**vuelvan**	**vuelvan**

Some examples:
poder → Puedes entrar. *You may come in.*
encontrar → Me encuentro bien. *I feel fine.*
costar → ¿Cuánto cuesta? *How much does it cost?*

4.3 Group 3: *e → i* (only certain *-ir* verbs)

pedir *to request, to ask for*

Present indicative	Present subjunctive	Imperative
pido *(I ask for)*	**pida** *(that I ask for)*	
pides	**pidas**	**pide** *(Ask!)*
pide	**pida**	
pedimos	**pidamos***	**pidamos** *(Let's ask!)*

pedís	**pidáis***	**pedid**
piden	**pidan**	**pidan**

* In the present subjunctive of **-ir** verbs, the **nosotros** and **vosotros** forms take the same stem change as that of the preterite.

Some examples:
servir → El camarero nos sirve. *The waiter serves us.*
repetir → Yo repito. *I repeat.*
vestirse → Mi abuela se viste de negro. *My grandmother dresses in black.*

Stem-changing verbs are covered in full detail in the grammatical appendix.

5 Cualquiera

Cualquiera means *any*, *whatever*, *whichever* in reference to things, or *anybody*, *anyone*, *whoever* in reference to people. It can be used as an adjective or a pronoun.

• As an adjective, it can come before or after the noun it modifies. If placed before the noun, it becomes **cualquier**.
Si tienes un problema, puedes llamarme en cualquier momento y cualquier día. *If you have a problem, you can call me at any time and any day.*
un pretexto cualquiera *any excuse.*

• As a pronoun, **cualquiera** replaces a noun:
cualquiera de nosotros *any of us* or *anybody among us*
¿Puedo elegir cualquiera? *Can I choose anyone?*

• The pronoun can also be used with **+ que** + clause with subjunctive verb:
Cualquiera que sea tu opinión … *Whatever your opinion may be ...*

In Spanish, most transitive verbs (i.e. those taking a direct object) can be made reflexive. While English commonly uses the passive voice, this is not the case in Spanish, in which the passive is mostly avoided. This is done:

• either by giving the sentence an active subject:

Venden tapas en muchos lugares. *Tapas are sold in many places.* ('They sell tapas in many places.')

• or by using what is called the passive 'se':

Se venden tapas en muchos lugares. 'Tapas sell themselves in many places', where **tapas** is now the grammatical subject.

Although it is possible in theory to use the passive voice in such sentences (in which case it exactly mirrors the English: **Las tapas son vendidas en muchos lugares.** *Tapas are sold in many places.*), in practice this is rare.

1 – Esta semana hay un puente de cuatro días.
2 – Podríamos ir a Santander; aprovecharíamos para ver el mar
3 e ir a visitar algunos pueblos que celebran las fiestas patronales.
4 – Me parece una excelente idea.
5 – No lejos de la playa del Sardinero,
6 conozco un pequeño restaurante en el que se come muy bien.
7 – Y… ¿qué nos vas a recomendar?
8 – ¡Ya veremos!
9 Por el momento, el plato fuerte consiste en:
10 ¡madrugar y cuatro horas de carretera!

---

71 Lección setenta y una

Inocentada ① (traída por los pelos)

1 – **Ho**la **bue**nas, pa**sa**ba por a**quí** y…
2 se me ha ocu**rri**do ② que el **ni**ño po**drí**a cor**tar**se el **pe**lo ③.
3 A**sí** que… ve**ni**mos sin **ci**ta.
4 ¿Es po**si**ble?

Notes

① **una inocentada** (from **inocente** *innocent*) is more or less the Spanish equivalent of *an April Fools' joke*, practiced on **el Día de los Santos Inocentes** *Holy Innocents' Day* on 28 December.

② When **ocurrir** is reflexive (indicated here by **se**), it means *to occur to someone*, *to come to mind*, *to have the idea to*, etc.
Se me ha ocurrido invitar a cenar a César.
It occurred to me to invite César to dinner.

Traducción

1 This week there is a four-day weekend. **2** We could go to Santander; we would take the opportunity to see the sea **3** and to go visit some towns that are celebrating their saints' days. **4** I think that's an excellent idea. **5** Not far from the beach at Sardinero, **6** I know a little restaurant where you can eat *(one eats)* very well. **7** And … what are you going to recommend to us? **8** We'll see! **9** For the moment, the main course consists of: **10** getting up early and four hours on the *(of)* road!

Second wave: 21st lesson

Lesson seventy-one 71

April Fools' joke (far-fetched *[brought by the hairs]*)

1 – Hello, I was passing by *(here)* and …
2 it occurred to me that the boy could get his hair cut *(to-have-cut the hair)*.
3 So … we['ve] come without [an] appointment.
4 Will that be *(Is it)* possible?

▸ In the non-reflexive form, **ocurrir** means *to happen* (lesson 55).

③ **cortarse el pelo** *to have one's hair cut, to get a haircut*. (Note that in Spanish, it's 'the hair', not 'my/his/your hair', etc.)
Tiene el pelo largo. *He/she has long hair.*
And if you want to get your hair cut:
ir a la peluquería *to go to the barber's/hairdresser's.*

5 – **Ll**egan a **pun**to, **den**tro de un ra**ti**to mi compa**ñ**era esta**rá li**bre.
6 ¿No les im**por**ta ④ espe**rar** diez mi**nu**tos o un **cuar**to de **ho**ra?
7 – Per**fec**to.
8 **Mi**re, **mien**tras le **lle**ga la vez ⑤ y le **cor**ta el **pe**lo,
9 yo voy a ir a ha**cer u**nas ⑥ lla**ma**das
10 y a to**mar** un ca**fé** en el bar de al **la**do.
11 ¿Le pa**re**ce? ⑦ ⑧
12 – Muy bien.

13 Una **ho**ra más **tar**de:

14 – **O**ye, **chi**co, **ha**ce ya **u**na **ho**ra que tu **pa**dre se ha **i**do y…

Notes

④ We've already seen the common expression **no importa** *it's not important, it doesn't matter* (lesson 67). Here we have **¿No le importa?** *Do you mind?* ('It doesn't matter to you?'). The word for *to bother*, **molestar** (lesson 45), is often replaced by **importar** *to matter* in a question. In this case, **importar** is preceded by a pronoun referring to the person one is asking.
¿No te importa que salgamos un poco más tarde?
Do you mind if we leave a little later?

⑤ **la vez** *time*, in the sense of *occasion*, *instance* or, as here, *turn* (**una vez** *once*). **Cuando me llegue la vez, avísame.** *When it's my turn, let me know.* Or you can say: **Cuando me toque, me avisas.** (lesson 50) (**llegue** and **toque** = present subjunctive)

⑥ Remember that the indefinite plural **unos/unas** is generally left out in Spanish. When it is expressed, it usually means *some*, *a few*. **Tomaremos unas pastas.** *We will eat some pastries.*

⑦ Whereas **¿Qué te/le parece?** means *What do you think? What do you say to that?*, the expression **¿Te/le parece?** means *Do you agree? Is that OK with you?* ▸

5 – You've arrived *(You[formal pl.] arrive)* [just] in time, in a moment *(within a little moment)* my colleague will be free.
6 Do you mind *(Not to-you[formal pl.] matters)* waiting ten minutes or a quarter of [an] hour?
7 – Perfect.
8 Look, until it's his turn *(while to-him arrives the time)* and you cut his hair,
9 I'm going to go make a few [phone] calls
10 and have a coffee in the bar next door *(bar of at-the side)*.
11 Is that OK with you *(To-you[formal sing.] it-seems)*?
12 – Fine.

13 One hour later *(more late)*:

14 – Hey, lad, it's been *(it-makes already)* an hour that your father's been *(has)* gone and …

▸ ⑧ **parecer** (like **aparecer**, line 15) conjugates like **conocer** *to know, to be familiar with*. All similar verbs take a **z** before the **c** that precedes an ending in **a** or **o**: **conozco** *I know*, but **conoces** *you know*. **Haz como te parezca.** *Do as you think best*. But: **Hago lo que me parece.** *I do what I think best.*

In other words, this change appears in the first-person present tense and in all present subjunctives. Check the grammatical appendix for more information.

15 ¡no apa**re**ce! ⑨
16 – No, no **e**ra mi **pa**dre,
17 era un se**ñor** que me ha **vis**to en la **ca**lle
18 y me ha pregun**ta**do si que**rí**a cor**tar**me el **pe**lo **gra**tis.

Notes

⑨ **aparecer** means *to appear* in the sense of *to become visible*, *to show up*, *to arrive*, etc. It is not a synonym of **parecer** *to seem.* ▸

* * *

Ejercicio 1: Traduzca

❶ Pasaba por allí y… he llamado a la puerta. ❷ Tengo que ir a la peluquería. ❸ ¿Qué te ocurre? ❹ Le he visto sólo una vez. ❺ Nos va a llegar la vez.

* * *

Ejercicio 2: Complete

❶ I don't know her family.
. . . . su . . . .

❷ Does it bother you *(formal)* if I smoke?
¿. . . . . ?

❸ Next month I'll take a few days of holiday *(holidays).*
El mes que viene . . . .
. . . .

❹ You're *(You[informal] arrive)* just in time, we were going to start eating.
. . . . , ... empezar . . . .

❺ He hasn't shown up *(He appears not)* here for *(since it makes)* a month.
. . . . por aquí . . . . un mes.

15 there's no sign of him *(he doesn't appear)*!
16 – No, [that] wasn't my father,
17 it was a man *(a sir)* who saw me in the street
18 and asked me if I wanted to get my hair cut [for] free.

▸ **Estamos esperándole desde esta mañana, pero no aparece.** *We've been waiting for him since this morning, but he hasn't shown up/turned up* ('doesn't appear').

* * *

Answers to Exercise 1

❶ I was passing by there and … I knocked at the door. ❷ I have to go to the hairdresser's/barber's. ❸ What's the matter with you? ❹ I have only seen him once. ❺ It's going to be our turn.

* * *

Answers to Exercise 2

❶ No conozco a – familia ❷ Le molesta si fumo ❸ – cogeré unos días de vacaciones ❹ Llegas a punto, íbamos a – a comer ❺ No aparece – desde hace –

On 28 December, Spain marks **los Santos Inocentes** Holy Innocents' Day, *which commemorates the massacre of the Innocents on the orders of King Herod. Over time, it has become a day for practical jokes with a festive air. At school, in the workplace, in the media, etc., people engage in silly pranks, spoofs or hoaxes intended to underscore* **la inocencia** innocence *or* naïvety *of friends and colleagues who are the butt of* **la broma** the joke. *These* **bromas** jokes, pranks *are called* **inocentadas***; the cultural equivalent of* April Fools' jokes.

Note: **gastar una broma** to play *(to spend)* a joke.

Second wave: 22nd lesson

Lenguas de España

1 – Juraría que en la señal ① que acabamos
de ② dejar atrás faltaba la ele;
2 quizás ③ me equivoque,
3 pero me ha parecido ver escrito
'A Coruña'.
4 – No, has leído perfectamente.
5 'La Coruña' se dice 'A Coruña' en gallego;
6 y la señalización de las carreteras gallegas
se hace igualmente en gallego.
7 – ¡No me digas!
8 – Y en el País Vasco encontrarás muchas
señales en eusquera ④.
9 Y… en Cataluña, en catalán.
10 – Pues… ¡menudo ⑤ rompecabezas ⑥!

Notes

① **señal** *signal*, *sign*; **dar la señal** *to give the signal*; **buena/mala señal** *good/bad sign*; **señal de tráfico** *roadsign*.
And another meaning: **dejar una señal** *to leave a deposit*.

② Reminder: **acabar de** *to finish from* + infinitive is the equivalent of the English *to have just* + past participle.

③ At the beginning of a phrase, **quizás** (or **quizá**) *perhaps* stresses the idea of doubt and is therefore here followed by the subjunctive (**equivoque** from **equivocarse**). In this case, **quizás** corresponds to **puede ser que** *it may be that*, *it is possible that* or *maybe*.

④ **eusquera** or **euskera** *Basque* (language).
Euskadi or **País Vasco** *Basque Country*.

Languages in Spain

1 – I could *(would)* swear that on the roadsign we've just passed *(we finish from leaving behind)* the 'l' was missing;
2 perhaps I'm mistaken,
3 but I thought it said *(to see written)* 'A Coruña'.
4 – No, you read [it] perfectly.
5 'La Coruña' is *(is said)* 'A Coruña' in Galician;
6 and the signs *(the signposting)* on Galician roads are also *(are made equally)* in Galician.
7 – Really! *(Don't tell me!)*
8 – And in the Basque Country, you'll find many signs in Basque.
9 And … in Catalonia, in Catalan.
10 – Well … how confusing *(what a head-breaker)*!

▸ ⑤ As indicated in lesson 39, **menudo/a** before a noun, usually in exclamations, has various translations along the lines of *What a* + noun, or *How* + adjective ending in *-ing*:
¡Menudo día! *What a day!* **¡Menuda faena!** *What a job!*
¡Menudo rollo! *How boring!*

The exclamation **¡Vaya!** can have a similar meaning:
¡Vaya lío! *What a mess!*

⑥ **rompecabezas** – **rompe** (from **romper** *to break*), **cabezas** *heads*. **un rompecabezas** *a jigsaw, puzzle, brainteaser*. Note in passing that **romper** is a regular verb that has an irregular past participle: *broken* → **roto**.
He roto las gafas. *I've broken my* (the) *glasses.*

11 – **To**do **tie**ne sus ven**ta**jas y sus inconve**nien**tes.
12 **Vis**to **des**de **fue**ra **pue**de pare**cer** compli**ca**do;
13 **pe**ro es más sen**ci**llo de lo que pa**re**ce ⑦.
14 – En **to**do **ca**so, Es**pa**ña es un pa**ís ri**co en **len**guas. □

Notes

⑦ **Es más sencillo de lo que parece.** ('It's more simple of what it seems.') *It's easier than it looks.*

* * *

Ejercicio 1: Traduzca

❶ Creo que me he equivocado. ❷ ¿Hay que dejar una señal? ❸ ¿Qué te ha parecido? ❹ No entiendo* lo que has escrito. ❺ Aún* no han dado la señal de salida.

* **entender** *to understand*; **aún** *still*

* * *

Ejercicio 2: Complete

❶ Really! *(informal)*

¡. . . . . !

❷ In the Basque Country, Basque can also be learned *(one can learn also the Basque)* in school.

. . . . País Vasco . . . . aprender . . . . el . . . . en el . . . .

❸ It's a good sign.

. . . .

❹ Seen from [the] outside, it doesn't seem complicated to me.

. . . . no me . . . .

❺ Everything has its advantages and disadvantages.

. . . .

11 – Everything has its pros and cons *(advantages and inconveniences)*.
12 Seen from [the] outside it may seem complicated,
13 but it's easier *(more easy)* than it seems.
14 – In any case, Spain has a wealth of *(is a country rich in)* languages.

* * *

Answers to Exercise 1

❶ I think that I was mistaken. ❷ Is it necessary to leave a deposit? ❸ What did you think of it? ❹ I don't understand what you have written. ❺ They still haven't given the signal for departure.

* * *

Answers to Exercise 2

❶ No me digas ❷ En el – se puede – también – eusquera – colegio ❸ Es una buena señal ❹ Visto desde fuera – parece complicado ❺ Todo tiene sus ventajas y sus inconvenientes

Besides **el castellano** Castilian*, which is more generally known as* **el español** Spanish*, the following are also recognized as official languages in Spain:* **el catalán** Catalan *in* **Cataluña** Catalonia*;* **el gallego** Galician *in* **Galicia** Galicia*;* **el vasco** *or* **euskera** Basque *in* **el País Vasco** the Basque Country*;* **el valenciano** Valencian Catalan *in* **la Comunidad Valenciana** the Region of Valencia *and* **el mallorquín** Majorcan Catalan **en las Islas Baleares** in the Balearic Islands. *For some decades now, these regional languages have been experiencing renewed interest. Many young people are relearning them, encouraged by official campaigns in the respective regions aimed at promoting them, and also motivated by an increasing desire to return to the region's cultural roots.*

73 Lección setenta y tres

Parecido inverosímil

1 – ¡Jo, **tí**o ①; no te **pue**des imagi**nar** lo que te pa**re**ces a mi mu**jer**!
2 **Ca**da vez que te **ve**o…
3 es **co**mo si la estu**vie**ra **vien**do ② a **e**lla ③.
4 ¡Es la re**pe**ra! ④
5 – ¡No me **di**gas!
6 ¡No se**rá** para **tan**to ⑤!

Notes

① In colloquial language, especially among young people, **tío** *uncle* or **tipo** *type* is similar to *man*, *bloke*, *guy*, *dude* or *mate* in English: **un tío estupendo** *a great guy*, *a fantastic bloke*.

② **como si la estuviera viendo (como si la viera)** *as if I were seeing her*: **estuviera** is the imperfect subjunctive of **estar** (**viera** is the imperfect subjunctive of **ver**). The imperfect subjunctive is always used after **como si** *as if*, since this indicates an unreal situation. More on the imperfect subjunctive soon. ▸

There are also two 'protected' dialects in Spain, although they are less widespread (limited mostly to rural areas): **el aragonés** Aragonese *spoken* **en Aragón** in Aragon*; and* **el bable** Asturian **en Asturias** in Asturias.

Second wave: 23rd lesson

The next lesson contains many colloquial expressions. In Spain, you'll hear these in different contexts – just try to remember them as they are without worrying too much about their literal translations.

Lesson seventy-three 73

Unlikely resemblance

1 – Wow, mate *(uncle)*; you can't imagine how much *(that which)* you look like my wife!
2 Every time I see you …
3 it's as if *(her)* I were looking at *(seeing)* her.
4 It's incredible!
5 – You're kidding!
6 Surely not as much as all that!

③ In this sentence, the pronoun *her* is included twice, once as **la** and again as **a ella**. In Spanish, pronouns can be repeated like this to give emphasis, but this is optional.

④ **¡Es la repera!** is a colloquial expression of astonishment or surprise; another is **¡Anda!** *Go on!* (literally, 'Walk!'). The translation can vary depending on the context; here it could just as easily be *It's too much! It's crazy!*, etc.

⑤ In lesson 52, we saw this expression with the meaning *No need to exaggerate!* Note that here the verb is in the future tense.

7 ¡No que**rrás** que me **tra**gue ⑥ **e**so!
8 – ¡**Co**mo lo **o**yes! ⑦
9 ¡**Bue**no, por su**pues**to, qui**tan**do ⑧ el bi**go**te!
10 – ¡No fas**ti**dies ⑨, **pe**ro si ⑩ yo no **ten**go bi**go**te!
11 – Ya lo sé; **pe**ro **e**lla sí. □

Notes

⑥ **tragar** *to swallow* is often used reflexively, as here. Like all verbs ending in **-gar**, to retain the same sound in all conjugated forms, a **u** is inserted after the **g** if the ending is **e**. This is merely a spelling change; the verb is considered regular.

pagar *to pay* → present subjunctive:
pag<u>u</u>e, pag<u>u</u>es, pag<u>u</u>e, etc.
apagar *to extinguish*, *turn off* → preterite:
apag<u>u</u>é, apagaste, apagó, etc.

⑦ **¡Como lo oyes!** ('As you hear it!') *I'm telling you! Believe me!*

⑧ **quitando** *taking away*, *removing* is very often used informally instead of **a/con excepción de** *with the exception of*, and can also be translated by *apart from* or *not counting*.

⑨ **¡No fastidies!** (from **fastidiar** *to bother*, *irritate*, *hassle*). This is heard a lot in colloquial speech to express annoyance, surprise, incredulity or denial.
Su desconfianza me fastidia. *His distrust annoys me.*
¡No fastidies! on its own or at the beginning of a sentence, *Stop! That's enough! Come on now! You're kidding!*, etc. ▸

* * *

Ejercicio 1: Traduzca

❶ ¿Es posible? ❷ Llegas a punto. ❸ ¡Menudo rompecabezas! ❹ ¡Es la repera! ❺ ¡Vaya día!

7 You don't expect me to *(You won't want that I)* swallow that!
8 – I'm telling you! *(As you hear it!)*
9 Well, of course, except for *(taking away)* the moustache!
10 – Get out of here *(Don't annoy me)*, *(but if)* I don't have [a] moustache!
11 – I know *(it)*; but she does *(but she yes)*.

⑩ **pero si …** is also a common expression of surprised disbelief, used to introduce an objection or to mitigate what has just been said. It often has the meaning of *How is that possible? How can that be?* **He perdido la cartera. – ¡Pero si la tenías ahora mismo en la mano!** *I've lost my wallet. – But you had it in your hand a moment ago!*

* * *

Answers to Exercise 1

❶ Is it possible? ❷ You've arrived just in time. ❸ What a headache! ❹ It's incredible! ❺ What a day!

Ejercicio 2: Complete

❶ There's no need to exaggerate!
¡.. .. ..!

❷ Get out of here!
¡.. ....!

❸ I'm telling you!
¡.... .. ....!

❹ Except for one or two people, everybody was happy.
...., todos .... contentos.

---

74 Lección setenta y cuatro

Con la carta de vinos

1 – ¿Qué pre**fe**rís ① **pa**ra acompa**ñar** la co**mi**da:
2 **tin**to ②, **blan**co o ro**sa**do?
3 – A mí me gusta**rí**a pro**bar** ③ un vi**ni**to **blan**co.
4 – Yo pre**fie**ro co**mer** con **tin**to.
5 – Yo tam**bién**.
6 **Mi**ra, a**quí** hay un Ri**be**ra del **Due**ro, re**ser**va ④ del 94,

Notes

① This is the second-person plural (**vosotros**) form of **preferir** in the present tense. Remember that this form is used to address more than one person informally. Check lesson 7 or the grammatical appendix if you need to refresh your memory.

② **vino tinto** *red wine*. Spain has a strong winemaking tradition. The origin and the quality of its wines are guaranteed by the classification **denominación de origen** *designation of origin*. In the evening, a popular pastime is **ir a tomar un vino** *to go for a glass of wine*. ▶

❺ You don't expect her to swallow that! *(You[informal] will not want that she herself swallows that!)*

¡.. ....!

Answers to Exercise 2

❶ No es para tanto (or ¡No hay que exagerar!) ❷ No fastidies ❸ Como lo oyes ❹ Quitando una o dos personas – estaban – ❺ No querrás que se trague eso

Second wave: 24th lesson

Lesson seventy-four 74

With the wine list

1 – What do you *(informal pl.)* prefer to go with *(accompany)* the meal:
2 red, white or rosé?
3 – Myself, I'd like to try a nice *(little)* white wine.
4 – I prefer *(to eat with)* red.
5 – Me too.
6 Look, here's a Ribera del Duero, reserve 94,

▸ ③ **probar** *to try, to test* and … *to taste!* (stem-changing verb **o → ue**)
Prueba este jamón. *Try this ham.*
Don't forget that *to try on* (clothes, shoes, etc.) = **probarse**.
Pruébate esta chaqueta. *Try on this jacket.*

④ On a wine label, the word **reserva** *reserve* means that the wine has been matured for at least three years, with a minimum of one year in an oak barrel. You might also see the word **cosecha** *vintage* between the word **reserva** and the year.

7 que pa**re**ce ser que ⑤ no es**tá** mal.
8 – ¡Ade**lan**te, en**ton**ces!
9 – ¿Y yo? ¿No **cuen**to?
10 – ¡Hoy te **to**ca condu**cir** ⑥!
11 O **se**a ⑦ que te ten**drás** que conten**tar** con el aperi**ti**vo y…
12 una bo**te**lla de **a**gua fres**qui**ta.
13 – ¡**Mi**ra qué ⑧ **lis**tos ⑨!
14 – Ya **sa**bes… si **be**bes, no con**duz**cas ⑩. □

Notes

⑤ **parece (ser) que** *it seems (to be) that*, *it appears that*, *it is said that* or *seemingly, apparently.*
Parece que va a nevar. *Apparently it's going to snow.*
All these constructions have the same meaning: **al parecer, a lo que parece** or **según lo que parece**.

⑥ **conducir** *to drive.* Verbs ending in **-ducir** (**introducir** *to introduce*; **producir** *to produce*; **seducir** *to seduce*; **traducir** *to translate*, etc.) are irregular in the present tense and the preterite. See lesson 77 for a full summary.

⑦ **o sea** can mean *that is to say* (**es decir**), *in other words* (**dicho de otra manera**, literally, 'said in another manner') or *so*, when summing up.

⑧ The exclamation **¡Mira qué …!** generally translates as *Look how* + adjective. **¡Mira qué fácil!** *Look how easy [it is]!* It can also express incredulity, surprise or, as here, annoyance. ▸

* * *

Ejercicio 1: Traduzca

❶ ¿Quieres probar este vino? ❷ No está mal. ❸ ¿Qué prefieres beber? ❹ A mí me gusta más el vino tinto. ❺ Compra un buen vino.

7 which apparently *(seems to be that)* is not bad.
8 – Go ahead *(Onwards)* then!
9 – What about me *(And me)*? I don't count?
10 – Today it's your turn to drive!
11 So you'll have to make do *(content yourself)* with the aperitif and …
12 a nice cold bottle of water.
13 – Very clever! *(Look how crafty!)*
14 – As *(Already)* you know … if you drink, don't drive!

⑨ **listo** *intelligent* (**inteligente**), *bright* (**vivo**), *sly, crafty* (**astuto**). **ser listo** *to be intelligent, smart, clever.* Not to be confused with **estar listo** *to be ready.*

⑩ **Si bebes, no conduzcas.** *If you drink, don't drive.* This is the slogan for Spanish road-safety campaigns.

A MÍ ME GUSTA MÁS
EL VINO TINTO.

* * *

Answers to Exercise 1

❶ Do you want to try this wine? ❷ It's not bad. ❸ What do you prefer to drink? ❹ Myself, I prefer red wine. ❺ Buy a good wine.

Ejercicio 2: Complete

❶ I'd like to try on those shoes.
Me .... esos ....

❷ Please could you bring me a bottle of water?
... ., ¿podría ....?

❸ Look how comfortable [it is]!
¡.... ... cómodo!

* * *

Grapevines have been cultivated on the Iberian Peninsula since Phoenician times, before the arrival of the Romans. Today, Spain is one of the most important wine-producing countries in the world, not only in terms of quantity, but also in the variety and quality of its wines. Its red wines fall into four main categories:
- **cosecha** – *young wines, bottled immediately*
- **crianza** – *wines of at least two years old that have been matured in oak barrels for six months before bottling*
- **reserva** – *wines of at least three years old that have been matured for a minimum of one year in oak barrels*
- **gran reserva** – *wines of at least four years old that have been matured for a minimum of two years in oak barrels.*

75 Lección setenta y cinco

Con pelos y señales ①

1 – **Ten**go un **dí**a muy compli**ca**do y me ha**rí**as un gran fa**vor**

Notes

① **con pelos y señales** (literally, 'with hairs and signs') means *in minute detail* or *down to the last detail*. **explicar algo con pelos y señales** *to explain something in great detail.*

❹ If you *(informal sing.)* drink, don't drive.

. . . . , ...

❺ Now it's your *(informal sing.)* turn to translate.

. . . . a ti.

Answers to Exercise 2

❶ – gustaría probarme – zapatos ❷ Por favor – traerme una botella de agua ❸ Mira qué – ❹ Si bebes, no conduzcas ❺ Ahora te toca traducir –

* * *

In addition, Spain produces a wide variety of **vinos blancos** white wines, **licores** liqueurs *and* **cavas** sparkling wines*, not to mention the famous* **jerez** sherry*, which itself comes in several varieties. And we can't leave out one of Spain's most well-known drinks,* **sangría** *(literally, 'bleeding'), a refreshing mixture of* **vino tinto** red wine *and* **gaseosa** lemon soda*, enhanced with sugar and/or pieces of fruit, according to the maker's personal taste.*

Second wave: 25th lesson

Lesson seventy-five 75

In great detail

1 – I have a very difficult *(complicated)* day [planned] and you'd be doing me a big favour

2 si **fue**ras ② a reci**bir** al direc**tor** de **nues**tra **Ca**sa Cen**tral**.

3 – **Pe**ro si… ¡ni si**quie**ra le co**noz**co!

4 – ¡No se**rá u**na ta**re**a muy di**fí**cil! Es**cu**cha:

5 Es más bien ba**ji**to ③, **mi**de un **me**tro cin**cuen**ta, **po**co más o **me**nos ④.

6 **Pe**sa alrede**dor** de los no**ven**ta **ki**los ⑤.

7 **Tie**ne el **pe**lo cas**ta**ño, ya un **po**co ca**no**so.

8 **Tie**ne los **o**jos a**zu**les y **lle**va bi**go**te, al es**ti**lo de Da**lí**.

9 En **cuan**to a ⑥ **có**mo esta**rá** ves**ti**do,

10 me ha **di**cho que se pon**drá al**go llama**ti**vo

11 **pa**ra que nos **se**a **fá**cil recono**cer**lo.

12 Lleva**rá u**na ca**mi**sa de **ra**yas **ne**gras y **blan**cas,

13 un panta**lón** de ⑦ **pa**na a**zul** y **u**nas zapa**ti**llas de de**por**te **ro**jas.

14 Ah, sí, me ha **di**cho tam**bién** que, por si a**ca**so, se pon**drá u**na **boi**na.

Notes

② **fueras** is the second-person singular imperfect subjunctive of **ir** (and also, incidentally, of **ser**). The imperfect subjunctive is used in the **si** *if* clause of a conditional sentence when the main clause is in the conditional mood (here, **me harías un gran favor** *you would be doing me a big favour*). See review lesson 77 for more about the imperfect subjunctive.

③ **bajo** *low* and *short* ≠ **alto** *high* and *tall*.

④ **poco más o menos** or **más o menos** *more or less*, *around* or *approximately*.

⑤ Spain uses the metric system for measurements: 1 m 50 cm is just under 5 feet, and 90 kilograms is almost 200 pounds! ▸

2 if you went to pick up *(receive)* the manager of our Head Office.

3 – But … I don't even know him *(not even him I know)*!

4 – It won't be a very difficult task! Listen:

5 He's rather *(more well)* short, *(he measures)* about 1 metre [and] 50 [centimetres tall] *(bit more or less)*.

6 He weighs around 90 kilos.

7 He has brown *(chestnut)* hair, already a little grey.

8 He has blue eyes and *(wears)* [a] moustache in the style of Dalí.

9 As for how he will be dressed,

10 he told me that he'll wear *(put on)* something eye-catching

11 so that it will be easy for us to recognize him.

12 He'll wear a shirt with *(of)* black and white stripes,

13 blue corduroy trousers and red sports shoes.

14 Oh, yes, he also told me that, just in case, he'll put on a beret.

▸ ⑥ **en cuanto a** *as for, as regards, as far as.*

⑦ Remember that in Spanish, the preposition **de** + noun is used to describe another noun; this is the equivalent to English noun + noun or adjective + noun constructions:
una chaqueta de lana *a wool jacket*
una camisa de rayas *a striped shirt*
un pantalón de pana azul *blue corduroy trousers.*

Another use of **de** is to describe a person or an object:
la mujer del sombrero *the woman in the hat.*

15 – No **hace fal**ta ⑧ que **di**gas más.
16 **Cre**o que po**dré** arre**glár**melas ⑨.

Notes

⑧ **no hace falta** *it's not necessary* (**no es necesario**).
No hace falta/No es necesario que vengas. *It's not necessary for you to come* ('that you come'). This construction requires the subjunctive (note the **que**). The idea of something being 'lacking' or 'missing', expressed with the phrase **hacer falta**, is similar to 'needing'. This can also be expressed with **necesitar** *to need.* **¿Necesitas ayuda?** or **¿Te hace falta ayuda?** *Do you need help?* Notice that here **hacer falta** must be preceded by an object pronoun.

* * *

Ejercicio 1: Traduzca

❶ Voy a pedirte un favor. ❷ Fui a recibirla al aeropuerto. ❸ ¿Cuánto mides? ❹ ¿De qué color son sus ojos? ❺ Es una persona muy alta.

* * *

Ejercicio 2: Complete

❶ It would be good if you came *(imperfect subjunctive, informal sing.)* tomorrow.
. . . . bien si . . . . mañana.

❷ She dresses in a very eye-catching way *(in a way very flashy).*
. . viste . . . .

❸ How much do you *(formal)* weigh?
¿. . . . . ?

15 – There's no need to say *(that you say)* [any] more.
16 I think that I'll be able to manage *(sort them out myself)*.

▸ ⑨ **arreglar** *to arrange, fix, sort out*; **arreglarse** *to get arranged, fixed, sorted out* or *to get ready, get dressed* (**vestirse**). Thus, a sentence like **se arregla con poca cosa** could have several meanings, from *it's easily arranged* (the reflexive use corresponding to the passive voice in English) to *he/she makes do with little.* Another example: **Se está arreglando para salir.** *She's getting ready to go out.*
arreglárselas (colloquial) *to manage, get by, cope.*
¡Arréglatelas como puedas! *Manage as best you can!*

* * *

Answers to Exercise 1

❶ I'm going to ask you a favour. ❷ I went to pick her up at the airport. ❸ How tall are you? *(How much do you measure?)* ❹ What colour are his/her/your/their eyes? ❺ She/He's a very tall person.

* * *

❹ Take the umbrella just in case.
Coge .. ..

❺ Do you need anything else?
¿Te .... algo ... ?

Answers to Exercise 2

❶ Estaría – vinieras – ❷ Se – de una forma muy llamativa ❸ Cuánto pesa ❹ – el paraguas por si acaso ❺ – hace falta – más

Second wave: 26th lesson

Una compra ①

1 – Voy a sa**lir** a ha**cer u**nas **com**pras;
2 ¿me acom**pa**ñas?
3 – Ya **sa**bes que me **po**ne **ma**lo ir de **tien**das.
4 – Ade**más**, tú nece**si**tas **u**nos panta**lo**nes ②.
5 ¡**A**le, a**sí** aprovecha**re**mos tam**bién pa**ra dar **u**na **vuel**ta!
6 En la **tien**da:
7 – Te**ne**mos tam**bién és**tos con un **cor**te más mo**der**no; es**tán** de **mo**da.
8 – ¿Qué **pre**cio **tie**nen ③?

Notes

① **compra** means *purchase*, but also refers to the act of shopping. It is used in many expressions: **hacer compras** *to do the shopping*; **ir de compras** *to go shopping* (usually referring to shopping for pleasure); **ir a hacer las compras/la compra** or **ir a la compra** *to do the shopping* (referring to errands, food shopping, etc.). And if you're just looking:
ir de escaparates *to go window shopping.*

② About a dozen Spanish words have two forms, singular or plural, to designate the same object. So you can say either **los pantalones** or **el pantalón** *trousers* (always plural in English). The speakers in this dialogue switch quite easily from one to the other; of course, the verb, pronouns and adjectives must agree with the form used.

③ There are several ways to ask the price:
¿Cuánto cuesta? *How much does it cost?*
¿Cuánto vale? *How much is it worth?* ▸

A purchase

1 – I'm going to go out to do some shopping *(make some purchases)*;
2 are you coming with me?
3 – You know that it makes *(puts)* me ill to go around the shops.
4 – Besides, you need some trousers.
5 Come on, that way we'll also get the chance to go for a walk!
6 At the shop:
7 – We also have these, with a more modern cut; they're in fashion.
8 – What price are they *(do they have)*?

¿QUIÉN VA A HACER LAS COMPRAS ?

To ask the price of something that fluctuates (in the market, for example), you can say **¿A cómo está?** *How much is it?* (Note that *to be* in this case is **estar**, not **ser**.) If you're talking about more than one object, **cuesta**, **vale** and **está** must change to the plural, of course. Other options include:
¿Cuánto/Qué le debo? *How much/What do I owe you?*
¿Cuánto es? *How much is it?*

9 – Ve**a**mos la eti**que**ta… Sí, **cues**tan dos**cien**tos **eu**ros.
10 – Son dema**sia**do **ca**ros.
11 – En**ton**ces, **pue**de pro**bar**se **és**tos.
12 – No, no me van; no es mi **ta**lla.
13 – ¿Y **és**te, de algo**dón**?
14 – Con **és**te es**toy** muy **có**modo. Me lo **que**do. ④
15 – Pues si es **to**do… ya **pue**den pa**sar** por **ca**ja.
16 – **Mu**chas **gra**cias.
17 – **Bue**no, **va**mos; es**toy** mare**a**do ⑤.
18 – Ven, te in**vi**to a to**mar** una hor**cha**ta ⑥. □

Notes

④ **Me lo quedo.** *I'll take it.* (when buying something) (literally, 'I keep it for myself.') **quedarse con algo** ('to remain with something') means *to keep something for oneself.* Another useful expression with this verb: **Quédese con las vueltas.** *Keep the change* (formal).

⑤ **estar mareado**, which we saw in lesson 43, can also mean, as here, *to be dizzy, to have one's head spinning.* ▸

* * *

Ejercicio 1: Traduzca

❶ ¿Quién va a hacer las compras? ❷ Tengo mucho que hacer, no puedo acompañarte. ❸ En mi casa tengo unos sellos para ti. ❹ ¿Cuánto cuestan esos pantalones? ❺ Son carísimos.

9 – Let's look at the tag … *(Yes)* they cost 200 euros.
10 – They're too expensive.
11 – Then you can try these.
12 – No, they don't suit me *(go with me)*; they're *(it's)* not my size.
13 – And these *(this)*, in *(of)* cotton?
14 – With these *(this)* I'm very comfortable. I'll take them *(it)*.
15 – Well, if that's everything … *(already)* you can go to *(pass by)* [the] till.
16 – Thank you very much.
17 – OK, let's go, I feel dizzy.
18 – Come [on], I'll buy you *(I invite you to take)* an 'horchata'.

⑥ **la horchata** is a sweet, refreshing drink that resembles milk, but is actually made from ground tigernuts. It is a speciality of the Valencia region. It is sometimes served in the form of crushed ice, in which case it is called **granizado de horchata**.

* * *

Answers to Exercise 1

❶ Who's going to do the shopping? ❷ I have a lot to do, I can't go with you. ❸ At home I have some stamps for you. ❹ How much do these trousers cost? ❺ They're very expensive.

Ejercicio 2: Complete

1. This haircut is in fashion.
   Ese . . . . pelo . . . .
2. Keep the change! *(informal)*
   ¡. . . . . !
3. This afternoon we'll go shopping.
   Esta . . . . . iremos . . . .
4. Do you *(formal)* want to try on this shirt?
   ¿. . . . . esta . . . . . . ?
5. Cotton – it's written on the label/tag.
   . . . . , está escrito en . . . .

---

77 Lección setenta y siete

Repaso

1 Imperfect subjunctive

The past form of the subjunctive is called the imperfect subjunctive.

1.1 Formation of the imperfect subjunctive

It has two forms, which are completely interchangeable:
- **-ar** verbs can end in **-ara** or **-ase**
- **-er** and **-ir** verbs can end in **-iera** or **-iese**.

-ar verbs, such as **hablar** *to speak*:
habl → ara / ase *(that I spoke)*
habl → aras / ases
habl → ara / ase
habl → áramos / ásemos

Answers to Exercise 2

❶ – corte de – está de moda ❷ Quédate con las vueltas ❸ – tarde – de compras ❹ Quiere probarse – camisa ❺ Algodón – la etiqueta

In the last few lessons, you've no doubt noticed that alongside new grammatical points, each text also includes constructions or expressions that aren't explained because they've been previously introduced. If at any time something doesn't seem clear, don't hesitate to go back and review the lesson where it first appeared or check the grammatical index or glossary. Even if you're sailing along in learning Spanish, these are useful resources if you're unsure of anything.

Second wave: 27th lesson

Lesson seventy-seven 77

habl → arais / aseis
habl → aran / asen

-er and **-ir** verbs, such as **comer** *to eat*, and **subir** *to climb, get on*:

com → iera / iese *(that I ate)*
com → ieras / ieses
com → iera / iese
com → iéramos / iésemos
com → ierais / ieseis
com → ieran / iesen

sub → iera / iese *(that I got on)*
sub → ieras / ieses
sub → iera / iese
sub → iéramos / iésemos
sub → ierais / ieseis
sub → ieran / iesen

Careful! When a verb is irregular in the third-person preterite tense (singular and plural), the same irregularity occurs in all persons of the imperfect subjunctive. For example:
pedir *to request, to ask for*:
preterite: **pedí, pediste, pidió, pedimos, pedisteis, pidieron**
I requested, you requested, etc.

77 imperfect subjunctive: **pidiera/pidiese, pidieras/pidieses, pidiera/pidiese, pidiéramos/pidiésemos, pidierais/pidieseis, pidieran/pidiesen**
that I requested, that you requested, etc.

The endings stay regular, but the root retains the irregularity from the third-person preterite. There are no exceptions to this rule!

1.2 Uses of the imperfect subjunctive

The subjunctive mood can be a bit tricky when learning Spanish because it is rarely used in English. The basic thing to remember is that it is used in various contexts to express things that are not certain, objective facts. As we've seen, it is often found in clauses following **que** *that* if the subject of the sentence changes. Some of the main uses of the imperfect subjunctive are summarized below.

• The imperfect subjunctive is generally used to express the same subjective attitudes as the present subjunctive (wish, emotion, doubt, denial), but with reference to an event in the past.
Quiero que vengas conmigo a la boda.
I want you to come with me to the wedding.
(present + **que** + present subjunctive)
Yo quería que vinieras/vinieses conmigo a la boda.
I wanted you to come with me to the wedding.
(past imperfect + **que** + imperfect subjunctive)

• The imperfect subjunctive is also used in a clause stating a condition beginning with **si** *if* when the conditional mood is used in the clause that expresses the outcome (which can be uncertain, improbable or impossible).
El señor llegaría más temprano si Ud. fuera/fuese a recogerlo.
The gentleman would arrive earlier if you went to pick him up.
(conditional + **si** + imperfect subjunctive)

As in English, the clauses can be inverted:
Si Ud. fuera/fuese a recogerlo, el señor llegaría más temprano.
If you went to pick him up, the gentleman would arrive earlier.
(**si** + imperfect subjunctive + conditional)

In this use, the imperfect subjunctive doesn't refer to a past action, but is simply required by the use of the conditional – the construction of English conditional sentences is similar.
Si no lloviera/lloviese, iríamos a dar una vuelta.
If it weren't raining, we would go for a walk.
Te acompañaría si no estuviera tan cansado.
I would go with you if I weren't so tired.

Note that a conditional sentence can also be formed using the present or future tense, in which case the condition (expressed in the **si** *if* clause) is in the present tense – no subjunctives are needed. Compare the following examples with those above:
Si no llueve, iremos a dar una vuelta.
If it doesn't rain, we will go for a walk.
Te acompañaré si no estoy cansado.
I will go with you if I'm not tired.

• A sentence starting with **si** might not have the conditional construction shown in bullet point 2, but instead describe an unreal, completely hypothetical situation in reference to the past. In this case, it has a similar construction as shown in bullet point 1.
¡Si supieras lo que me ocurrió ayer!
If you knew what happened to me yesterday!
(imperfect subjunctive + **lo que** + past imperfect)

• Likewise, the expression **como si** *as if* is always followed by the imperfect subjunctive.
Es como si la viera … *It's as if I were seeing her …*
(**como si** + imperfect subjunctive)

• The imperfect subjunctive is also sometimes used instead of the conditional to express a polite request (lesson 56).
Quisiera unas tapas, por favor. *I would like some tapas, please.*

2 Verbs ending in *-ducir*

Verbs ending in **-ducir** are irregular and, like most verbs ending in **-cer** or **-cir** (**conocer** *to know, to meet*; **parecer** *to seem, to appear*; **agradecer** *to thank*, etc.), they take a **z** before the **c** if the **c** precedes an **a** or an **o** (in the present indicative, present subjunctive and imperative).

77 **conduzco** *(I drive)*	**conduzca** *(that I drive)*
conduces	**conduzcas**
conduce	**conduzca**
conducimos	**conduzcamos**
conducís	**conduzcáis**
conducen	**conduzcan**

In addition (and this is why they are irregular), in the preterite they take **-duje**, and consequently the imperfect subjunctive becomes **-dujera** or **-dujese**:

conduje *(I drove)*	**condujera** / **condujese** *(that I drove)*
condujiste	**condujeras** /**condujeses**
condujo	**condujera** / **condujese**
condujimos	**condujéramos** / **condujésemos**
condujisteis	**condujerais** / **condujeseis**
condujeron	**condujeran** / **condujesen**

The other forms of the verb (and all other verbs ending in **-ducir**) are conjugated on the model of **vivir**.

3 Spelling changes in verbs

Some verbs undergo a spelling change in certain persons. This does not, however, mean that they are irregular verbs. In fact, the change in spelling allows the verb to stay regular by retaining the same sound in all cases. So for example, **convencer** *to convince* keeps the same sound in the present tense as in the infinitive by becoming **convenzo** (and not **convenço**) *I convince.*

• Spelling changes in **-ar** verbs
(verbs ending in **-car**, **-gar**, **-guar**, **-zar**)

The change takes place in the preterite (first-person singular), in the present subjunctive (in all persons) and in some forms of the imperative.

Verbs ending in		becomes	
-car	**c**	→	**qu**
-gar	**g**	→	**gu**
-guar	**gu**	→	**gü**
-zar*	**z**	→	**c**

* Verbs ending in **-zar** change the **z** to **c** simply because there is never a **z** before **e** or **i** in Spanish.

Examples:

Infinitive	Preterite	Present subjunctive
indicar *to indicate*	**indiqué**	**indique, indiques**, etc.
pagar *to pay*	**pagué**	**pague, pagues**, etc.
apaciguar *to appease, pacify*	**apacigüé**	**apacigüe, apacigües**, etc.
adelgazar *to lose weight*	**adelgacé**	**adelgace, adelgaces**, etc.

• Changes in **-er** and **-ir** verbs
(verbs ending in **-cer**, **-cir**, **-ger**, **-gir**, **-guir**, **-quir**)

The change takes place in the present indicative (first-person singular), in the present subjunctive (all persons) and in some forms of the imperative.

Verbs ending in			becomes	
-cer **-cir**	}	**c**	→	**z**
-ger **-gir**	}	**g**	→	**j**
-guir		**gu**		**g**
-quir		**qu**		**c**

77 Examples:

Infinitive	Present indicative	Present subjunctive
convencer *to convince*	**convenzo**	**convenza, convenzas**, etc.
esparcir *to scatter, sprinkle*	**esparzo**	**esparza, esparzas**, etc.
coger *to take*	**cojo**	**coja, cojas**, etc.
dirigir *to direct*	**dirijo**	**dirija, dirijas**, etc.
distinguir *to distinguish*	**distingo**	**distinga, distingas**, etc.
delinquir *to commit a crime*	**delinco**	**delinca, delincas**, etc.

* * *

Diálogo recapitulativo

1 – Pareces cansado. ¿Qué te pasa?
2 – ¡Si supieras lo que me ocurrió ayer!
3 Por la mañana, fui a recibir a la madre de mi mujer al aeropuerto;
4 al verme, me dijo que tenía mal aspecto
5 y que así no podíamos ir a ninguna parte.
6 Primero me llevó a la peluquería;
7 luego, fuimos de tiendas porque quería comprarse un traje;
8 y, para terminar, se le ocurrió ir a tomar unos vinos.
9 A la vuelta tuvimos un accidente.
10 ¡Menudo día!

* * *

Traducción

1 You look tired. What's the matter with you? **2** If you knew what happened to me yesterday! **3** In the morning, I went to pick up my wife's mother at the airport; **4** when she saw me, she told me that I looked bad **5** and that [looking] like that, we couldn't go anywhere. **6** First, she took me to the barber's; **7** then, we went around the shops because she wanted to buy herself a suit; **8** and, finally, it came into her head to go have a few glasses of wine. **9** On the way back, we had an accident. **10** What a day!

Second wave: 28th lesson

Una llamada equivocada ①

1 – Me gustar**í**a visit**ar** la re**gión** de los **Pi**cos de Eu**ro**pa ② y…
2 quis**ie**ra ③ alqui**lar u**na **ca**sa ru**ral**.
3 ¿Po**drí**a aconse**jar**me al**gu**na por ④ esa **zo**na?
4 – Sé de ⑤ **u**na que es**tá** muy bien **cer**ca de A**re**nas de Ca**bra**les ⑥.
5 – ¿**Tie**ne i**de**a del **pre**cio?
6 – No, ten**drí**a que po**ner**se en con**tac**to con los propie**ta**rios…
7 – ¿**Sa**be si la al**qui**lan en tempo**ra**da **ba**ja?

Notes

① **una llamada equivocada** *a wrong number*, but **un dato erróneo** *wrong information*. The adjective **equivocado/a** has the notion of being mistaken about something (**equivocarse** *to make a mistake, get it wrong, be wrong*), whereas **erróneo** is used to mean something is erroneous.

② **Los Picos de Europa** is a mountain chain with rivers, gorges, mountain streams, caves and lakes that straddles the regions of Asturias, Cantabria and Castile-León. It is **un parque nacional**, the biggest natural reserve in Europe (nearly 700 km^2), and is a paradise for hikers, climbers and other nature lovers.

③ Remember: to politely express a wish using **querer** *to want*, the imperfect subjunctive rather than the conditional is used.
Quisiera un vaso de agua, por favor.
I'd like a glass of water, please.
Quisiéramos reservar una mesa para cuatro personas.
We'd like to reserve a table for four people.
Compare with **me gustaría** (conditional) *I would like* in line 1. The two can be used interchangeably. ▸

Wrong number

1 – I would like to visit the Picos de Europa region and …
2 I'd like to rent a country cottage *(a house rural)*.
3 Could you advise me [of] any around that region?
4 – I know of one that's very nice near Arenas de Cabrales …
5 – Do you have [any] idea of the price?
6 – No, you would have to get in contact *(put yourself in contact)* with the owners …
7 – Do you know if they rent it in [the] low season?

④ **por** is used here in the sense of *around* to express an inexact area within a location; it is also found in the expression **por ahí** *somewhere*.
Los niños corrían por el pueblo.
The kids were running around the village.
Los niños están por ahí, en el pueblo.
The kids are somewhere in the village.

⑤ Why **'Sé …'** and not **'Conozco …'** here (lesson 42)? Well, **saber de** *to know of* is interchangeable with **conocer**.
Sé de/Conoczo un médico que te recibirá inmediatamente, sin cita. *I know of a doctor who will see you immediately, without an appointment.*
Sé de/Conoczo una tienda donde encontrarás lo que buscas.
I know of a store where you'll find what you're looking for.

⑥ The region of Cabrales, one of the gateways to the **Picos de Europa**, is located on its northern slopes. It is a very welcoming spot famous for its **queso** *(cheese)* **de Cabrales**, a powerfully scented goat cheese with a strong, sharp taste.

8 – **Cre**o que sí, **pe**ro no es**toy** seguro, tend**rí**a
que pregun**tar** a…

9 – ¿**Sa**be si hay posibili**dad** de mon**tar** a
ca**ba**llo en los alrede**do**res ⑦?

10 – Sé que las activi**da**des son muy di**ver**sas,
pero…

11 – ¿**Po**d**rí**a proporcio**nar**me **o**tros de**ta**lles?

12 – **Oi**ga, **es**to es **u**na ferrete**rí**a y…

13 ¡no la ofi**ci**na de tu**ris**mo! □

Notes

⑦ **alrededor** *around* (adverb): **mirar alrededor** *to look around*
alrededor de *around* (preposition): **alrededor de la mesa**
around the table
alrededor de *around*, *about*, *approximately* (adverb): ▶

* * *

Ejercicio 1: Traduzca

❶ ¿Qué me aconsejarías? ❷ Podríamos alquilar
un coche. ❸ ¿Sabes de un buen restaurante en
ese pueblo? ❹ Ponte en contacto con la oficina de
turismo. ❺ Quisiera hablar con el propietario.

* * *

Ejercicio 2: Complete

❶ What do you *(informal sing.)* advise *(me)*?
¿ · · · · · · · · · · · · · ?

❷ We can rent a country cottage.
· ·

❸ I don't know all the details.
· · · · · · · · · · · · · · · · · detalles.

8 – I think so *(I believe that yes)*, but I'm not sure; you would have to ask *(to)* …
9 – Do you know if it's possible *(if there is possibility)* to go horse riding *(to mount to horse)* in the surrounding area?
10 – I know that there are a wide range of activities *(the activities are very varied)*, but …
11 – Could you provide me [with any] other details?
12 – Listen, this is a hardware shop and …
13 not the tourist office!

▸ **Ese viaje costará alrededor de mil euros.**
This trip will cost around 1000 euros.
Or as a plural noun, **alrededores** *surrounding area, vicinity*: **en los alrededores de la ciudad** *in the vicinity of the town.*

* * *

Answers to Exercise 1

❶ What would you advise *(me)*? ❷ We could rent a car. ❸ Do you know of a good restaurant in the village? ❹ Get in contact with the tourist office. ❺ I'd like to speak with the owner.

* * *

❹ Allow me to say *(that I say to you[informal])* that …
Permíteme que . . . . . . que…

❺ We'll ask at the tourist office.
. . . . en . . . .

Answers to Exercise 2

❶ Qué me aconsejas ❷ Podemos alquilar una casa rural ❸ No conozco todos los – ❹ – te diga – ❺ Preguntaremos – la oficina de turismo

The boom in rural tourism has led to a proliferation of **casas rurales** country cottages *and* **casas rústicas** farms *throughout Spain for those seeking an alternative to mass tourism and looking for somewhere to stay that's off the beaten track. This type of tourism, well suited to holidays with families or friends, makes it easier to get to know the local people and customs.*

79 Lección setenta y nueve

In this lesson, we invite you to discover some colloquial expressions that you might hear in a range of contexts.

Sin respetar ni rey ni roque ①

1 – **Pe**ro… ¿qué es**tás** ha**cien**do a**hí**?
2 – **Na**da, e**char** una oje**a**da ②;
3 **an**do mi**ran**do ③ a ver lo que **tie**nes a**quí** **den**tro.
4 – ¡**Có**mo que **an**das mi**ran**do?
5 Y… ¿quién te ha **da**do a ti per**mi**so ④
6 **pa**ra an**dar** regis**tran**do en el ca**jón** de mi des**pa**cho?
7 ¿Con qué de**re**cho?
8 ¡Son mis **co**sas!

Notes

① **No temer ni rey ni roque** *To fear neither God nor man*, *To accept no master* is a saying that makes reference to the king and the rook in **el ajedrez** *chess. The rook*, or *castle*, **la torre**, is also called **roque**, from the Persian 'rokh'. From the same root comes the verb **enrocar** *to castle*, a term well known to chess players.

② **una ojeada** *a look*, *peek*, *glance*, from **el ojo** *the eye*. As we saw in lesson 54, the suffix **-ada** often expresses the idea of a blow or strike. Here, we have a 'blow' from the eye.

Las oficinas de turismo tourist offices, *as well as official bodies that promote* **turismo rural** rural tourism, *can provide information to travellers and holidaymakers who wish to experience Spain in this less conventional and more authentic way.*

Second wave: 29th lesson

Lesson seventy-nine 79

Fearing neither God nor man
(Without respecting neither king nor rook)

1 – But … what are you doing there?
2 – Nothing, [just] taking *(throwing)* a quick look;
3 I'm checking to see *(I walk looking to see)* what you have in there.
4 – What do you mean *(How that)*, you're checking?
5 And who has given you permission
6 to go *(to walk)* searching through my desk drawer *(the drawer of my study)*?
7 With what right?
8 They're my things!

▸ ③ Note the use of **andar** + present participle (see lesson 70 for a reminder on present participles). This is a frequently used colloquial construction that expresses vagueness when referring to a particular action.
¿Dónde está tu hermano? - Anda preparando el viaje. *Where is your brother? – He is off (somewhere) preparing for the trip.*

④ **el permiso** *permission* and *permit, licence*. So, **con su permiso** *with your permission*; **permiso de conducir** (also, **carnet de conducir**) *driving licence.*

9 – De **to**das **for**mas ⑤, no **ve**o por qué te mo**les**ta;
10 si no tu**vie**ras **na**da que escon**der**…
11 – ¡No se **tra**ta de ⑥ escon**der** o no!
12 ¡No fal**ta**ba más! ⑦
13 ¡Es **u**na cues**tión** de prin**ci**pios!
14 – ¡Los prin**ci**pios me dan i**gual**! ⑧
15 ¡A**ba**jo los prin**ci**pios!
16 ¡**Dé**jate de ⑨ his**to**rias!
17 – No, **pe**ro… ¡tú no es**tás** bien!
18 ¡Si no lo **ve**o, no lo **cre**o! ⑩

Notes

⑤ The frequently used expression **de todas formas** (or **maneras**) *anyway, in any event, in any case*, has a negative equivalent: **de ninguna forma** (or **manera**) *in no way, by no means.*
De todas formas (maneras), en la carretera hay que ser prudente. *In any case, on the road one must be cautious.*
¡De ninguna forma (manera)! *No way!*

⑥ **tratarse de** *to be about, to concern, to be a question/matter of.*
¿De qué se trata? *What's it about?*

⑦ **¡No faltaba más!** from **faltar** *to be missing, to be lacking* is a commonly heard sarcastic remark roughly equivalent to *That's all we needed! Whatever next!*, etc., used in response to an offensive or ridiculous statement.

* * *

Ejercicio 1: Traduzca

❶ Voy a echar una ojeada. ❷ ¿Qué estás comiendo? ❸ El pasaporte está dentro, en la maleta. ❹ No sé dónde he dejado el permiso de conducir. ❺ ¿Has mirado en el bolsillo de la chaqueta?

9 – Anyway, I don't see why it should bother *(bothers)* you
10 if you didn't have anything to hide …
11 – It's not a matter *(It isn't about)* of hiding or not!
12 That's all we needed *(It wasn't lacking more)*!
13 It's a question of principle*(s)*!
14 – I don't care about principles *(Principles give me equal)*!
15 Down with principles!
16 Stop [making] excuses *(stories)*!
17 – No, but … you're crazy *(you're not well)*!
18 I can't believe it *(If I don't see it, I don't believe it)*!

⑧ **Me da igual** *It's all the same to me*, *I don't care*, or, more colloquially, *I couldn't care less*, *I don't give a damn*.

⑨ **dejarse** (or **dejar**) followed by **de** + a noun (or a verb in the infinitive) often translates as *to stop*, *to leave off*:
¡Deja de hablar! *Stop talking!*
¡Déjate de bobadas! *Stop that nonsense! Stop saying silly stuff!* (**Deja de decir bobadas.**)

⑩ **¡Si no lo veo no lo creo!** *I can't believe my eyes! Unbelievable!*

* * *

Answers to Exercise 1

❶ I'm going to take a quick look. ❷ What are you eating? ❸ The passport is inside, in the suitcase. ❹ I don't know where I've left my driving licence. ❺ Have you looked in your jacket pocket?

Ejercicio 2: Complete

❶ He's off doing some shopping.
.... unas ....

❷ No, it's not all the same to me.
No, ...

❸ That's all we needed!
¡.. ....!

❹ What's it about?
¿.. ... .?

❺ Stop playing with my things!
¡.... .. jugar ... ...!

---

80 Lección ochenta

Hacia Santiago

1 El Ca**mi**no de San**tia**go, conste**la**do de re**fu**gios y al**ber**gues
2 que ja**lo**nan las dife**ren**tes e**ta**pas,
3 consti**tu**ye hoy **día** ① la pri**me**ra **ru**ta tu**rís**tica euro**pe**a.
4 A un **rit**mo de **u**nos **trein**ta ② ki**ló**metros **dia**rios,

Notes

① **hoy día** or **hoy en día** *nowadays*, *at the present time*, *today.*

② **unos treinta kilómetros** (or **una treintena de kilómetros**) *some thirty kilometres.*

NO SÉ DÓNDE HE DEJADO EL PERMISO DE CONDUCIR.

Answers to Exercise 2
❶ Anda haciendo – compras ❷ – no me da igual ❸ No faltaba más ❹ De qué se trata ❺ Deja de – con mis cosas

Second wave: 30th lesson

Lesson eighty 80

On the way to *(Towards)* Santiago [de Compostela]

1 The Way of St. James, studded with shelters and inns
2 that mark out the various stages,
3 is *(constitutes)* today the first European [Cultural] *(tourist)* Route.
4 At a rate of some thirty kilometres per day *(daily)*,

Había unas veinte personas (or **una veintena de personas**).
There were some twenty people.
The first construction in each example is more usual.

5 har**á** **fal**ta ③ un mes **pa**ra reco**rrer** los ocho**cien**tos kil**ó**metros

6 que se**pa**ran Ronces**va**lles ④ de San**tia**go de Compos**te**la.

7 **Pa**ra los nume**ro**sos pere**gri**nos que **ca**da **a**ño lo fre**cuen**tan,

8 ya **se**a por ra**zo**nes de **or**den espiri**tual**,

9 por afi**ción** al sende**ris**mo,

10 por el pla**cer** de encon**trar**se en con**tac**to con la natura**le**za

11 o por **sim**ple **gus**to por la aven**tu**ra,

12 su reco**rri**do ⑤, a me**nu**do de ca**rác**ter ini**ciá**tico,

13 consti**tu**ye ⑥ una expe**rien**cia inolvi**da**ble. □

Notes

③ **hará falta un mes** *it will take a month*, *a month will be needed.* As we saw in lesson 75, the idea of needing, which is related to that of lacking or missing something, can be translated either by **hacer falta** or **necesitar**. *A* [noun] *is needed* = **hace falta**/ **se necesita** + noun. When the noun is plural, so is the verb: **Hacen falta** (or **Se necesitan**) **tres vasos más.** *We need three more glasses.* ('Three more glasses are needed.')

④ Of all the routes that formerly led to Santiago de Compostela from every corner of Europe, there remain today only three once the Pyrenees have been crossed: the northern route, through Asturias, formerly considered the most dangerous; and those starting from Somport and from Roncesvalles, which meet up at Puente la Reina to become **el Camino Francés** (the French Way). Today, the Roncesvalles route, which is shorter, is by far the most frequented.

⑤ **un recorrido** *a trip*, *tour*, *journey*, *route* comes from **recorrer** *to cover*, *to travel* (line 5), whose past participle is also **recorrido** *travelled.* ▸

5 it will take a month to cover the 800 km
6 that separate Roncesvalles from Santiago de Compostela.
7 For the numerous pilgrims who traverse *(frequent)* it each year,
8 whether it be for reasons of a spiritual nature *(order)*,
9 for love of hiking,
10 for the pleasure of being *(finding oneself)* in contact with nature
11 or simply for a taste *(or by simple taste)* of adventure,
12 their journey, often a voyage of discovery *(often of character initiatory)*,
13 is an unforgettable experience.

▸ ⑥ Verbs ending in **-uir** undergo a spelling change, adding a **y** after the **u** of the stem before the vowels **a**, **e** and **o**. This change takes place in the present indicative, the present subjunctive and the imperative.
construir → **construyo** *I build* (present indicative)
contribuir → **contribuya** *that I contribute* (present subj.)
distribuir → **distribuye** *Distribute!* (imperative)
But: **construimos** *we build/built* (present indicative, preterite).

Ejercicio 1: Traduzca

❶ Pasaremos la noche en un refugio. ❷ Ayer noche el cielo estaba constelado de estrellas. ❸ Ha sido un placer. ❹ Numerosos peregrinos recorren cada año el Camino de Santiago. ❺ La marcha a pie constituye un excelente ejercicio.

* * *

Ejercicio 2: Complete

❶ How many kilometres have you *(informal plural)* covered?
¿. . . . . habéis . . . . ?

❷ Several hours will be needed to finish that job.
. . . . varias horas . . . . ese trabajo.

❸ I need ten minutes more.
. . . .

❹ Alberto hands out *(distributes)* the presents.
Alberto . . . .

* * *

The spreading of the news of the discovery of the tomb of St. James *(***Santiago** *in Spanish, derived from* **santo** saint *combined with* **Iago**, *a Spanish or Galician form of the name* James*) at the farthest western point of the Iberian Peninsula at the beginning of the 9th century triggered a huge mobilization of Medieval Christendom. Streams of* **peregrinos** pilgrims, *more than half a million each year, made their way to Santiago de Compostela (from the Latin 'campus stellae',* field of stars), *particularly from the 11th century, to worship the relics of James the Apostle. All along* **el Camino** the Way, *inns, hospices, leper-houses and the like sprang up. Towns were founded as skilled craftsmen – blacksmiths, masons, carpenters – and merchants of all kinds settled along the route. As these towns were made up of and visited by foreigners with different customs, the Way became a melting pot and an important cultural channel,*

Answers to Exercise 1

❶ We will spend the night in a shelter. ❷ Last night the sky was studded with stars. ❸ It has been a pleasure. ❹ Numerous pilgrims travel the Way of St. James every year. ❺ Walking *(The walk on foot)* is excellent exercise.

* * *

❺ There's an inn *(at)* some ten kilometres from here.
… .. …….. a …. …. ……….
.. ….. .

Answers to Exercise 2

❶ Cuántos kilómetros – recorrido ❷ Harán falta – para acabar – ❸ Necesito diez minutos más ❹ – distribuye los regalos ❺ Hay un albergue – unos diez kilómetros de aquí

* * *

laying the foundations that made possible the birth of Spanish Romanesque art, followed by Gothic art.

Today, **el Camino***, dotted with* **catedrales** cathedrals, **monasterios** monasteries, **iglesias** churches, **santuarios** sanctuaries, **hospitales** hospitals, *etc., several of which have become* **paradores***, is a protected historical site. In 1987, the Council of Europe declared it the first European Cultural Route, and it has also been named a UNESCO World Heritage Site. Modern* **peregrinos***, on foot, horseback or bicycle, travel a well-charted route that allows them to reach one of the most beautiful architectural treasures in Spain: the city of Santiago de Compostela.*

Second wave: 31st lesson

81 Lección ochenta y una

Concordancia

1 Un hombre**zue**lo ① **ca**si analfa**be**to
2 **pe**ro sin **du**da al**gu**na despabi**la**do,
3 lo**gró** que le nom**bra**ran ② ma**es**tro de es**cue**la.
4 Un alde**a**no bas**tan**te pa**tán**, que por su **la**do
5 ha**bí**a conse**gui**do que le eli**gie**ran ③ al**cal**de,
6 se diri**gió** ④ a él y le **di**jo:
7 – **Ten**go un **tí**o que emi**gró** de a**quí** **ha**ce **a**ños

Notes

① The diminutive suffix **-uelo** denotes smallness and often has a pejorative or contemptuous connotation; use it with care (also, it can't be used with all nouns). **un bribonzuelo** *a little rascal.* **un actorzuelo** *a bit-part actor of no importance.*

Certain words with the suffix **-uelo** have become words in their own right over time: **un pañuelo** *a handkerchief* (from **paño** *cloth, piece of fabric*).

② **logró que le nombraran** *he managed to get them to appoint him* ('he managed that they named him'). The English infinitive construction *to get* is here replaced by a subordinate clause introduced by **que** + imperfect subjunctive. As you know, the subjunctive is often found after **que** when the subject changes. Here the imperfect (past) subjunctive is used in the subordinate clause because the main clause is in the past tense. This tense sequence is strictly observed in Spanish.
Le pedí que viniera. *I asked him to come.*
('I ask<u>ed</u> that he <u>came</u>.')

③ **había conseguido que le eligieran** *he had managed to get himself elected.* This construction is very similar to that in ▸

Agreement

1 A pitiable little man, almost illiterate
2 but definitely *(without doubt any)* resourceful,
3 managed to get himself appointed *(managed that they named him)* schoolmaster.
4 A village bumpkin *(villager rather boorish)*, who in turn *(for his side)*
5 had managed to get himself elected *(managed that they elected him)* mayor,
6 addressed himself to him and *(to him)* said:
7 – I have an uncle who emigrated from here years ago

▸ note 2. Note the tense sequence: the main clause verb is in a past (past perfect) tense (**había conseguido** *he had managed*) → the subordinate clause verb is therefore in the imperfect subjunctive (**que le eligieran** *to get himself elected* – 'that they elected him').

④ **dirigir** *to direct*; **dirigirse** *to make one's way to, to address, to speak to, to contact.*

8 y del que (5) no **ten**go no**ti**cias (6);
9 ¿po**drí**a escri**bir**le **u**na **car**ta por mí?
10 **Lue**go (7), tras ha**ber**sela dic**ta**do,
11 el alde**a**no le pi**dió** que se la rele**ye**ra (8):
12 – **Quie**ro es**tar** se**gu**ro de no ha**ber** olvi**da**do **na**da.
13 El hombre**zue**lo, con**fu**so **an**te su garaba**te**o, se excu**só**:
14 – Lo **sien**to, **pe**ro no con**si**go (9) desci**frar** lo que he es**cri**to.
15 – Pues… si us**ted** no **pue**de le**er**la,
16 ¿**có**mo po**drá** ha**cer**lo mi **tí**o?
17 – **E**so no es a**sun**to **mí**o (10);
18 mi tra**ba**jo con**sis**te en escri**bir** y no en le**er**.

Notes

(5) **de quien** or **de quienes** *of/from whom*, may also be rendered by **del que**, **de la que**, **de los que**, **de las que**, according to the gender and number of the noun it refers to.
La mujer de quien (or **de la que**) **hablé.**
The woman of whom (of the which) *I spoke.*
Los jóvenes de quienes (or **de los que**) **me ocupo.**
The young people whom I look after.

(6) **las noticias** *news* is also used to refer to TV and radio news (the singular **una noticia** is *a piece of news*, *news item*).
Voy a escuchar las noticias.
I'm going to listen to the news. (radio)
Quiero ver el telediario or **las noticias.**
I want to watch the news. (TV)

(7) **luego** *then*, *afterwards* (**después**), *later* (**más tarde**) is also found in the expression **¡Hasta luego!** *See you later!*

(8) Again, note the tense sequence (see notes 2 and 3). Here we have the imperfect subjunctive of **releer** *to reread*. It has a ▸

8 and from whom I have no news;
9 could you write him a letter for me?
10 Afterwards, after having dictated it to him *(to-have-to-him-it dictated)*,
11 the bumpkin asked him to read it back to him *(that to-him it was reread)*:
12 – I want to be sure not to have forgotten anything *(nothing)*.
13 The little man, confused by *(before)* his [own] scribble, apologized *(excused himself)*:
14 – I'm sorry, but I can't figure out *(don't manage to decipher)* what I have written.
15 – Well … if you can't read it,
16 how will my uncle be able to *(do it)*?
17 – That's not my concern *(affair)*;
18 my job is to write, not to read *(consists in to write and not in to read)*.

spelling change – the 'i' of the imperfect subjunctive ending changes to 'y'.

(9) Three verbs in this lesson, **consigo** (**conseguir** *to obtain*, *to manage to*, *to succeed in*), **eligieran** (**elegir** *to choose*, *to elect*) in line 5 and **pidió** (**pedir** *to request*, *to ask for*) in line 11, are verbs that undergo a stem change (**e** to **i**) in both the present and preterite tenses. More on this in review lesson 84.

(10) **mío** *my*, *[of] mine*. Remember that in Spanish there are two forms of possessive adjective (lesson 63): the standard forms (**mi** *my*, **tu** *your*, **su** *his*, *her*, *its*, *your*, *their*) come before the noun, the emphatic forms **mío**, **tuyo**, **suyo** are always placed after the noun.
No es tu asunto. *It's not your concern.*
Eso no es asunto tuyo. *That's not your concern.* or *That's no concern of yours.*

19 – Y, por **o**tra **par**te… es ver**dad** – aña**dió** el alde**a**no conven**ci**do –
20 ¿con qué de**re**cho va a le**er u**na **car**ta que no es **pa**ra us**ted**? □

* * *

Ejercicio 1: Traduzca

❶ Durante los años cincuenta muchos emigraron a América. ❷ Hace años que no le veo. ❸ ¿Habéis hecho un dictado en el colegio? ❹ Le pedí que me acompañara. ❺ ¿En qué consiste tu trabajo?

* * *

Ejercicio 2: Complete

❶ Are you *(masc. informal sing.)* sure you haven't forgotten anything *(to not have forgotten nothing)*?
¿. . . . . haber . . . . ?

❷ I didn't manage to arrive on time.
. . . . llegar . . . .

❸ The friends I spoke to you about *(of the which to-you[informal sing.] I have spoken)* are going to arrive immediately.
Los amigos . . . . van a llegar . . . .

❹ To whom is that letter addressed *(directed)*?
¿. . . . . esa carta?

❺ See you later!
¡. . . . . !

19 – Actually *(And by another part)* … that's true – added the bumpkin, convinced –
20 what gives you the right to read *(with what right are you going to read)* a letter that isn't for you?

* * *

Answers to Exercise 1

❶ In the 1950s, many [people] emigrated to America. ❷ I haven't seen him for years. ❸ Have you *(informal pl.)* done a dictation at school? ❹ I asked him to accompany me. ❺ What does your work involve *(consist of)*?

* * *

Answers to Exercise 2

❶ Estás seguro de no – olvidado nada ❷ No he conseguido – a tiempo ❸ – de los que te he hablado – enseguida ❹ A quién está dirigida – ❺ Hasta luego

Second wave: 32nd lesson

En el museo

1 – **Cua**tro en**tra**das ①, por fa**vor**.
2 – **Ten**ga ②, los **ni**ños no **pa**gan.
3 Les dese**a**mos **u**na agra**da**ble vi**si**ta.
4 – **Gra**cias. ¿**Has**ta qué **ho**ra es**tá** a**bier**to el mu**se**o?
5 – Hoy, **jue**ves, **has**ta las **sie**te.
6 **Llé**vese tam**bién es**te pe**que**ño fo**lle**to;
7 encontra**rá** en él ③ un **pla**no del mu**se**o
8 con las indica**cio**nes nece**sa**rias **pa**ra orien**tar**se,
9 a**sí co**mo **u**na **se**rie de informa**cio**nes ④ **prác**ticas:
10 ho**ra**rio de vi**si**tas con **guí**a,
11 **lis**ta de ca**tá**logos que se **pue**den adqui**rir** ⑤ en la **tien**da del mu**se**o,

Notes

① **una entrada** *ticket* (also *entrance* for a museum, theatre, etc.), but **un billete** *ticket* (for a bus, train, etc.). Another distinction that might be useful to remember in a museum is that Spanish has different words for 'room' depending on their size: **una sala** *large room*, *hall* (in a museum, theatre, etc.), **una habitación** *room*, *bedroom* (in a home, hotel, etc.), **un cuarto** *small room* (bathroom, cloakroom, etc.).

② When handing something to someone, you can use:
• **aquí** or **ahí** + the present tense of **tener** *to have*, *hold*:
Aquí tiene./Aquí tienes. *Here you are.* (form./inf.)
• the command form of **tener**:
Tenga!/Ten! *Here you are.* (form./inf.)

At the museum

1 – Four tickets, please.
2 – Here you are *(Have)*; children don't pay.
3 We wish you a pleasant visit.
4 – Thank you. Until what time is the museum open?
5 – Today, Thursday, until seven o'clock.
6 Take this little leaflet, too;
7 you will find in it a map *(plan)* of the museum
8 with the directions necessary to guide you *(to orient yourselves)*,
9 as well as *(so as)* a list *(a series)* of practical information*(s)*:
10 [a] schedule of guided visits *(hours of visits with guide)*,
11 [a] list of catalogues that can be purchased *(acquired)* in the museum shop,

▸ ③ The pronoun **él** *he* (note the written accent) also means *it* when referring to a masculine noun (here, **el folleto** *leaflet*).

④ **la información** *information* can also be used in the plural in Spanish, **informaciones**.

⑤ **adquirir** *to acquire, to obtain, to purchase* has a stem change from **i** to **ie** in the present tense (apart from the **nosotros** and **vosotros** forms): **adqu<u>ie</u>ro**, **adqu<u>ie</u>res**, **adqu<u>ie</u>re**, **adquirimos**, **adquirís**, **adqu<u>ie</u>ren**. All verbs ending in **-irir** change in the same way. You can check the grammatical appendix to review stem-changing verbs any time you need to.

12 **u**na pe**que**ña descrip**ción** de las princi**pa**les **o**bras ex**pues**tas, et**cé**tera.
13 – Se lo agra**dez**co.
14 – ¿**Sa**bes, E**duar**do?
15 Es**toy** encan**ta**da ⑥ de ha**ber** ve**ni**do a ver **to**das **es**tas mara**vi**llas;
16 Ve**láz**quez, el **Gre**co, Zurba**rán**, **Go**ya, Da**lí**, Pi**ca**sso, Mi**ró**…
17 Esta**ría** bien te**ner** **cua**dros a**sí** en **ca**sa …
18 – **Pe**ro, **Mai**te ⑦, con **to**do el tra**ba**jo que **ten**go…
19 ¿de **dón**de **quie**res que **sa**que ⑧ **tiem**po **pa**ra pin**tar**? □

Notes

⑥ Don't forget that the form of an adjective changes depending on whether a man or a woman is speaking:
Encantado/Encantada de conocerle/la.
Delighted to meet you. (m./f.)
¡Encantado/Encantada! *It's a pleasure!* (m./f.)

⑦ **Maite** (or **Mayte**) originated as a diminutive of **María Teresa**, but is now a full first name in its own right.

⑧ We've seen **sacar** meaning *to get out*, *to take out* (lesson 61). It also means *to obtain*, *to get*, *to gain*, as here, where it is used in the first-person present subjunctive form, **saque**.

* * *

Ejercicio 1: Traduzca

❶ Todavía no he sacado las entradas. ❷ Creo que los niños no pagan. ❸ ¿Has cogido el folleto con todas las informaciones? ❹ Compraremos un plano de la ciudad. ❺ ¿En qué piso se encuentra la sala de Goya?

12 a short description of the key works exhibited, etcetera.

13 – I thank you *(You for-it I-thank)*.

14 – You know, Eduardo?

15 I'm delighted that I came *(enchanted to have come)* to see all these wonderful things *(marvels)*;

16 Velázquez, El Greco, Zurbarán, Goya, Dalí, Picasso, Miró …

17 It would be great to have paintings like these at home …

18 – But, Maite, with all the work that I have …

19 where do you want me to find *(want that I get)* [the] time to paint?

* * *

Answers to Exercise 1

❶ I haven't got(ten) the tickets yet. ❷ I believe that children don't pay. ❸ Did you take the leaflet with all the information? ❹ We'll buy a map of the city. ❺ What floor is the Goya room on?

Ejercicio 2: Complete

❶ I'll ask what the opening hours are *(what is the schedule of opening).*

. . . . cuál . . . . apertura.

❷ Here are your catalogues.

. . . . sus . . . .

❸ I thank you *(formal) (for it).*

. . . .

* * *

There is such a wealth of **patrimonio cultural** cultural heritage *in Spain that it's difficult for the traveller to ignore the many signs inviting him or her to enter* **un museo** a museum*, to visit* **una exposición** an exhibition, *or to venture into* **una iglesia** a church.

Los horarios (or **el horario**) **de apertura** opening hours *and* **los días de cierre** closing days *may vary from place to place; in addition, some may open only in the morning or close* **a la hora de la siesta** *(2 pm to 4 or 5 pm). It's wise to get information in advance! In many sites listed as* **Patrimonio Nacional** National Heritage, *entry is free for EU citizens. Also, many museums and* **monumentos** monuments *have certain times when entry is free* (**entrada gratuita**).

83 Lección ochenta y tres

Alta tecnología

1 Señoras y señores pasajeros:
2 nos disponemos ① a atravesar una zona de turbulencias.
3 Abróchense el cinturón

Notes

① **disponer** *to set out, to arrange*; **disponer de** *to have at one's disposal*; **disponerse** *to prepare.*

❹ This evening I'd like to watch the news.

....

❺ I'm purchasing *(acquiring)* a new car.

....

Answers to Exercise 2

❶ Preguntaré – es el horario de – ❷ Aquí tiene – catálogos ❸ Se lo agradezco ❹ Esta noche me gustaría ver el telediario ❺ Adquiero un nuevo coche

* * *

In small towns, villages and more isolated places, churches, sanctuaries, castles and other sites worth a detour are often closed; however, don't hesitate to try and get the key. You could seek out the caretaker, a neighbour, a nearby bar, or enquire at the town hall or even the **farmacia**. *Generally, it's worth the effort, as often these 'unofficial' guides give personalized, colourful explanations with details that you won't find in books.*
¡Le deseamos una agradable visita!

Second wave: 33rd lesson

Lesson eighty-three 83

High technology

1 Ladies and gentlemen *(passengers)*:
2 we are preparing to go through *(cross)* an area of turbulence.
3 Fasten your seat belts *(the seat belt)*

4 y perma**nez**can ② en su a**sien**to.
5 **Gra**cias por su aten**ción**.
6 Nos com**pla**ce ③ recor**dar**les que se en**cuen**tran a **bor**do
7 del **nue**vo apa**ra**to de **ti**po '**Na**ve **dro**ne',
8 que **vue**la de ma**ne**ra au**tó**noma ④,
9 sin tripula**ción** ⑤ al**gu**na ⑥.
10 El pilo**ta**je es com**ple**tamente auto**má**tico.

Notes

② We've seen that after verbs that express a wish, request, order, etc., the subjunctive is often used in the subordinate clause. And remember (lesson 81), tense sequence is applied strictly in Spanish. So here, since the imperative A**bróchense** *Fasten* (formal plural) refers to the present, the verb in the second command is in the present subjunctive (**permanezcan** is the third-person plural present subjunctive of **permanecer** *to stay, remain*). We've seen this with constructions using **que** + subordinate clause:
Le pide (present) **que venga** (present subjunctive)**.**
He asks him to come. ('He asks that he come.')
Le pidió (preterite) **que viniera** (imperfect subjunctive)**.**
He asked him to come. ('He asked that he came.')

③ **complacer** *to please*, **complacerse en algo** *to take pleasure in something* are verbs you're only likely to come across in very formal contexts, such as announcements or invitations.
Nos complace anunciarles que aterrizaremos en breves instantes. *We are pleased to announce that we will land shortly.*
Nos complacemos en anunciar la boda de nuestra hija.
We have great pleasure in announcing the wedding of our daughter.

④ **de manera autónoma** *independently* ('in an autonomous manner'). One way to form adverbs in Spanish is by adding the suffix **-mente** to the feminine form of the adjective: ▶

4 and stay in your seats *(seat)*.
5 Thank you for your attention.
6 We are pleased *(Us it-pleases)* to remind you that you are *(find yourselves)* on board
7 the new 'Drone Ship' type aircraft *(apparatus)*,
8 which flies independently *(of manner autonomous)*;
9 without any crew.
10 Piloting is completely automatic.

EL CIERRE DE LAS PUERTAS SE EFECTUARÁ AUTOMÁTICAMENTE.

absoluto *complete* → **absolutamente** *completely* (line 11). But this isn't possible with all adjectives (such as **autónomo/a**), so another way is to form an adverbial phrase using **de manera** + adjective (or **de forma/de modo** + adjective).

⑤ **los miembros de la tripulación** *the members of the crew*. Among **el personal de a bordo** *the on-board personnel*: **el piloto** *the pilot*, **las azafatas** *the air hostesses* and **los auxiliares de vuelo** *the flight attendants*.

⑥ Remember, **alguno/a** means *none*, *not any* when placed after a noun preceded by **sin** or another negative word (lesson 57). **Sin ninguna duda** = **Sin duda alguna.** *Without any doubt.*

11 La seguri**dad** es**tá** abso**lu**tamente garanti**za**da,
12 ya que el con**trol** del apa**ra**to
13 se efec**tú**a, **des**de la esta**ción** espa**cial** 'At**lan**tis',
14 por **me**dio de un com**ple**jo sis**te**ma elec**tró**nico
15 teledirigido por **ra**yos **lá**ser.
16 Les dese**a**mos un fe**liz** viaj…, liz viaj…, liz via…, liz vi… □

* * *

Ejercicio 1: Traduzca

❶ Les recordamos que está prohibido fumar a bordo. ❷ Nos disponíamos a sentarnos a la mesa. ❸ Los miembros de la tripulación recibieron a los pasajeros. ❹ ¡Abróchate el cinturón! ❺ El cierre de las puertas se efectuará automáticamente.

* * *

Ejercicio 2: Complete

❶ Speak *(Address yourself[formal])* to the air hostess who is *(located)* at the entrance of the aircraft.
. . . . que se encuentra . . . . del aparato.

❷ She advised me to come see her.
Me aconsejó . . . .

❸ The aircraft has an electronic security system.
. . . . dispone de . . . . electrónico.

11 Safety is totally guaranteed,
12 since the control of the aircraft
13 is carried out from the space station 'Atlantis',
14 by means of a complex electronic system
15 remote-controlled by laser beams.
16 We wish you a good *(happy)* tri …, ood trip …, ood tr …, od t …

* * *

Answers to Exercise 1

❶ We remind you that it is forbidden to smoke on board. ❷ We were getting ready *(preparing ourselves)* to sit down at the table. ❸ The members of the crew welcomed *(received)* the passengers. ❹ Fasten your seat belt! ❺ The closing of the doors will be carried out automatically.

* * *

❹ Our plane is late.
.... lleva ....

❺ Thank you for your *(formal)* attention.
....

Answers to Exercise 2

❶ Diríjase a la azafata – a la entrada – ❷ – que viniera a verla ❸ El aparato – un sistema de seguridad – ❹ Nuestro avión – retraso ❺ Gracias por su atención

Second wave: 34th lesson

84 Lección ochenta y cuatro

Repaso

1 Tense sequence

Tense sequence is strictly observed whenever a sentence includes a subordinate clause introduced by **que** + subjunctive.

• When the main clause verb is in the present or future tense, the verb in the subordinate clause must be in the present subjunctive.
Dile (present) **que conduzca** (present subj.) **con precaución.**
Tell him to drive carefully.
Me dirá (future) **que tenga** (present subj.) **cuidado.**
He will tell me to be careful.

• When the main clause verb is in the past tense or conditional, the verb in the subordinate clause must be in the imperfect (past) subjunctive.
Le dije (preterite) **que leyera** (imperfect subj.) **el periódico.**
I told him to read the newspaper.
¿Le aconsejarías (conditional) **que lo leyera** (imperfect subj.)**?**
Would you advise him to read it?

• Even for the English verbs that require a similar structure (*that* + subordinate clause instead of an infinitive), the tense sequence described above still applies in Spanish.
Recomiendo que digas la verdad.
I recommend that you tell the truth.
Recomendaría que dijeras la verdad.
I would recommend that you tell ('you told') *the truth.*

2 Expressing a need

There are various ways to say that something is needed or necessary in Spanish. As in English, the idea can either be expressed actively with a subject or impersonally.

• **tener que** + infinitive *to have to ...*:
Tengo que estudiar. *I have to study.* (active)

• **hay que** + infinitive *it is necessary to ..., one should ...*:
Hay que estudiar. *It is necessary to study.* (impersonal)

• **necesitar** *to need*:
Necesito un destornillador. *I need a screwdriver.* (active)

• **necesitarse** *to be necessary, required*:
Se necesita una persona competente.
A competent person is needed. (impersonal)

• **hacer falta** *to be necessary* (synonymous with **necesitar**):
Me hace falta un destornillador. *I need a screwdriver.*
Hace falta una persona competente.
A competent person is needed.

• The construction with **falta** actually indicates that something is missing (**faltar** *to be lacking, missing*), which is another way of expressing need:
Falta un ordenador en la sala de informática. *We're lacking one computer* ('It-is-lacking a computer') *in the IT room.*
which has the same meaning as:
Necesitamos/Nos hace falta un ordenador más en la sala de informática. *We need one more computer in the IT room.*

Note that **faltar** and **hacer falta** conjugate like **gustar**; singular if the subject (what is missing) is singular, and plural if the subject is plural: **Faltan dos ordenadores.** *We need two computers.*
(See also lessons 21, 75, 80.)

3 Presenting or indicating something

There are several ways to present or indicate something, depending on the situation:

84 • To indicate or point something out → **éste**, **ése** or **aquél es**:
Éste es mi vaso y ése es el tuyo.
This is my glass and that one is yours.

• To situate something or someone → **aquí** and **ahí/allí**:
Aquí viene Juan. *Here comes Juan.*
Ahí va la pelota. *There goes the ball.*

• To hand something over → **aquí/ahí** + the present tense or the imperative form of **tener**:
¡Aquí tienes!/¡Aquí tiene! *Here you go!*
¡Ten!/¡Tenga! *Here you go!*

4 Irregular verbs (by tense)

Now that you've had a fairly complete overview of Spanish verb conjugation, here is a summary with a few simple guidelines that will help you begin to make sense of the irregularities. Some verbs are regular in one tense, but irregular in another, so the irregular patterns are shown according to tense. Don't worry about trying to retain all this information; just note it for now – you can always refer to the verb tables in the grammatical appendix.

4.1 Present tense

If a verb is irregular in the first-person present indicative, this irregularity is also found in the present subjunctive and the imperative. (Note that the first-person present indicative is the base of the present subjunctive of all verbs, irregular or not.)
conozco → **conozca** *I know* (present), *that I know* (present subj.)
vengo → **no vengas** *I come* (present), *Don't come!* (imperative)

There are some exceptions to this rule (**haber**, **ser**, **estar**, **ir**, **saber**, etc.), which need to be learned individually.

4.2 Preterite tense

If a verb is irregular in the third-person plural preterite, this irregularity is also found in the imperfect subjunctive. (Note that the third-person plural preterite is the base of the imperfect subjunctive of all verbs, irregular or not.)

pidieron → pidieran or **pidiesen** *they requested* (preterite), *that they request* (imperfect subj.)

4.3 Future tense

If a verb is irregular in the future (all persons), it will also be irregular in the conditional.
diré → diría *I will say* (future), *I would say* (conditional)

4.4 Imperfect tense

In the imperfect indicative, only the verbs **ir** *to go*, **ser** *to be* and **ver** *to see*, all of which you already know, are irregular.

5 Stem-changing *-ir* verbs

Certain **-ir** verbs (e.g. **pedir** *to request*, *ask for*; **servir** *to serve*; **conseguir** *to get*, *manage to*, *succeed in*; **vestirse** *to get dressed*, etc.) have a stem vowel change from **e** to **i** whenever the **e** is stressed or when the verb ending starts with a diphthong or with **a**. This change takes place in all persons in the present (except for **nosotros** and **vosotros**), in the third-person (sing. and pl.) preterite, in the subjunctive, in the imperative and in the present participle.
Siga (seguir) las instrucciones. *Follow the instructions.*
Me visto (vestirse) después de ducharme.
I get dressed after showering.
Consiguieron (conseguir) llegar a tiempo.
They managed to arrive on time.
¡Sírvete (servir)! *Serve yourself!*
Está pidiendo (pedir) la cuenta. *He/she's asking for the bill.*

Note that only **-ir** verbs (and not **-ar** and **-er** verbs) have a stem change in the third-person preterite and present participle. You'll find a list of verb irregularities by group (including stem and spelling changes) in section 16 of the grammatical appendix.

1 – Y si alquiláramos una casita en Galicia,
2 sacáramos tres billetes de avión,
3 nos fuéramos a Santiago,
4 cogiésemos allí un coche y…
5 cambiáramos de aire durante unos días,
6 ¿qué diríais?
7 – ¡Estupendo!
8 – ¿Cuándo nos vamos?
9 – ¡No tan deprisa!
10 ¡Parece ser que va a haber una huelga general!

---

85 Lección ochenta y cinco

Quién sabe… si… quizás… es posible...

1 – Voy a pro**bar** for**tu**na, voy a com**prar** un bi**lle**te de lote**rí**a.
2 – Ten cui**da**do, no desa**fí**es a la **suer**te ①,
3 **pue**de ser peli**gro**so.
4 – ¿**Có**mo, peli**gro**so?
5 – Si nos **to**ca el **gor**do ②,

Notes

① **desafiar (a)** *to challenge someone/something, to dare, to defy*: **desafiar a la suerte** *to tempt fate*; **desafiar el peligro** *to defy danger.*

② **tocar**, as we've seen, can mean *to touch* (lesson 29) or *to be one's turn* (lesson 50). It can also mean *to win the lottery* or, in a wider sense, *to win something in a draw* (**un sorteo**). Yet another meaning is *to play music/a musical instrument* (as opposed to **jugar** *to play a game/sport*). ▸

Traducción

1 And if we were to rent *(imperfect subj.)* a little house in Galicia, **2** we could get *(imperfect subj.)* three airline tickets, **3** we could go *(imperfect subj.)* to Santiago, **4** we could get *(imperfect subj.)* a car there and … **5** we could have a change *(imperfect subj.)* of scenery *(we could change of air)* for a few days, **6** what do *(would)* you *(informal pl.)* say? **7** Fantastic! **8** When are we leaving? **9** Not so fast! **10** It seems that there's going to be a general strike!

Second wave: 35th lesson

Lesson eighty-five 85

Who knows … if … perhaps … it's possible ...

1 – I'm going to try [my] luck *(fortune)*, I'm going to buy a lottery ticket.
2 – Be careful *(Have care)*, don't tempt fate *(challenge luck)*,
3 it can be dangerous.
4 – How [so], dangerous?
5 – If we win the jackpot *(If us it-touches the fat-one)*,

▸ **No tocar, recién pintado.** *Do not touch: fresh paint.*
¿Me toca a mí? *Is it my turn?*
¿Te ha tocado el gordo? *Have you won the jackpot?*
Te puede tocar un viaje. *You may win a trip.* (in a draw)
Toca el violín. *She plays the violin.*

6 es po**si**ble que nos ape**tez**ca ③ cam**biar**nos de **pi**so.

7 – Sí, segu**ra**mente, ¿y qué?

8 – Pues, que ha**brá** que acondicio**nar**lo: pin**tar**lo, deco**rar**lo y…

9 a**ca**so ④ discu**ta**mos por ⑤ no es**tar** de a**cuer**do

10 con res**pec**to al ⑥… co**lor** de las cor**ti**nas, por e**jem**plo;

11 y **lue**go nos senti**re**mos mal y nos deprimi**re**mos y…

12 qui**zás**… ¿qué sé yo? ¡I**gual** ⑦ nos da por ⑧ be**ber**!

Notes

③ **apetecer** *to feel like* conjugates like **gustar** (according to whether what one feels like is singular or plural) – i.e. in a similar way as *to appeal to*. Here it is used in the present subjunctive because it follows an impersonal expression introducing something hypothetical: **es posible que** (see review lesson 91 for further details). Note that it takes a spelling change like that of **conocer** *to know, to meet*.
¿Te apetece un helado? *Do you feel like an ice cream?* ('Does an ice cream appeal to you?')
Me apetecen tostados. *I feel like some toast.*
Hoy no me apetece nada salir a cenar. *Today I don't feel at all like going out to dinner.*

④ **discutamos** is the first-person plural present subjunctive of **discutir** *to argue, to discuss, to dispute*. When the adverbs of doubt **acaso**, **tal vez**, **quizá/s** *perhaps*, *maybe* are followed by the subjunctive (expressing the meaning **puede ser que** ...), this often translates in English to *may/might* or *maybe* + future tense. (See also note 9.)
Tal vez llame. *He might call./Maybe he will call.* ▸

6 it's possible that we'll feel like changing apartments *(to-us it-appeals to-change-us of apartment)*.

7 – Yes, surely, and [so] what?

8 – Well, we'll have to *(that it will be necessary to)* fix it up: paint it, decorate it and …

9 maybe we'll argue because we don't agree *(for not to-be of agreement)*

10 with respect to the … colour of the curtains, for example;

11 and then we'll feel bad and we'll get depressed and …

12 perhaps … what do I know? Maybe we'll start *(give ourselves to)* drinking!

⑤ Here **por** translates to *because*, though it generally means *for*. Remember that both **por** and **para** can mean *for*. They have various uses, but in general **por** tends to look back to the cause (*because of*), while **para** looks forward, to the effect:
Gracias por jugar. *Thanks for playing.*
Esto es para ti. *This is for you.*

⑥ Some useful phrases: **con respecto a** *regarding*, **con relación a** *in relation to*, **en cuanto a** *as regards, as for*, **en lo que concierne a** *concerning, with regard to.*

⑦ When **igual** *equal* introduces a hypothetical statement, it can mean *probably* or *maybe* (synonymous with **a lo mejor**, lesson 41). **Igual/A lo mejor tus amigos no beben.** *Perhaps your friends don't drink.*

⑧ **dar por** *to get into, to take to, to take up* followed by an infinitive implies the idea of 'giving oneself up' to something: to fall into a habit or to succumb to temptation by taking up an activity that becomes a mania; to start doing something excessively. It conjugates like **gustar**.
¿Le ha dado por beber? *Has he taken up drinking?*
Ahora le da por levantarse a las cinco de la mañana para hacer gimnasia. *Now she has taken to getting up at five o'clock in the morning to do exercises.*

13 Y… ¡quién **sa**be incluso si no ha**re**mos una lo**cu**ra!

14 – ¡Qué ho**rror**!

15 Sí, tal vez es ⑨ me**jor** no ju**gar** a la lote**rí**a! □

Notes

⑨ If the adverbs of doubt **tal vez**, **acaso**, **quizá/s** *perhaps* are followed by the indicative, what follows is considered as 'real' or factual as opposed to hypothetical.

* * *

Ejercicio 1: Traduzca

❶ Vamos a probar fortuna. ❷ ¿A quién le toca? ❸ Quizá lleguemos con retraso. ❹ Igual no bebe. ❺ Le ha dado por la informática.

* * *

Ejercicio 2: Complete

❶ Do you *(informal sing.)* feel like going to the cinema?
¿. . . . . ?

❷ Perhaps I'll stay at home. *(factual, not hypothetical)*
. . . .

❸ It's not worth the trouble *(hardship)* to argue over such a small thing.
. . . . . . la pena . . . . por . . . poca cosa.

❹ This year we haven't won the lottery.
. . . . la lotería.

❺ Be *(informal sing.)* careful, it's a very dangerous road.
. . . . , ... carretera . . .
. . . .

13 And … who even knows if we won't do something crazy *(a madness)*!
14 – How awful!
15 Yes, perhaps it's better not to play the lottery!

▸ **Tal vez, acaso, quizá/s** (or **probablemente**) **es** (or **será**) **mejor no jugar a la lotería.** *Perhaps* (or *probably*) *it is* (or *it will be*) *better not to play the lottery.*

* * *

Answers to Exercise 1

❶ We are going to try our luck. ❷ Whose turn is it? ❸ Perhaps we'll arrive late. ❹ Maybe he doesn't drink. ❺ He has got(ten) into computers *(IT)*.

* * *

Answers to Exercise 2

❶ Te apetece ir al cine ❷ Quizás me quedaré en casa ❸ No vale – discutir – tan – ❹ Este año no nos ha tocado – ❺ Ten cuidado, es una – muy peligrosa

Spain is one of the European countries where gambling fever is highest, with its **lotería nacional** national lottery*;* **lotería de la ONCE** *or* **cupón pro ciegos** daily lottery benefitting the blind*;* **quinielas** sports betting *and* **máquinas tragaperras** one-armed bandits, slot machines *in bars.*

Among these, **el sorteo extraordinario de la lotería de Navidad: el Gordo** the special Christmas lottery draw*: also known as* 'the Big One' (**gordo/a** fat)*, takes pride of place. This takes place each year on 22 December, marking the start of the end-of-year festive period and often coinciding with the first day of the school holidays. The draw is accompanied by singing children and is broadcast*

86 Lección ochenta y seis

Del buen comer

1 La co**ci**na espa**ño**la, de sa**bo**res ① muy va**ria**dos
2 y caracteri**za**da por un sin**nú**mero de especiali**da**des regio**na**les,
3 es excepcio**nal**mente **ri**ca.
4 Los de **fi**no pala**dar** ②,

Notes

① **sabor**, literally, *savour*, but also *flavour, taste.*
un pastel con sabor a canela *a cinnamon-flavoured cake* ('a cake with taste of cinnamon')
un cuento con sabor oriental *a story with an Oriental flavour.*

The word **gusto** *taste* is a synonym, but can additionally be used to mean a liking or preference for something.
sabores/gustos de helado *flavours of ice cream.*
No es a mi gusto. *It's not to my taste.* ▸

live on television, with radio stations repeating it throughout the morning. Wherever you are that day, it's hard to get away from those droning voices first chanting the numbers and the matching prizes and then suddenly shaking off their lethargy to shout out the biggest prizes and, in a burst of excitement, the winning number for the jackpot. Many participate in this **sorteo extraordinario** *in groups – as a family, a group of friends or workmates, etc. – and then share any winnings.*
¡Buena suerte!

Second wave: 36th lesson

Lesson eighty-six 86

About eating well

1 Spanish cuisine, with its *(of)* greatly varied flavours,
2 and characterized by an infinite number *(a 'without-number')* of regional specialities,
3 is exceptionally tasty *(rich)*.
4 Those with refined palate[s],

② **paladar** *palate* can also mean **gusto** or **sabor**.
tener el paladar fino (or **delicado**) *to have a refined palate, to be a gourmet.*
No tengo paladar para apreciar una cocina tan picante.
I don't have the taste for appreciating such spicy cuisine.

5 **co**mo ③ **bue**nos gas**tró**nomos ④,
6 **aun**que ⑤ tam**bién** a**pre**cian la lla**ma**da **nue**va co**ci**na,
7 y no **du**dan en palade**ar** ⑥ **nue**vos sa**bo**res,
8 se de**lei**tan ⑦ **so**bre **to**do con las re**ce**tas tradicio**na**les,
9 de las más sen**ci**llas a las más sofisti**ca**das.
10 Un fe**nó**meno cu**rio**so, **tí**picamente espa**ñol**:
11 la crea**ción** de socie**da**des gastro**nó**micas ⑧,
12 de ma**yor** so**le**ra ⑨ en el Pa**ís Vas**co,
13 **pe**ro **cu**ya ⑩ multiplica**ción** es cons**tan**te en **o**tras re**gio**nes,
14 particu**lar**mente en el **nor**te. □

Notes

③ Here, **como** *as, like* translates to 'being', in the sense of **en calidad de** *in one's capacity as*, **en tanto que** *acting as* (generally introducing one's role or function).
Saludó al vencedor, como buen deportista que es. *He shook hands with* ('greeted') *the winner, being a good sport* ('like good sportsman that he is').

④ **gastrónomo** *gourmet*. The word *gourmet*, of French origin, is also used in Spanish, especially among food connoisseurs.

⑤ Here, **aunque** *although*, *even though*, *even if* is followed by the indicative mood, indicating certainty. To express something hypothetical, it would be **aunque** + subjunctive.
Aunque llueve (indicative)**, vamos a salir.**
Although it's raining, we are going to go out.
Aunque llueva (subjunctive)**, vamos a salir.**
Even if it rains, we are going to go out.

⑥ **paladear** (from **paladar** *palate*) *to taste, savour* (**saborear**).

5 being *(as)* good gourmets,
6 although they also appreciate what is known as *(the so-called)* new cuisine
7 and have no hesitation *(do not doubt)* in savouring new tastes,
8 delight above all in *(with the)* traditional recipes,
9 from the simplest to the most sophisticated.
10 [There is] a curious phenomenon, typically Spanish:
11 the creation of gastronomic clubs,
12 more established *(of greater tradition)* in the Basque Country,
13 but which are steadily multiplying *(but whose multiplication is constant)* in other regions,
14 particularly in the north.

▸ (7) **deleitarse** *to take delight (in)*, *to enjoy very much*, when eating or otherwise. **Juan se deleita con la literatura del Siglo de Oro.** *Juan enjoys the literature of the 'Golden Age'.* (The **Siglo de Oro** – literally, 'Century of Gold' – of Spanish literature straddles the 16th and 17th centuries.)

(8) **las sociedades gastronómicas** *gastronomic clubs* are groups whose main aim is getting together to eat quality meals prepared by **socios** *club members*. The idea began in the Basque Country and dates back to the 1800s. Traditionally, their members are almost exclusively men.

(9) **solera** has the figurative sense of *tradition* (**tradición**), *age/seniority* (**antigüedad**), *pedigree* or *vintage* and applies particularly to wines: **un vino de solera** *an aged wine*.

(10) **cuyo(s)**, **cuya(s)** *whose* agrees in gender and number with the noun that immediately follows it.
Es la mujer cuyos hijos son socios aquí.
She's the woman whose sons are members here.

Ejercicio 1: Traduzca

❶ Me gusta la buena cocina. ❷ ¿Qué quieres probar? ❸ No duda en probar lo que le presentan. ❹ Prueba esta salsa y saboréala, ¡está deliciosa! ❺ La receta es muy sencilla.

* * *

Ejercicio 2: Complete

❶ When I travel, I like to try the regional specialities.
...... viajo, ...
....

❷ He helps his sister, like [the] good brother that he is.
...., ... buen ....
... .. .

❸ This cake has a lemony taste.
.... pastel tiene ...... limón.

❹ Although it's not very nice [out], we are going for a walk.
.... muy bueno, nos ..... a pasear.

❺ The taxi driver whose vehicle is parked on the right.
El taxista ....
.. ..

LA RECETA ES MUY SENCILLA.

Answers to Exercise 1

❶ I like good cooking. ❷ What do you want to try? ❸ He/she has no hesitation in trying whatever they give him/her. ❹ Taste this sauce and savour it, it's delicious! ❺ The recipe is very simple.

* * *

Answers to Exercise 2

❶ Cuando – me gusta probar las especialidades regionales ❷ Ayuda a su hermana, como – hermano que es ❸ Este – sabor a – ❹ Aunque no hace – vamos – ❺ – cuyo vehículo está aparcado a la derecha

Spain has a rich and varied gastronomic culture, and the Spanish take great pleasure in eating well, which goes hand in hand with their love of social gatherings.

There is a long tradition of getting together to enjoy local foods, and people may spend hours at the table. This philosophy of sharing food and drink in a convivial atmosphere is exemplified by tapas, but there are many other examples. Wherever you go in Spain, you'll see different versions of this eating culture, depending on the specific lifestyle of the various regions. For example, for many, **la época de la matanza** slaughter season [for pigs] *is the occasion to return* **al pueblo** to the village *to prepare cuts of meat and cured meats and share them out between family members, friends and neighbours so they can be enjoyed throughout the year.*

Of course, changes in lifestyles mean traditional customs have to adapt. Today, in some towns and cities you can still find men-only **sociedades gastronómicas**, *particularly in the Basque Country, where they are called* **txokos**. *For a less exclusive experience, throughout Spain you can find* **merenderos** picnic spots *or* outdoor bars *of varying sophistication, which are places to get together for a friendly* barbecue **una parrillada** *or to share a variety of delicious small (or large!) dishes.* **¡A saborear!** Tuck in!

Second wave: 37th lesson

En todas partes cuecen habas ①

1 – **Aun**que es**toy** ② con**ti**go,
2 me a**bu**rro en **es**te club nu**dis**ta.
3 ¡Es**toy** can**sa**do de **es**te **ti**po de vaca**cio**nes!
4 **Ha**ce **trein**ta y dos **a**ños que ve**ni**mos a pa**sar** los ve**ra**nos a**quí**
5 y **siem**pre es lo **mis**mo.
6 ¿Tú no es**tás has**ta las na**ri**ces ③?
7 Te pro**pon**go que ju**gue**mos ④ al **jue**go de **pren**das ⑤,
8 **pe**ro en vez de qui**tar**nos **ca**da vez **u**na **pren**da

Notes

① **En todas partes cuecen habas** (literally, 'Everywhere they cook beans') is a proverb that more or less means *It's the same anywhere you go*. Here the implication is that even free-spirited nudists still worry about what people will think!

② A reminder: **aunque** + indicative always refers to something real rather than hypothetical. **Aunque estoy contigo …** *Even though/Although I'm with you …*

③ **Estar hasta las narices** or **Estar hasta la coronilla** (literally, 'To be up to the nostrils' or 'To be up to the crown [of the head]') is a colloquial expression that means 'to have it up to here': *to be fed up (with)* or *to be sick and tired (of)*. Another common, more formal, expression is **estar harto/a** *to have had enough (of), to be fed up.* ▸

It's the same the whole world over

1 – Even though I'm with you,
2 I'm bored in this nudist club.
3 I'm tired of this kind of holiday!
4 For thirty-two years we've been coming to spend the summer*(s)* here
5 and it's always the same.
6 Aren't you fed up with it *(Aren't you up to the nostrils)*?
7 I suggest *(propose to you)* that we play strip poker *(the game of forfeits)*,
8 but instead of taking off an item of clothing each time,

④ **juguemos** is the first-person plural present subjunctive of **jugar** *to play*. It is a stem-changing verb (the only verb with a stem change from **u** → **ue**, a variant of **o** → **ue**), so in the present indicative it conjugates as **juego**, **juegas**, **juega**, **jugamos**, **jugáis**, **juegan**. As with other stem-changing verbs, the change does not occur in the **nosotros** and **vosotros** forms, but here because the subjunctive ending starts with **-e**, a spelling change (**g** → **gu**) is necessary in order to retain the hard **g** sound.

⑤ **juego de prendas** translates in this context as *strip poker*, but its wider meaning is any game in which the loser has to pay some type of penalty. Note also that another meaning of **una prenda** is *an item of clothing* (see line 8).

9 hacemos lo contrario:

10 nos vamos poniendo ⑥ el calzoncillo,
la braga, los calcetines,

11 las medias, la camiseta ⑦, el sujetador y…
así sucesivamente.

12 – ¡Tú no estás bien de la cabeza!

13 ¿Te das cuenta de lo que estás diciendo?

14 ¿Y si nos ven?

15 ¿Qué va a decir la gente? ☐

Notes

⑥ Remember that **ir** + present participle (lesson 70) expresses
the idea of a sequence of events, with the implied meaning
of *progressively*, *one after the other*, etc. Note also in line
11 the use of **sucesivamente** *successively*, preceded by the
conjunction **y** and the adverb **así**, meaning *and so on, and so
forth*.

⑦ **camiseta** can also mean *undershirt* or *sport jersey*.

* * *

Ejercicio 1: Traduzca

❶ Hace mucho tiempo que no le escribo. ❷ ¿Te
aburres? ❸ No estoy cansado, estoy en forma.
❹ ¡Estoy harta! ❺ Me han propuesto un empleo
que me gusta.

9 we do the opposite:
10 we'll put on [one by one] underpants, panties, socks,
11 stockings, T-shirt, bra and so forth like that *(like that successively)*.
12 – You're not right in the head!
13 Do you realize what you're saying?
14 And [what] if they see us?
15 What are people going to say?

* * *

Answers to Exercise 1

❶ I haven't written to him/her for a long time. ❷ Are you bored? ❸ I'm not tired; I'm in [good] shape *(on form)*. ❹ I'm fed up! ❺ I've been offered *(They have proposed to me)* a job that I like.

Ejercicio 2: Complete

❶ We are accustomed to spending the weekends there.
Solemos . . . . . allí los . . . .

❷ Even though it's raining, I'm going to do the shopping.
. . . . , ... hacer . . . .

❸ Where are you *(informal sing.)* going to spend the summer this year?
¿. . . . . ?

❹ Do you *(informal sing.)* have a headache?
¿. . duele . . . . ?

---

88 Lección ochenta y ocho

A la vuelta ①

1 – ¡Qué mo**re**nos es**táis**!
2 – Nos ha **he**cho un **tiem**po estu**pen**do.
3 Te**néis** que ir a **Mé**xico.
4 Nos lo **he**mos pa**sa**do en **gran**de ②.
5 Vol**ve**mos un **po**co can**sa**dos

Notes

① **a la vuelta** *upon return* (**del viaje** *from the trip*, or **de México** *from Mexico*). Other meanings include:
a la vuelta de + time, *at the end of/after* + time (**a la vuelta de tres meses** *at the end of/after three months*)
a la vuelta de la esquina *around the corner* (**Encontrarás un quiosco a la vuelta de la esquina.** *You'll find a newspaper stand just around the corner.*) ▸

❺ Take off *(formal sing.)* your overcoat, make yourself comfortable *(m.)*!

¡ . . . . el abrigo, póngase . . . . . . !

Answers to Exercise 2

❶ – pasar – fines de semana ❷ Aunque llueve, voy a – las compras ❸ Dónde vas a pasar el verano este año ❹ Te – la cabeza ❺ Quítese – cómodo

Second wave: 38th lesson

Lesson eighty-eight 88

Back home *(At the return)*

1 – How tanned *(brown)* you *(informal pl.)* are!
2 – We had *(To-us it-has made a)* fantastic weather.
3 You [just] have to go to Mexico.
4 We had a great time.
5 We've come back *(We return)* a bit tired

▸ ② **pasárselo bien** *to have a good time, to have fun* (**divertirse**). **pasárselo mal** *to not have fun, to be very bored* (**aburrirse**). **pasarlo** or **pasárselo en grande** *to have a great time, to really enjoy oneself.* And more colloquial, but very common: **pasarlo** or **pasárselo bomba** *to have a fantastic time.* **¿Te lo estás pasando bien?** *Are you having a good time? Are you enjoying yourself?*

6 **por**que nos **he**mos mo**vi**do ③ **mu**cho;
7 **pe**ro ha va**li**do la **pe**na.
8 – ¿Qué es lo que más ④ os ha gus**ta**do?
9 – Es di**fí**cil de de**cir**…
10 Las pi**rá**mides az**te**cas son impresio**nan**tes.
11 – La ma**ne**ra de ha**blar** nos ha resul**ta**do ⑤ a me**nu**do cu**rio**sa:
12 al**gu**nas expre**sio**nes son **pa**ra no**so**tros muy llama**ti**vas.
13 – Yo qui**zá** destaca**rí**a ⑥ el ca**rác**ter acoge**dor** de los mexi**ca**nos ⑦.
14 – Ve**nid**, **va**mos a sen**tar**nos a to**mar al**go y…
15 char**la**mos y os ense**ña**mos ⑧ las **fo**tos del **via**je. □

Notes

③ **moverse** *to move* is often used reflexively. Its stem changes from **o** to **ue** in the present tense, like **volver**.
No te muevas, voy a hacerte una foto.
Don't move – I'm going to take your photo.

④ **lo que más me gusta** *what I like most*, and its opposite: **lo que menos me gusta** *what I like least.*

⑤ **resultar** is a commonly used verb that has several different meanings, including *to result (in/from)*, *to turn out to be*, *to work out*, and here, in the sense of **parecer** *to seem to*, *to appear to.* You could say either **nos ha resultado** or **nos ha parecido** *it seemed to us*: they mean the same thing.

⑥ **destacar** *to highlight*, *to stress*, *to emphasize*, *to bring out*, *to underline* (also **subrayar**). **En su discurso ha destacado (subrayado) tres ideas principales.** *In her speech, she stressed three main ideas.* ▸

6 because we travelled around *(have moved ourselves)* a lot;
7 but it was worth it *(has-been worth the hardship)*.
8 – What did you like most?
9 – It's hard to say …
10 The Aztec pyramids are impressive.
11 – [People's] way of speaking often seemed odd to us:
12 certain expressions are *(for us)* very striking.
13 – I would perhaps highlight the welcoming nature of the Mexicans.
14 – Come on, let's go sit down and have something [to eat or to drink], and …
15 we['ll] chat and show you the photos from the trip.

▸ Used intransitively (without an object), **destacar** means *to stand out*, *to excel*. **Julia destaca por su inteligencia.** *Julia stands out because of her intelligence.*

⑦ And some other nationalities: **los americanos (América)** *Americans (America)*; **los australianos (Australia)** *Australians (Australia)*; **los franceses (Francia)** *French (France)*; **los alemanes (Alemania)** *Germans (Germany)*; **los irlandeses (Irlanda)** *Irish (Ireland)*; **los ingleses (Inglaterra)** *English (England)*; **los canadienses (Canadá)** *Canadians (Canada)*. Nouns of nationality are not capitalized in Spanish.

⑧ In Spanish, the use of the present tense to refer to the immediate future is very common. It makes the statement more active. **Hoy estoy ocupado, te llamo mañana.** *Today I'm busy, I['ll] call you tomorrow.* (Note that it is also possible to put the verb in the future tense.)

Ejercicio 1: Traduzca

❶ Lo supe* a la vuelta de un año. ❷ Nos hizo un tiempo muy malo. ❸ ¿Te has movido mucho? ❹ Es muy difícil de decir. ❺ Su manera de hablar me resulta familiar.

* Preterite form (irregular) of **saber**.

* * *

Ejercicio 2: Complete

❶ Did you *(informal sing.)* have fun?

¿.. .. ..?

❷ What did you *(informal sing.)* like least about that film?

¿... .. .. de esa película?

❸ Is it worth it *(Is-it-worth the hardship)*?

¿.... .. ....?

❹ Do you *(informal sing.)* want me to show you the photos?

¿....... que .. enseñe ... .?

❺ There's a taxi stand around the corner.

... ... parada .. ..

¡NOS HA HECHO UN TIEMPO ESTUPENDO!

Answers to Exercise 1

❶ I found out *(I knew it)* after a year. ❷ We had very bad weather. ❸ Did you move around a lot? ❹ It's very hard to say. ❺ His/Her/Your/Their manner of speaking seems familiar to me.

* * *

Answers to Exercise 2

❶ Te lo has pasado bien ❷ Qué es lo que menos te ha gustado – ❸ Vale la pena ❹ Quieres – te – las fotos ❺ Hay una – de taxis a la vuelta de la esquina

The **lengua española** Spanish language *is the second most spoken language in the world, with its use set to continue to increase with the growing population* **en Iberoamérica** in Latin America.

La comunidad hispanohablante the Spanish-speaking community *is not made up exclusively of Spaniards and* **hispanoamericanos** Spanish-speaking Latin Americans*; Spanish is also spoken in Asia, especially in the Philippines, in the former areas of Spanish influence in Africa, and in many islands in the Caribbean. In the United States, Spanish has become the second most-used language, with an estimated 45 million people speaking it as a first or second language. Some advocates argue that Spanish should be made the country's second* **lengua oficial** official language. *The worldwide Spanish community also includes the Sephardim, the descendants of Jews who left the Iberian Peninsula after their 1492 expulsion by the Catholic monarchs of Spain. They mainly settled around the Mediterranean, in North Africa, the Near East and the Balkans. Their language (Judeo-Spanish, or Ladino) derives from the Old Castilian spoken in the 16th century.*

This diversity of cultures, lifestyles and traditions is, not surprisingly, reflected in language differences. So, for example, in **América Latina** *you will encounter accents, words and expressions that are not only different from those in Spain, but also vary from one country to another.* **La diversidad** the diversity *is further enriched by the Native American peoples who have retained their ancestral languages.*

Second wave: 39th lesson

89 Lección ochenta y nueve

You're making amazing progress! This next lesson is a little longer than usual and has quite a bit of new vocabulary. Don't worry, we'll make up for it by making lesson 90 shorter and more of a review.

¡Que gane el mejor!

1 – Te **ve**o muy exci**ta**do.
2 – **Sal**go **es**ta **tar**de con mi **hi**jo **pa**ra Barce**lo**na.
3 Ma**ña**na se **jue**ga la fi**nal** de la Euro**li**ga de balon**ces**to,
4 y **co**mo mi **hi**jo es un gran aficio**na**do ①, le **lle**vo al par**ti**do.
5 – Cre**í**a que ju**ga**ba a balon**ma**no ②.
6 – Sí, en el co**le**gio; le **gus**ta **mu**cho el de**por**te.
7 Tam**bién jue**ga al **te**nis y prac**ti**ca la nata**ción**.
8 – ¿No te queja**rás**? ③
9 – **Só**lo me **que**jo **cuan**do me **ha**ce co**rrer** a mí; me **ma**ta.
10 Me **gus**ta ju**gar** con él, **pe**ro…

Notes

① **aficionado/a** *fan, enthusiast.*
aficionado/a a la música *a music lover.*
ser muy aficionado a *to like very much, to be passionate about, to be keen on.* **Es un gran aficionado a la lectura** or **Tiene una gran afición a la lectura.** *He loves reading.*
Similarly, **afición** is also used to mean *hobby, pastime.*
¿Cuál es tu afición principal? *What's your main hobby?* ▸

May the best team win!
(That may win the best!)

1 – You look *(I see you)* very excited.
2 – I'm leaving this afternoon with my son for Barcelona.
3 Tomorrow it's *(is played)* the Euroleague basketball final,
4 and since my son is a big fan I'm taking him to the game.
5 – I thought *(that)* he played handball.
6 – Yes, at school; he really loves sports.
7 He also plays tennis and swims *(practices swimming)*.
8 – You can't complain about that, can you *(You won't complain)*?
9 – I only complain when he makes me run; he's killing me.
10 I like to play with him, but …

▸ ② **balonmano** *handball* (i.e. European handball – a team sport with seven players per side); **baloncesto** (line 3) *basketball*; **balonvolea** and **voleibol** *volleyball* (literally, 'ball-hand', 'ball-basket' and 'ball-volley' respectively). An exception to this construction is **el fútbol** *football* (i.e. soccer), which has superseded the term **balompié** 'ball-foot', which is correct but rarely used.

③ **quejarse** *to complain*. The verb is in the future tense in this idiomatic expression that translates to 'you can't complain'.

11 ¡mi de**por**te favo**ri**to es la par**ti**da ④!
12 – ¿Vais **so**los?
13 – No, el Ma**drid** ha organi**za**do un **via**je en auto**car pa**ra los **so**cios ⑤ del club.
14 **Es**te **a**ño, no**so**tros es**ta**mos elimi**na**dos y…
15 **va**mos a ani**mar** al **Bar**ça ⑥.
16 **Pa**se por **u**na vez ⑦.
17 – **Bue**no, pues… ¡a pa**sar**lo bien! Y que ten**gáis** un buen **via**je.
18 – **Gra**cias. Que te **va**ya bien. **Pá**salo bien tú tam**bién** ⑧.

Notes

④ **una partida** *a game* (**de cartas** *of cards*; **de damas** *checkers*, *draughts*; **de dominó** *of dominoes*, etc.). **La partida**, without specifying which game, implies a game that is played regularly. Other meanings of **una partida** include *departure*, *certificate*, *party (a group)* and *shipment*. Don't confuse with **un partido** *a match*, *a game* (of sports).

⑤ **un/a socio/a** *member* (of a club or organization), *partner* (in a business). Compare:
un/a afiliado/a (literally, 'affiliated') *member* (political party), *holder* (insurance policy)
un/a abonado/a or **suscriptor/ora** *subscriber*.

⑥ **el Barcelona** or **el Barça** (in Catalan) is the Barcelona team. In sports parlance, it's common to simply add the article **el** to the name of a team (usually the city); the article refers to **equipo** (m.) *team*, which is understood. We also see this in line 13: **el Madrid** (or, less often, **el Real**) is **el equipo del Real Madrid** *the Real Madrid team.*

11 my favourite sport is a game of cards or chess *(the game)*!
12 – Are you going by yourselves *(alone)*?
13 – No, [Real] Madrid has organized a coach trip for club members.
14 This year we were *(are)* eliminated, and [so] …
15 we're going to cheer on Barcelona's team *(the Barça)*!
16 Just once won't hurt *(Pass for one time).*
17 – Well, then … have a good time! And [I hope] that you have a good trip.
18 – Thanks. All the best *(That it may go well with you)*. You enjoy yourself, too.

El Celta (de Vigo) y el Valencia han empatado.
Celta (of [the city of] Vigo) *and Valencia have drawn.*

⑦ **Pase por una vez** (literally, 'Pass for one time') means *Just this once. Just once won't hurt.*

⑧ There are various ways of wishing someone well when taking leave of them. Three of the most common are:
• **A** + infinitive: **A pasarlo bien, A divertirse** or **A disfrutar** *Enjoy yourself!* (all-purpose: formal, informal, sing. or pl.).
• **Que** + present subjunctive (indirect command): **Que tengáis (un) buen viaje.** *[I hope] that you* (informal pl.) *have a good trip.* **Que te vaya bien.** *All the best.* ('That it may go well with you.'). See also the lesson title: **¡Que gane el mejor!**
• As a direct command: **Pásalo bien, Diviértete** … *Enjoy yourself!*; **Cuídate mucho.** *Take good care of yourself.*

89 **Ejercicio 1: Traduzca**

❶ Voy a ver la final en la tele. ❷ El partido comienza a las nueve de la noche. ❸ ¿Haces deporte? ❹ Juego mucho a baloncesto. ❺ ¿Quieres jugar una partida a las cartas?

* * *

Ejercicio 2: Complete

❶ Our team is eliminated; they *(it)* won't play the final.
. . . . está . . . . , ...
. . . .

❷ What was she complaining about?
¿. . . . . ?

❸ After the match, her leg was hurting.
Después . . . . , le dolía . . . .

❹ Enjoy yourself. *(That you[informal sing.] may amuse yourself.)*
Que . . . .

❺ We have a small company; the three of us are partners *(we are three partners).*
. . . . pequeña . . . . , ...
. . . .

Answers to Exercise 1

❶ I'm going to watch the final on TV. ❷ The match begins at 9:00 pm. ❸ Do you practice a sport? ❹ I play a lot of basketball. ❺ Do you want to play a game of cards?

* * *

Answers to Exercise 2

❶ Nuestro equipo – eliminado, no jugará la final ❷ De qué se ha quejado ❸ – del partido – la pierna ❹ – te diviertas ❺ Tenemos una – empresa, somos tres socios

Spain has an excellent network of **autocares** coaches, long-distance buses *that serve the whole country. This mode of transport is quite fast and inexpensive; moreover, the coaches, which are generally safe and comfortable, also serve small towns that may not have a railway station. Each* **ciudad** city *has at least one* **estación de autobuses** coach/bus station*, which, as an added benefit, is usually located in the centre of the city and not on the outskirts.*

Second wave: 40th lesson

90 Lección noventa

¿Hay que ①... mirar de otra manera ②?

1 ¿Hay que suble**var**se **an**te ③ la pe**re**za de un **co**che que se **nie**ga ④ a arran**car**?
2 ¿Hay que admi**rar** la pa**cien**cia de **u**na bu**ta**ca que, **cuan**do nos **va**mos, se **que**da a**hí**, in**mó**vil, en es**pe**ra de ⑤ **nues**tra **vuel**ta?
3 ¿Hay que alte**rar**se **an**te la provoca**ción** que consti**tu**ye **u**na **ca**ma va**cí**a en **u**na habita**ción**?

Notes

① **hay que** + infinitive is an extremely common construction, which we first saw in lesson 18. It expresses obligation in an impersonal way (meaning the subject is not specified). There are a variety of ways to express this in English: *one must*, *one should*, *one has to*, *it is necessary to* or *it must be* + past participle. Spanish also has various other ways to express obligation (**tener que**, **deber**, **hacer falta**, some of which specify the subject: **tengo que** ... *I have to*, etc.) To review these, take a quick look at review lessons 21 and 84.

② **de otra manera** *in another way* and **de otro modo** *otherwise*. **dicho de otra manera** *in other words*, *put another way*.

③ Like **bajo** *under(neath)*, *below*, the preposition **ante** *before*, *in front of* is almost always used figuratively. To refer to a specific physical position in space, the forms **delante de** and **debajo de** are used. Compare:
iguales ante la ley *equal before the law*
delante de la cabina telefónica *in front of the telephone booth*
bajo las órdenes del Alto Mando *under the orders of High Command* (in the army) or *senior management* (business)
debajo de la silla *underneath the chair*. ▸

Should one … look [at things] differently?

1 Should one rebel against *(before)* the laziness of a car that refuses to start?
2 Should one admire the patience of an armchair that, when we get up, stays there, immobile, waiting for our return?
3 Should one get annoyed at *(before)* the provocation of *(that constitutes)* an empty bed in a room?

④ **negar**, whose primary meaning is *to deny*, means *to refuse* when used reflexively (**negarse**); it is then followed by the preposition **a**.
negar la verdad *to deny the truth*
Esta factura no está a mi nombre; hay un error, me niego a pagar. *This invoice is not in my name; there's a mistake, I refuse to pay.*

⑤ In a letter, this phrase is used in the formula **en espera de su respuesta** *awaiting your reply.*

4 ¿Hay que mos**trar**se tole**ran**te ⑥ **fren**te a la **fal**ta de compren**sión** de un ordena**dor** que, ne**gán**dose a obede**cer**, nos **de**ja plan**ta**dos ⑦?

5 ¿Se **de**be reaccio**nar an**te el servi**lis**mo de los fel**pu**dos en que ⑧ se **plan**tan los vende**do**res a domi**ci**lio?

6 ¿Hay que mi**rar** ce**rran**do los **o**jos para perci**bir** qué es la clari**dad**? □

Notes

⑥ The verb **mostrar** *to show*, *to display* is a stem-changing verb (**o** → **ue**) that has several useful synonyms: **dar pruebas/muestras** *to give proof*, **demostrar** *to prove*, *to demonstrate*, **manifestar** *to demonstrate*, *to express*, etc.
Dio muestras de / Demostró / Mostró / Manifestó una gran sangre fría. *He showed great composure* ('sang-froid').

⑦ **dejar plantado/a** (literally, 'to leave planted') *to leave helpless*, or, more colloquially, *to leave in the lurch/high and dry/out in the cold/stranded*, *to stand up*, etc. (*to abandon* **abandonar**). ▸

* * *

Ejercicio 1: Traduzca

❶ Hacía frío y el coche no arrancaba. ❷ No se puede negar que es una persona con muchas cualidades. ❸ ¡Qué pereza esta mañana para levantarme! ❹ Es demasiado pequeña, está bajo la autoridad de sus padres. ❺ ¡Abre los ojos!

4 Should one show oneself tolerant faced with the lack of comprehension of a computer that, refusing to obey, leaves us high and dry *(planted)*?
5 Ought one to react to the servility of the doormat*(s)* on which travelling salesmen *(sellers to domicile)* plant themselves?
6 Should one look [by] closing one's eyes in order to perceive what clarity is?

▸ **plantar** *to plant* (line 5) can also be used reflexively with the colloquial meaning *to turn up.* **Se ha plantado en mi casa sin avisar.** *He turned up at my house without warning.*

⑧ Don't forget that the relative pronoun *in/on which*, *where* (lesson 70) is translated by **en que**.
La casa en que nací. *The house where/in which I was born.*
Los ríos en que me bañaba. *The rivers where/in which I used to swim.*

* * *

Answers to Exercise 1

❶ It was cold and the car didn't start. ❷ It cannot be denied that he/she is a person with many [good] qualities. ❸ How lazy I was this morning in getting up! ❹ She's too young *(small)*; she's [still] under the authority of her parents. ❺ Open your eyes!

Ejercicio 2: Complete

As we've seen, there are various ways to say should, must, to have to, it is necessary to *in Spanish. Use the clues in parentheses to help you complete this exercise. For bonus points, try to get the pronoun right!*

❶ Is it necessary to warn him? *(impersonal obligation)*
¿... ... .?

❷ Do we have to warn her? *(personal obligation – subject specified)*
¿....... ... .?

❸ Should we warn them *(masc. plural)*? *(moral obligation)*
¿....... ....?

91 Lección noventa y una

Repaso

1 Uses of the subjunctive

As we've been pointing out, the subjunctive is widely used in Spanish. Just to recap: the subjunctive mood is used to express doubt, subjectivity or uncertainty, as opposed to the indicative mood, which is used to state something as an objective fact.

To help you increase your understanding of when it is needed, here are the uses of the subjunctive that appeared in this set of lessons.

1.1 After impersonal expressions

In expressions such as 'It is possible that …', the construction **ser/estar** + **que** usually requires the subjunctive. This follows the rule we've already seen that the subjunctive is needed after **que** when

❹ Do we need to warn them *(fem. plural)*? *(need)*
¿. . . . . ?

❺ Is it necessary to warn him? *(need/lack)*
¿. ?

Answers to Exercise 2

❶ Hay que avisarle ❷ Tenemos que avisarla ❸ Debemos avisarles ❹ Necesitamos avisarlas ❺ Hace falta avisarle

Second wave: 41st lesson

Lesson ninety-one 91

there is a change of subject in a subordinate clause introducing something hypothetical:
Es posible que nos apetezca salir.
It's possible that we may feel like going out.
Es bueno que tú quieras salir. *It's good that you want to come.*

1.2 After 'perhaps'

Although words such as **acaso**, **tal vez**, **quizá(s)** *perhaps*, *maybe* would seem by nature to indicate doubt and uncertainty, they can in fact be followed either by the subjunctive or the indicative. Basically, the mood chosen depends on how much you want to stress the doubtfulness of the situation.

Acaso discutamos (subjunctive) **por no estar de acuerdo.**
Maybe we'll argue because we won't agree. (relatively uncertain)
Sí, tal vez es (indicative) **mejor no jugar a la lotería.**
Yes, perhaps it's better not to play the lottery. (relatively certain)

91 If you weren't sure that playing the lottery is a bad idea, you could also say: **Sí, tal vez <u>sea</u>** (subjunctive) **mejor no jugar a la lotería.**

1.3 After 'although', 'even if'

There are certain other words, such as the conjunction **aunque** *although, even though, even if,* which can be followed either by the indicative or the subjunctive, depending on whether the situation is certain or uncertain.

• **aunque** + indicative, if the event is definitely going to happen:
Aunque es tarde, voy a ir a bailar.
Although it's late, I'm going to go dancing.

• **aunque** + subjunctive, it the event is hypothetical:
Aunque sea tarde, iré a bailar.
Even if gets late, I shall go dancing.
Aunque mañana nieve, iré a buscarte a la estación. *Although it may snow tomorrow, I'll come and pick you up at the station.*

Note that if the sentence is in the past tense, the indicative must be used, since the event definitely happened (there is no uncertainty in this case!).
Aunque se lo recordabas todos los días, le daba igual.
Even though you reminded him about it every day, he didn't care.

2 *Cuyo, cuya, cuyos, cuyas*

• This relative pronoun corresponds to *whose, of which.* Its form (**cuyo**, **cuya**, **cuyos** or **cuyas**) needs to agree with the noun that immediately follows it.
El Quijote, cuyo autor es Cervantes, es una novela…
Don Quixote*, of which the author is Cervantes, is a novel ...*
Aquellos señores cuya invitación a cenar nos sorprendió…
Those gentlemen whose invitation to dinner surprised us …
El niño cuyos pantalones están manchados…
The boy whose trousers are stained ...
El árbol cuyas hojas iban cayendo…
The tree whose leaves were falling one after the other ...

• This relative pronoun may also be preceded by a preposition.
El amigo en cuya casa pasé unos días...
The friend in whose house I spent a few days ...
El árbol a cuyo pie estábamos sentados...
The tree at whose foot we were seated ...
La mujer delante de cuya tienda nos besamos...
The woman in front of whose shop we kissed ...
Los bosques por cuyos senderos nos paseábamos...
The forests along whose paths we walked ...
Las montañas en cuyas laderas las ovejas pastaban...
The mountains on whose slopes the sheep grazed ...

3 The irregular verbs *salir* and *valer*

The verbs **salir** *to leave, go out, come out* and **valer** *to be worth* share the same irregularities.

• In the first-person singular present indicative a **g** is added: **salgo** *I leave* (but **sales** *you leave*), **valgo** *I am worth* (but **vale** *it is worth*).

• In the present subjunctive (which is formed using the first-person present indicative as a base) a **g** is added:
Ella quiere que yo salga. *She wants me to leave.*
No hay pero que valga. *There are no ifs, ands or buts about it.*

• In the future and conditional, a **d** replaces the vowel of the verb ending: **saldré** *I will leave*, **saldrás** *you will leave*, **saldría** *I would leave*, **valdrá** *it will be worth*, **valdría** *it would be worth.*

• In the second-person singular command forms, the final vowel disappears: **sal** *Leave!* and the rarely used **val** *Be worthy!* (although **vale** is also correct).

1 – ¡Me han tocado veintidós euros en la lotería!
2 – ¡Hay que celebrarlo!
3 – Te propongo que nos lleves a un buen restaurante
4 para que podamos deleitarnos con una buena receta tradicional y beber a tu salud.
5 – ¡Lo pasaremos en grande!
6 – Aunque reconozco que es una buena idea,
7 tengo que deciros que estoy harto de ir al restaurante.
8 Pero no os preocupéis, lo celebraremos.
9 Tengo aquí unos huevos de las gallinas del pueblo de mi tía; biológicos.
10 ¡Nos haremos una tortillita!

---

92 Lección noventa y dos

El español en el mundo

1 En los al**bo**res ① del **si**glo XXI,
2 el espa**ñol** es la **len**gua ma**ter**na de cuatro**cien**tos mi**llo**nes de per**so**nas.
3 A**sí**, se pre**sen**ta **co**mo

Notes

① **el albor** *dawn* (also **el alba** [f.]), *daybreak* and *beginning* (also **el principio**) is generally used in the plural, especially when speaking about historical events.
En los albores del Renacimiento *At the dawn of the Renaissance.*

Traducción

1 I won 22 euros in the lottery! **2** We must celebrate that! **3** I suggest that you take us to a good restaurant **4** so that we can enjoy a good traditional dish *(recipe)* and drink to your health! **5** We'll have a great time! **6** Although I admit *(recognize)* that it's a good idea, **7** I have to tell you that I'm fed up of going to restaurants. **8** But don't worry, we'll celebrate it. **9** I have here some eggs from the hens in my aunt's village; [they're] organic. **10** We'll make ourselves a little omelette!

Second wave: 42nd lesson

Lesson ninety-two 92

Spanish in the world

1 At the dawn of the 21st century,
2 Spanish is the mother tongue of 400 million people.
3 Thus, it ranks *(presents itself)* as

EL ESPAÑOL ES EL ÍDIOMA OFICIAL DE NUMEROSOS PAÍSES LATINOAMERICANOS.

4 la **cuar**ta **len**gua más ha**bla**da en el **mun**do,
5 tras el **chi**no, el in**glés** y el **hin**di ②.
6 Es tam**bién** la se**gun**da **len**gua de comunica**ción** internacio**nal**.
7 En e**fec**to, el espa**ñol** es el i**dio**ma ③ ofi**cial** de **u**na vein**te**na de pa**í**ses.
8 Su difu**sión** es**tá** en cons**tan**te au**men**to,
9 y su impor**tan**cia en el **pla**no de las rela**cio**nes **en**tre los **pue**blos,
10 a ni**vel** eco**nó**mico, po**lí**tico y cultu**ral**,
11 no **ce**sa de cre**cer**.

Notes

② In terms of total number of speakers, Spanish is the second most spoken language in the world. It ranks fourth in terms of native speakers. Also note that, like nationalities, the names of languages are not capitalized. Usually they are preceded by a definite article. However, after verbs such as **hablar**, **aprender**, **entender**, **estudiar**, etc. the article does not have to be used if the name of the language immediately follows the verb: **Yo hablo español.** *I speak Spanish.* But, **Yo hablo muy bien el español.** *I speak Spanish very well.*

* * *

Ejercicio 1: Traduzca

❶ Y ahora, ¿qué idioma te gustaría aprender? ❷ Me gustaría aprender chino, iré a una escuela de idiomas. ❸ El español es el idioma oficial de numerosos países latinoamericanos. ❹ Vivimos siete años en Egipto, mis hijos hablan árabe. ❺ En algunos países, la difusión de la lengua constituye hoy en día un objetivo cultural.

4 the fourth most spoken language in the world,
5 behind Chinese, English and Hindi.
6 It is also the second language of international communication.
7 Indeed, Spanish is the official language of about 20 *(a twenty-odd of)* countries.
8 It is constantly spreading *(Its diffusion is in constant increase)*,
9 and its importance for *(on the plane of the)* relationships between peoples
10 at the economic, political and cultural level
11 never stops growing *(does not cease to grow)*.

③ **el idioma** *language*: **Estoy estudiando japonés en una escuela de idiomas.** *I am studying Japanese at a language school.* However, the term **la lengua** *tongue* may also be used: **Mi lengua materna es el árabe, pero también hablo vietnamita; soy bilingüe.** *My mother tongue is Arabic, but I also speak Vietnamese; I am bilingual.*

* * *

Answers to Exercise 1

❶ And now, which language would you like to learn? ❷ I would like to learn Chinese; I will go to a language school. ❸ Spanish is the official language of numerous Latin American countries. ❹ We lived in Egypt for seven years; my children speak Arabic. ❺ In some countries, the spread of the language is nowadays a cultural objective.

Ejercicio 2: Complete

❶ How many languages do you *(informal sing.)* speak?
¿....... ....?

❷ I am learning German.
.... alemán.

❸ What is your *(informal sing.)* mother tongue?
¿.... .. ..?

❹ I would also like to learn Chinese.
También .. ..

❺ The Soley family speaks Spanish, Catalan, French and Dutch.
.. .. Soley ...., ..., ... neerlandés.

93 Lección noventa y tres

España agreste

1 Es**pa**ña es **u**no de los pa**í**ses de Eu**ro**pa occiden**tal** ①

Notes

① Like most adjectives ending in a consonant, **occidental** *western* and **oriental** *eastern* don't change for gender. Note also: **occidente** *west*; **oriente** *east*.

Answers to Exercise 2

❶ Cuántos idiomas/Cuántas lenguas hablas ❷ Estoy aprendiendo – ❸ Cuál es tu lengua materna ❹ – me gustaría aprender chino ❺ La familia – habla español, catalán, francés y –

Among the many organizations, public and private, dedicated to aiding the spread of Spanish culture throughout the world, the **Instituto Cervantes** *holds pride of place. Created by the Spanish Parliament in 1991 and today established across four continents, its aim is not only to teach the Spanish language, but also to promote and disseminate Spanish and Latin American culture.*

Its responsibilities include organizing language courses as well as granting diplomas and certificates, for example, the **DELE** *(***Diploma de Español como Lengua Extranjera** Diploma of Spanish as a Foreign Language*); supporting research by Hispanicists; conducting cultural events in association with other Spanish and Latin American organizations and host countries; and making available a vast network of resources.*

Second wave: 43rd lesson

Lesson ninety-three 93

Wild Spain

1 Spain is one of the countries in Western Europe

ESPAÑA ES UN PARAÍSO
PARA LOS AFICIONADOS AL SENDERISMO.

2 que dis**po**ne de ma**yor** ② superficie a**gres**te ③ prote**gi**da.

3 Mon**ta**ñas, hume**da**les, **bos**ques, pai**sa**jes vol**cá**nicos,

4 **is**las que al**ber**gan impor**tan**tes co**lo**nias de **a**ves ④ y **plan**tas…

5 con**for**man **u**na gran diversi**dad** de ecosis**te**mas.

6 A**sí**, el pa**ís** **cuen**ta con más de dos**cien**tas re**ser**vas natu**ra**les,

7 de las que una do**ce**na han **si**do decla**ra**das **par**ques nacio**na**les ⑤,

Notes

② **mayor** can be used in several ways. Here it is the comparative of **grande** and means *larger, bigger, greater* (**más grande**). But when it is preceded by a definite article, it becomes the superlative *the greatest*. Compare:
un material de mayor flexibilidad *a more flexible material*
Es la mayor autoridad en ese campo.
He is the greatest authority in that field.

mayor also means *major, main* and *older*:
la calle mayor *the main street*
Francisco es mayor que su hermana.
Francisco is older than his sister.
una persona mayor *an elderly person* (Note: it is considered impolite to call an elderly person **viejo/a**.)
Ya tiene dieciocho años, es mayor.
He is already 18 years old; he is an adult.
el hermano mayor *the elder brother*
el mayor de los hermanos *the oldest of the brothers.*

③ **agreste** can mean *rugged, wild* (**salvaje**), as in unspoiled by people, or simply *rural, of the countryside* (**campestre**). ▸

2 with the largest surface area of protected wilderness *(that has-at-its-disposal greater surface-area wild protected)*.
3 Mountains, wetlands, forests, volcanic landscapes,
4 [and] islands that shelter large *(important)* bird colonies and [numerous species of] plants
5 form a great diversity of ecosystems.
6 Thus the country has *(counts with)* more than two hundred nature reserves,
7 of which a dozen have been declared national parks,

④ **ave** *bird* refers to any avian species, including poultry.
La gallina es un ave de corral. *The hen is a domestic fowl* ('a bird of farmyard'). (Note: a different word is used to refer to the bird and to its meat: **pollo de corral** *free-range chicken*, i.e. meat.)
El águila es un ave de presa. *The eagle is a bird of prey.*

However, when referring to any small bird, **pájaro** is used:
Cada vez se ven menos pájaros, como golondrinas y gorriones, en las grandes aglomeraciones. *Fewer and fewer birds such as swallows and sparrows are seen in big cities.*

⑤ National parks in Spain (with the exception of ***Aigüestortes i Estany de Sant Maurici***, which is administered by the Catalonian Department of Agriculture) are managed by the **Ministerio de Medio Ambiente**, the *Department of the Environment*. Regional nature reserves are managed by *the regional governments*, **las Comunidades Autónomas**.

8 y **mu**chas **o**tras **par**ques natu**ra**les.
9 Se**gun**do pa**ís** más monta**ño**so del conti**nen**te, tras **Sui**za,
10 Es**pa**ña es un para**í**so **pa**ra los aficio**na**dos al sende**ris**mo ⑥
11 y de**más** a**man**tes ⑦ de la natura**le**za, de la **fau**na y de la **flo**ra. □

Notes

⑥ As we've seen, **aficionado/a** means *fan* or *enthusiast* (lesson 89): **Es muy aficionada a los deportes de nieve.** *She is a big winter sports fan./She loves winter sports* ('sports of snow').
The noun **senderismo**, which comes from **el sendero** *path, track*, means *hiking, trekking*.

⑦ **amante** (m./f.) is both the noun *lover* and the adjective *loving*. It has various meanings:
un amante de la naturaleza *a nature lover*
una esposa amante *a loving wife*
un amante de la libertad *a lover of freedom, freedom-loving.* ▸

* * *

Ejercicio 1: Traduzca

❶ España, Italia y Francia son países mediterráneos de Europa occidental. ❷ ¿De cuánto tiempo dispones? ❸ Muchas aves salvajes viven en las reservas naturales protegidas. ❹ España es un país montañoso. ❺ ¿Tiene un pollo de corral para cuatro personas?

8 and many other natural parks.
9 The second most mountainous country on the continent, after Switzerland,
10 Spain is a paradise for hiking enthusiasts
11 and other lovers of nature [and] fauna and flora.

▸ Colloquially, **amante** can mean either a licit or illicit *lover.*
Tiene una amante. *He has a mistress.*
Él es su amante. *He is her lover.*

Most adjectives ending in **-ente**/**-ante** used as nouns in this way are gender neutral, like all adjectives ending in **-e**.

* * *

Answers to Exercise 1

❶ Spain, Italy and France are Mediterranean countries in Western Europe. ❷ How much time do you have [available]? ❸ Many wild birds live in the protected nature reserves. ❹ Spain is a mountainous country. ❺ Do you have a free-range chicken that will serve *(for)* four people?

Ejercicio 2: Complete

❶ His grandparents are very old.
... .

❷ My elder sister is a big fan of the opera.
.. hermana ..... es muy .... a la ópera.

❸ They say that swallows announce the spring.
Dicen ... ... anuncian la ....

❹ The national parks shelter numerous species of birds.
... . nacionales .... numerosas especies de ..... .

---

94 Lección noventa y cuatro

A vueltas con ① el ordenador

1 – No sé lo que **pa**sa con mi por**tá**til ② **pe**ro…
2 ¡hay **al**go que no **mar**cha!
3 Y no es la pri**me**ra vez; a**yer** ya me pa**só**.
4 Ten**dré** que lla**mar** a un **téc**nico
5 o lle**var**lo a repa**rar** a la **tien**da.

Notes

① The colloquial expression **andar a vueltas con un problema** *to struggle* ('walk in circles') *with a problem* is often abbreviated to **a vueltas con** + the problem in question (a thing, situation, person, etc.). ▸

❺ The Picos de Europa National Park is the largest nature reserve in Europe.
. . Parque Nacional de los Picos de Europa . .
. . . .

Answers to Exercise 2

❶ Sus abuelos son muy mayores ❷ Mi – mayor – aficionada – ❸ – que las golondrinas – primavera ❹ Los parques – albergan – aves ❺ El – es la mayor reserva natural de Europa

Second wave: 44th lesson

Lesson ninety-four 94

Computer problems

1 – I don't know what's happening with my laptop *(portable)*, but …
2 there's something that's not working *(doesn't function)*!
3 And it's not the first time; it already happened to me yesterday.
4 I'll have to call *(to)* a technician
5 or take it to the store to be repaired *(to repair)*.

▸ ② **ordenador portátil** *portable computer, laptop* is usually just called **el portátil** *portable*; not to be confused with **el móvil** *mobile* (telephone), *cell phone*. Other useful computer words: **la impresora** *printer*; **el ratón** *mouse*; **el teclado** *keyboard*; **la pantalla** *screen*; **el disco duro** *hard disk*; **el escáner** *scanner*.

6 El pro**ble**ma es que **ten**go que ha**cer u**na con**sul**ta en Inter**net** ③.
7 – Pues, ten cui**da**do, he le**í**do en el pe**rió**dico que hay un **vi**rus **ra**ro ④ en circula**ción**.
8 El ar**tí**culo **di**ce que son las **mis**mas em**pre**sas que pro**du**cen los pro**gra**mas
9 las que **lan**zan los **vi**rus **pa**ra **lue**go ven**der** los anti**vi**rus y…
10 ¡ma**tar** a**sí** dos **pá**jaros de un **ti**ro! ⑤
11 – ¡No lo **pue**do cre**er**!
12 – Hoy en **dí**a… ¡**ve**te a sa**ber**!
13 Si **quie**res te **pue**do pres**tar** mi **nue**vo anti**vi**rus.
14 Lo **ten**go a**quí**, lo a**ca**bo de com**prar**.
15 **Mi**ra a ver, ¡pro**bar** no **cues**ta **na**da ⑥!
16 – Muy bien, ¡**va**mos a ver si hay **suer**te! □

Notes

③ **hacer una consulta en Internet, en la biblioteca**, etc. *to search the Internet, to look something up in the library*, etc. Similarly, **consultar el diccionario** *to consult the dictionary.* Other useful words: **el servidor** *server*; **el sitio (Web)** *website*; **el portal** *the portal.*

④ **raro** *rare* is frequently used to mean *strange, bizarre* or *odd.*
un fenómeno raro *a strange phenomenon*
Es raro que se haya ido sin despedirse. *It's strange that he should have left without saying goodbye.*
¡Qué cosa más rara! *How strange!* ▸

6 The problem is that I have to do a search *(consultation)* on the Internet.
7 – Well, be careful – I read in the newspaper that there's a strange virus going around *(in circulation)*.
8 The article says that it's *(they are)* the same companies that produce the programmes
9 who launch the viruses in order to then sell the antiviruses and
10 so kill two birds with one stone *(shot)*!
11 – I can't believe it!
12 – These days … who knows *(go to know)*!
13 If you want, I can lend you my new antivirus.
14 I have it here, I just bought it.
15 Look *(Look to see)*, it doesn't cost anything to try *(to try doesn't cost nothing)*!
16 – Very well, let's see if we have any luck *(we'll see if there is luck)*!

⑤ **Matar dos pájaros de un tiro** is almost the same as the English saying *To kill two birds with one stone*, apart from the last word: **tiro** *shot*.

⑥ The Spanish requires a double negative here: **no cuesta nada** 'it doesn't cost nothing'.

Ejercicio 1: Traduzca

❶ Se ha puesto a llover, tendremos que salir más tarde. ❷ ¿Qué pasa, no te sientes bien? ❸ Ten cuidado, hace mucho frío. ❹ ¿Tienes Internet en casa? ❺ ¿Qué haces? – Ando a vueltas con la impresora, hay algo que no marcha.

* * *

Ejercicio 2: Complete

❶ Do you *(informal sing.)* like this CD *(disc)*? I can lend it to you.
¿. . . . . . . este . . . . . ? . . . .

❷ The technician couldn't come yesterday; he will come today.
. . . . pudo venir . . . . , ...

❸ It's the first time that something like that has happened *(happens)* to me.
. . . . me ocurre . . . . así.

❹ I can't believe it.
. . . .

❺ It doesn't cost anything to try.
. . . .

---

95 Lección noventa y cinco

El flamenco

1 El fla**men**co es un **gri**to ar**tís**tico espon**tá**neo que ex**pre**sa,

Answers to Exercise 1

❶ It has started to rain – we'll have to leave later. ❷ What's wrong, don't you feel well? ❸ Be careful, it's very cold. ❹ Do you have the Internet at home? ❺ What are you doing? – I'm struggling with the printer, there's something that's not working.

* * *

TEN CUIDADO, HACE MUCHO FRÍO.

Answers to Exercise 2

❶ Te gusta – disco – Te lo puedo prestar ❷ El técnico no – ayer, vendrá hoy ❸ Es la primera vez que – algo – ❹ No lo puedo creer ❺ Probar no cuesta nada

Second wave: 45th lesson

Lesson ninety-five 95

Flamenco

1 Flamenco is a spontaneous artistic declaration *(cry)* that expresses,

2 particu**lar**mente a tra**vés** “del **can**te **jon**do” ①,
3 su **for**ma más desgarra**do**ra,
4 los senti**mien**tos **ín**timos de sufri**mien**to, injus**ti**cia, tris**te**za y ale**grí**a
5 **pro**pios de la exis**ten**cia.
6 Sus o**rí**genes se si**tú**an en la **ba**ja Andalu**cí**a,
7 **don**de los gi**ta**nos proce**den**tes del ② **nor**te de la **In**dia,
8 combi**nan**do su **mú**sica con la **á**rabe, la ju**dí**a y la cris**tia**na,
9 se van estable**cien**do.
10 **Mez**cla de **can**te, gui**ta**rra y **bai**le ③,
11 univer**sal**mente aso**cia**do a la cul**tu**ra espa**ño**la,
12 el fla**men**co es **an**te **to**do la **que**ja del **al**ma anda**lu**za.
13 Cual**quie**ra que **fue**ren ④ sus va**rian**tes,

Notes

① The term **‘cante jondo’**, ‘deep singing’, refers specifically to flamenco. **jondo** is a variant spelling of **hondo** *deep, profound*, and comes from the way the letter **h** was pronounced by older generations of Andalusians. Outside the context of Andalusian song, the word for *singing* is generally **canto**.
Voy a clases de canto. *I’m taking singing lessons.*

② **procedente de** *originating from, coming from.*
El tren procedente de Burgos con destino a Irún, va efectuar su salida. *The train from Burgos to Irún is about to leave.* (‘The train originating from Burgos with destination to Irún is going to carry out its departure.’)

2 particularly through 'el cante jondo' *(deep singing)*,
3 its most heart-rending form,
4 the innermost feelings of suffering, injustice, sadness and joy
5 inherent in *(typical of)* [our] existence.
6 Its origins are found *(are situated)* in lower Andalusia,
7 where gypsies coming from the north of India
8 combined *(combining)* their music with Arabian, Jewish and Christian [music]
9 as they settled progressively over time.
10 [A] mixture of song, guitar and dance
11 universally associated with Spanish culture,
12 flamenco is above all the cry of despair *(the complaint)* of the Andalusian soul.
13 In all of its variants *(Whatever that may be its variants)*,

③ **bailar** *to dance.*
Elena y José han ido a bailar a una discoteca.
Elena and José have gone out dancing at a night club.
el baile can mean *dancing, dance* or *ball.*

④ Grammatically speaking, this should be **cualesquiera que fueren** because the noun is plural, but **cualquiera** is often heard in spoken language. An even more common form is **cual(es)quiera que sean** *whatever they may be*. Both verbs are forms of **ser**. The former, **fueren**, is the future subjunctive, which is now rare and is replaced by the present subjunctive (**sean**). We've included it here just so you know it exists. You may come across it in classical literature, in legal language or in idiomatic expressions: **sea lo que fuere** (more commonly **sea lo que sea**) *whatever happens, whatever may be.*

95 **14** la expre**sión** ar**tís**tica al**can**za su paro**xis**mo
15 cuando **sur**ge el "**duen**de": ⑤
16 la comu**nión** de senti**mien**tos **en**tre el ar**tis**ta y su **pú**blico. □

Notes

⑤ **el duende** *goblin*, *imp*, *spirit* can be used in the sense of *spell* (**el hechizo**), *magic* (**la magia**) or *charm* (**el encanto**) – here, ▸

* * *

Ejercicio 1 : Traduzca

➊ Esta noche asistiremos a un espectáculo de flamenco. ➋ El "cante jondo" expresa sentimientos íntimos. ➌ ¿De qué te quejas? ➍ ¿Sabes tocar la guitarra? ➎ Me gustaría ir a bailar esta noche.

* * *

Ejercicio 2: Complete

➊ She expresses her feelings easily.
. . . . fácilmente . . . .

➋ She is very spontaneous.
. . . .

➌ Moors, Jews and Christians lived in peace in Andalusia.
Moros, ... vivieron . . paz en Andalucía.

➍ The plane from Shanghai will arrive late.
. . . . Shanghai . . . .

➎ I feel a great joy.
. . . .

14 the artistic expression reaches its climax
15 with the emergence of *(when arises)* the 'duende':
16 the communion of feeling*(s)* between the artist and his public.

▸ it is the sort of mystical connection that can arise between a performer and the audience. The verb for attending a concert, show or performance (**un espectáculo**) is **asistir** *to attend.*

* * *

Answers to Exercise 1

❶ This evening we will attend a flamenco show. ❷ 'Cante jondo' expresses innermost feelings. ❸ What are you complaining about? ❹ Do you know how to play the guitar? ❺ I would like to go dancing tonight.

* * *

Answers to Exercise 2

❶ Expresa – sus sentimientos ❷ Es muy espontánea ❸ – judíos y cristianos – en – ❹ El avión procedente de – llegará con retraso ❺ Siento una gran alegría

ME GUSTARÍA IR A BAILAR
ESTA NOCHE.

Flamenco as we know it today – as a form of entertainment – developed mainly towards the end of the 18th century, in parallel with changes to the classical guitar that allowed the musician to better keep the rhythm. Gradually, it became a recognized art form. In 1915, the Spanish composer Manuel de Falla took it as inspiration for his gypsy-influenced ballet **El Amor Brujo**, *known in English as* Love, the Magician *(***el brujo** sorcerer, wizard; **la bruja** witch*), contributing to its increase in popularity.*

The cornerstones of flamenco are **el cante** singing, **la guitarra** guitar *and* **la bailaora y/o el bailaor** the female dancer and/or male dancer, *who employ with great passion* **la voz** voice, **la música**

---

96 Lección noventa y seis

Incompresión

1 – ¿Qué **ha**ces a**hí** pa**rao** ① mi**rán**dome a**sí**?
2 – Por más **vuel**tas que le doy ②,
3 no con**si**go compren**der**lo.
4 Me lo pre**gun**to y me lo **vuel**vo a pregun**tar**, **pe**ro…
5 ¡No hay tu **tí**a! ③
6 ¡No me **ca**be en la ca**be**za! ④

Notes

① In everyday speech, **parado**, the past participle of **parar** *to stop*, *to stand*, is often pronounced **parao**. In fact, when speaking, the **d** of the ending **-ado** in regular past participles is barely audible and is often completely omitted. In this case, the **a** and the **o** are pronounced as a single syllable: *[ow]*.

② **por más que** (or **por mucho que**) *no matter how (much)*, *however (much)*, etc. is used in the same way as **aunque** *although* or *even if/though* (lesson 91, section 1.3): ▸

music, **el baile** dance, *as well as* **las palmas** handclapping, **las castañuelas** castanets *and impressive footwork involving stamping of feet and clicking of heels.*

Each generation brings new singers, guitarists and dancers who contribute to flamenco's evolution by introducing elements from other influences, for example, from rock or jazz music, Latin American or Arabic culture, or contemporary dance, taking the form to new heights of virtuosity.

Second wave: 46th lesson

Lesson ninety-six 96

Incomprehension

1 – What are you doing standing *(stopped)* there looking at me like that?
2 – No matter how I look at it *(For more turns that I give it)*,
3 I can't *(I don't manage to)* understand it.
4 I keep asking myself *(I ask myself about it and I return to ask myself about it)*, but …
5 It's no use!
6 I can't get it into my head!

▸ **Por más que se lo repetías, le daba igual.** *No matter how much you repeated it to him, it was all the same to him.*
Por más que digas, le dará igual. *No matter what you may say, he won't care.*

③ The expression **¡No hay tu tía!** (literally, 'There isn't your aunt!') means *It can't be helped! There's nothing to be done!*

④ **¡No me cabe en la cabeza!** ('It doesn't fit in my head!') *I can't get my head around it! It's too much for me to understand!*

7 – **Bue**no, **pe**ro ¿de qué se **tra**ta?
8 – Pues, me es**ta**ba pregun**tan**do
9 **có**mo es po**si**ble que yo **ha**ya po**di**do encon**trar**te a mi **gus**to.
10 No lo en**tien**do ⑤.
11 – ¿**Pe**ro tú no es**tás** bien o qué?
12 Es evi**den**te.
13 ¡Yo te**ní**a se**sen**ta **a**ños **me**nos!

Notes

⑤ There are two ways to say *to understand*: **entender** (line 10) and **comprender** (line 3).
Perdone, no le he entendido; ¿puede repetir, por favor?
Sorry, I didn't understand you; can you please repeat that?

* * *

Ejercicio 1: Traduzca

❶ Me pregunto a qué hora va a llegar. ❷ Hay demasiado ruido, no se oye nada. ❸ No entiendo lo que me dice. ❹ No sé de qué se trata. ❺ ¡No me cabe en la cabeza!

* * *

Ejercicio 2: Complete

❶ No matter how much I explain it to him, he doesn't understand it.
... . que .. .., no lo entiende.

❷ It seems obvious to me.
.. ..

❸ It's all the same to me.
.. ..

❹ I stayed at home watching a film.
.. .. en casa ....

7 – OK, what are you talking about *(of what is it about)*?
8 – Well, I was wondering *(asking myself)*
9 how it's possible that I could have fancied you *(found you to my taste)*.
10 I don't understand it.
11 – But, have you taken leave of your senses *(are you not well)* or what?
12 It's obvious.
13 I was sixty years younger *(I had sixty years less)*!

▸ **No comprendo su actitud.** *I don't understand his/her attitude.* To say you didn't hear someone correctly, the verb **oír** *to hear* is used: **No he oído lo que decía.** *I didn't hear what he said.*

* * *

Answers to Exercise 1

❶ I wonder what time he/she is going to arrive. ❷ There's too much noise, you can't hear anything. ❸ I don't understand what he/she is telling me. ❹ I don't know what it's about. ❺ I can't get it into my head!

* * *

❺ But have you *(informal sing.)* taken leave of your senses or what?
¿. . . . . ?

Answers to Exercise 2

❶ Por mucho – se lo explico – ❷ Me parece evidente ❸ Me da igual ❹ Me he quedado – viendo una película ❺ Pero tú no estás bien o qué

Second wave: 47th lesson

Apuntes ① de geografía

1 España **tie**ne **u**na superfi**ci**e
2 de quin**ien**tos **cua**tro mil sete**cien**tos o**chen**ta y dos kil**ó**metros cua**dra**dos,
3 in**clui**dos los archi**pié**lagos bale**ar** y ca**na**rio.
4 **Tie**ne **u**na pobla**ción** que su**pe**ra ② los cua**ren**ta mi**llo**nes de habi**tan**tes.
5 Li**mi**ta al **Nor**te con el mar Can**tá**brico ③ y **Fran**cia;
6 al Sur con el conti**nen**te afri**ca**no,
7 del que **só**lo la se**pa**ran **u**nos **quin**ce kil**ó**metros:
8 el es**tre**cho ④ de Gibral**tar**;
9 al **Es**te con el mar Medite**rrá**neo
10 y al O**es**te con Portu**gal** y el oc**é**ano At**lán**tico.
11 Los princi**pa**les **rí**os son el **E**bro y el **Due**ro, al **nor**te;
12 el **Ta**jo, en el **cen**tro;
13 y el Gua**dia**na y el Guadalqui**vir**, al sur.

Notes

① **un apunte** *note*. It is generally used in the plural:
Los alumnos toman apuntes. *The students take notes.*

② **superar** can mean *to exceed*, *to go beyond* or *to overcome*, *to get through something.*
Nos superan en número. *They outnumber us.* ▸

Geography notes

1 Spain has a surface area
2 of 504,782 square kilometres,
3 including the Balearic Islands and the Canary Islands.
4 It has a population that exceeds 40 million inhabitants.
5 In the north, it borders *(It limits to the north with)* the Bay of Biscay *(Cantabrian Sea)* and France;
6 in the south, *(with)* the African continent,
7 from which it is separated by only some 15 kilometres
8 [by] the Strait of Gibraltar;
9 to the east, the Mediterranean Sea
10 and to the west, Portugal and the Atlantic Ocean.
11 The main rivers are the Ebro and the Duero in the north;
12 the Tagus in the centre;
13 and the Guadiana and the Guadalquivir in the south.

▸ **Ya hemos superado la etapa más dificil.**
We've already got(ten) through the most difficult stage.

③ **el mar Cantábrico** *the Cantabrian Sea* is also known as **el golfo de Vizcaya** *the Bay of Biscay.*

④ As an adjective, **estrecho** means *narrow, tight.*

14 Administra**ti**vamente, el pa**ís** es**tá** divi**di**do
15 en dieci**sie**te Comuni**da**des Au**tó**nomas, que **su**man ⑤ cin**cuen**ta y dos pro**vin**cias.
16 Por es**tar** ⑥ situ**a**da **en**tre dos conti**nen**tes y dos **ma**res,
17 por su ca**rác**ter peninsu**lar**, su re**lie**ve acciden**ta**do
18 y un **cli**ma que **ro**za los ex**tre**mos,
19 Es**pa**ña o**cu**pa un lu**gar** singu**lar** en Eu**ro**pa. □

Notes

⑤ **sumar** *to add up to, to equal.*

⑥ The construction **por** *for, by* + infinitive means *because of, due to* + present participle, or *owing to* (the fact that).
Le dieron un trofeo por haber ganado.
They gave her a trophy for having won.

Remember that while both **por** and **para** can mean *for*, in general **por** is used to indicate a cause (in the past), while **para** is used to indicate an effect (in the future).

* * *

Ejercicio 1: Traduzca

❶ ¿Qué superficie tiene España? ❷ ¿Cuántos millones de habitantes tiene Europa? ❸ El estrecho de Gibraltar separa los continentes europeo y africano. ❹ Me gusta también bañarme en el río. ❺ Los archipiélagos balear y canario se encuentran en el mar Mediterráneo y en el océano Atlántico respectivamente.

14 Administratively, the country is divided
15 into 17 'Autonomous Communities', comprising *(which total)* 52 provinces.
16 Because it is *(Because of being)* situated between two continents and two seas,
17 [as well as] because of its peninsular character, its rugged terrain *(rough relief)*
18 and a climate that verges on *(brushes)* the extremes,
19 Spain holds *(occupies)* a unique position *(place)* in Europe.

ME GUSTA TAMBIÉN BAÑARME EN EL RÍO.

* * *

Answers to Exercise 1

❶ What is the surface area of Spain? ❷ How many millions of inhabitants does Europe have? ❸ The Strait of Gibraltar separates the European and African continents. ❹ I also like to swim in the river. ❺ The Balearic and Canary Islands are located in the Mediterranean Sea and [in the] Atlantic Ocean respectively.

Ejercicio 2: Complete

❶ I didn't arrive on time because I missed the bus *(because of having missed the bus).*
.. .. haber perdido .. ..

❷ He lives near the sea, at [a distance of] some twelve kilometres.
...., a ....

❸ Andalusia takes up *(occupies)* the southern part of Spain.
Andalucía ..... la parte ... .

❹ At university, one often works with notes.
En la .... trabaja . ...

❺ The Iberian Peninsula is located in the extreme south of Europe.
La península Ibérica .. .. el extremo ... .

---

98 Lección noventa y ocho

Repaso

1 Accentuation and stress

1.1 Word stress

All Spanish words of more than one syllable include a syllable that is stressed in speech (that is, pronounced with more emphasis). We've indicated this accentuation in bold type throughout the lessons. Apart from one-syllable words, we've seen four types of words (**palabras**) in terms of their accentuation.

Answers to Exercise 2
❶ No llegué a tiempo por – el autobús ❷ Vive cerca del mar – unos doce kilómetros ❸ – ocupa – sur de España ❹ – universidad se – a menudo con apuntes ❺ – se encuentra en – sur de Europa

Spain is famous for its mild climate. However, it is less well known that temperatures there can range from one extreme to the other. In fact, far from the Mediterranean coast, on the central plateau, it is not at all uncommon for **el termómetro** the thermometer *to register well below zero,* **bajo cero** – *that is, 0 °C (32 °F) – for weeks at a time, with icy* **inviernos** winters *giving way to scorching* **veranos** summers.

Second wave: 48th lesson

Lesson ninety-eight 98

• **Palabras agudas**: words with the stress on the last syllable: **ver<u>dad</u>** *truth*; **intensi<u>dad</u>** *intensity*; **sa<u>lud</u>** *health*; **adi<u>ós</u>** *goodbye*; **hu<u>mor</u>** *humour*, etc.

• **Palabras llanas**: words with the stress on the penultimate syllable (the most common type): **<u>li</u>bro** *book*; **a<u>mi</u>go** *friend*; **<u>ár</u>bol** *tree*; **<u>som</u>bra** *shade*; **<u>lá</u>piz** *pencil*; **com<u>ple</u>to** *complete, full*, etc.

• **Palabras esdrújulas**: words with the stress on the antepenultimate syllable (i.e. before the next-to-last): **<u>sí</u>laba** *syllable*; **<u>dá</u>melo** *give it to me*; **<u>ár</u>boles** *trees*; **<u>pá</u>jaro** *bird*; **<u>có</u>gelo** *take it*, etc.

• **Palabras sobresdrújulas**: words with the stress on any syllable preceding the antepenultimate syllable: **cuéntamelo** *tell it to me*; **irónicamente** *ironically*, etc.

1.2 General rules for accentuation

• Words ending in a vowel, an **n** or an **s** have the stress on the next-to-last syllable (**palabras llanas**): **hoja** *leaf*; **familia** *family*; **padre** *father*; **madre** *mother*, etc.

• Words ending in a consonant other than **n** or **s** have the stress on the last syllable (**palabras agudas**): **estudiar** *to study*; **amistad** *friendship*; **papel** *paper*, etc.

• Any word that breaks these two rules takes a written accent on the stressed syllable (always written as [´]): **fácil** *easy*; **sílaba** *syllable*; **también** *also*; **árbol** *tree*, etc.

• Words with the stress on or before the antepenultimate syllable (**palabras esdrújulas** or **sobresdrújulas**) always take a written accent: **pájaro** *bird*; **cantándotelo** *singing it to you*; **paradójicamente** *paradoxically*, etc.

You can also review the pronunciation section of the introduction and the explanations given in lessons 3, 7, 15, 16 and 35.

2 More verb irregularities

2.1 Verbs ending in *-eír* or *-eñir*

The verb **reír** *to laugh* is the most common example. (Note: the reflexive form **reírse** is more generally used.) These verbs have the following irregularities:
• the **e** of the stem is replaced by **i** when the **e** is stressed or when the ending begins with a diphthong or with **a**.
• in **-eír** verbs, the stem vowel is lost in the present participle, in the third-person singular and plural of the preterite and, consequently, in the imperfect subjunctive.
• in **-eñir** verbs the unstressed **i** in the ending is lost in the present participle, in the third-person singular and plural of the preterite and, consequently, in the imperfect subjunctive.

Some examples:
sonríes *you smile* (present indicative of **sonreír**)
No le riñas. *Don't scold him.* (present subjunctive/imperative of **reñir**)
Estoy friendo las patatas. *I am frying the potatoes.* (present participle of **freír**)
(Ella) se rió. *She laughed.* (preterite of **reír**)
And last but not least:
Quien ríe el último ríe mejor. ('Who laughs the last laughs better.') *He who laughs last laughs longest.*

2.2 Verbs (in the *-ir* group) where the *e* of the stem is followed by *r* or by *nt*

Two examples are **divertirse** *to enjoy oneself* and **sentir** *to feel, to regret* (**servir** *to serve*, which conjugates like **pedir** *to request, to ask for*, is the only exception). The irregularities include:

- the **e** preceding the ending changes to **ie** in all persons except **nosotros/vosotros** in the present tenses (present indicative and present subjunctive/imperative).
- the **e** of the stem changes to **i** if the **e** is stressed or if the ending begins with a diphthong or with **a** (in the present, the preterite and the present participle).

Lo siento. *I'm sorry.* (present indicative of **sentir**)
¿Qué prefieres? *What do you prefer?* (present indicative of **preferir**)
¿Cómo te sientes? *How do you feel?* (present indicative of **sentirse**)
No mientas. *Don't lie.* (present subjunctive/imperative of **mentir**)
Me advirtió con antelación. *He/she warned me in advance.* (preterite of **advertir**)
Nos estamos divirtiendo. *We are having fun.* (present participle of **divertirse**)

You don't need to memorize this information; just read through it for now. You can always refer to the irregular verb groups in section 16 of the grammatical appendix if you need to.

99 Diálogo recapitulativo

1 – Sí, ¿qué desean?
2 – Mire, estamos aprendiendo árabe
3 y quisiéramos poder estudiar también por ordenador.
4 – Pues tenemos justamente un CD-ROM muy interesante.
5 Se lo voy a enseñar.
6 ¡De todas formas, han elegido ustedes un idioma difícil!
7 ¿Cómo así les ha dado por el árabe?
8 – Pues hemos adoptado un niño libanés que tiene ya dos años;
9 y como pronto empezará a hablar…
10 ¡nos gustaría poder entender lo que dice!

99 Lección noventa y nueve

And now, all that's left for us to say is **¡Enhorabuena y… hasta la vista!** Congratulations and … see you soon!

¡Enhorabuena!

1 ¡Enhora**bue**na!
2 Por ha**ber** afron**ta**do con **é**xito las dificul**ta**des de la **len**gua,
3 por su tenaci**dad**, por su perseve**ran**cia;
4 en **u**na pa**la**bra: por el tra**ba**jo reali**za**do.
5 **Pe**ro…¿y a**ho**ra?
6 A**ho**ra**,** se **tra**ta de ¡mante**ner** el con**tac**to!

Traducción

1 Yes, can I help you *(what do you desire)*? **2** Look, we are learning Arabic **3** and we would like to be able to study by computer as well. **4** Well, in fact we have a very interesting CD-ROM. **5** I'm going to show it to you. **6** In any case, you have chosen a difficult language! **7** And how did you get into Arabic? **8** Well, we adopted a Lebanese child who is already two years old; **9** and since he will soon begin to talk … **10** we would like to be able to understand what he says!

Second wave: 49th lesson

You're almost at the end of the 'first wave'. Can you believe how far you've come? In the final two lessons of the book, enjoy the two-part text that we've provided and try to keep in mind at least some of the tips that it recommends.

Lesson ninety-nine 99

Congratulations!

1 Congratulations!
2 For having successfully faced *(confronted with success)* the difficulties of the language,
3 for your tenacity, [and] for your perseverance;
4 in a word: for the work achieved.
5 But … what now?
6 Now, it's a question of keeping in contact!

7 No **du**de en ① **echar**se al **rue**do ②
8 y po**ner**se **an**te el **to**ro: la **prác**tica **dí**a a **dí**a,
9 con mo**ti**vo de ③ **u**na conversa**ción** con un hispanoa**blan**te,
10 **vien**do **u**na pe**lí**cula en ver**sión** origi**nal**,
11 nave**gan**do por Inter**net**,
12 tra**tan**do de ④ ver **u**na ca**de**na espa**ño**la de televi**sión**,
13 le**yen**do un pe**rió**dico o **u**na re**vis**ta;
14 en **su**ma, aprove**chan**do cual**quier** oportuni**dad** ⑤ **pa**ra en**trar** en rela**ción** di**rec**ta con el espa**ñol**...
15 ¡a**hí** es**tá** el verda**de**ro test! □

Notes

① **dudar** *to doubt*, but **dudar en** + infinitive *to hesitate to.*

② In the figurative sense, **echarse al ruedo** (literally, 'to throw oneself into the bullring') is the equivalent of *throwing one's hat into the ring*, *entering the fray* (**entrar en liza**). The word **el ruedo** ('the ring') denotes something that is round, which, in bullfighting terminology, is *the bullfighting arena* (**la arena**). (But the primary meaning of **arena** is *sand*. **La arena de esta playa es muy fina.** *The sand on this beach is very fine.*) A well-known expression: **Coger el toro por los cuernos.** *Take the bull by the horns.*

③ **con motivo de** *on the occasion of*, *because of*, *owing to*, or as here, *by way of*, *by means of.*

④ **tratar** *to treat*, *handle*, *deal with*, when followed by **de** + infinitive, is translated by *to try to.*
Trataré de pedir una cita. *I'll try to request an appointment.*

And don't forget **tratarse de** *to be about*, *to be a matter of* (line 6). **¿De qué se trata?** *What's it about?*

7 Don't hesitate *(doubt in)* to throw yourself into the *(bull)*ring,
8 and take the bull by the horns *(put yourself before the bull)*: daily practice
9 by means of *(with motive of)* a conversation with a Spanish speaker,
10 watching an undubbed film in Spanish *(original version)*,
11 surfing the *(navigating by)* Internet,
12 trying to watch a Spanish television channel,
13 reading a newspaper or a magazine;
14 in short *(in sum)*, seizing any opportunity to enter into direct contact *(relation)* with Spanish ...
15 there's the true test!

⑤ **aprovechando cualquier oportunidad** *taking advantage of any opportunity* or *seizing any opportunity.* Note that **cualquier**, which we looked at in detail in lesson 70, can also be translated by *every* (**todo**): **aprovechando toda oportunidad** *making the most of every opportunity.* And … with the same sense: **No dejar escapar/pasar la oportunidad.** *Don't let the opportunity slip away.*

Ejercicio 1: Traduzca

❶ ¡Enhorabuena! ¡Buen trabajo! ❷ ¿Qué vas a hacer ahora? ❸ Quiero mantener el contacto; voy a seguir estudiando. ❹ Si me necesitas, no dudes en llamarme. ❺ ¡No dejes escapar la oportunidad!

* * *

Ejercicio 2: Complete

❶ There has been [a bit] of everything – ups and downs *(highs and lows).*

.. .. todo, ...

❷ But we have managed to overcome the difficulties.

.... hemos ....

❸ Now, one must throw one['s hat] into the ring; with gusto, without fear.

Ahora ...... echarse .. .., con brío, ... miedo.

❹ She may arrive at any moment.

..... llegar .. ..

100 Lección cien

¡Hasta la vista!

1 En ade**lan**te ① prac**ti**que en **cuan**to ② la oca**sión** se pre**sen**te;

Notes

① We've seen **adelante** *forward*; **adelantar** *to overtake, to move forward*; **¡Adelante!** *Carry on! Go on!*, and here we have **en adelante** *from now on, as of today.*

Answers to Exercise 1

❶ Congratulations! Good work! ❷ What are you going to do now? ❸ I want to keep in contact; I'm going to continue studying. ❹ If you need me, don't hesitate to call me. ❺ Don't let the opportunity slip away!

* * *

❺ Congratulations! You've known [how] to make the most of the opportunity!
¡ . . . . ! ¡Ha sabido . . . . !

Answers to Exercise 2

❶ Ha habido de – altos y bajos ❷ Pero – conseguido superar las dificultades ❸ – hay que – al ruedo – sin – ❹ Puede – en cualquier momento ❺ Enhorabuena – aprovechar la oportunidad

Second wave: 50th lesson

Lesson one hundred 100

See you again *(Until the view)*!

1 From now on, practice whenever *(as soon as)* the occasion presents itself;

② **en cuanto** *as soon as.* **Te llamaremos en cuanto lleguemos.** *We'll call you as soon as we arrive.* (Note that **lleguemos** here and **se presente** in line 1 are in the present subjunctive, which is used after **en cuanto** if the action that follows is not yet completed.)

100 **2** es ha**cien**do **fren**te ③ con tranquili**dad** a lo que se pre**sen**te de ma**ne**ra impre**vis**ta,
3 sin te**ner mie**do de no es**tar** a la al**tu**ra,
4 de no enten**der**, de ha**cer fal**tas, etc.,
5 **co**mo po**drá** evalu**ar** ④ su verda**de**ra **fuer**za,
6 la ampli**tud** de sus conoci**mien**tos, el ni**vel** que ha alcan**za**do.
7 ¡Queda**rá** sorpren**di**do!
8 A**sí mis**mo, **cuan**do **sien**ta la necesi**dad**,
9 **vuel**va a**quí pa**ra repo**ner fuer**zas:
10 re**le**a **u**na lec**ción** en voz **al**ta, tra**ba**je **u**na **fra**se,
11 re**pa**se **u**na **no**ta, **vuel**va a ha**cer** un ejer**ci**cio,
12 **e**che **u**na oje**a**da a la conjuga**ción**,
13 **bus**que en el **lé**xico, con**sul**te un **pun**to de gra**má**tica…
14 Practi**car**, practi**car**, practi**car**, ¡**é**se es el se**cre**to de **to**do **ar**te!

Notes

③ **el frente** *front*, *forehead*; **hacer frente** *to confront*, *to face* (**afrontar**), *to take on/meet* (challenges), *to cope/deal with*. **Es una persona que no rehúye la dificultad, siempre hace frente.** *She is a person who does not shy away from difficulty, she always faces [it].*

④ Other useful words with related meanings: **medir** *to measure*, *to consider*, *to weigh up*; **estimar** *to consider*, *to value*, *to esteem;* **apreciar** *to perceive*, *to appreciate*, etc.

2 it is [by] facing calmly *(with tranquillity)* whatever suddenly *(in an unexpected way)* presents itself,
3 without being afraid of not being equal to the task *(at the height)*,
4 of not understanding, of making mistakes, etc.,
5 that *(as)* you will be able to judge *(evaluate)* your true strength,
6 the extent of your knowledge [and] the level that you have attained.
7 You will be *(remain)* surprised!
8 Likewise *(Like same)*, when you feel the need,
9 come back *(here)* to recharge your batteries *(to recover strength)*:
10 reread a lesson aloud *(in high voice)*, work on a phrase,
11 review a note, repeat *(return to do)* an exercise,
12 take a quick look at the conjugation,
13 look up [a word] in the glossary, check *(consult)* a grammar point …
14 Practice, practice, practice – that's the secret to any skill *(of all art)*!

15 Es a tra**vés** de la **prác**tica, del con**tac**to a**si**duo,
16 **co**mo ⑤ la **len**gua llega**rá** a **ser**le ⑥ fami**liar**,
17 **co**mo se ha**rá ca**da vez más **due**ño ⑦ de sus conoci**mien**tos
18 y **co**mo esta**rá** en condi**cio**nes de ⑧ afron**tar nue**vos desa**fí**os.
19 A**hí** esta**re**mos para ayu**dar**le a conse**guir**lo.
20 ¡Buen **via**je y… **has**ta **pron**to ⑨!

Notes

⑤ **es … como** *it is ... that* ('it is … as'): there are several examples of this construction in this lesson. Whereas in English, we would use *that* in this context, in Spanish, **como** *as*, *like* is used to express the way something is done, **donde** *where* to express a place, **cuando** *when* to express a time and **por … que** *why* to express a cause. For example:
Fue en Nueva Zelanda donde conocí a mi mujer.
It was in New Zealand that I met my wife.

⑥ **llegar a ser** *to become* ('to come to be') is used to express the idea of a transformation that involves effort. **llegar a ser presidente, médico, abogado** *to [manage to] become president, [a] doctor, [a] lawyer.*

* * *

Ejercicio 1: Traduzca

❶ Ven en cuanto puedas. ❷ Voy a echar una ojeada al periódico. ❸ Practicar y practicar; ésa es la mejor manera de familiarizarse con la lengua. ❹ Cada vez conozco más expresiones. ❺ ¿Qué te gustaría llegar a ser?

15 It is through practice [and] regular *(assiduous)* contact
16 that *(as)* the language will become familiar to you,
17 that you will increasingly master your knowledge,
18 and that you will be capable *(in conditions)* of meeting new challenges.
19 We will be here to help you achieve it.
20 Have a great trip and … see you soon!

▸ **hacerse** *to become*, *to grow* is used to express a change regarding someone's ideology, habits or lifestyle: **Se hizo vegetariano.** *He became a vegetarian.* **Se hizo famosa.** *She became famous.*

⑦ **el dueño** *master*, *owner*; **hacerse dueño** *to take control.*

⑧ **estar en condiciones de** *to be capable of, to be able to, to be in a position to.* **No estoy en condiciones de acompañaros.** *I am not able to accompany you* (informal pl.).

⑨ And finally, some ways to say 'Until we meet again!': **¡Hasta la vista!** *See you next time!* is an informal way to say **adiós** *goodbye*. Another option is **¡Hasta pronto!** *See you soon!*

* * *

Answers to Exercise 1

❶ Come as soon as you can. ❷ I'm going to take a quick look at the newspaper. ❸ Practicing and practicing; that's the best way to become familiar with the language. ❹ I know more and more expressions [every day]. ❺ What would you like to be *(become)*?

100 Ejercicio 2: Complete

❶ It's [by] studying that one learns.

.. ..

❷ Review, look up, check: in a word, study! *(informal sing.)*

......, ..., ...; .. ..: ¡estudia!

❸ Come back to see us, we'll be waiting *(we wait)* for you.

...., le ....

❹ To face up to [it] and to be equal to the task.

....

❺ You can do it! See you soon!

¡.....! ¡..... ......!

Answers to Exercise 2

❶ Es estudiando como se aprende ❷ Repasa, busca, consulta; en una palabra – ❸ Vuelva a vernos – esperamos ❹ Hacer frente y estar a la altura ❺ Ánimo – Hasta pronto

Second wave: 51st lesson

Don't forget to carry on with the 'second wave', revisiting each lesson right up to lesson 100!

Grammatical appendix

Contents

1 Articles

Spanish has four forms of the definite article (*the*) and of the indefinite article (*a*, *an*, *some*) in order to show gender (masculine or feminine) and number (singular or plural):

		Masculine	Feminine
Definite article	Singular	**el chico** *the boy*	**la chica** *the girl*
	Plural	**los chicos** *the boys*	**las chicas** *the girls*
Indefinite article	Singular	**un chico** *a boy*	**una chica** *a girl*
	Plural	**unos chicos** *some boys*	**unas chicas** *some girls*

2 Nouns and adjectives

2.1 Nouns

In Spanish, all nouns are either masculine or feminine in gender. As a general rule, nouns referring to males are masculine, while nouns referring to females are feminine, but remember that nouns referring to inanimate objects and abstract concepts also have grammatical gender.

In general, masculine nouns end in **-o**, while feminine nouns end in **-a**. Adding **s** makes these nouns plural. Other noun endings that are typically masculine are **-r**, **-s** and **-l**, while typically feminine noun endings include **-ión**, **-dad**, **-tad**, **-tud** and **-umbre**. However, it is wise to learn a noun together with its article because the ending of a noun does not always allow you to predict its gender.

2.2 Adjectives

An adjective that accompanies a noun generally agrees with it in both gender and number. Thus, many adjectives have four forms:
el árbol alto *the tall tree*; **los árboles altos** *the tall trees*;
la montaña alta *the high mountain*; **las montañas altas** *the high mountains*.

However, adjectives whose masculine form does not end in **-o** usually agree only in number and have just two forms:
un asunto/una decisión importante/difícil
an important/difficult matter/decision;
unos asuntos/unas decisiones importantes/difíciles
(some) important/difficult matters/decisions.
Exceptions to this rule are many adjectives of nationality, which also show gender and therefore have four forms, even when the masculine singular ends in a consonant:
Mi padre es español y mi madre es española también.
My father is Spanish and my mother is Spanish, too.

Descriptive adjectives used literally are generally placed after the noun in Spanish.
Madrid es una ciudad grande. *Madrid is a big city.*
However, adjectives used figuratively precede the noun.
Madrid es una gran ciudad. *Madrid is a great city.*

Adjectives indicating quantity or number, as well as possessive adjectives, also precede the noun.
Muchas personas visitan el país. *Many people visit the country.*
Mis padres viven en Barcelona. *My parents live in Barcelona.*

3 Personal pronouns

3.1 Overview

Subject	Direct object	Indirect object	Reflexive (direct and indirect object)	Prepositional (emphatic)
yo *I*	**me**	**me**	**me**	**mí**
tú *you* (inf. sing.)	**te**	**te**	**te**	**ti**
él *he/it* (m.)	**lo (le)***	**le (se)****	**se**	**él**
ella *she/it* (f.)	**la**	**le (se)****	**se**	**ella**
usted *you* (formal sing.)	**lo (le)*/la**	**le (se)****	**se**	**usted**
nosotros/as *we* (m./f.)	**nos**	**nos**	**nos**	**nosotros/as**
vosotros/as *you* (inf. pl.)	**os**	**os**	**os**	**vosotros/as**
ellos *they* (m.)	**los (les)**	**les (se)****	**se**	**ellos**
ellas *they* (f.)	**las**	**les (se)****	**se**	**ellas**
ustedes *you* (formal pl.)	**los (les)/ las**	**les (se)****	**se**	**ustedes**

* The use of **le** instead of **lo** as a direct object pronoun is quite common, but there exists a certain amount of confusion in this regard. The Real Academia Española authorizes the use of the pronoun **le** instead of **lo** as a direct object when it refers to a person, so we can say **No lo conozco** or **No le conozco.** *I don't know him/ you* (formal sing.). (For the feminine, the use of **la** is obligatory: **No la conozco.** *I don't know her/you.*).

** When there are two consecutive third-person object pronouns, the indirect object (**le** or **les**) becomes **se**. See also section 3.2.

3.2 Word order with object pronouns

Spanish object pronouns, including reflexives, normally precede the conjugated verb, unlike in English:
Yo <u>los</u> vi. *I saw <u>them</u>.*

However, in some circumstances they may be placed afterwards, in which case they are attached to the verb to form one word.

- Object of an infinitive

If an infinitive is immediately preceded by a conjugated verb, the position of the object pronoun(s) is optional:
Yo <u>los</u> quiero ver. *I want to see them.*
Yo quiero ver<u>los</u>. *I want to see them.*

If the infinitive is <u>not</u> immediately preceded by a conjugated verb, the object pronoun(s) must be attached:
Tienes que ir a España para ver<u>los</u>.
You have to go to Spain to see them.

- Object of a present participle

If a present participle is immediately preceded by a conjugated verb, the position of the object pronoun(s) is optional:
Yo <u>los</u> estoy mirando. *I am watching them.*
Yo estoy mirándo<u>los</u>. *I am watching them.*

If the present participle is <u>not</u> immediately preceded by a conjugated verb, the object pronoun(s) must be attached:
Estudiándo<u>lo</u>, vosotros lo entenderéis mejor.
By studying it, you will understand it better.

- Object of an imperative

With negative imperatives, object pronouns must precede the conjugated verb:
¡No <u>me</u> hables! *Don't speak to me!*

With affirmative imperatives, object pronouns must be attached to the verb:
¡Hábla<u>me</u>! *Speak to me!*

• Double object pronouns

If a direct object pronoun and an indirect object pronoun are used together, the **indirect object pronoun** (usually a person) comes first. Note that the **direct object pronoun** is then very often a thing and not a person:

¡Dámelo! *Give it to me!*

Mi padre no quería dárselos. *My father didn't want to give them to him.*

4 Possessive adjectives and pronouns

The possessive adjectives (*my*, *your*, *his*, *her*, *its*, *our*, *their*) and the possessive pronouns (*mine*, *yours*, *his*, *hers*, *its*, *ours*, *theirs*) in Spanish need to agree in gender and number with the noun they are used with.

Subject	Possessive adjective (placed before the noun)			
	masc. sing.	masc. pl.	fem. sing.	fem. pl.
yo	**mi**	**mis**	**mi**	**mis**
tú	**tu**	**tus**	**tu**	**tus**
él, ella, usted	**su**	**sus**	**su**	**sus**
nosotros/as	**nuestro**	**nuestros**	**nuestra**	**nuestras**
vosotros/as	**vuestro**	**vuestros**	**vuestra**	**vuestras**
ellos, ellas, ustedes	**su**	**sus**	**su**	**sus**

Subject	Emphatic possessive adjective (placed after the noun)*			
	masc. sing.	masc. pl.	fem. sing.	fem. pl.
yo	**mío**	**míos**	**mía**	**mías**
tú	**tuyo**	**tuyos**	**tuya**	**tuyas**
él, ella, usted	**suyo**	**suyos**	**suya**	**suyas**
nosotros/as	**nuestro**	**nuestros**	**nuestra**	**nuestras**
vosotros/as	**vuestro**	**vuestros**	**vuestra**	**vuestras**
ellos, ellas, ustedes	**suyo**	**suyos**	**suya**	**suyas**

* Possessive pronouns are identical in form to the emphatic possessive adjective, but are preceded by the appropriate definite

article: **Mi hermano tiene sus libros y yo tengo los míos.** *My brother has his books and I have mine.* However, the use of the article after the verb **ser** is optional: **Estos libros son (los) míos.** *These books are mine.*

5 Conjugation groups

There are three types of verbs in Spanish, which conjugate in slightly different ways:

- First conjugation: verbs in which the infinitive ends in **-ar**
- Second conjugation: verbs in which the infinitive ends in **-er**
- Third conjugation: verbs in which the infinitive ends in **-ir**.

There are different verb forms for tense, which indicates when the action took place (e.g. past, present or future). There are also different verb forms for mood, which indicates how likely the action is. The indicative mood is used to express something as a fact, the subjunctive is used to indicate something subjective or uncertain, the conditional is used to express hypothetical or contingent actions, and the imperative is used to give commands.

6 Forming the simple tenses of regular verbs

A simple tense is a tense formed by adding an ending on the verb itself (making a one-word verb).

The following tenses/moods of Spanish verbs are simple, formed by adding an ending to the three bases indicated below:

Base of verb	Tense/mood formed by adding an ending to this base
a) the verb stem	present indicative present subjunctive imperative imperfect indicative preterite (simple past) present participle past participle

b) the infinitive	future conditional
c) the preterite (simple past)	imperfect subjunctive* future subjunctive*

* For more information on these verb forms, see lessons 77, 78, 81, 83 and 84 and section 10 in this appendix.

7 Compound tenses

A compound tense is a tense formed with an auxiliary verb and a participle (so the full verb has more than one word).

There are two main types of Spanish compound tenses: perfect tenses and progressive tenses, and both are formed in a similar way as in English.

7.1 Perfect tenses

The perfect tenses use a conjugated form (in the appropriate tense) of the auxiliary verb **haber** *to have* + past participle. For example, here are a few of the forms:
Present perfect: **Mi hija ha llamado.** *My daughter has called.*
Past perfect: **Mi hijo había llamado.** *My son had called.*
Future perfect: **Mi hija habrá llamado.** *My daughter will have called.*
Conditional perfect: **Mi hijo habría llamado.** *My son would have called.*

7.2 Progressive tenses

The progressive (or continuous) tenses use a conjugated form (in the appropriate tense) of the auxiliary verb **estar** *to be* + present participle. For example, here are a few of the forms:
Present progressive: **Estoy trabajando.** *I am working.*
Imperfect progressive: **Estaba trabajando cuando ...** *I was working when ...*
Future progressive: **Estaré trabajando.** *I will be working.*
Conditional progressive: **Estaría trabando si ...** *I would be working if ...*

There is also a passive voice (which is not a tense), which uses a conjugated form (in the appropriate tense) of the auxiliary verb **ser** + past participle. In this case, because the participle actually serves as an adjective, it needs to agree with the subject in both number and gender:
El puente fue complet<u>ado</u> en 1990.
The bridge was completed in 1990.
Los puentes fueron complet<u>ados</u> en 1990.
The bridges were completed in 1990.
La casa fue complet<u>ada</u> en 1990.
The house was completed in 1990.
Las casas fueron complet<u>adas</u> en 1990.
The houses were completed in 1990.

8 Forming present and past participles

8.1 Present participle

To form the present participle of regular verbs, you replace the infinitive ending with the endings below.

Verb group	Ending
First conjugation (**-ar** verbs) e.g. **estudiar** *to study*	→ stem of the verb + **-ando** e.g. **estudiando** *studying*
Second conjugation (**-er** verbs) Third conjugation (**-ir** verbs) e.g. **comer** *to eat*, **vivir** *to live*	→ stem of the verb + **-iendo** e.g. **comiendo** *eating*, **viviendo** *living*

Spelling rules cause some exceptions, e.g.:
i becomes **y** in **construir** → **construyendo**.

Irregular present participles occur with **-ir** verbs that take a stem-change (**e** → **i** or **o** → **u**) in the third-person preterite. This change is maintained in the present participle, e.g.:
servir: **sirvió/sirvieron** *he/they served*, **sirviendo** *serving*
dormir: **durmió/durmieron** *he/they slept*, **durmiendo** *sleeping*

8.2 Past participle

To form the past participle of regular verbs, you simply replace the infinitive ending with the endings that follow.

Verb group	Ending
First conjugation (**-ar** verbs) e.g. **estudiar** *to study*	→ stem of the verb + **-ado** e.g. **estudiado** *studied*
Second conjugation (**-er** verbs) Third conjugation (**-ir** verbs) e.g. **comer** *to eat*, **vivir** *to live*	→ stem of the verb + **-ido** e.g. **comido** *eaten*, **vivido** *lived*

Most irregular past participles end in **-to**, **-so** or **-cho**:
abrir → abierto *to open*, *opened*; **imprimir → impreso** *to print*, *printed*; **hacer → hecho** *to do*, *done*.

9 Usage of the past tenses in Spanish

• The present perfect and past perfect (pluperfect) tenses are used in essentially the same way as in English:
Yo he comido. *I have eaten.*
Yo había comido. *I had eaten.*

However, note that in Spanish (though not in Latin America), the present perfect is sometimes used where in English we might use the simple past. So, in fact, **Yo he comido** could translate to *I have eaten* or *I ate*, depending on the context.

• The preterite tense is a simple (single word) tense, indicating a completed action in the past:
Yo comí en aquel restaurante. *I ate at that restaurant.*

• The imperfect tense is also a simple (single word) tense, indicating a regular, repeated action or a continuous description. In English, it is often rendered by *was/were* + present participle or by *used to* + infinitive, depending on the context:
Yo comía en aquel restaurante. *I was eating at that restaurant./ I used to eat at that restaurant.*

Note also the use of the imperfect continuous tense, which corresponds exactly to English:
Yo estaba comiendo en aquel restaurant.
I was eating at that restaurant.

In some cases, Spanish uses the imperfect for situations in which the preterite could be used in English:
Yo comía en aquel restaurante cada día.
I ate ('used to eat') *at that restaurant every day.*

Generally, the imperfect is used to describe something in the past (**El cielo era azul.** *The sky was blue.*), while the preterite expresses specific events. Thus, the two are sometimes used in the same sentence, with the imperfect describing the context, and the preterite used to report the event:
Roberto llamó [preterite] **mientras tú trabajabas** [imperfect].
Roberto called while you were working.
Era [imperfect] **tarde cuando llegó** [preterite].
It was late when she arrived.

10 Usage of the subjunctive mood

The subjunctive is a verb form that is used much more frequently in Spanish than in English. It is not a tense, but what is known as a grammatical mood. The subjunctive mood is used chiefly to express situations of 'unreality' (wish, possibility, opinion or an action that has not yet occurred) – think 'subjective'. The verb form used to express statements as objective fact is called the indicative mood.

The subjunctive mood has three tenses: present subjunctive, past subjunctive (or imperfect subjunctive) and future subjunctive, which is now used only very rarely.

The following are some of the situations in which the subjunctive may be used. This list is not exhaustive.

10.1 In subordinate clauses

The most frequent use of the subjunctive is in subordinate clauses, usually after the word **que** *that*, when there is a change in subject.

• After verbs expressing commands, wishes, advice, requests, etc.:
Quiero que me hables. *I want you to speak to me.*
Dile que me llame mañana. *Tell her to call me tomorrow.*

Me recomienda que lea este libro.
He recommends that I read this book.
Te pido que vengas. *I'm asking you to come.*

• After certain conjunctions:
Te lo digo para que lo sepas. *I'm telling you so that you will know.*
No sé qué voy a hacer cuando se muera. *I don't know what I'm going to do when he dies.* (The subjunctive is used after **cuando** here because the main clause expresses the unknown future.)

• After an indefinite pronoun (such as *whatever*, *whoever*, *whenever*, etc.):
Coge lo que quieras. *Take whatever you wish.*
Bienvenidos, cualquiera que sea su religión.
Welcome, whatever your religion may be.

• After impersonal expressions that introduce uncertainty (e.g. *it's likely that*, *it's doubtful that*, *it could be that*):
Es posible que nos apetezca cambiar de piso.
It's possible that we'll feel like changing apartments.

• In 'if' clauses (if the condition is unlikely or contrary to fact; note that this is the imperfect subjunctive):
Si tuviera dinero, lo compraría. *If I had money I would buy it.*

10.2 In main clauses

• To form all commands except affirmative informal commands:
Hágame un favor. *Do me a favour.* (formal sing.)

• To make polite requests (the imperfect subjunctive can be used to replace the conditional):
Quisiera hablar con el señor Martínez.
I would like to speak with Mr Martínez.

• After **quizá(s)**, **acaso**, etc. (if what follows is doubtful or improbable):
Quizás tengas razón. *Perhaps you are right.*

• In certain fixed expressions:
Ya sea… *Whether it be …*

11 First conjugation: verbs ending in *-ar*

- **cantar** *to sing*

Present indicative	Imperative (affirmative informal)	Present subjunctive
cant o *I sing*		**cant e** *that I sing*
cant as *you sing* (informal sing.)	**canta** *sing* (singular)	**cant es**
cant a *he/she/it sings, you* (formal sing.) *sing*		**cant e**
cant amos *we sing*		**cant emos**
cant áis *you sing* (informal plural)	**cant ad** (plural)	**cant éis**
cant an *they sing, you* (formal plural) *sing*		**cant en**

Imperfect indicative	Present participle
cant aba *I was singing, I used to sing*	**cant ando** *singing*
cant abas	
cant aba	**Past participle**
cant ábamos	**cant ado** *sung*
cant abais	
cant aban	

Future	Conditional
cantar é *I will sing*	**cantar ía** *I would sing*
cantar ás	**cantar ías**
cantar á	**cantar ía**
cantar emos	**cantar íamos**
cantar éis	**cantar íais**
cantar án	**cantar ían**

Preterite/ Simple past	Imperfect subjunctive	Future subjunctive
cant é *I sang*	**cant ara** or **cant ase**	**cant are**
cant aste	**cant aras / -ases**	**cant ares**
cant ó	**cant ara / -ase**	**cant are**
cant amos	**cant áramos / -ásemos**	**cant áremos**
cant asteis	**cant arais / -aseis**	**cant areis**
cant aron	**cant aran / -asen**	**cant aren**

12 Second conjugation: verbs ending in *-er*

• **comer** *to eat*

Present indicative	Imperative (affirmative informal)	Present subjunctive
com o *I eat*		**com a** *that I eat*
com es	**com e** *eat*	**com as**
com e		**com a**
com emos		**com amos**
com éis	**com ed**	**com áis**
com en		**com an**

Imperfect indicative	Present participle
com ía *I was eating, I used to eat*	**com iendo** *eating*
com ías	
com ía	**Past participle**
com íamos	
com íais	**com ido** *eaten*
com ían	

Future	Conditional
comer é *I will eat*	**comer ía** *I would eat*
comer ás	**comer ías**
comer á	**comer ía**
comer emos	**comer íamos**
comer éis	**comer íais**
comer án	**comer ían**

Preterite/ Simple past	Imperfect subjunctive	Future subjunctive
com í *I ate*	**com iera** or **com iese**	**com iere**
com iste	**com ieras / -ieses**	**com ieres**
com ió	**com iera / -iese**	**com iere**
com imos	**comi éramos / -iésemos**	**com iéremos**
com isteis	**com ierais / -ieseis**	**com iereis**
com ieron	**com ieran / -iesen**	**com ieren**

13 Third conjugation: verbs ending in *-ir*

- **vivir** *to live*

Present indicative	Imperative (affirmative informal)	Present subjunctive
viv o *I live*		**viv a** *that I live*
viv es	**viv e** *live*	**viv as**
viv e		**viv a**
viv imos		**viv amos**
viv ís	**viv id**	**viv áis**
viv en		**viv an**

Imperfect indicative	Present participle
viv ía *I was living, I used to live*	**viv iendo** *living*
viv ías	
viv ía	**Past participle**
viv íamos	
viv íais	**viv ido** *lived*
viv ían	

Future	Conditional
vivir é *I will live*	**vivir ía** *I would live*
vivir ás	**vivir ías**
vivir á	**vivir ía**
vivir emos	**vivir íamos**
vivir éis	**vivir íais**
vivir án	**vivir ían**

Preterite/ Simple past	Imperfect subjunctive	Future subjunctive
viv í *I lived*	**viv iera** or **viv iese**	**viv iere**
viv iste	**viv ieras / -ieses**	**viv ieres**
viv ió	**viv iera / -iese**	**viv iere**
viv imos	**viv iéramos / -iésemos**	**viv iéremos**
viv isteis	**viv ierais / -ieseis**	**viv iereis**
viv ieron	**viv ieran / -iesen**	**viv ieren**

• **haber** *to have* (mainly an auxiliary verb)

Present indicative	Imperative (affirmative informal)	Present subjunctive
he *I have* **has** **ha** (impersonal **hay**) **hemos** **habéis** **han**	 **he** *have* **hab ed**	**haya** *that I have* **hayas** **haya** **hayamos** **hayáis** **hayan**

Imperfect indicative	Present participle / Past participle
hab ía *I was having, I used to have* **hab ías** **hab ía** **hab íamos** **hab íais** **hab ían**	Present participle: **hab iendo** *having* Past participle: **hab ido** *had*

Future	Conditional
habr é *I will have* **habr ás** **habr á** **habr emos** **habr éis** **habr án**	**habr ía** *I would have* **habr ías** **habr ía** **habr íamos** **habr íais** **habr ían**

Preterite/ Simple past	Imperfect subjunctive	Future subjunctive
hub e *I had* **hub iste** **hub o** **hub imos** **hub isteis** **hub ieron**	**hub iera** or **hub iese** **hub ieras / -ieses** **hub iera / -iese** **hub iéramos / -iésemos** **hub ierais / -ieseis** **hub ieran / -iesen**	**hub iere** **hub ieres** **hub iere** **hub iéremos** **hub iereis** **hub ieren**

• **tener** *to have* (meaning *to possess*)

Present indicative	Imperative (affirmative informal)	Present subjunctive
tengo *I have*		**teng a** *that I have*
tien es	**ten** *have*	**teng as**
tien e		**teng a**
ten emos		**teng amos**
ten éis	**ten ed**	**teng áis**
tien en		**teng an**

Imperfect indicative	Present participle
ten ía *I was having, I used to have*	**ten iendo** *having*
ten ías	
ten ía	**Past participle**
ten íamos	**ten ido** *had*
ten íais	
ten ían	

Future	Conditional
tendr é *I will have*	**tendr ía** *I would have*
tendr ás	**tendr ías**
tendr á	**tendr ía**
tendr emos	**tendr íamos**
tendr éis	**tendr íais**
tendr án	**tendr ían**

Preterite/ Simple past	Imperfect subjunctive	Future subjunctive
tuv e *I had*	**tuv iera** or **tuv iese**	**tuv iere**
tuv iste	**tuv ieras / -ieses**	**tuv ieres**
tuv o	**tuv iera / -iese**	**tuv iere**
tuv imos	**tuv iéramos / -iésemos**	**tuv iéremos**
tuv isteis	**tuv ierais / -ieseis**	**tuv iereis**
tuv ieron	**tuv ieran / -iesen**	**tuv ieren**

• **ser** *to be* (used to describe unchanging characteristics)

Present indicative	Imperative (affirmative informal)	Present subjunctive
soy *I am*		**se a** *that I be*
eres	**sé** *be*	**se as**
es		**se a**
somos		**se amos**
sois	**sed**	**se áis**
son		**se an**

Imperfect indicative	Present participle
era *I was being, I used to be*	**s iendo** *being*
eras	
era	**Past participle**
éramos	
erais	**s ido** *been*
eran	

Future	Conditional
ser é *I will be*	**ser ía** *I would be*
ser ás	**ser ías**
ser á	**ser ía**
ser emos	**ser íamos**
ser éis	**ser íais**
ser án	**ser ían**

Preterite/ Simple past	Imperfect subjunctive	Future subjunctive
fu i *I was*	**fu era** or **fu ese**	**fu ere**
fu iste	**fu eras / -eses**	**fu eres**
fu e	**fu era / -ese**	**fu ere**
fu imos	**fu éramos / -ésemos**	**fu éremos**
fu isteis	**fu erais / -eseis**	**fu ereis**
fu eron	**fu eran / -esen**	**fu eren**

• **estar** *to be* (used to describe changing characteristics or location)

Present indicative	Imperative (affirmative informal)		Present subjunctive
estoy *I am*			**est é** *that I be*
est ás	**est á** *be*		**est és**
est á			**est é**
est amos			**est emos**
est áis	**est ad**		**est éis**
est án			**est én**
Imperfect indicative			Present participle
est aba *I was being, I used to be*			**est ando** *being*
est abas			
est aba			Past participle
est ábamos			
est abais			**est ado** *been*
est aban			
Future		Conditional	
estar é *I will be*		**estar ía** *I would be*	
estar ás		**estar ías**	
estar á		**estar ía**	
estar emos		**estar íamos**	
estar éis		**estar íais**	
estar án		**estar ían**	
Preterite/ Simple past	Imperfect subjunctive		Future subjunctive
estuv e *I was*	**estuv iera** or **estuv iese**		**estuv iere**
estuv iste	**estuv ieras / -ieses**		**estuv ieres**
estuv o	**estuv iera / -iese**		**estuv iere**
estuv imos	**estuv iéramos/ -iésemos**		**estuv iéremos**
estuv isteis	**estuv ierais / -ieseis**		**estuv iereis**
estuv ieron	**estuv ieran / -iesen**		**estuv ieren**

15 Irregular verbs

The tables in sections 11, 12 and 13 show the conjugations for regular **-ar**, **-er** and **-ir** verbs. Unfortunately, there are a number of irregular verbs. There are different types of irregularities a verb can have, which themselves can be categorized to make it easier to learn them. A verb is considered irregular if it diverges from the regular conjugations in the three following forms:
• in the first-person singular of the present indicative
• in the third-person plural of the preterite (simple past)
• in the first-person singular of the future indicative.

If a verb is regular in these three tenses and persons, it is regular in all tenses.

However:
• If the verb is irregular in the first-person singular of the present indicative, it will also be irregular in the present subjunctive and the imperative.
• If the verb is irregular in the third-person plural of the preterite, it will also be irregular in the imperfect subjunctive and the future subjunctive.
• If the verb is irregular in the first-person future indicative, it will also be irregular in the conditional.

This means that we can form three categories that allow us to know where the irregularity will appear:
• **Present:** in the present indicative, the present subjunctive and the imperative
• **Preterite:** in the preterite, the imperfect subjunctive and the future subjunctive
• **Future:** in the future indicative and the conditional.

The imperfect indicative is an exception, but in this tense only the following verbs are irregular: **ir** *to go*, **ser** *to be* and **ver** *to see*.

16 Irregular verb groups

16.1 Group 1

Many verbs with **e** as the final (or only) vowel in the stem.

Irregularity: stem change **e** → **ie**

Category affected: present

Examples: **pensar** *to think*; **perder** *to lose* (lesson 70)

16.2 Group 2

Many verbs with **o** as the final (or only) vowel in the stem.

Irregularity: stem change **o** → **ue**

Categories affected: present

Examples: **contar** *to count*, *to tell*; **volver** *to return*, *to come back* (lessons 49 and 53)

16.3 Group 3

Verbs ending in **-acer**, **-ecer**, **-ocer**, **-ucir**.

Irregularity: change **c** → **zc**

Category affected: present

Examples: **nacer** *to be born*; **agradecer** *to thank*; **conocer** *to know*, *meet*; **lucir** *to shine* (lessons 40, 71 and 77)

16.4 Group 4

Verbs ending in **-ducir**.

Irregularities: change **c** → **zc** (present)
ends in **-duje** (preterite)

Categories affected: present, preterite

Example: **conducir** *to lead to*, *drive* (lesson 77)

16.5 Group 5

Verbs ending in **-añer**, **-añir**, **-iñir**, **-uñir**, **-eller**, **-ullir**. (These verbs are quite uncommon.)

Irregularity: **i** in conjugation ending is dropped

Categories affected: preterite, present participle

Examples: **tañer** *to strum*, *ring (a musical instrument or bell)*; **engullir** *to guzzle*, *gobble*

16.6 Group 6

servir *to serve*, and verbs ending in **-ebir**, **-edir**, **-egir**, **-eguir**, **-emir**, **-enchir**, **-endir**, **-estir**, **-etir**.

Irregularity: stem change **e** → **i** (final or only **e**)

Categories affected: present, preterite, present participle

Examples: **pedir** *to request*; **elegir** *to elect*; **seguir** *to follow*; **gemir** *to groan*; **henchir** *to swell*; **rendir** *to render*; **vestir** *to dress*; **repetir** *to repeat* (lesson 84)

16.7 Group 7

reír *to laugh*, and verbs ending in **-eír**, **-eñir**.

Irregularities: stem change **e** → **i**
e of the stem is dropped (**reír**)
i in conjugation ending is dropped (**teñir**)

Categories affected: present, preterite, present participle

Examples: **reír** *to laugh*; **teñir** *to dye* (lesson 98)

16.8 Group 8

Verbs ending in **-entir**, **-erir**, **-ertir**.

Irregularities: stem change **e** → **ie** (final or only **e**) (present)
stem change **e** → **i** (final or only **e**) (preterite, present participle, present subj. **nosotros/vosotros**)

Categories affected: present, preterite, present participle

Examples: **sentir** *to feel*; **preferir** *to prefer*; **divertir** *to amuse, entertain* (lesson 98)

16.9 Group 9

jugar *to play*, and verbs ending in **-irir**.

Irregularities: stem change **u** → **ue**
stem change **i** → **ie**

Category affected: present

Examples: **jugar** *to play*; **adquirir** *to acquire* (lesson 82 and 87)

16.10 Group 10

Verbs ending in **-uir**.

Irregularity: + **y** before **a**, **e** and **o** in endings

Categories affected: present, present participle

Example: **construir** *to build* (lesson 80)

16.11 Group 11

dormir *to sleep* and **morir** *to die.*

Irregularities: stem change **o** → **ue** (present)
stem change **o** → **u** (preterite, present participle, present subj. **nosotros/vosotros**)

Categories affected: present, preterite, present participle

16.12 Group 12

salir *to leave* and **valer** *to be worth* (lesson 91).

Irregularities: + **g** before **a** and **o** in endings (present)
the vowel in the infinitive ending is replaced with a **d** (future/conditional)
short form in the imperative

Categories affected: present, future/conditional, imperative

17 Uniquely irregular verbs

There are around 20 Spanish verbs that are irregular in a unique way and can't be neatly categorized in any of the irregular verb groups presented in the previous pages. Although it would be nice to gloss over these, as with most languages, many are very commonly used verbs that are needed to form all kinds of basic everyday phrases. Here is an alphabetical list of those that are used most often:

andar	*to walk*
caber	*to fit*
caer	*to fall*
dar	*to give*
decir	*to say, to tell*
estar	*to be* (used to describe changing characteristics or location)
haber	*to have* (auxiliary verb)
hacer	*to do, to make*
ir	*to go*
oír	*to hear*
poder	*to be able to*
poner	*to put*
querer	*to want, to love*
saber	*to know*
ser	*to be* (used to describe unchanging characteristics)
tener	*to have* (meaning *to possess*)
traer	*to bring*
venir	*to come*
ver	*to see*

The following tables show the conjugations for each of these verbs, but only for the irregular forms. If a form is missing, it conjugates normally according to the respective **-ar**, **-er** or **-ir** model (see sections 11, 12 and 13 respectively). In these tables, in most cases we have not considered spelling changes as irregularities.

• **andar** *to walk*

Preterite	Imperfect subjunctive	Future subjunctive
anduve *I walked*	**anduv iera** or **anduv iese**	**anduviere**
anduviste	**anduv ieras /-ieses**	**anduvieres**
anduvo	**anduv iera / -iera**	**anduviere**
anduvimos	**anduv iéramos / -iésemos**	**anduviéremos**
anduvisteis	**anduv ierais / -ieseis**	**anduviereis**
anduvieron	**anduv ieran / -iesen**	**anduvieren**

• **caber** *to fit*

Present indicative	Present subjunctive
quepo *I fit*	**quepa** *that I fit*
cabes	**quepas**
cabe	**quepa**
cabemos	**quepamos**
cabéis	**quepáis**
caben	**quepan**
Future	Conditional
cabré *I will fit*	**cabría** *I would fit*
cabrás	**cabrías**
cabrá	**cabría**
cabremos	**cabríamos**
cabréis	**cabríais**
cabrán	**cabrían**

Preterite	Imperfect subjunctive	Future subjunctive
cupe *I fitted*	**cupiera** or **cupiese**	**cupiere**
cupiste	**cupieras / cupieses**	**cupieres**
cupo	**cupiera / cupiese**	**cupiere**
cupimos	**cupiéramos / cupiésemos**	**cupiéremos**
cupisteis	**cupierais / cupieseis**	**cupiereis**
cupieron	**cupieran / cupiesen**	**cupieren**

- **caer** *to fall*

Present indicative	Present subjunctive
caigo *I fall*	**caiga** *that I fall*
caes	**caigas**
cae	**caiga**
caemos	**caigamos**
caéis	**caigáis**
caen	**caigan**

- **dar** *to give*

Present indicative		
doy *I give* **das** **da** **damos** **dais** **dan**		
Preterite	Imperfect subjunctive	Future subjunctive
di *I gave*	**diera** or **diese**	**diere**
diste	**dieras / dieses**	**dieres**
dio	**diera / diese**	**diere**
dimos	**diéramos / diésemos**	**diéremos**
disteis	**dierais / dieseis**	**diereis**
dieron	**dieran / diesen**	**dieren**

• **decir** *to say, to tell*

Present indicative	Imperative (affirmative informal)	Present subjunctive
digo *I say* **dices** **dice** **decimos** **decís** **dicen**	 **di** *say* **decid** 	**diga** *that I say* **digas** **diga** **digamos** **digáis** **digan**
Future	Conditional	
diré *I will say* **dirás** **dirá** **diremos** **diréis** **dirán**	**diría** *I would say* **dirías** **diría** **diríamos** **diríais** **dirían**	
Preterite	Imperfect subjunctive	Future subjunctive
dije *I said* **dijiste** **dijo** **dijimos** **dijisteis** **dijeron**	**dijera** or **dijese** **dijeras / dijeses** **dijera / dijese** **dijéramos / dijésemos** **dijerais / dijeseis** **dijeran / dijesen**	**dijere** **dijeres** **dijere** **dijéremos** **dijereis** **dijeren**
Present participle	Past participle	
diciendo *saying*	**dicho** *said*	

• **estar** *to be* (used to describe changing characteristics or location)

See conjugation on page 497

• **haber** *to have* (auxiliary verb)

See conjugation on page 494

• **hacer** *to do, make*

Present indicative	Imperative (affirmative informal)	Present subjunctive
hago *I do, I make* **haces** **hace** **hacemos** **hacéis** **hacen**	 **haz** *do, make* **haced** 	**haga** *that I do* **hagas** **haga** **hagamos** **hagáis** **hagan**
Future	Conditional	
haré *I will do, make* **harás** **hará** **haremos** **haréis** **harán**	**haría** *I would do, make* **harías** **haría** **haríamos** **haríais** **harían**	
Preterite	Imperfect subjunctive	Future subjunctive
hice *I did, I made* **hiciste** **hizo** **hicimos** **hicisteis** **hicieron**	**hiciera** or **hiciese** **hicieras / hicieses** **hiciera / hiciese** **hiciéramos / hiciésemos** **hicierais / hicieseis** **hicieran / hiciesen**	**hiciere** **hicieres** **hiciere** **hiciéremos** **hiciereis** **hicieren**
Past participle		
hecho *done, made*		

• **ir** *to go*

Present indicative	Imperative (affirmative informal)	Present subjunctive
voy *I go* **vas** **va** **vamos** **vais** **van**	 **ve** *go* **id** 	**vaya** *that I go* **vayas** **vaya** **vayamos** **vayáis** **vayan**
Imperfect indicative		
iba *I went* **ibas** **iba** **íbamos** **ibais** **iban**		
Preterite	Imperfect subjunctive	Future subjunctive
fui *I went* **fuiste** **fue** **fuimos** **fuisteis** **fueron**	**fuera** or **fuese** **fueras / fueses** **fuera / fuese** **fuéramos / fuésemos** **fuerais / fueseis** **fueran / fuesen**	**fuere** **fueres** **fuere** **fuéremos** **fuereis** **fueren**
Present participle		
yendo *going*		

• **oír** *to hear*

Present indicative	Imperative (affirmative informal)	Present subjunctive
oigo *I hear*		**oiga** *that I hear*
oyes	**oye** *hear*	**oigas**
oye		**oiga**
oímos		**oigamos**
oís	**oíd**	**oigáis**
oyen		**oigan**
Present participle		
oyendo *hearing*		

• **poder** *to be able to, can*

Present indicative	Imperative (affirmative informal)	Present subjunctive
puedo *I am able to, I can*		**pueda** *that I be able, that I can*
puedes	**puede**	**puedas**
puede		**pueda**
podemos		**podamos**
podéis	**poded**	**podáis**
pueden		**puedan**

Future	Conditional
podré *I will be able to*	**podría** *I would be able to*
podrás	**podrías**
podrá	**podría**
podremos	**podríamos**
podréis	**podríais**
podrán	**podrían**

Preterite	Imperfect subjunctive	Future subjunctive
pude *I was able to*	**pud iera** or **pudiese**	**pudiere**
pudiste	**pud ieras** / **-ieses**	**pudieres**
pudo	**pud iera** / **-iese**	**pudiere**
pudimos	**pud iéramos** / **-iésemos**	**pudiéremos**
pudisteis	**pud ierais** / **-ieseis**	**pudiereis**
pudieron	**pud ieran** / **-iesen**	**pudieren**
Present participle		
pudiendo *being able to*

• **poner** *to put*

Present indicative	Imperative (affirmative informal)	Present subjunctive
pongo *I put*		**ponga** *that I put*
pones	**pon** *put*	**pongas**
pone		**ponga**
ponemos		**pongamos**
ponéis	**poned**	**pongáis**
ponen		**pongan**

Future	Conditional
pondré *I will put*	**pondría** *I would put*
pondrás	**pondrías**
pondrá	**pondría**
pondremos	**pondríamos**
pondréis	**pondríais**
pondrán	**pondrían**

Preterite	Imperfect subjunctive	Future subjunctive
puse *I put*	**pusiera** or **pusiese**	**pusiere**
pusiste	**pus ieras / -ieses**	**pusieres**
puso	**pus iera / -iese**	**pusiere**
pusimos	**pus iéramos / -iésemos**	**pusiéremos**
pusisteis	**pus ierais / -ieseis**	**pusiereis**
pusieron	**pus ieran / -iesen**	**pusieren**

Past participle
puesto *put*

• **querer** *to want, to like*

Present indicative	Imperative (affirmative informal)	Present subjunctive
quiero *I want, I like*		**quiera** *that I want*
quieres	**quiere** *want*	**quieras**
quiere		**quiera**
queremos		**queramos**
queréis	**quered**	**queráis**
quieren		**quieran**

Future	Conditional
querré *I will want, like*	**querría** *I would like*
querrás	**querrías**
querrá	**querría**
querremos	**querríamos**
querréis	**querríais**
querrán	**querrían**

Preterite	Imperfect subjunctive	Future subjunctive
quise *I wanted*	**quisiera** or **quisiese**	**quisiere**
quisiste	**quis ieras / -ieses**	**quisieres**
quiso	**quis iera / -iese**	**quisiere**
quisimos	**quis iéramos / -iésemos**	**quisiéremos**
quisisteis	**quis ierais / -ieseis**	**quisiereis**
quisieron	**quis ieran / -iesen**	**quisieren**

• **saber** *to know*

Present indicative	Present subjunctive
sé *I know*	**sepa** *that I know*
sabes	**sepas**
sabe	**sepa**
sabemos	**sepamos**
sabéis	**sepáis**
saben	**sepan**

Future	Conditional
sabré *I will know*	**sabría** *I would know*
sabrás	**sabrías**
sabrá	**sabría**
sabremos	**sabríamos**
sabréis	**sabríais**
sabrán	**sabrían**

Preterite	Imperfect subjunctive	Future subjunctive
supe *I knew*	**supiera** or **supiese**	**supiere**
supiste	**sup ieras / -ieses**	**supieres**
supo	**sup iera / -iese**	**supiere**
supimos	**sup iéramos / -iésemos**	**supiéremos**
supisteis	**sup ierais / -ieseis**	**supiereis**
supieron	**sup ieran / -iesen**	**supieren**

• **ser** *to be* (used to describe unchanging characteristics)

See conjugation on page 496

• **tener** *to have* (meaning *to possess*)

See conjugation on page 495

• **traer** *to bring*

Present indicative	Present subjunctive
traigo *I bring* **traes** **trae** **traemos** **traéis** **traen**	**traiga** *that I bring* **traigas** **traiga** **traigamos** **traigáis** **traigan**

Preterite	Imperfect subjunctive	Future subjunctive
traje *I brought*	**trajera** or **trajese**	**trajere**
trajiste	**traj eras / -eses**	**trajeres**
trajo	**traj era /-ese**	**trajere**
trajimos	**traj éramos / -ésemos**	**trajéremos**
trajisteis	**traj erais / -eseis**	**trajereis**
trajeron	**traj eran / -esen**	**trajeren**

• **venir** *to come*

Present indicative	Imperative (affirmative informal)	Present subjunctive
vengo *I come* **vienes** **viene** **venimos** **venís** **vienen**	 **ven** *come* **venid** 	**venga** *that I come* **vengas** **venga** **vengamos** **vengáis** **vengan**
Future	Conditional	
vendré *I will come* **vendrás** **vendrá** **vendremos** **vendréis** **vendrán**	**vendría** *I would come* **vendrías** **vendría** **vendríamos** **vendríais** **vendrían**	
Preterite	Imperfect subjunctive	Future subjunctive
vine *I came* **viniste** **vino** **vinimos** **vinisteis** **vinieron**	**viniera** or **viniese** **vin ieras / -ieses** **vin iera / -iese** **vin iéramos / -iésemos** **vin ierais / -ieseis** **vin ieran / -iesen**	**viniere** **vinieres** **viniere** **viniéremos** **viniereis** **vinieren**
Present participle		
viniendo *coming*		

- **ver** *to see*

Present indicative	Present subjunctive
veo *I see* **ves** **ve** **vemos** **veis** **ven**	**vea** *that I see* **veas** **vea** **veamos** **veáis** **vean**
Imperfect indicative	
veía *I saw* **veías** **veía** **veíamos** **veíais** **veían**	
Past participle	
visto *seen*	

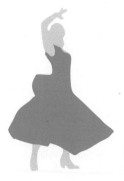

Grammatical index

The reference numbers for each entry occur in pairs: the first number refers to the lesson, the second to the note or section of the lesson in which the explanation can be found. Reference numbers in bold indicate review lessons.

Glossary of expressions

Greetings

Buenos días. (1)	Good morning. ('good day')
¡Buenas! / ¡Muy buenas! (32)	Hello!
Buenas noches. (10)	Good night.
Buenas tardes. (10)	Good evening. / Good afternoon.
¡Diga! / ¡Dígame! (31)	Hello! (answering the phone)
¡Hola! (2)	Hi!

Taking leave

¡Adiós! (1)	Goodbye!
¡Hasta la vista! (100)	See you next time!
¡Hasta luego! (81)	See you later!
¡Hasta mañana! (10)	See you tomorrow!
¡Hasta pronto! (100)	See you soon!

Making conversation

¿Cómo estás? (16)	How are you?
¿Cómo te va / te ha ido? (47)	How is it going with you?
¿Cuántos años tienes? (22)	How old are you?
Da gusto… (9)	It's nice … / It's a pleasure …
¡Encantado/a de conocerle! (36)	Delighted to meet you.
¿Qué edad tienes? (22)	How old are you?
¿Qué es de ti? (51)	How are things with you?
¿Qué tal? (3)	How are you? / How's it going?

Thanking, excusing or apologizing

De nada. (5)	Don't mention it. / It's nothing.
Disculpe. (44)	Excuse me.
Gracias. (1)	Thank you.
¿Le molesta si...? (45)	Does it bother you if …?
¡Lo siento! / ¡Lo siento muchísimo! (48)	I'm sorry! / I beg your pardon. / I'm very sorry!
Muchas gracias. (23)	Many thanks.

¿No le importa? (71)	Do you mind?
Perdón. / Perdone. (5)	Sorry. / Excuse me.
Por favor ... (1)	Please ...
Se lo agradezco. (82)	I thank you.

Service transactions

¿Algo más? (50)	Anything else?
Aquí tiene. (1)	Here it is. / Here you are.
Eso es. (33)	That's it.
Está comunicando. (54)	The line is engaged/busy.
¿Le atienden? (32)	Is someone serving you?
¿Le parece? (71)	Do you agree? / Is that OK with you?
Nada más. (50)	That's all. / Nothing else.
¿Qué desea? (50)	How can I help you?
Son... euros. (1)	That's ... euros.
¡Ten! (82, 84)	Here you are! / Here you go!

Asking or giving opinions

a lo mejor (41, 42)	perhaps / maybe / it might be
¿A que...? (36)	Isn't it true that ... / I bet that ...
¡Claro! / ¡Claro que sí! (3)	Certainly! / Of course! / Absolutely right!
Creo que sí. (78)	I think so.
de acuerdo (10)	OK / agreed
en absoluto (40, 68)	not at all
En efecto. (92)	Indeed.
Es verdad. (9)	It's true.
Eso es. (33)	That's it.
Está bien. (13)	That's fine. / Very well.
¿Está claro? (3)	Is that clear?
Me da igual. (79)	I don't mind.
Me da que... (64)	I feel that ... / I have the impression that ...
No cabe duda. (57)	There is no doubt.
No hace falta. (75)	It's not necessary.
No importa. (52, 71)	It doesn't matter. / It's OK.
No pasa nada. (52)	It doesn't matter. / It's OK.
Nunca se sabe. (20)	You never know.
¡Ojalá! (62)	Hopefully!

por supuesto (68)	of course
Pues… (41)	Well …
¿Qué te parece? (16, 71)	How does that seem? / What do you think about …?
sea lo que sea (95)	whatever happens
sin duda alguna / sin ninguna duda (57)	without any doubt
¡Vale! (10)	OK!
¿Verdad? (9)	Right?
¿Verdad que…? (36)	Isn't it true that …

Talking about actions or states

amargarse la vida / amargarle la vida a alguien (51)	to make one's life a misery / to make someone else's life a misery
andar a vueltas con… (94)	to struggle with a problem
caerse de espaldas (55)	to fall [flat] on one's back
comer como una fiera / un león (60)	to eat like a horse
comer una barbaridad (52)	to eat a huge amount
comportarse como un caballero (32)	to behave like a gentleman
cortar(se) el pelo (71)	to get one's hair cut
cumplir años (23)	to turn/be … years old
dar la espalda (43)	to turn one's back
dar un telefonazo (54)	to give someone a ring/call
darse cuenta (55)	to realize
darse una vuelta (29)	to turn around
dejar plantado/a (90)	to leave in the lurch / to leave high and dry
dormir como una marmota (60)	to sleep like a log
echar una carta al correo (50)	to post a letter
echar una ojeada (79)	to have a quick look
echarse al ruedo (99)	to throw one's hat into the ring
estar a la altura (100)	to be equal to
estar de vuelta / de regreso (49)	to be back
estar en condiciones de (100)	to be capable of
estar harto/a (87)	to have had enough
estar hasta la coronilla (87)	to be fed up [with]
estar hasta las narices (87)	to be sick and tired [of]

gastar una broma (71)	to play a joke
hacer cola (50)	to queue/line up
hacer una consulta en Internet (94)	to search the web
hacerse dueño (100)	to take control
ir a dar una vuelta (49)	to go for a walk
ir al médico (29)	to go to the doctor's
ir de compras (76)	to go shopping
ir de copas (16)	to go for a drink
ir de escaparates (76)	to go window shopping
ir de tapas (1)	to go for tapas
llegar con retraso (18)	to arrive late
llegar la vez (71)	to be one's turn
llevar… (55)	to take [amount of time]
llevar retraso (18)	to be late
llevarse una bronca (55)	to get a telling-off
mantenerse en sus trece (66)	to stick to one's guns
matar dos pájaros de un tiro (94)	to kill two birds with one stone
no dejar escapar la oportunidad (99)	to not let the opportunity slip away
no parar quieto (67)	to be unable to stay still
parecer traído por los pelos (71)	to seem far-fetched
pasárselo en grande (88)	to have a great time
poner buena cara / poner mala cara (11)	to put on a brave face / to balk at
poner cara de… (64)	to make a face
poner cara de entierro (64)	to look gloomy
poner enfermo/malo a... (43)	to make one sick
ponerse enfermo/malo (43)	to get sick
quitarse la ropa (55)	to take off one's clothes
saber nadar y guardar la ropa (55)	to sit on the fence
saltarse un semáforo (38)	to run a traffic light
tener buena/mala cara (11)	to look well/unwell
tener dinero suelto (6)	to have change (coins)
tener en cuenta (52)	to keep in mind
tener ganas (51)	to feel like / to have the urge to
tener mala pata (11)	to have bad luck
tener mucha cara (41)	to have a lot of nerve
trabajar como una mula (60)	to work like a mule/dog

valer la pena (88)	to be worth it
volver la cabeza (49)	to turn one's head
volver loco (36)	to drive crazy

Celebrations

celebrar el cumpleaños (23)	to celebrate a birthday
¡Felices fiestas! (23)	Happy Holidays!
¡Felicidades! (23)	Congratulations!
¡Feliz Año Nuevo! (23)	Happy New Year!
¡Feliz cumpleaños! (23)	Happy Birthday!
¡Feliz Navidad! (23)	Merry Christmas!

Asking questions

¿Cuánto…? (22)	How much/many …?
¿De qué se trata? (96)	What's it about?
¿Para qué? (20)	Why? / What for?
¿Por qué? (12)	Why?
¿Qué hora es? (17)	What time is it?
¿Qué me dices? (51)	What are you telling me? / What do you mean?
¿Qué ocurre? (55)	What's going on? / What's happening?
¿Qué pasa? (20)	What's going on? / What's happening?
¿Qué quiere decir eso? (55)	What does that mean?
¿Qué te ocurre? (55)	What happened to you?
¿Qué te pasa? (20)	What's the matter with you? / What's wrong?
¿Tienes hora? (17)	Do you have the time?
¿Y ahora? (17)	Now what? / What's next?

Giving encouragement and good wishes

¡A pasarlo bien! (89)	Enjoy yourself!
¡Adelante! (28, 50, 57)	Carry on! / Onwards! / Keep going!
¡Ale! (67)	Come on!
¡Ánimo! (20, 50)	You can do it! / Go for it!
¡Buen provecho! (1)	Enjoy your meal!
¡Buen viaje! (100)	Have a great trip!

¡Confíe en sí mismo! (40)	Have confidence in yourself!
¡Enhorabuena! (23, 99)	Congratulations!
¡Eso es lo que cuenta! (29)	That's what counts!
¡Felicidades! (23)	Best wishes!
¡Feliz viaje! (23)	Have a good trip!
¡Más vale tarde que nunca! (23)	Better late than never!
¡Mira qué fácil! (74)	Look how easy!
¡No se preocupe! (31, 40)	Don't worry!
Pase por una vez. (89)	Just once won't hurt.
¡Que te vaya bien! (89)	All the best!
¡Vamos! (18, 48)	Let's go! / Come on!
¡Ya verás! (41)	You'll see!

Showing surprise

¡Ay! (5)	Oh!
¡Cuánto tiempo! (16)	It's been ages!
¡De cine! / ¡De película! (39)	Fantastic!
¡Dios de mi vida! / ¡Dios mío! (36)	Oh my goodness!
¡Es la repera! (73)	It's incredible! / It's too much!
¡Estupendo! (4)	Great!
¡Hombre! / ¡Mujer! (16)	Hey! / No way!
¡Jo! (73)	Wow!
¡Menudo…! (39)	How / What a …!
¡Mira esto! (33)	Look at this!
¡No es para tanto! (52, 73)	No need to exaggerate! / You're kidding!
¡No es posible! (47)	It's not possible!
No me cabe en la cabeza. (96)	I can't get my head around it.
¡No me digas! (20)	Really! / You don't say!
¡Oye! (46, 71)	Hey!
¡Qué…! (19)	How ...! / What a ...!
¡Qué cosa más rara! (94)	How strange!
¡Qué extraño! (29)	How odd!
¡Qué raro! (17)	How strange!
¡Si no lo veo, no lo creo! (79)	I can't believe my eyes!

Expressing annoyance, disappointment or worry

¡Abajo…! (79)	Down with …!
¡Ahí va! (54)	Oh no!
¡Anda! (18)	Well I never! / Come on!
¡Caramba! (30)	Good heavens!
Como lo oyes. (73)	I'm telling you!
¡Estamos apañados! (17)	We're in trouble!
¡Estoy hasta las narices! (87)	I've have had enough!
¡Mala pata! (11)	Tough luck!
¡Malísimamente! (47)	Extremely badly!
¡Menudo… ! / ¡Menudo jaleo! / ¡Menudo lío! (39)	What a …! / What a racket! / What a mess!
¡Menudo rollo! / ¡Menudo tostón! (39)	What boring rubbish! / How boring!
¡Mira qué ...! (74)	Look how ...!
¡Nada de nada! (39)	Absolutely not! / No way!
¡Ni te cuento! (39)	I can't even tell you!
¡No aguanto más! (27)	I can't stand it anymore!
¡No faltaba más! (79)	That's all we needed!
¡No fastidies! (73)	Come on now! / That's enough!
¡No hables! (39)	Don't even ask!
¡No hay pero que valga! (40)	There are no ifs, ands or buts about it!
¡No hay tu tía! (96)	It's no use!
Por más que… / Por mucho que… (96)	No matter how …
¡Qué barbaridad! (52)	How awful! / It's outrageous!
¡Qué cara dura! (41)	What a cheek! / What a nerve!
¡Qué mala pata! (11)	What bad luck!
¿Qué más da? (41)	So what?
¡Que te den morcilla! (39)	Get lost!
¡Qué tostón! (39)	How boring!
¡Tampoco es para tanto! (52)	No need to exaggerate!
¡Vaya! (6)	Oh dear! / Oh no!
¡Y dale! (44)	There you go again!
¡Y dale que dale! (44)	Always the same old thing!

Giving advice or orders

¡Atención! (38)	Watch out!
Cuéntame. / Cuénteme. (53)	Tell me.
¡Cuidado! (5, 38)	Careful!
Deja de… / Deje de… (79)	Leave off … / Stop ...
¡Deprisa! (6, 38)	Hurry up!
¡Mira! / ¡Mire! (13)	Look!
¡No te muevas! (67)	Don't move!
¡Oiga! (46, 48, 78)	Listen! / Excuse me! (to attract someone's attention)
¡Rápido! (67)	Quick!
¡Ten/Tenga cuidado! (85)	Be careful!
¡Tranquilo/a! (45)	Stay calm! / Don't worry about it!

Useful phrases

a casa de… (27)	to ...'s house
a la vuelta (88)	on [one's] return
a la vuelta de… (88)	around [the] …
a menudo (80)	often
a pesar de (38)	in spite of
a última hora (18)	at the last minute
ahí está... (99)	there's … / that's …
cada vez más (36)	more and more
cada vez peor (47)	from bad to worse
con destino a (95)	going to (the destination of)
con pelos y señales (75)	in great detail
continuará (57)	to be continued …
de segunda mano (26)	secondhand
emilio (59)	email
en metálico (61)	in cash
en vez de (87)	instead of
hoy en día (80)	nowadays
idas y venidas (65)	comings and goings
procedente de (95)	originating from
un buen negocio (26)	a good deal / a bargain

Various expressions

¡De tal palo, tal astilla! (27)	He/She's a chip off the old block!
En todas partes cuecen habas. (87)	It's the same the whole world over.
¡Hace un frío que pela! (67)	It's absolutely freezing!
¿Qué va a ser de mí? (51)	What will become of me?
Quien ríe el último ríe mejor. (98)	He who laughs last laughs longest.
Se hace camino al andar. (57)	The road is made by walking.
Sin noticias, buenas noticias. (50)	No news is good news.
Sin respetar ni rey ni roque. (79)	Fearing neither God nor man.

Glossaries

We've provided a two-way glossary in which you'll find all the Spanish words used in this book.
• Spanish – English
• English – Spanish

The glossary lists only the meanings found in the lessons; it is not a dictionary that lists all possible meanings.

The gender of each Spanish noun is indicated. Adjectives are given in the masculine singular form. An asterisk (*) indicates feminine nouns that require the article **el** in the singular because they begin with a stressed **a** (or **ha**) (see lesson 68, note 2). Note that **ñ** is a letter in its own right and comes between **n** and **o** in the Spanish alphabet.

Key to abbreviations:

(m.) masculine	*(f.)* feminine
(sing.) singular	*(pl.)* plural
(adj.) adjective	*(prep.)* preposition
(dir. obj.) direct object	*(indir. obj.)* indirect object

Each word is followed by the number of the lesson in which it first appears. The reference GA refers to the Grammatical Appendix. Certain words refer to more than one lesson if they are used with a different meaning or in a different context, or if a note gives additional explanations.

Spanish-English

A

a	to 4; at 34
abandonar	to abandon 37
abeja *(f.)*	bee 68
abierto	open 14
abogado/-a *(m./f.)*	lawyer 100
abonado/-a *(m./f.)*	subscriber 89
abrigo *(m.)*	coat 67
abrir	to open 14
abrochar	to buckle up, to fasten 38
absolutamente	absolutely 40; totally 83
absoluto (en ~)	absolutely not, not at all 40
abuelo/-a *(m./f.)*	grandfather/grandmother 24
aburrirse	to be bored 87
acabar	to end, to finish 13
acabar de *(+ infinitive)*	to have just + -ed 19
acampada *(f.)*	camping 63
acaso	maybe 85
acaso (por si ~)	just in case 75
accidentado	rough, rugged 97
accidente *(m.)*	accident 38
acción *(f.)*	deed 64
acelerador *(m.)*	accelerator 45
acera *(f.)*	sidewalk 54
acercarse	to approach 37; to near 65
acogedor	friendly 88
acompañar	to accompany 69
acomplejado	have a complex 53
acondicionar	to remodel 85
aconsejar	to recommend 56; to advise 78
acontecimiento *(m.)*	event 69
acordarse	to remember 63
acostarse	to go to bed 60
actitud *(f.)*	attitude 57; bearing 58
actividad *(f.)*	activity 78
acto *(m.)*	act 8
acudir	to go (with a specific purpose) 57
acuerdo (de ~)	all right (agreed), OK 10
acuerdo *(m.)*	agreement 10
adelantar	to overtake, to pass someone 38
adelante	forward 28
adelante (en ~)	from now on 100
adelgazar	to lose weight 77
además	in addition, moreover 44
adiós	goodbye 1
¿Adónde?	Where? *(with movement)* 5
adonde/a donde	where 5
adquirir	to acquire 82
aduana *(f.)*	customs 34
adulto/-a *(m./f.)*	adult 22
advertencia *(f.)*	warning 48

advertir	to inform, to warn 48
aeropuerto *(m.)*	airport 18
afición *(f.)*	pastime 46; interest 80; hobby 89
aficionado/-a *(m./f.)*	fan (enthusiast) 89
afilar	to sharpen 68
afiliado/-a *(m./f.)*	member (of a political party) 89
afrontar	to face, to meet (a challenge) 100
agarrar	to grab 6
agencia *(f.)*	agency 25
agitación *(f.)*	agitation 67
aglomeración *(f.)*	urban area 69
agradable	pleasant 82
agradecer	to thank 82
agreste	rugged, wild 93
agua* *(f.)*	water 34
agua* *(f.)* con gas	water (fizzy/sparkling) 68
agua* *(f.)* mineral	water (mineral) 68
agua* *(f.)* sin gas	water (still) 68
aguantar	to bear, to endure, to tolerate 27
águila* *(f.)*	eagle 93
agujero *(m.)*	hole 6
ahí	there 33
ahora	now 1
ahora mismo	right away 1; immediately 13; right now 31
aire *(m.)*	air 84
ajedrez *(m.)*	chess 79
ajo *(m.)*	garlic 52
al	to the 4
alba* *(f.)*	dawn 65
albergar	to shelter 93
albergue *(m.)*	inn 80
albor *(m.)*	dawn 92
alcalde *(m.)*	mayor 37
alcaldía *(f.)*	town hall 37
alcanzar	to reach 95; to attain 100
alcohol *(m.)*	alcohol 31
alcohólico	alcoholic 65
aldea *(f.)*	village 69
aldeano/-a *(m./f.)*	villager 81
alegre	happy 65
alegría *(f.)*	joy 95
algazara *(f.)*	jubilation 67
algo	something 34
algodón *(m.)*	cotton 76
alguien	someone 47
algún/alguno/-a/-os/-as	some 57; any 59
allí	there 41
alma* *(f.)*	soul 24
almohada *(f.)*	pillow 53
alquilar	to rent 26
alquiler *(m.)*	rental 26
alrededor (de)	around 52; about, approximately 78
alrededores *(m.)*	surrounding area, vicinity 78

alterarse	to get annoyed 90
alto	high 60; tall 75
altura (estar a la ~)	to be equal to the task 100
altura *(f.)*	height 100
alumno/-a *(m./f.)*	student 97
amable	nice 43
amante	loving 93
amante *(m./f.)*	lover 93
amar	to love 51
amargarse	to spoil, to become upset/embittered 51
amargo	bitter 51
amarillo	yellow 32
ambiente *(m.)*	environment 93
ambulancia *(f.)*	ambulance 31
americano	American 2
amigo/-a *(m./f.)*	friend 4
amistad *(f.)*	friendship 98
amonestación *(f.)*	caution 48
amor *(m.)*	love 9
amplitud *(f.)*	extent 100
añadir	to add 69
analfabeto	illiterate 81
andar	to walk 44
animar	to cheer on 89
ánimo *(m.)*	energy, spirit 20
aniversario *(m.)*	anniversary 23
año *(m.)*	year 16
anoche	last night 28
anochecer	to get dark 61
ante	before 81, 90; in front of 90
antelación (con ~)	in advance 98
antes	before 13
antigüedad *(f.)*	seniority 86
antiguo	old (former) 58
anular	to cancel 47
anunciar	to announce 83
anuncio *(m.)*	advertisement 41
anzuelo *(m.)*	bait 46
apaciguar	to appease, to pacify 77
apagar	to extinguish, to switch off 73
apañado	in trouble 17
aparato *(m.)*	aircraft 83
aparcar	to park 44
aparecer	to appear, to show up 71
apellido *(m.)*	family/last name (surname) 30
aperitivo *(m.)*	appetizer 1
apertura *(f.)*	opening 82
apetecer	to feel like 85
apilar	to stack 65
apostar	to bet 36
apreciar	to appreciate 86
aprender	to learn 69
apretar	to press 29

aprovechar	to take advantage 26; to get the chance 76
apuntes *(m.)*	notes 97
aquel/aquella	that (over there) *(adj.)* 35
aquél/aquélla	that one (over there) *(pronoun)* 35
aquello *(neuter)*	that (over there) *(non-specific)* 35
aquellos/aquellas	those (over there) *(adj.)* 35
aquéllos/aquéllas	those (over there) *(pronoun)* 35
aquí	here 1
árabe	Arabian (also Arab and Arabic) 95
árbol *(m.)*	tree 41
arena *(f.)*	sand 65
arrancar	to start (a car/computer) 45
arreglar	to repair 26
arreglarse	to arrange 59; to fix (sort out) 75
arreglárselas	to cope, to manage 75
arreglo *(m.)*	alteration, repair 26
arte* *(f.)*	art 100
artículo *(m.)*	article 94
artista *(m./f.)*	artist 95
artístico	artistic 95
asado	roasted 62
asar	to roast 62
ascensor *(m.)*	elevator, lift 57
así	thus 92; like this/that 96
así como	as well as 82
así mismo	likewise 100
así pues	so 66
así que	so (that) 66
asiduo	regular 100
asiento *(m.)*	seat 43
asistir	to attend 95
asociar	to associate 95
aspecto (tener mal ~)	to look bad 77
aspecto *(m.)*	appearance 77
astilla *(f.)*	splinter 27
asunto *(m.)*	issue 11; business 49; concern 81
atar	to attach 38
atasco *(m.)*	traffic jam 18
atención *(f.)*	attention 83
¡Atención!	Warning! 38
atender a	to help (serve) 32
aterrizar	to land 27
atracción *(f.)*	attraction 64
atraer	to attract 64
atrás	behind 57
atravesar	to cross 48; to go through 83
aumento *(m.)*	increase 92
aún	still 72
aunque	although, even if/though 86
australiano	Australian 2
autobús *(m.)*	bus 6
autocar *(m.)*	bus (long-distance), coach (bus) 89
automóvil *(m.)*	automobile 20

autónomo	independent 83; autonomous 97
autopista *(f.)*	motorway/highway 38
autor/a *(m./f.)*	author 14
autoridad *(f.)*	authority 93
autovía *(f.)*	motorway/highway 38
auxiliar de vuelo *(m./f.)*	flight attendant 83
ave* *(f.)*	bird 93
aventura *(f.)*	adventure 80
avión *(m.)*	airplane 18
avisar	to warn 48
ayer	yesterday 39
ayudar	to help 53
ayunar	to fast 3
ayuntamiento *(m.)*	city government, town hall 37
azafata *(f.)*	flight attendant 83
azul	blue 32

B

bailar	to dance 95
baile *(m.)*	dance 95
bajar	to descend, to go down 27
bajo	low 60; short 75
baloncesto *(m.)*	basketball 89
balonmano *(m.)*	handball 89
bamboleante	rickety 65
bañarse	to bathe, to go swimming 46
banco *(m.)*	bank 15; bench 65
bañista *(m./f.)*	bather, swimmer 37
baño *(m.)*	bathroom 37
bar *(m.)*	bar 54
barato	cheap 52
barbaridad *(f.)*	atrocity, huge amount, outrage 52
bárbaro	barbaric 52
barco *(m.)*	boat 43
barrio *(m.)*	neighbourhood 63
bastante	rather 40
beber	to drink 35
bebida *(f.)*	drink 61; beverage 65
besar	to kiss 91
beso *(m.)*	kiss 19
biblioteca *(f.)*	library 94
bici *(f.)*	bike 57
bicicleta *(f.)*	bicycle 57
bien	well 3; OK 10
bien…o bien	whether … or 70
bigote *(m.)*	moustache 73
billete *(m.)*	ticket (for transport) 49
biológico	organic 52
blanco	white 32
bobada *(f.)*	nonsense 79
bocadillo *(m.)*	sandwich 3
boda *(f.)*	wedding 23
boina *(f.)*	beret 75

bolígrafo *(m.)*	pen 50
bolsa *(f.)*	bag 33
bolsillo *(m.)*	pocket 6
bombón *(m.)*	chocolate candy 64
bonito	pretty 36
bordo (a ~)	on board 83
bosque *(m.)*	forest 48
botella *(f.)*	bottle 68
braga *(f.)*	panties 87
breve	short (brief) 83
brisa *(f.)*	breeze 62
broma *(f.)*	joke, prank 71
bromista *(m./f.)*	joker 54
bronca *(f.)*	quarrel, telling-off 55
broncear	to tan 62
brujo/-a *(m.)*	wizard/witch 95
buen	good 14
buenísimo	very good 8
bueno	good 4; nice (weather) 62
buenos días	good morning ('good day') 1
bufanda *(f.)*	scarf 67
buscar	to look for 42; to get (fetch) 61; to pick someone up 91
butaca *(f.)*	armchair 90
buzón *(m.)*	letterbox, mailbox 50

C

cabalgar	to ride a horse 67
cabalgata *(f.)*	parade 67
caballero *(m.)*	gentleman, knight 32
caballo *(m.)*	horse 32
caber	to fit, to hold (have room for) 57
cabeza *(f.)*	head 6
cabina *(f.)*	booth 54
cada	each 30
cada vez más	more and more 36; increasingly 100
cada vez mejor	better and better 47
cada vez menos	less and less 47
cada vez peor	worse and worse 47
cadena *(f.)*	channel (TV or radio) 99
caducado	expired 18
caer	to fall 55
café *(m.)*	coffee 3
caja *(f.)*	till (cash register) 76
cajero/-a *(m./f.)*	cashier 61
cajón *(m.)*	drawer 79
calcetín *(m.)*	sock 87
calendario *(m.)*	calendar 69
calidad *(f.)*	quality 68
caliente	hot (food or drink) 64
calle *(f.)*	street 5
calor *(m.)*	heat 35; hot (weather) 62
calzada *(f.)*	road 38
calzado *(m.)*	footwear 32

calzar	to take a shoe size 32
calzoncillo *(m.)*	underpants 87
cama *(f.)*	bed 59
cama de matrimonio *(f.)*	double bed 59
camarero/-a *(m./f.)*	waiter/waitress 41
cambiar	to change 26
camello *(m.)*	camel 67
caminar	to walk 57
camino *(m.)*	road, way 57
camisa *(f.)*	shirt 35
camiseta *(f.)*	T-shirt 87
campestre	rural 93
campo *(m.)*	field 93
caña *(f.)*	fishing rod 46
canadiense	Canadian 2
candidato/-a *(m./f.)*	applicant 41
canela *(f.)*	cinnamon 86
canoso	grey-haired 75
cansado	tired 7
cantar	to sing 21
canto *(m.)*	song 60
capital *(f.)*	capital 69
cara *(f.)*	face 11; cheek (nerve) 41
cara o cruz (echar a ~)	to toss for heads or tails 41
carácter *(m.)*	character (nature) 69
caracterizar	to characterize 86
caramelo *(m.)*	candy, sweet 64
cargar	to load 67
carnaval *(m.)*	Mardi Gras 69
carne *(f.)*	meat 61
carne picada *(f.)*	ground beef 61
caro	expensive 52
carrete *(m.)*	reel, spool 46
carretera *(f.)*	road 58
carro *(m.)*	cart 61
carroza *(f.)*	float (parade) 67
carta *(f.)*	letter 50; menu 74; card 89
carta de vinos *(f.)*	wine list 74
cartera *(f.)*	wallet 11
casa (a ~)	home 27
casa (en ~)	at home 27
casa *(f.)*	house 1
casa central *(f.)*	head office 75
casado/-a *(m./f.)*	married man/woman 9
casarse	to marry/get married 12
casi	nearly 41; almost 81
caso *(m.)*	case 72
castaña *(f.)*	chestnut 62
castaño	brown 75
castellano	Castilian 72
casualidad (por ~)	by chance 62
catálogo *(m.)*	catalogue 82
cava *(m.)*	sparkling wine 74

cebolla *(f.)*	onion 52
celebración *(f.)*	celebration 69
celebrar	to celebrate 23
cena *(f.)*	dinner 8
cenar	to dine/have dinner 16
centro *(m.)*	centre 97
centro comercial *(m.)*	shopping centre 61
cerca	near 54
cereal *(m.)*	cereal 61
cereza *(f.)*	cherry 50
cero *(m.)*	zero 54
cerrar	to close, to bring to an end 67
cesar	to cease 92
champiñón *(m.)*	mushroom 13
chaqueta *(f.)*	jacket 38
charcutería *(f.)*	deli (for cured meats) 52
charlar	to chat 30
chica *(f.)*	girl 46
chico	small 46
chico *(m.)*	boy 46
chino	Chinese 30
chiringuito *(m.)*	chiringuito (open-air refreshment stand) 65
chocolate *(m.)*	chocolate 3
chollo *(m.)*	bargain 26
churrería *(f.)*	churro stand/shop 3
churro *(m.)*	churro (a cylindrical doughnut) 3
ciego	blind 85
cielo *(m.)*	sky 41
cien/ciento	hundred 21
cierre *(m.)*	closing 61
cierto	certain (true) 36; certain 62
cierto (por ~)	by the way 62
cigarro *(m.)*	cigarette 44
cine *(m.)*	cinema 4
cinta (adhesiva) *(f.)*	tape (adhesive) 33
cinta (transportadora) *(f.)*	belt (conveyor) 33
cinta *(f.)*	ribbon 33
cintura *(f.)*	waist 43
cinturón *(m.)*	seat belt 38
circulación *(f.)*	circulation 94
circular	to drive 38
circunstancia *(f.)*	circumstance 26
cita *(f.)*	appointment, date (social engagement), meeting 10
ciudad *(f.)*	city 38
claridad *(f.)*	clarity 90
claro	certainly, clear 3
clase *(f.)*	class (lesson) 95
cliente *(m./f.)*	customer 47
clima *(m.)*	climate 97
cocer	to cook 87
coche *(m.)*	car 26
cocina *(f.)*	cooking, cuisine, kitchen 86

código postal *(m.)*	post code 50
coger	to take, to take hold of 6; to grab 33
cola *(f.)*	line (of people), queue 39
colegio *(m.)*	school 25
colgar	to hang (up) 54
colonia *(f.)*	colony 93
color *(m.)*	colour 35
combinar	to combine 95
comenzar	to begin, to start 42
comer	to eat 13
comercio *(m.)*	business 61
comestibles *(m.)*	groceries 52
cometido *(m.)*	mission (commitment) 65
comida *(f.)*	food, meal 34
comisaría *(f.)*	police station 45
como	like 13; as 42
cómo	what 2; how 96
cómo así	how come 30
cómodo	comfortable 40
compañero/-a *(m./f.)*	companion 57; colleague 71
compañía *(f.)*	company 40
comparar	to compare 53
compensar	to make up for 60
complacerse	to be pleased, to take pleasure 83
complejo	complex 83
completamente	completely 83
completo	complete, full 98
complicado	complicated 72
comportarse	to behave 32
compra *(f.)*	purchase 76
comprar	to buy 25
compras (hacer las ~)	to do the shopping/errands 76
compras (ir de ~)	to go shopping 76
compras *(f.)*	shopping 76
comprender	to understand 43
comprensión *(f.)*	comprehension 90
comunicación *(f.)*	communication 92
comunicando	busy (phone), engaged (phone) 54
comunidad *(f.)*	community 97
comunión *(f.)*	communion 95
con	with 3
conceder	to grant 59
concejo *(m.)*	council 37
concentrado	concentrated 61
concentrarse	to concentrate, to focus 61
concierne (en lo que ~ a)	concerning 85
concordancia *(f.)*	agreement 81
condición *(f.)*	condition 100
conducir	to drive 38, 77
confiar	to trust 40
confirmar	to confirm 59
conformar	to form 93
confundir	to confuse 9

confundirse	to make a mistake, to mix up 54
confundirse de número	to misdial 54
confuso	confused 81
congelador *(m.)*	freezer 61
congelados *(m.)*	frozen foods 61
congelar	to freeze 61
conjugación *(f.)*	conjugation 100
conllevar	to involve 66
conmemoración *(f.)*	commemoration 69
conmigo	with me 12
conocer	to know (to be familiar with), to meet 42; to know of 78
conocimiento *(m.)*	knowledge 100
conque	so (that) 66
conseguir	to manage to, to obtain, to succeed in 81
consejo *(m.)*	advice (piece of) 60
consigo	with himself/herself/itself/oneself/yourself *(formal)*/themselves 66
consistir	to consist 68
constante	constant 86
constelado	studded 80
constituir	to constitute 80
construir	to build 80
consulta *(f.)*	doctor's office/surgery 29; consultation 53; search (e.g. on the Internet) 94
consultar	to consult 100
consumición *(f.)*	consumption 38
contacto *(m.)*	contact 19
contar	to count 29; to tell (recount) 98
contentarse	to make do 74
contento	happy 9
contestar	to reply 44
contigo	with you *(informal sing.)* 12
continente *(m.)*	continent 93
continuar	to continue 34
contrario (al ~)	on the contrary 53
contrato *(m.)*	contract 40
contribuir	to contribute 80
convencer	to convince 81
conversación *(f.)*	conversation 99
convocar	to convene (convoke) 40
copa *(f.)*	glass (for drinking) 16
corazón *(m.)*	heart 29
coronilla *(f.)*	crown (of the head) 87
corral (de ~)	free-range 93
corral *(m.)*	farmyard 93
correcto	correct 30
correo *(m.)*	post (mail) 50
correo electrónico *(m.)*	e-mail 50
correo urgente *(m.)*	express mail 50
correos *(m.)*	post office 50
correr	to drive (fast) 38; to speed 42; to run 65
corretear	to run around 65

corriente	current 13
cortar	to cut 41
cortarse el pelo	to cut one's hair 71
corte *(m.)*	cut 76
cortina *(f.)*	curtain 85
cosa *(f.)*	thing 13
cosecha *(f.)*	harvest 69; vintage (year of a wine) 74
coser	to sew 30
costar	to cost 22
coto *(m.)*	reserve (preserve) 46
creación *(f.)*	creation 86
crecer	to grow 38
crédito *(m.)*	credit 61
creer	to think 11; to believe 94
crema protectora *(f.)*	sunscreen 62
cretino/-a *(m./f.)*	idiot 30
cristiano	Christian 95
cruce *(m.)*	crossing (intersection) 38
cruz *(f.)*	cross 41
cruzarse	to cross paths 57
cuadrado	square 97
cuadro *(m.)*	painting 82
cuál	what 2; which 15
cualidad *(f.)*	quality 90
cualquier	any 36
cualquier cosa	anything 36
cualquiera	anybody/anyone 70
cualquiera (que)	whatever 48
cuando	when 29; as (at the same time as) 31
cuánto	how much 10
cuanto (en ~ a)	as far as, as for 75; as regards 85
cuanto (en ~)	as soon as 100
cuanto antes	as soon as possible 59
cuarto *(m.)*	quarter 17; room (small) 82
cubierto	cloudy, covered 68
cubierto *(m.)*	table setting 68
cubrir	to cover 68
cuchara *(f.)*	spoon 68
cucharilla *(f.)*	teaspoon 68
cuchillo *(m.)*	knife 68
cuenta (en ~)	in mind 52
cuenta *(f.)*	account, bill (check) 13
cuento *(m.)*	story 53
cuerno *(m.)*	horn 99
cuerpo *(m.)*	body 29
cuestión *(f.)*	question (matter) 11
cuidado	careful 5
cuidado (tener ~)	to be careful 38
cuidado *(m.)*	care 38
cultura *(f.)*	culture 95
cumpleaños *(m.)*	birthday 23
cumplir	to fulfill (accomplish) 23; to complete 65
cuñada *(f.)*	sister-in-law 63

cuñado *(m.)*	brother-in-law 63
curiosidad *(f.)*	curiosity 22
curioso	curious 29; odd 88
curso *(m.)*	course 40
cuyo/-a/-os/-as	whose (of which) 91

D

dar	to give 29
dar con	to find 57
dar las gracias	to thank 63
darse cuenta	to realize 87
darse la mano	to shake hands 29
darse la vuelta	to turn around 29
dátil *(m.)*	date (fruit) 67
dato *(m.)*	piece of information 78
de	of 1; from 2; about (a subject) 79
debajo de	underneath 90
deber	to have to 54; to owe 76
decidir	to decide 70
decir	to say 14; to tell 14, 22
decisión *(f.)*	decision 48
declarar	to declare 34
decorar	to decorate 85
dedicar	to dedicate, to devote 15
dedicarse	to devote oneself, to do for a living 15
deficiente	inadequate 40
dejar	to leave 31; to let (allow) 35
dejarse	to leave behind (accidentally) 54
del	of the 8
delante	in front 24
delatar	to betray 57
deleitarse con	to delight in 86
delicado	delicate 86
delinquir	to commit a crime 77
demás	other 93
demasiado	too much 33
demostrar	to demonstrate 90
dentro (de)	in, inside, within 71
deporte *(m.)*	sport 89
deportista *(m./f.)*	sportsman/-woman 86
deprimirse	to get depressed 85
deprisa	quick 6
derecha (a la ~)	on the right 5
derecho *(m.)*	right (prerogative) 79
desafiar	to dare, to defy 85
desafío *(m.)*	challenge 100
desastre *(m.)*	disaster 39
desatar	to unleash 67
desayunar	to have breakfast 3
desayuno *(m.)*	breakfast 3
descansar	to rest 65
descarado	brazen 44
descifrar	to figure out 81

desconfianza *(f.)*	distrust 73
desde	from 37; since 67
desde entonces	since then 67
desear	to desire 50; to wish 82
desenlace *(m.)*	ending (of a film/book etc.) 39
desfile *(m.)*	parade 67
desgarrador	heartbreaking 95
desnudarse	to undress 46
desnudo	naked 46
desocupado	idle 62
despabilado	resourceful 81
despacho *(m.)*	office (room) 59
despacio	slowly 38
despedirse	to say goodbye 94
despertar	to wake up 39
después	afterwards 81
después (de)	after 8
destacar	to emphasize, to highlight, to stand out 88
destino *(m.)*	destination 95
destornillador *(m.)*	screwdriver 84
desvestirse	to take off one's clothes 46
detalle *(m.)*	detail 78
detrás (de)	behind 24
devolver	to refund, to return something 47
día *(m.)*	day 1
día festivo *(m.)*	day off, holiday 69
diario	daily 80
diccionario *(m.)*	dictionary 94
dicho	said 14
dictar	to dictate 81
diente *(m.)*	tooth 46; clove (of garlic) 52
diferencia *(f.)*	difference 21
difícil	difficult 88
dificultad *(f.)*	difficulty 40
difusión *(f.)*	spread (diffusion) 92
dinámico	dynamic 30
dinero *(m.)*	money 6
dios *(m.)*	god 36
dirección *(f.)*	address 57
directo	direct 99
director/a *(m./f.)*	director 40; manager 75
dirigir	to direct 40, 81
dirigirse	to head over to 44; to address, to go to speak to someone 81
disco *(m.)*	record (vinyl) 47
disco *(m.)* compacto	compact disc 47
disco *(m.)* duro	hard disk 94
discoteca *(f.)*	night club 95
disculpar	to excuse 44
disculpas (pedir ~)	to beg someone's pardon 44
discurso *(m.)*	speech 88
discutir	to argue, to discuss 27
disponer	to get ready 31; to set up 65; to arrange 83

disponer de	to have (available) 83
disponerse	to prepare 31
distinguir	to distinguish 77
distraído	absent-minded 45
distribuir	to distribute 80
diversidad *(f.)*	diversity 88
diverso	varied 78
divertirse	to have fun 98
dividir	to divide 97
docena *(f.)*	dozen 52
doctor/a *(m./f.)*	doctor (someone with a doctorate) 29
doler	to hurt (have pain) 29
dolor *(m.)*	pain 29
doméstico	domestic 34
domingo *(m.)*	Sunday 14
donde	where 70
¿Dónde?	Where? *(without movement)* 5
donde (en ~)	where 5
dormir	to sleep 3
dos	two 1
droga *(f.)*	drug 31
ducharse	to shower 46
duda *(f.)*	doubt 57
dudar	to doubt 86
dudar en	to hesitate 86
duende *(m.)*	spirit (magical creature) 95
dueño/-a *(m./f.)*	master, owner 100
durante	during 84
duro	difficult, hard 41

E

e	and (before words starting with **i** or **hi**) 67
echar	to pour, to throw 34
echar marcha atrás	to go back on (reconsider) 57
echarse	to throw oneself 99
echarse (crema)	to put on (a cream/lotion) 62
económico	economic 92
ecosistema *(m.)*	ecosystem 93
edad *(f.)*	age 22
efecto *(m.)*	effect 24
efectuar	to carry out 83
ejemplo *(m.)*	example 49
él	he 7; him *(after prep.)* 12
el	the *(m. sing.)* 3
el/la/los/las que	the one(s) that 32
elección *(f.)*	election 37; choice 69
electrónico	electronic 50
elegir	to choose 68; to elect 81
eliminar	to eliminate 89
ella	she 7; her *(after prep.)* 12
ellos/ellas *(m./f.)*	them *(after prep.)* GA3; they 7
embarcar	to embark 14
embrague *(m.)*	clutch (in a car) 45

emergencia *(f.)*	emergency 31
emigrar	to emigrate 81
emilio *(m.)*	e-mail 59
empatar	to draw (end in a tie) 89
empezar	to start 22
empleado/-a *(m./f.)*	employee 30
empleo *(m.)*	employment 41
empresa *(f.)*	company 30
empujar	to prompt, to push, to shove 64
en	in 6; on 17; at 34
en efecto	indeed 92
en el que	where (in which) 65
en que	where (in which) 65
encantado	delighted 36
encantador	charming 36
encantar	to delight, to enchant 36
encanto *(m.)*	charm 36
encender	to turn/switch on 45
encima	above, in addition, on top of 44
encontrar	to find 12
encontrarse con	to come across 57
enfermo	sick 43; ill 51
enfrente	opposite 54
enganchado	addicted 31
enganchar	to hook 31
enhorabuena *(f.)*	congratulations 49
enorme	huge 39
ensalada *(f.)*	salad 68
enseguida	immediately 13; quickly 62
enseñar	to show, to teach 46
entender	to understand 96
entierro *(m.)*	funeral 64
entonces	then (so) 25
entrada *(f.)*	entrance 62; ticket (for admission) 82
entrar	to go into 27; to come in 70; to enter 99
entrar en liza	to enter the fray 99
entre	between 92
entretanto	in the meantime, meanwhile 50
entusiasmo *(m.)*	enthusiasm 67
enviar	to send 31
época *(f.)*	period 86
equipaje *(m.)*	luggage 33
equipo *(m.)*	team 89
equis *(f.)*	x (the letter) 23
equivocado	wrong (mistaken) 78
equivocarse	to make a mistake, to get wrong 54
erróneo	wrong (erroneous) 78
error *(m.)*	mistake 90
escapar	to escape 99
escaparates (ir de ~)	to go window-shopping 76
esconder	to hide 79
escribir	to write 14
escrito	written 14

escritor/a *(m./f.)*	writer 15
escuchar	to listen 75
escuela *(f.)*	school 40
ese/esa	that *(adj.)* 35
ése/ésa	that (one) *(pronoun)* 35
eso *(neuter)*	that *(non-specific)* 35
esos/esas	those *(adj.)* 35
ésos/ésas	those (ones) *(pronoun)* 35
espacio *(m.)*	space 83
espalda *(f.)*	back (part of the body) 43
espaldas (de ~)	facing backwards 43
español	Spanish 2
esparcir	to scatter, to sprinkle 77
especialidad *(f.)*	speciality 1
especialista *(m./f.)*	specialist 53
especie *(f.)*	sort (type) 64; species 93
específico	specific 69
espectáculo *(m.)*	show (performance) 95
espectador/a *(m./f.)*	spectator 39
espejo *(m.)*	mirror 24
espera *(f.)*	wait 67
esperar	to wait 6
espiritual	spiritual 80
espontáneo	spontaneous 95
esposo/-a *(m./f.)*	spouse (husband/wife) 93
esquí *(m.)*	ski 65
esquina *(f.)*	corner 88
establecerse	to settle 95
estación *(f.)*	station 6
estadounidense	American (from the United States) 40
estanco *(m.)*	tobaconnist's/newsagent's 50
estar	to be *(for locations and temporary states)* 5, 7
este *(m.)*	east 97
este/esta	this *(adj.)* 35
éste/ésta	this (one) *(pronoun)* 35
estilo *(m.)*	style 2
estimar	to consider (something as) 100
esto *(neuter)*	this *(non-specific)* 35
estos/estas	these *(adj.)* 35
éstos/éstas	these (ones) *(pronoun)* 35
estrecho	narrow, tight 97
estrecho *(m.)*	strait 97
estrella *(f.)*	star 48
estrés *(m.)*	stress 60
estudiar	to study 22
estupendamente	marvellously 47
estupendo	great 4; fantastic 59
etapa *(f.)*	stage (phase) 80
etiqueta *(f.)*	tag 76
euro *(m.)*	euro 1
Europa *(f.)*	Europe 93
europeo	European 80
eusquera/euskera *(m.)*	Basque (language only) 72

evaluar	to evaluate 100
evidente	obvious 96
exactamente	exactly 68
exagerar	to exaggerate 52
examinar	to examine 29
excelente	excellent 60
excepcionalmente	exceptionally 86
exceso *(m.)*	excess 38
excitado	excited 89
excusa *(f.)*	excuse 69
existencia *(f.)*	existence 95
éxito *(m.)*	success 99
experiencia *(f.)*	experience 41
explicación *(f.)*	explanation 45
explicar	to explain 45
exponer	to exhibit 82
exposición *(f.)*	exhibition 82
expresar	to express 95
expresión *(f.)*	expression 88
extender	to spread out 62
extrañado	surprised 58
extranjero/-a *(m./f.)*	foreigner 15
extraño	strange 29
extraordinario	extraordinary 53; special 85
extremo	extreme 65

F

fácil	easy 98
factura *(f.)*	invoice 90
faena *(f.)*	job 72
falda *(f.)*	skirt 35
falta (hacer ~)	to be necessary, to need 75; to have to 90
falta *(f.)*	lack 90; mistake 100
faltar	to be missing something 61; to lack 79
familia *(f.)*	family 14
familiar	familiar 100
famoso	famous 100
fanático/-a *(m./f.)*	fan (enthusiast), fanatic 31
farmacia *(f.)*	drugstore, pharmacy 29
fastidiar	to annoy, to bother 73
favor (hacer un ~)	to do a favour 75
favor (por ~)	please 1
favor *(m.)*	favour 75
favorito	favourite 89
febrilidad *(f.)*	feverishness 67
fecha *(f.)*	date (day) 69
felicidad *(f.)*	happiness 23
felicidades *(f.)*	congratulations 23
feliz	happy 66
felpudo *(m.)*	doormat 90
fenómeno *(m.)*	phenomenon 86
feo	ugly 53
ferretería *(f.)*	hardware shop, ironmonger's 78

ferrocarril *(m.)*	railway 43
festejar	to celebrate 69
festivo	festive 69
ficha *(f.)*	token 61
fiebre *(f.)*	fever 68
fiera *(f.)*	wild animal 60
fiesta *(f.)*	party 16; holiday 23; celebration 67
fijo	fixed (unchanging) 53
filete *(m.)*	fillet, steak 68
filme *(m.)*	film 39
fin *(m.)*	end 10
fin *(m.)* de semana	weekend 10
final *(m.)*	end 39
final *(f.)*	final 89
fino	refined 86
firma *(f.)*	business, company, firm, signature 40
firmar	to sign 25
física *(f.)*	physics 2
físico	physical 19
flor *(f.)*	flower 28
folleto *(m.)*	leaflet 82
forma *(f.)*	form (shape) 10
formas (de todas ~)	anyway (in any case) 10
fortuna *(f.)*	luck 85
foto *(f.)*	photo 88
francamente	frankly 40
francés	French 2
frase *(f.)*	sentence 26; phrase 100
fraudulento	fake 34
frecuentar	to frequent 80
freír	to fry 98
freno *(m.)*	brake 45
frente (a) (hacer ~)	to confront 100
frente *(m.)*	front 100
frente a	faced with 90
fresco	cool 62
frío	cold 62
fritas (patatas ~) *(f.)*	fries, chips 68
frontera *(f.)*	border 34
fuegos artificiales *(m.)*	fireworks 67
fuera	out 60
fuerte	strong 68
fuerza *(f.)*	strength 100
fumador/a *(m./f.)*	smoker 44
fumar	to smoke 44
funcionar	to work/function 41
fútbol *(m.)*	football (soccer) 89
futuro *(m.)*	future 12

G

gafas *(f.)*	glasses (spectacles) 72
galleta *(f.)*	biscuit, cookie 14

gallina *(f.)*	hen 52
gallo *(m.)*	rooster 60
gana *(f.)*	desire 51
ganar	to earn 26; to win 97
ganas (tener ~)	to feel like (doing something) 51
ganga *(f.)*	bargain 26
garabateo *(m.)*	scribble 81
garantizar	to guarantee 83
gaseosa *(f.)*	soda 74
gastrónomo/-a *(m./f.)*	gourmet 86
gato *(m.)*	cat 34
gaviota *(f.)*	seagull 65
generoso	generous 64
gente *(f.) (sing.)*	people (general) 39
geografía *(f.)*	geography 97
gimnasia *(f.)*	exercises (physical) 85
gira *(f.)*	tour 59
gitano/-a *(m./f.)*	gypsy 95
golfo *(m.)*	gulf 97
golondrina *(f.)*	swallow (bird) 93
golosina *(f.)*	candy 25; sweet 65
gordo	fat 85
gorrión *(m.)*	sparrow 93
gozar	to enjoy 66
gracias	thank you 1
gramática *(f.)*	grammar 100
grande	big, great 14
granizado *(m.)*	slush (crushed-ice drink) 76
gratuito	free (of charge) 82
grave	serious 11
gris	grey 35
grito *(m.)*	shout 43
grupo *(m.)*	group 65
guante *(m.)*	glove 46
guapo	good-looking 24
guardar	to keep 55
guía *(f.)*	guide 62
guitarra *(f.)*	guitar 95
gusano *(m.)*	worm 46
gustar	to appeal to (be pleasing), to like 9
gusto *(m.)*	pleasure 9; taste 69

H

haba* *(f.)*	bean 87
haber *(auxiliary verb)*	to have + -ed 3, 6, 7, 14
habitación *(f.)*	room (bedroom or hotel room) 59
habitante *(m./f.)*	inhabitant 97
hablar	to speak 14; to talk 42
hace	it's been … (referring to time) 16; ago 21
hace *(+ time)*	for (+ period of time) 71
hacer	to do 8; to make 24
hacer (calor/frío)	to be (hot/cold) (weather) 62
hacha* *(f.)*	axe 68

hacia — towards 80
hall *(m.)* — lobby 48
hallar — to find 57
harto — fed up 87
hasta — to 39; until 82; up to 87
hay — there is/are 21
hay que — it is necessary 9; one must, one should 90
hechizo *(m.)* — spell (magic) 95
hecho — done, made 14
helado *(m.)* — ice cream 85
hermana *(f.)* — sister 63
hermano *(m.)* — brother 63
hermoso — beautiful 42
hielo *(m.)* — ice 67
hierro *(m.)* — iron (the metal) 51
higo *(m.)* — fig 67
hija *(f.)* — daughter 10
hijo *(m.)* — son 25
hijos *(m.)* — children (offspring) 25
hispanohablante — Spanish-speaking 88
historia *(f.)* — story 79
histórico — historical 69
hogar *(m.)* — home 27
hoja *(f.)* — leaf 91
hola — hello 2
hombre *(m.)* — man 12
hombro *(m.)* — shoulder 43
hondo — deep 29; profound 95
honor *(m.)* — honour 40
honrado — honourable 57
hora *(f.)* — hour 2, 11; time 10; o'clock 21
hora punta *(f.)* — rush hour 2
horario *(m.)* — hours (timetable) 82
horario de apertura *(m.)* — opening times 61
hospital *(m.)* — hospital 29
hotel *(m.)* — hotel 48
hoy — today 6
hoy día — today 80
hoy en día — nowadays 80
huelga *(f.)* — strike 7
huella *(f.)* — track (footprint) 65
huella dactilar/digital *(f.)* — fingerprint 65
hueso *(m.)* — bone 34
huevo *(m.)* — egg 52
humedal *(m.)* — wetland 93
humor *(m.)* — humour 35

I

ida *(f.)* — one-way/single ticket 9
ida y vuelta *(f.)* — return ticket 9
idas y venidas *(f.)* — comings and goings 9
idea *(f.)* — idea 4
idioma *(m.)* — language 40

iglesia *(f.)*	church 80
igual	same 68; perhaps, probably 85
imaginar	to imagine 66
imitación *(f.)*	imitation 34
importa (no ~)	it's not important 67
importancia *(f.)*	importance 92
importante	important 26; large 93
importe *(m.)*	amount 47
imposible	impossible 45
impresionante	impressive 88
impreso *(m.)*	form (sheet) 50
impresora *(f.)*	printer 94
imprevisto	unexpected 100
imprimir	to print GA8
incluido	including 97
incluso	even, including 40
incomprensión *(f.)*	incomprehension 96
inconveniente *(m.)*	disadvantage 72
indecisión *(f.)*	hesitation 41
indicación *(f.)*	instruction 82
indicar	to indicate 50
infinidad *(f.)*	infinity 69
información/informaciones *(f.)*	information 82
informática *(f.)*	information technology (IT) 84
infusión *(f.)*	herbal tea 43
Inglaterra	England 30
inglés	English 2, 40
iniciático	initiatory 80
injusticia *(f.)*	injustice 95
inmediatamente	immediately 31
inmóvil	still (immobile) 90
inmueble *(m.)*	apartment block 57
inocencia *(f.)*	innocence 71
inocente	innocent 71
inolvidable	unforgettable 80
insistir	to insist 44
instante *(m.)*	instant 41
instituto *(m.)*	institute 41
instrucción *(f.)*	instruction 84
inteligencia *(f.)*	intelligence 88
inteligente	intelligent 42
intensidad *(f.)*	intensity 98
intensivo	intensive 40
interesante	interesting 41
interesar	to interest 66
internacional	international 92
íntimo	intimate 95
introducir	to introduce 74
inverosímil	unlikely 73
invierno *(m.)*	winter 97
invitación *(f.)*	invitation 91
invitado/-a *(m./f.)*	guest 70
invitar	to invite 4

ir	to go 5; to suit 76
irónicamente	ironically 98
irse	to go away, to go/be off 4; to leave 27
isla *(f.)*	island 72
izquierda (a la ~)	on the left 32

J

jaleo *(m.)*	racket (din) 39
jalonar	to mark out 80
jamás	never 13
jamón *(m.)*	ham 52
jardín *(m.)*	garden 38
jarra *(f.)*	jug 68
jefe/jefa *(m./f.)*	boss 55
jerez *(m.)*	sherry 74
joven	young 81
joven *(m./f.)*	young person (youth) 81
judío	Jewish 95
juego *(m.)*	game 87
jueves *(m.)*	Thursday 14
jugar	to play (a game) 41, 87
julio *(m.)*	July 63
junto a	next to 30
juntos	together 16
jurar	to swear 72
justo	just 32
juzgar	to judge 57

K

kilo *(m.)*	kilogram 75
kilómetro *(m.)*	kilometer 65

L

la	the *(f. sing.)* 4; her *(indir. obj.)*, it *(f.)* *(dir. obj.)*, you *(formal sing. f.)* *(dir. obj.)* 49
labio *(m.)*	lip 24
ladera *(f.)*	slope 91
lado (al ~)	at the side 32; next door 71
lado *(m.)*	side 32
lado *(m.)* (por su ~)	for his/her/its part 81
ladrón/ladrona *(m./f.)*	thief 57
lana *(f.)*	wool 75
lana (de ~)	woollen 75
lanzar	to launch 94
lápiz *(m.)*	pencil 98
largo	long 36
las	the *(f. pl.)* 7; them *(f.)* *(dir. obj.)*, you *(formal pl. f.)* *(dir. obj.)* 49
láser *(m.)*	laser 83
latinoamericano	Latin American 40
lavar	to wash 41
le	her *(indir. obj.)*, him *(dir./indir. obj.)*, it *(dir./indir. obj.)*, you *(formal sing.)* *(dir./indir. obj.)* 49

leche *(f.)*	milk 13
lectura *(f.)*	reading 89
leer	to read 16
lejos	far 65
leñador/a *(m./f.)*	woodcutter 41
lengua *(f.)*	language 72; tongue 92
lengua *(f.)* materna	mother tongue (first language) 92
les	them *(dir./indir. obj.)*, you *(formal pl.) (dir./indir. obj.)* 49
letrero *(m.)*	sign 44
levantarse	to get up 46; to rise 65
léxico *(m.)*	glossary 100
ley *(f.)*	law 90
libre	free (available) 15
libro *(m.)*	book 47
licencia *(f.)*	licence, permit 46
licor *(m.)*	liqueur 74
ligar	to join, to tie 62
ligar con	to pick up (get together with someone) 62
lila *(f.)*	lilac 32
limitar	to border 97
limón *(m.)*	lemon 52
limpiar	to clean 61
limpieza *(f.)*	cleaning, cleanliness 61
limpieza *(f.)* en seco	dry cleaning 61
línea *(f.)*	line 54
lío *(m.)*	mess 39
lista *(f.)*	list 61
listo	ready 18; clever, sly 74
literatura *(f.)*	literature 86
llamada *(f.)*	call 54
llamado	called 4
llamar	to call 4
llamarse	to be called/named 2
llamativo	eye-catching 75; striking 88
llave *(f.)*	key 6
llegada *(f.)*	arrival 33
llegar	to arrive 10
llegar a ser	to become 100
llevar	to wear 44; to take 55; to have been + -ing, to lead 60
llorar	to cry (weep) 14
llover	to rain 64
lluvioso	rainy 49
lo	it *(m.) (dir. obj.)* 6; him *(dir. obj.)*, you *(formal sing. m.) (dir. obj.)* 49
lo que	what 29
lo siento	I'm sorry 48
local	local 54
local *(m.)*	premises 57
loco	crazy 36
locura *(f.)*	madness 36
locutorio *(m.)*	call shop 54

… *(f.)*	logic 44
…r	to manage to 81
…briz *(f.)*	earthworm 46
…ncha *(f.)*	slice (thin) 52
los	the *(m. pl.)* 4; them *(m.) (dir. obj.)*, you *(formal pl. m.) (dir. obj.)* 49
lotería *(f.)*	lottery 85
lucidez *(f.)*	perceptiveness 53
lucir	to shine GA16
luego	then 16
lugar *(m.)*	place 60; position 97
lunes *(m.)*	Monday 10

M

madera *(f.)*	wood (the material) 68
madre *(f.)*	mother 27
madrugada *(f.)*	daybreak, early morning 65
madrugar	to get up early 65
maestro/-a *(m./f.)*	teacher 10
magia *(f.)*	magic 95
mal	bad 14; badly 47
malecón *(m.)*	jetty 65
maleta *(f.)*	suitcase 18
maletero *(m.)*	boot (of a car), trunk (of a car) 57
malísimo	very bad 8
malo	bad 14; ill 43; badly 47
mañana	tomorrow 10
mañana *(f.)*	morning 10
manchado	stained 91
mando *(m.)*	control 31; command 90
manera (de otra ~)	differently 90
manera *(f.)*	way (method) 88; manner 100
manera que (de ~)	so (that) 66
mango *(m.)*	handle 68
manifestación *(f.)*	event 69
manifestar	to demonstrate 90
mano *(f.)*	hand 19
mantener	to maintain, to support 66
mantequilla *(f.)*	butter 52
maquillarse	to put on make-up 24
máquina *(f.)*	machine 30
mar *(m.)*	sea 97
maravilla (de ~)	wonderfully 49
maravilla *(f.)*	marvel 19; wonder 82
maravilloso	wonderful 36
marca *(f.)*	brand 69
marcar	to dial 54
marcha (en ~)	in operation/motion 33
marcha *(f.)*	motion (progress) 43
marcha *(f.)* a pie	walking 80
marchar	to work/operate 94
marea *(f.)*	tide 65
mareado	dizzy 76

marearse	to feel queasy, to be seasick 43
marido *(m.)*	husband 25
mariscos *(m.)*	seafood 46
marrón	brown 35
martes *(m.)*	Tuesday 14
martillo *(m.)*	hammer 54
más	more 33
más bien	rather 75
más o menos	more or less 75
más…que	more … than 42
matar	to kill 89
matrimonio *(m.)*	married couple 59
mayo *(m.)*	May 69
mayor	bigger, elderly, older 38; greater 47; main, major 93
me	myself 2, 10; me 49
mear	to piss 37
media (y ~)	half past 17
media *(f.)*	stocking 87
médico/-a *(m./f.)*	doctor (medical) 29
medio (por ~ de)	by means of 83
medio *(m.)*	means 66
medir	to measure 75, 100; to weigh up 100
mejicano	Mexican 88
Méjico	Mexico 88
mejor	better 47
mejor (a lo ~)	perhaps, possibly 41
melón *(m.)*	melon 52
menor	lesser/smaller, younger 47; least 57
menos	less, minus 17
menos… que	less … than 42
mentir	to lie 22
mentira *(f.)*	lie (falsehood) 28
menú *(m.)*	menu (set menu) 68
menudo	slight, small 39
merendar	to snack 4
merienda *(f.)*	snack 7
mes *(m.)*	month 14
mesa *(f.)*	table 14
metálico *(m.)*	cash 61
metro *(m.)*	metre 75
mezcla *(f.)*	mixture 95
mí	me *(after prep.)* 14
mi/mis	my 28
miedo *(m.)*	fear 99
miembro *(m.)*	member 83
mientras	meanwhile, while 50; until 71
mientras tanto	in the meantime 50
miércoles *(m.)*	Wednesday 14
militar *(adj.)*	military 67
millón *(m.)*	million 92
ministerio *(m.)*	ministry 59
ministro/-a *(m./f.)*	minister 15

minuto *(m.)*	minute 11
mío/-a/-os/-as	mine, my *(after noun)* 36
mirar	to look (at) 13
mismo	even 1; same 31; self 40
mismo (lo ~)	the same thing 87
mochila *(f.)*	backpack/rucksack 33
moda *(f.)*	fashion 76
modelo *(m.)*	style (model) 32
moderno	modern 76
modo *(m.)*	way (manner) 66
modo que (de ~)	so (that) 66
mojado	wet 38
molde *(m.)*	baking pan 61
molestar	to bother, to disturb, to trouble 45
momento *(m.)*	moment 17
moneda *(f.)*	coin 6
monedero *(m.)*	wallet/purse (for coins) 6
montaña *(f.)*	mountain 91
montañoso	mountainous 93
montar a caballo	to ride a horse 78
monumento *(m.)*	monument 82
moreno	brown, dark 62
morir	to die 39
mostrar	to display 90
motivo (con ~ de)	by means of, by way of 99
motivo *(m.)*	motive, reason 46
motor *(m.)*	engine 26
moverse	to move (around) 67, 88
móvil *(m.)*	mobile phone 20
muchacha *(f.)*	girl 22
muchacho *(m.)*	boy 22
muchísimo	very much 25
mucho/-a	a lot, much 9
muchos/-as	many 23
mueble *(m.)*	piece of furniture 26
muerte *(f.)*	death 11
mujer *(f.)*	woman 14; wife 100
mula *(f.)*	mule 60
multa *(f.)*	fine (penalty) 38
multinacional *(adj.)*	multinational 30
multiplicación *(f.)*	multiplication 86
mundo *(m.)*	world 30
municipio *(m.)*	municipality 37
museo *(m.)*	museum 82
música *(f.)*	music 95
muy	very 3

N

nacer	to be born 30
nacional	national 41
nada	nothing 5
nada más	nothing else/more 44
nadar	to swim 42

nadie	nobody 43
naranja *(f.)*	orange 3
nariz *(f.)*	nostril 87
natación *(f.)*	swimming 89
naturaleza *(f.)*	nature 80
nave *(f.)*	ship 83
navegar	to navigate 99
Navidad *(f.)*	Christmas 67
necesario	necessary 82
necesidad *(f.)*	need 100
necesitar	to need 12
negar	to deny 90
negarse	to refuse 90
negociación *(f.)*	negotiation 40
negociar	to negotiate 40
negocio *(m.)*	business, deal 26
negro	black 35
nevar	to snow 74
ni	neither 39
ni siquiera	not even 39
nietos *(m.)*	grandchildren 38
nieve *(f.)*	snow 65
niña *(f.)*	girl (child) 63
ningún/ninguno/-a/-os/-as	no 29, 57; none 40; not … any 57
ninguna parte (en ~)	nowhere 29
niño *(m.)*	boy (child) 71
niño/-a *(m./f.)*	child 4
nivel *(m.)*	level 92
no	no 6
noche (de la ~)	at night 21
noche *(f.)*	night 10
nombrar	to appoint (name) 81
nombre *(m.)*	name 30
norte *(m.)*	north 86
norteamericano	North American 40
nos	us *(dir./indir. obj.)* 49
nosotros/-as	us *(after prep.)* GA3; we 7
nota *(f.)*	note 100
noticia *(f.)*	piece of news 81
noticias *(f.)*	news 81
novela *(f.)*	novel 16
nuestro/-a/-os/-as	our 28; ours 63
nuevo	new 26
nuevo (de ~)	anew 49
número *(m.)*	number 2
numeroso	large (numerous) 25
nunca	never 13
nunca jamás	never ever 13

O

o	or 11
obedecer	to obey 90

objetivo *(m.)*	aim 92
obra *(f.)*	play (theatre) 8; work (of art) 82
obsesionar	to obsess 53
ocasión (de ~)	second-hand 26
ocasión *(f.)*	occasion 100
occidental	western 93
occidente *(m.)*	west 93
océano *(m.)*	ocean 97
ocio *(m.)*	free time, leisure 62
ocioso	idle 62
ocupado	busy 88
ocupar	to occupy 97
ocuparse	to look after 81
ocurrir	to happen, to occur 55
ocurrirse	to come to mind, to occur (to one) 71
oeste *(m.)*	west 97
oficina *(f.)*	office (agency) 41
oficio *(m.)*	trade (profession) 15
oír	to listen 46; to hear 96
ojalá	hopefully 62
ojeada *(f.)*	glance 79
ojo *(m.)*	eye 24
ola *(f.)*	wave (water) 65
olvidar	to forget 6
oportunidad *(f.)*	opportunity 99
órbita *(f.)*	orbit 23
orden *(f.)*	order (command) 90
orden *(m.)*	order 80
ordenador *(m.)*	computer 90
organizar	to organize 69
oriental	eastern 93
orientar	to guide 82
orientarse	to orient oneself 82
oriente *(m.)*	east 93
origen *(m.)*	origin 69
original	original 99
oro *(m.)*	gold 86
os	you *(informal pl.) (dir./indir. obj.)* 49
otra vez *(f.)*	again 49
otro	other 29
oveja *(f.)*	sheep 91

P

paciencia *(f.)*	patience 90
padre *(m.)*	father 27
padres *(m.)*	parents 38
pagar	to pay 13
país *(m.)*	country 92
paisaje *(m.)*	landscape 93
pájaro *(m.)*	bird (songbird) 93
palabra *(f.)*	word 98
paladar *(m.)*	palate, taste 86
paladear	to savour, to taste 86

palanca *(f.)* de cambio	gearstick 45
pálido	pale 43
palo *(m.)*	stick 27
palomitas *(f.)* de maíz	popcorn 62
pan *(m.)*	bread 28
pana *(f.)*	corduroy 75
panadería *(f.)*	bakery 17
panadero/-a *(m./f.)*	baker 15
pantalla *(f.)*	screen 94
pantalón/pantalones *(m.)*	trousers 76
pañuelo *(m.)*	handkerchief, shawl 34
papel *(m.)*	paper 34
par *(m.)*	pair 32
para	for 10, 85; in order to 12
parada *(f.)*	stop (for buses/taxis etc.) 19
paradójicamente	paradoxically 98
parador *(m.)*	parador (historic site renovated into a hotel) 59
paraguas *(m.)*	umbrella 46
paraíso *(m.)*	paradise 93
parar	to stay/keep 67
parar(se)	to stop 96
parecer	to seem 10; to think 71
parecerse	to look like 73
parecido *(m.)*	resemblance 73
paréntesis *(m.)*	interval 67
paro *(m.)*	unemployment 41
paroxismo *(m.)*	climax 95
parque *(m.)*	park 78
parquímetro *(m.)*	parking meter 38
parrillada *(f.)*	barbecue 86
parte (por otra ~)	actually 81
parte *(f.)*	part 29
particular	particular 38; private (personal) 40
particularmente	particularly 86
partida *(f.)*	game (of cards) 89
partido *(m.)*	game (match) 89
partir	to leave 27
pasado	last (referring to time), past 10
pasajero/-a *(m./f.)*	passenger 83
pasaporte *(m.)*	passport 18
pasar	to happen 20; to pass (by) 36; to spend (time) 87
pasár(se)lo bien/mal	to have a good/bad time 88
pasear	to go for a walk 48
pasta *(f.)*	pastry 71
pasta *(f.)* de dientes	toothpaste 2
pastar	to graze 91
pastel *(m.)*	cake 86
pata *(f.)*	leg (animal or furniture), paw 11
patán/patana *(m./f.)*	bumpkin 81
patata *(f.)*	potato 68
patrimonio *(m.)*	heritage 82
paz *(f.)*	peace (Intro.)
peaje *(m.)*	toll 38

pedal *(m.)*	pedal 45
pedir	to ask for 13, 70; to request 64
pedir disculpas	to apologize 44
pegar	to keep/stick to 38
peinarse	to comb one's hair 46
pelar	to peel 67
película *(f.)*	film 39
peligro *(m.)*	danger 38
peligroso	dangerous 85
pelo *(m.)*	hair 71
pelota *(f.)*	ball 84
peluquería *(f.)*	barber's, hairdresser's 71
pena *(f.)*	hardship 88
pendiente *(m.)*	earring 44
pensar	to think 40, 70
pensar de	to think of (opinion) 48
pensar en	to think about (ponder) 48
peor	worse 8
pequeño	little, small 25
percibir	to perceive 90
perder	to lose, to miss (fail to catch) 6
pérdida *(f.)*	loss 6
perdonar	to excuse 5
peregrinación *(f.)*	pilgrimage 69
peregrino/-a *(m./f.)*	pilgrim 80
pereza *(f.)*	laziness 90
perfectamente	perfectly 72
perfecto	perfect 71
periódico *(m.)*	newspaper 39
período *(m.)*	period 69
permanecer	to stay 83
permiso *(m.)*	leave (time off work), permission 59; licence 79
permitir	to permit 48
pero	but 13
perro *(m.)*	dog 34
perseverancia *(f.)*	perseverance 99
persona *(f.)*	person 21
personal *(m.)*	personnel 83
personas *(f.) (pl.)*	people (a specific or countable group) 78
persuadir	to persuade 57
pesar	to weigh 33
pesar de (a ~)	despite (in spite of) 38
pesca *(f.)*	fishing 46
pescadería *(f.)*	fish market, seafood counter 61
pescado *(m.)*	fish (seafood) 46
pescar	to fish 46
petición *(f.)*	petition, proposal, request 66
petróleo *(m.)*	oil (petroleum) 62
pez *(m.)*	fish (live) 61
picante	spicy 86
pie *(m.)*	foot 29
piel *(f.)*	skin 62
pierna *(f.)*	leg (part of the body) 29

pijama *(m.)*	pyjamas 48
pila *(f.)*	battery 31
piloto *(m./f.)*	pilot 83
pincho *(m.)*	tapa (bite-size) 13
pintar	to paint 82
pintarse	to put on make-up 24
pintarse los labios	to put on lipstick 24
pirámide *(f.)*	pyramid 88
pis *(m.)* (hacer ~)	to pee 37
pisar	to step/tread 58
piscina *(f.)*	swimming pool 27
piso *(m.)*	floor (of a building) 55; apartment 25; flat 85
placer *(m.)*	pleasure 80
plancha (a la ~)	grilled 62
plano *(m.)*	map 82
planta *(f.)*	plant 38
plantado (dejar ~)	to leave stranded 90
plantar	to plant 90
plato *(m.)*	course (of a meal), plate 68
plato combinado *(m.)*	combination plate 68
plato fuerte/segundo *(m.)*	main course 68
playa *(f.)*	beach 16
plaza *(f.)*	square (in a town) 67
población *(f.)*	population 97
pobre	poor 64
poco más o menos	around (approximately) 75
poco/-a/-os/-as	little 11
poder	to be able to, can/may 4
policía *(f.)*	police/policewoman 38
policía *(m.)*	policeman 38
político	political 92
pollo *(m.)*	chicken (meat) 93
pomada *(f.)*	ointment 62
poner	to put 11
ponerse	to make oneself 40; to put oneself 42; to get (become) 43; to put on 67
ponerse en marcha	to start up 33
por	by 1; in 10; because of 12; for 36, 85; on 42; around (in the vicinity of) 78
por favor	please 1
por poco	just, by a little 11
por qué	why 12
por supuesto	of course 66
porque	because 12
portal *(m.)*	entranceway 57
portátil (ordenador ~) *(m.)*	laptop (computer) 94
portero/-a *(m./f.)*	caretaker 57
posible	possible 47
postre *(m.)*	dessert 68
práctica *(f.)*	practice 99
practicar	to practice 70
práctico	practical 20
pradera *(f.)*	meadow 35

precaución (con ~)	carefully 84
precavido	warned 13; cautious 38
precio *(m.)*	price 38
preferencia *(f.)*	preference 38
preferir	to prefer 74
pregunta *(f.)*	question 11
preguntar	to ask (a question) 17, 64
preguntarse	to wonder 96
prenda *(f.)*	item of clothing, forfeit 87
preocuparse	to worry 31
preparar	to prepare 55
presa *(f.)*	prey 93
presentar	to present 41
presentarse	to appear 92
prestado	borrowed 47
prestar	to lend 94
previsto	planned 46
primavera *(f.)*	spring 69
primer	first 14
primero	first 5
primero (lo ~)	the first thing 41
principal	key (principal), main 82
principalmente	mainly 41
principio *(m.)*	principle 79; beginning 92
prisa *(f.)*	hurry 38
prisa (tener ~)	to be in a hurry 38
probablemente	probably 85
probar	to try (on) 32; to taste, to test 74
problema *(m.)*	matter, problem 11
procedente de	originating from 95
producir	to produce 74
producto *(m.)*	product 61
profesión *(f.)*	profession 15
profesor/a *(m./f.)*	teacher 15
programa *(m.)*	programme 94
prohibido	forbidden 37
pronto	soon 40
propietario/-a *(m./f.)*	owner 78
propina *(f.)*	tip (for service) 21
propio	typical 95
proponer	to suggest 25; to propose 87
proporcionar	to provide 78
protagonista *(m./f.)*	protagonist 39
proteger	to protect 93
provincia *(f.)*	province 97
provocación *(f.)*	provocation 90
próximo	next 14
proyecto *(m.)*	plan 9
pruebas/muestras de (dar ~)	to show proof of 90
público *(m.)*	public 95
pueblo *(m.)*	town 69; people (nation) 92
puente *(m.)*	bridge 69
puerta *(f.)*	door 42

pues	well … 46
puesto *(m.)*	post (position) 41
puñado *(m.)*	handful 65
punta *(f.)*	peak 2; point (tip or end) 65
punto (a ~)	on time 71
punto (en ~)	on the dot 18
punto *(m.)*	point 100

Q

que	that 13; than 42
¿Qué?	What? 3
que (del ~)	from whom 81
quedar	to arrange (to meet), to be/have left (remaining), to meet (up) 10; to remain 57
quedarse	to stay 10
quedarse con	to keep for oneself 76
queja *(f.)*	complaint 95
quejarse	to complain 44
quemar	to burn 62
quemarse	to get sunburned 62
querer	to want 3; to like 19; to love 51
querer decir	to mean 55
queso *(m.)*	cheese 78
¿Qué tal?	How are you? 3
quien (de ~)	of whom 81
quien/quienes	who 12
quiosco *(m.)*	kiosk/stand 54
quitando	except for 73
quitar	to remove, to take 45
quitarse	to take off 87
quizá(s)	perhaps 68

R

ración *(f.)*	portion 13
radio *(f.)*	radio 45
radio *(m.)*	radius 45
raja *(f.)*	slice 52
rápido	quickly 21
raro	strange 17; bizarre, rare 94
ratito *(m.)*	brief moment 22
rato *(m.)*	moment 15
ratón *(m.)*	mouse 94
raya *(f.)*	stripe 32
rayo *(m.)*	ray 83
razón (no tener ~)	to be wrong GA10
razón (tener ~)	to be right GA10
razón *(f.)*	reason 80
reaccionar	to react 90
realizar	to achieve 99
rebanada *(f.)*	slice 52
receta *(f.)*	recipe 86
recibir	to receive, to welcome 75
recibo *(m.)*	receipt 21

recién	newly, recently 9
recién llegado/-a *(m./f.)*	newcomer 44
recientemente	recently 9
recinto *(m.)*	premises 37
recoger	to pick up (collect) 77
recomendar	to recommend 68
reconocer	to recognize 60
reconstitución *(f.)*	reenactment 69
recordar	to remind 83
recorrer	to cover (traverse) 80
recorrido *(m.)*	route 67; journey 80
red *(f.)*	network 38
redactar	to write (a draft) 55
reducir	to reduce 38
refresco *(m.)*	cold drink 65
refugio *(m.)*	shelter 80
regalo *(m.)*	present (gift) 23
región *(f.)*	region 69
registrar	to record 69; to search (through) 79
regresar	to return 49
regreso (de ~)	back from (returned) 40
regreso *(m.)*	return 40
rehuir	to shy away 100
reír(se)	to laugh 98
relación (con ~ a)	regarding 85
relación *(f.)*	relationship 92
relativo	relative 11
releer	to reread 81
relieve *(m.)*	relief (topography) 97
religión *(f.)*	religion 48
religioso	religious 69
rellenar	to fill in/out 50
reloj *(m.)*	watch 17
reñir	to scold 98
reparar	to repair 94
repasar	to review 100
repaso *(m.)*	review 7
repetir	to repeat 26
reponer	to replace 100
resbalar	to slip 57
reserva *(f.)*	reservation 59
reservado	reserved 44
reservar	to reserve 78
resistir	to resist 64
respecto (con ~ a)	regarding 85
respetar	to respect 38
respirar	to breathe 29
responder	to answer 57
responsabilidad *(f.)*	responsibility 66
respuesta *(f.)*	reply 90
restaurante *(m.)*	restaurant 44
resultar	to result, to seem, to turn out (to be) 88
retirar	to remove, to withdraw 52

retraso *(m.)*	delay 18
retraso (con ~)	late (delayed) 18
reunión *(f.)*	meeting 63
reunirse	to meet (gather) 66
revista *(f.)*	magazine 99
revolotear	to flutter 65
rey *(m.)*	king 62
rico	rich 12; tasty 86
río *(m.)*	river 97
ritmo *(m.)*	rate (pace) 80
robar	to rob 45
rodaja *(f.)*	slice (round) 52
rogar	to request 37; to beg 44
rojo	red 5
rollo *(m.)*	bore, reel, roll 39
romería *(f.)*	procession (religious) 69
rompecabezas *(m.)*	brainteaser, puzzle 72
romper	to break 20
ropa *(f.)*	clothes/clothing 55
ropa interior *(f.)*	underwear 55
rosado (vino ~)	rosé wine 74
roto	broken 29
rozar	to brush (against), to verge on 97
rubio	blond 62
ruedo *(m.)*	ring (circle) 99
ruido *(m.)*	noise 43
ruta *(f.)*	route 80

S

sábado *(m.)*	Saturday 10
saber	to know (a fact or how to do something) 5
saber de	to know of 78
sabor *(m.)*	flavour 86
saborear	to savour 86
sacar	to take out 61; to get 82
sala *(f.)*	room (large) 84
salchichón *(m.)*	sausage (cured) 52
salida *(f.)*	departure 14; exit 43
salida *(f.)* de socorro	emergency exit 43
salir	to go out 6; to leave 6, 91
salpicadero *(m.)*	dashboard 45
salsa *(f.)*	sauce 8
saltar	to jump, to run (a traffic light) 38
salud *(f.)*	health 98
saludar	to greet 57
salvaje	wild 93
sandía *(f.)*	watermelon 52
sangre *(f.)*	blood 90
sangre fría *(f.)*	composure 90
santo	holy 69
santo/-a (patrón/a ~) *(m./f.)*	patron saint 69
sarta *(f.)*	string (of identical things) 52

se	herself *(reflexive)*, himself *(reflexive)*, itself *(reflexive)*, oneself *(reflexive)*, themselves *(reflexive)* GA3; yourself *(reflexive) (formal)* 45; her *(dir. obj.)*, him *(indir. obj.)*, them *(indir. obj.)*, you *(formal) (indir. obj.)* 49
sección *(f.)*	department 32; section 61
secreto *(m.)*	secret 100
seducir	to seduce 74
seguida (en ~)	immediately 13
seguir	to continue to be (still …) 41; to follow 84
segundo	second 8
seguridad *(f.)*	safety 38
seguro	sure 40
sello *(m.)*	stamp (postage) 14
semáforo *(m.)*	traffic light 5
semana *(f.)*	week 10
señal *(f.)*	deposit, sign, signal 72
señal *(f.)* de tráfico	road sign 38
señalización *(f.)*	signposting 72
sencillo	simple 72
senda *(f.)*	path 57
senderismo *(m.)*	hiking 80
sendero *(m.)*	path 57
señor *(m.)*	sir 32; gentleman 44; Mr 55
señora *(f.)*	madam, Mrs 17; lady 49
señorita *(f.)*	Miss, young lady 31
sentado	seated 43
sentar bien/mal	to agree/not agree with one, to suit/not suit one 43
sentarse	to sit down 40
sentido *(m.)*	sense 20
sentimiento *(m.)*	feeling 95
sentir	to be/feel sorry 48
sentirse	to feel 53
separar	to separate 80
ser	to be *(unchanging characteristics)* 1, 2, 7
serie *(f.)*	series 82
serio	serious 46
servicio *(m.)*	restroom, toilet (lavatory) 37
servidor *(m.)*	server (computer) 94
servilismo *(m.)*	servility 90
servilleta *(f.)*	napkin (table) 62
servir	to serve 13
seta *(f.)*	mushroom (wild) 13
si	if 12
sí	yes 1; yourself *(formal) (after prep.)* 40; herself *(after prep.)*, himself *(after prep.)*, itself *(after prep.)*, oneself *(after prep.)*, themselves *(after prep.)*, yourselves *(formal) (after prep.)* 66
si no	if not, otherwise 18
siempre	always 10

sierra *(f.)*	mountain range, saw (carpentry) 52
siesta *(f.)*	nap 28
siglo *(m.)*	century 21
significar	to mean 55
siguiente día (al ~)	the next/following day 58
sílaba *(f.)*	syllable 2
silbotear	to whistle 65
silla *(f.)*	chair 65
simpático	nice 7
simple	simple 80
sin	without 36
sinfín *(m.)*	myriad 69
singular	unique 97
sinnúmero *(m.)*	endless number 69
sino	but (only) 63
sistema *(m.)*	system 83
sitio *(m.)*	site 29; place 43
situación *(f.)*	situation 43
situado	situated 97
situarse	to be situated 95
sobre	on 54
sobre todo	above all 86
sociedad *(f.)*	company 40; club 86
socio *(m.)*	member (of a club), partner (business) 89
socorrista *(m./f.)*	lifeguard 37
sofisticado	sophisticated 86
sol *(m.)*	sun 65
soler	to be used to, to usually do something 43
solera *(f.)*	tradition 86
solo	alone 89
sólo	only 26
solsticio *(m.)*	solstice 69
soltar	to let loose 31; to blurt out 41
sombra *(f.)*	shade 98
sombrero *(m.)*	hat 75
sonámbulo/-a *(m./f.)*	sleepwalker 48
sonar	to ring 31
sonreír	to smile 98
sonriente	smiling 9
soportar	to bear 27
sorprender	to surprise 91
sorpresa *(f.)*	surprise 19
sorteo *(m.)*	draw (for a prize) 85
sospecha *(f.)*	suspicion 57
sospechar	to suspect 57
su/sus	her, his *(adj.)*, its, their, your *(formal)* 28
subir	to climb, to rise (in height) 65
sublevarse	to rebel 90
subrayar	to underline 88
sucesivamente	successively 87
sudamericano	South American 40
suelo *(m.)*	floor (ground) 65

suelto	loose 6
suelto *(m.)*	change (loose coins) 6
sueño *(m.)*	sleep 55
suerte *(f.)*	fate 85; luck 94
suficiente	sufficient 66
sufrimiento *(m.)*	suffering 95
sujetador *(m.)*	bra 87
suma (en ~)	in short 99
sumar	to total 97
superar	to exceed, to overcome 97
superficie *(f.)*	surface area 93
supermercado *(m.)*	supermarket 52
suplemento *(m.)*	surcharge 21
suponer	to suppose 52
sur *(m.)*	south 97
surgir	to arise, to emerge 95
suyo/-a/-os/-as	hers, his *(pronoun)*, theirs, yours *(formal)* 63

T

tal	such 3, 27
tal vez	maybe, perhaps 85
talla *(f.)*	size 76
también	also 52
tampoco	neither 52
tan	so 11; as 14
tan… como	as … as 42
tanto	so 11
tanto/-a/-os/-as	so much/many 14
tapa *(f.)*	tapa 1
tardar	to delay 24; to take (a long) time 61
tarde	late 23
tarde *(f.)*	afternoon 10
tarea *(f.)*	task 75
tarjeta *(f.)*	card 54
tarjeta *(f.)* de crédito	credit card 61
tarjeta *(f.)* de visita	business card 61
tarjeta *(f.)* postal	postcard 61
tarjeta *(f.)* telefónica	telephone card 61
taxi *(m.)*	taxi 18
taxista *(m./f.)*	taxi driver 19
te	yourself *(informal sing.)* 2; you *(informal sing.) (dir./indir. obj.)* 49
té *(m.)*	tea 13
teatro *(m.)*	theatre 8
teclado *(m.)*	keyboard 94
técnico/-a *(m./f.)*	technician 94
tecnología *(f.)*	technology 83
telediario *(m.)*	news (TV) 81
teledirigido	remote-controlled 83
telefonazo *(m.)*	telephone call 54
telefonear	to telephone 4
teléfono *(m.)*	telephone 2
televisión/tele *(f.)*	television/TV 31

temer	to fear 27
temerse que	to be afraid that 27
temporada *(f.)*	period, season, spell 60
temprano	early 65
¡Ten!/¡Tenga!	Here you go! *(informal/formal)* 84
tenacidad *(f.)*	tenacity 99
tender (la ropa)	to hang out (the laundry) 55
tenedor *(m.)*	fork 68
tener	to have (possess) 1, 7
tener que	to have to 21
tener… años	to be … years old (age) 96
teñir	to dye GA16
tenis *(m.)*	tennis 89
tensión *(f.)*	blood pressure 60
terminal *(m.)*	terminal 33
terminar	to end, to finish 55
término *(m.)*	end 67
termómetro *(m.)*	thermometer 97
ternera *(f.)*	veal 68
test *(m.)*	test 99
ti	you *(informal sing.) (after prep.)* 14
tía *(f.)*	aunt 91
tiempo *(m.)*	time 10; weather 49
tienda *(f.)*	shop 47; store 94
tinto (vino ~)	red wine 74
tío *(m.)*	bloke, guy, uncle 73
típicamente	typically 86
tipo *(m.)*	type 43; kind 69
tirarse	to throw oneself 68
tiro *(m.)*	shot 39
toalla *(f.)*	towel 62
tobogán *(m.)*	slide 63
tocar	to touch 29; to be one's turn 50; to play (a musical instrument) 85
tocino *(m.)*	bacon 9
todas partes (en ~)	everywhere 29
todavía	even 8; still 25; yet 49
todo	everything 11
todo/-a/-os/-as	all 10; every 14
tolerante	tolerant 90
tomar	to take 6; to have (eat or drink) 33
tomate *(m.)*	tomato 61
tonto	stupid 12
torno (en ~ a)	around (with regard to) 69
toro *(m.)*	bull 99
tortilla *(f.)*	omelette 1
tostado *(m.)*	toast 85
trabajar	to work 15
trabajo *(m.)*	job 9; work 15
tradición *(f.)*	tradition 86
traducir	to translate 74
traer	to bring 13
tráfico *(m.)*	traffic 38

tragar(se)	to swallow 31, 73
traje *(m.)*	suit 77
trampolín *(m.)*	diving board 37
tranquilidad *(f.)*	calm 100
tranquilizar	to calm 31
tranquilizarse	to stay calm 31
tranquilo	quiet 25
tras	after 57
trasero	rear 45
trasnochar	to stay out all night 16
tratar de	to try to 99
tratarse de	to be about (to concern) 79
través de (a ~)	across, through 95
tren *(m.)*	train 11
tripulación *(f.)*	crew (airplane/ship) 83
tristeza *(f.)*	sadness 95
trofeo *(m.)*	trophy 97
tú	you *(informal sing.)* 2
tu/tus	your *(informal sing.)* 2, 28
tumbona *(f.)*	deck chair 65
turismo *(m.)*	tourism 59
turno *(m.)*	turn (in a game/line) 50
tuyo/-a/-os/-as	yours *(informal sing.)* 63

U

último	last (final) 18
un/una *(m./f.)*	a(n) 1
único	only (unique) 53
único (el ~)	the only one 37
universalmente	universally 95
universidad *(f.)*	university 46
uno	one 8
unos/unas	some 7; a few 71
urgencias *(f.)*	emergency ward (hospital) 29
usted/Ud.	you *(formal sing.)* 5
ustedes/Uds.	you *(formal pl.)* 5

V

vacaciones *(f.)*	holidays, vacation 52
vacío	vacant 43; empty 90
¡Vale!	OK! 10
valer	to be worth 13, 91
valor *(m.)*	value 35
variado	varied 86
variante *(f.)*	variant 95
vasco	Basque 72
vaso *(m.)*	glass (for drinking) 34
vecino/-a *(m./f.)*	neighbour 59
vegetariano/-a *(m./f.)*	vegetarian 100
velocidad *(f.)*	speed 9
vencedor/a *(m./f.)*	winner 86
vendedor/a *(m./f.)*	salesperson 90
vender	to sell 34

venenoso	poisonous 13
ventaja *(f.)*	advantage 72
ventana *(f.)*	window 28
ventanilla *(f.)*	window (car/counter etc.) 28
ver	to see 9
ver la televisión	to watch television 99
verano *(m.)*	summer 40
verdad *(f.)*	true, truth 9
verdadero	true 99
verde	green 32
versión *(f.)*	version 99
vestíbulo *(m.)*	lobby 48
vestido	dressed 75
vestido *(m.)*	clothing 75
vestir	to dress 37
vez *(f.)*	time (occasion) 36; turn (in line) 71
viajar	to travel 43
viaje *(m.)*	trip (voyage) 23
vida *(f.)*	life 11
vídeo *(m.)*	video 47
viento *(m.)*	wind 62
vientre *(m.)*	stomach 29
viernes *(m.)*	Friday 14
vino *(m.)*	wine 16
visera *(f.)*	cap (peaked) 65
visita *(f.)*	visit 82
visitar	to visit 78
víspera *(f.)*	eve 67
vista *(f.)*	view 100
visto	seen 14
vivir	to live 21
vivo	bright (clever) 74
volante *(m.)*	steering wheel 45
volar	to fly 83
volcánico	volcanic 93
voluntario/-a *(m./f.)*	volunteer 49
volver	to come back 9; to go back 49; to return 49, 70
volver a *(+ infinitive)*	to repeat something (do again) 31
volver loco	to drive crazy 36
vosotros/-as	you *(informal pl.)* 7
voz *(f.)*	voice 31
voz (en alta ~)	aloud 100
vuelta (de ~)	back from (returned) 49
vuelta *(f.)*	spin, turn 49; change (after paying) 76
vuestro/-a/-os/-as	your *(informal pl.)* 28; yours *(informal pl.)* 63

Y

y	and 2
ya	already 18
ya no	no longer 58; not … anymore 63
ya que	since 83
ya sea… o ya sea	on the one hand … on the other 70
ya… ya	either … or 70

yo	I 2
yogur *(m.)*	yoghurt 61

Z

zapatillas de deporte *(f.)*	sports shoes 75
zapato *(m.)*	shoe 32
zona *(f.)*	zone 38; area 44
zumo *(m.)*	juice 3
zumo *(m.)* de naranja	orange juice 3

English-Spanish

A

a(n)	un/una *(m./f.)* 1
abandon (to ~)	abandonar 37
able to (to be ~)	poder 4
about	alrededor (de) 78
about (a subject)	de 79
above	encima 44
above all	sobre todo 86
absent-minded	distraído 45
absolutely	absolutamente 40
absolutely not	en absoluto 40
accelerator	acelerador *(m.)* 45
accident	accidente *(m.)* 38
accompany (to ~)	acompañar 69
account	cuenta *(f.)* 13
achieve (to ~)	realizar 99
acquire (to ~)	adquirir 82
across	a través de 95
act	acto *(m.)* 8
activity	actividad *(f.)* 78
actually	por otra parte 81
add (to ~)	añadir 69
addicted	enganchado 31
addition (in ~)	además, encima 44
address	dirección *(f.)* 57
address (to ~)	dirigirse 81
adult	adulto/-a *(m./f.)* 22
advance (in ~)	con antelación 98
advantage	ventaja *(f.)* 72
adventure	aventura *(f.)* 80
advertisement	anuncio *(m.)* 41
advice (piece of)	consejo *(m.)* 60
advise (to ~)	aconsejar 78
afraid that (to be ~)	temerse que 27
after	después (de) 8; tras 57
afternoon	tarde *(f.)* 10
afterwards	después 81
again	otra vez *(f.)* 49
age	edad *(f.)* 22
agency	agencia *(f.)* 25
agitation	agitación *(f.)* 67
ago	hace 21
agree/not agree with one (to ~)	sentar bien/mal 43
agreement	acuerdo *(m.)* 10; concordancia *(f.)* 81
aim	objetivo *(m.)* 92
air	aire *(m.)* 84
aircraft	aparato *(m.)* 83
airplane	avión *(m.)* 18
airport	aeropuerto *(m.)* 18
alcohol	alcohol *(m.)* 31
alcoholic	alcohólico 65

all	todo/-a/-os/-as 10
all right (agreed)	de acuerdo 10
almost	casi 81
alone	solo 89
a lot	mucho/-a 9
aloud	en alta voz 100
already	ya 18
also	también 52
alteration	arreglo *(m.)* 26
although	aunque 86
always	siempre 10
ambulance	ambulancia *(f.)* 31
American	americano 2
American (from the United States)	estadounidense 40
amount	importe *(m.)* 47
and	y 2
and (before words starting with **i** or **hi**)	e 67
anew	de nuevo 49
anniversary	aniversario *(m.)* 23
announce (to ~)	anunciar 83
annoy (to ~)	fastidiar 73
annoyed (to get ~)	alterarse 90
answer (to ~)	responder 57
any	cualquier 36; algún/alguno/-a/-os/-as 59
anybody/anyone	cualquiera 70
anything	cualquier cosa 36
anyway (in any case)	de todas formas 10
apartment	piso *(m.)* 25
apartment block	inmueble *(m.)* 57
apologize (to ~)	pedir disculpas 44
appeal to (to ~) (be pleasing)	gustar 9
appear (to ~)	aparecer 71; presentarse 92
appearance	aspecto *(m.)* 77
appease (to ~)	apaciguar 77
appetizer	aperitivo *(m.)* 1
applicant	candidato/-a *(m./f.)* 41
appoint (to ~) (name)	nombrar 81
appointment	cita *(f.)* 10
appreciate (to ~)	apreciar 86
approach (to ~)	acercarse 37
approximately	alrededor (de) 78
Arabian (also Arab and Arabic)	árabe 95
area	zona *(f.)* 44
argue (to ~)	discutir 27
arise (to ~)	surgir 95
armchair	butaca *(f.)* 90
around	alrededor (de) 52
around (approximately)	poco más o menos 75
around (in the vicinity of)	por 78
around (with regard to)	en torno a 69
arrange (to ~)	arreglarse 59; disponer 83
arrange (to meet) (to ~)	quedar 10

arrival	llegada *(f.)* 33
arrive (to ~)	llegar 10
art	arte* *(f.)* 100
article	artículo *(m.)* 94
artist	artista *(m./f.)* 95
artistic	artístico 95
as	tan 14; como 42
as (at the same time as)	cuando 31
as … as	tan… como 42
as far as	en cuanto a 75
as for	en cuanto a 75
as regards	en cuanto a 85
as soon as	en cuanto 100
as soon as possible	cuanto antes 59
as well as	así como 82
ask (a question) (to ~)	preguntar 17, 64
ask for (to ~)	pedir 13, 70
associate (to ~)	asociar 95
at	a, en 34
atrocity	barbaridad *(f.)* 52
attach (to ~)	atar 38
attain (to ~)	alcanzar 100
attend (to ~)	asistir 95
attention	atención *(f.)* 83
attitude	actitud *(f.)* 57
attract (to ~)	atraer 64
attraction	atracción *(f.)* 64
aunt	tía *(f.)* 91
Australian	australiano 2
author	autor/a *(m./f.)* 14
authority	autoridad *(f.)* 93
automobile	automóvil *(m.)* 20
autonomous	autónomo 97
axe	hacha* *(f.)* 68

B

back (part of the body)	espalda *(f.)* 43
back from (returned)	de regreso 40; de vuelta 49
backpack/rucksack	mochila *(f.)* 33
backwards (facing ~)	de espaldas 43
bacon	tocino *(m.)* 9
bad	mal, malo 14
badly	mal, malo 47
bag	bolsa *(f.)* 33
bait	anzuelo *(m.)* 46
baker	panadero/-a *(m./f.)* 15
bakery	panadería *(f.)* 17
baking pan	molde *(m.)* 61
ball	pelota *(f.)* 84
bank	banco *(m.)* 15
bar	bar *(m.)* 54
barbaric	bárbaro 52
barbecue	parrillada *(f.)* 86

barber's	peluquería *(f.)* 71
bargain	chollo *(m.)*, ganga *(f.)* 26
basketball	baloncesto *(m.)* 89
Basque (language only)	eusquera/euskera *(m.)* 72
Basque	vasco 72
bathe (to ~)	bañarse 46
bather	bañista *(m./f.)* 37
bathroom	baño *(m.)* 37
battery	pila *(f.)* 31
be (hot/cold) (to ~) (weather)	hacer (calor/frío) 62
be (to ~) *(for locations and temporary states)*	estar 5, 7
be (to ~) *(unchanging characteristics)*	ser 1, 2, 7
be … years old (to ~) (age)	tener… años 96
be about (to ~) (to concern)	tratarse de 79
beach	playa *(f.)* 16
bean	haba* *(f.)* 87
bear (to ~)	aguantar, soportar 27
bearing	actitud *(f.)* 58
beautiful	hermoso 42
because	porque 12
because of	por 12
become (to ~)	llegar a ser 100
bed	cama *(f.)* 59
bee	abeja *(f.)* 68
before	antes 13; ante 81, 90
beg (to ~)	rogar 44
beg someone's pardon (to ~)	pedir disculpas 44
begin (to ~)	comenzar 42
beginning	principio *(m.)* 92
behave (to ~)	comportarse 32
behind	detrás (de) 24; atrás 57
believe (to ~)	creer 94
belt (conveyor)	cinta (transportadora) *(f.)* 33
bench	banco *(m.)* 65
beret	boina *(f.)* 75
bet (to ~)	apostar 36
betray (to ~)	delatar 57
better	mejor 47
better and better	cada vez mejor 47
between	entre 92
beverage	bebida *(f.)* 65
bicycle	bicicleta *(f.)* 57
big	grande 14
bigger	mayor 38
bike	bici *(f.)* 57
bill (check)	cuenta *(f.)* 13
bird	ave* *(f.)* 93
bird (songbird)	pájaro *(m.)* 93
birthday	cumpleaños *(m.)* 23
biscuit	galleta *(f.)* 14
bitter	amargo 51

bizarre	raro 94
black	negro 35
blind	ciego 85
bloke	tío *(m.)* 73
blond	rubio 62
blood	sangre *(f.)* 90
blood pressure	tensión *(f.)* 60
blue	azul 32
blurt out (to ~)	soltar 41
boat	barco *(m.)* 43
body	cuerpo *(m.)* 29
bone	hueso *(m.)* 34
book	libro *(m.)* 47
boot (of a car)	maletero *(m.)* 57
booth	cabina *(f.)* 54
border	frontera *(f.)* 34
border (to ~)	limitar 97
bore	rollo *(m.)* 39
bored (to be ~)	aburrirse 87
born (to be ~)	nacer 30
borrowed	prestado 47
boss	jefe/jefa *(m./f.)* 55
bother (to ~)	molestar 45; fastidiar 73
bottle	botella *(f.)* 68
boy	muchacho *(m.)* 22; chico *(m.)* 46
boy (child)	niño *(m.)* 71
bra	sujetador *(m.)* 87
brainteaser	rompecabezas *(m.)* 72
brake	freno *(m.)* 45
brand	marca *(f.)* 69
brazen	descarado 44
bread	pan *(m.)* 28
break (to ~)	romper 20
breakfast	desayuno *(m.)* 3
breakfast (to have ~)	desayunar 3
breathe (to ~)	respirar 29
breeze	brisa *(f.)* 62
bridge	puente *(m.)* 69
bright (clever)	vivo 74
bring (to ~)	traer 13
broken	roto 29
brother	hermano *(m.)* 63
brother-in-law	cuñado *(m.)* 63
brown	marrón 35; moreno 62; castaño 75
brush (against) (to ~)	rozar 97
buckle up (to ~)	abrochar 38
build (to ~)	construir 80
bull	toro *(m.)* 99
bumpkin	patán/patana *(m./f.)* 81
burn (to ~)	quemar 62
bus	autobús *(m.)* 6
bus (long-distance)	autocar *(m.)* 89

business	negocio *(m.)* 26; firma *(f.)* 40; asunto *(m.)* 49; comercio *(m.)* 61
business card	tarjeta *(f.)* de visita 61
busy	ocupado 88
busy (phone)	comunicando 54
but	pero 13
but (only)	sino 63
butter	mantequilla *(f.)* 52
buy (to ~)	comprar 25
by	por 1
by the way	por cierto 62

C

cake	pastel *(m.)* 86
calendar	calendario *(m.)* 69
call	llamada *(f.)* 54
call (to ~)	llamar 4
call shop	locutorio *(m.)* 54
called	llamado 4
called/named (to be ~)	llamarse 2
calm	tranquilidad *(f.)* 100
calm (to ~)	tranquilizar 31
calm (to stay ~)	tranquilizarse 31
camel	camello *(m.)* 67
camping	acampada *(f.)* 63
can/may	poder 4
Canadian	canadiense 2
cancel (to ~)	anular 47
candy	golosina *(f.)* 25; caramelo *(m.)* 64
cap (peaked)	visera *(f.)* 65
capital	capital *(f.)* 69
car	coche *(m.)* 26
card	tarjeta *(f.)* 54; carta *(f.)* 89
care	cuidado *(m.)* 38
careful	cuidado 5
careful (to be ~)	tener cuidado 38
carefully	con precaución 84
caretaker	portero/-a *(m./f.)* 57
carry out (to ~)	efectuar 83
cart	carro *(m.)* 61
case	caso *(m.)* 72
cash	metálico *(m.)* 61
cashier	cajero/-a *(m./f.)* 61
Castilian	castellano 72
cat	gato *(m.)* 34
catalogue	catálogo *(m.)* 82
caution	amonestación *(f.)* 48
cautious	precavido 38
cease (to ~)	cesar 92
celebrate (to ~)	celebrar 23; festejar 69
celebration	fiesta *(f.)* 67; celebración *(f.)* 69
centre	centro *(m.)* 97
century	siglo *(m.)* 21

cereal	cereal *(m.)* 61
certain	cierto 62
certain (true)	cierto 36
certainly	claro 3
chair	silla *(f.)* 65
challenge	desafío *(m.)* 100
chance (by ~)	por casualidad 62
change (after paying)	vuelta *(f.)* 76
change (loose coins)	suelto *(m.)* 6
change (to ~)	cambiar 26
channel (TV or radio)	cadena *(f.)* 99
character (nature)	carácter *(m.)* 69
characterize (to ~)	caracterizar 86
charm	encanto *(m.)* 36
charming	encantador 36
chat (to ~)	charlar 30
cheap	barato 52
cheek (nerve)	cara *(f.)* 41
cheer on (to ~)	animar 89
cheese	queso *(m.)* 78
cherry	cereza *(f.)* 50
chess	ajedrez *(m.)* 79
chestnut	castaña *(f.)* 62
chicken (meat)	pollo *(m.)* 93
child	niño/-a *(m./f.)* 4
children (offspring)	hijos *(m.)* 25
Chinese	chino 30
chips	patatas fritas *(f.)* 68
chiringuito (open-air refreshment stand)	chiringuito *(m.)* 65
chocolate	chocolate *(m.)* 3
chocolate candy	bombón *(m.)* 64
choice	elección *(f.)* 69
choose (to ~)	elegir 68
Christian	cristiano 95
Christmas	Navidad *(f.)* 67
church	iglesia *(f.)* 80
churro (a cylindrical doughnut)	churro *(m.)* 3
churro stand/shop	churrería *(f.)* 3
cigarette	cigarro *(m.)* 44
cinema	cine *(m.)* 4
cinnamon	canela *(f.)* 86
circulation	circulación *(f.)* 94
circumstance	circunstancia *(f.)* 26
city	ciudad *(f.)* 38
city government	ayuntamiento *(m.)* 37
clarity	claridad *(f.)* 90
class (lesson)	clase *(f.)* 95
clean (to ~)	limpiar 61
cleaning	limpieza *(f.)* 61
cleanliness	limpieza *(f.)* 61
clear	claro 3
clever	listo 74

climate	clima *(m.)* 97
climax	paroxismo *(m.)* 95
climb (to ~)	subir 65
close (to ~)	cerrar 67
closing	cierre *(m.)* 61
clothes/clothing	ropa *(f.)* 55
clothing	vestido *(m.)* 75
clothing (item of ~)	prenda *(f.)* 87
cloudy	cubierto 68
clove (of garlic)	diente *(m.)* 52
club	sociedad *(f.)* 86
clutch (in a car)	embrague *(m.)* 45
coach (bus)	autocar *(m.)* 89
coat	abrigo *(m.)* 67
coffee	café *(m.)* 3
coin	moneda *(f.)* 6
cold	frío 62
cold drink	refresco *(m.)* 65
colleague	compañero/-a *(m./f.)* 71
colony	colonia *(f.)* 93
colour	color *(m.)* 35
comb one's hair (to ~)	peinarse 46
combination plate	plato combinado *(m.)* 68
combine (to ~)	combinar 95
come across (to ~)	encontrarse con 57
come back (to ~)	volver 9
come in (to ~)	entrar 70
come to mind (to ~)	ocurrirse 71
comfortable	cómodo 40
comings and goings	idas y venidas *(f.)* 9
command	mando *(m.)* 90
commemoration	conmemoración *(f.)* 69
commit a crime (to ~)	delinquir 77
communication	comunicación *(f.)* 92
communion	comunión *(f.)* 95
community	comunidad *(f.)* 97
compact disc	disco *(m.)* compacto 47
companion	compañero/-a *(m./f.)* 57
company	empresa *(f.)* 30; compañía *(f.)*, firma *(f.)*, sociedad *(f.)* 40
compare (to ~)	comparar 53
complain (to ~)	quejarse 44
complaint	queja *(f.)* 95
complete	completo 98
complete (to ~)	cumplir 65
completely	completamente 83
complex	complejo 83
complex (have a ~)	acomplejado 53
complicated	complicado 72
composure	sangre fría *(f.)* 90
comprehension	comprensión *(f.)* 90
computer	ordenador *(m.)* 90
concentrate (to ~)	concentrarse 61

concentrated	concentrado 61
concern	asunto *(m.)* 81
concerning	en lo que concierne a 85
condition	condición *(f.)* 100
confirm (to ~)	confirmar 59
confront (to ~)	hacer frente (a) 100
confuse (to ~)	confundir 9
confused	confuso 81
congratulations	felicidades *(f.)* 23; enhorabuena *(f.)* 49
conjugation	conjugación *(f.)* 100
consider (something as) (to ~)	estimar 100
consist (to ~)	consistir 68
constant	constante 86
constitute (to ~)	constituir 80
consult (to ~)	consultar 100
consultation	consulta *(f.)* 53
consumption	consumición *(f.)* 38
contact	contacto *(m.)* 19
continent	continente *(m.)* 93
continue (to ~)	continuar 34
continue to be (to ~) (still …)	seguir 41
contract	contrato *(m.)* 40
contrary (on the ~)	al contrario 53
contribute (to ~)	contribuir 80
control	mando *(m.)* 31
convene (to ~) (convoke)	convocar 40
conversation	conversación *(f.)* 99
convince (to ~)	convencer 81
cook (to ~)	cocer 87
cookie	galleta *(f.)* 14
cooking	cocina *(f.)* 86
cool	fresco 62
cope (to ~)	arreglárselas 75
corduroy	pana *(f.)* 75
corner	esquina *(f.)* 88
correct	correcto 30
cost (to ~)	costar 22
cotton	algodón *(m.)* 76
council	concejo *(m.)* 37
count (to ~)	contar 29
country	país *(m.)* 92
course	curso *(m.)* 40
course (of a meal)	plato *(m.)* 68
cover (to ~)	cubrir 68
cover (to ~) (traverse)	recorrer 80
covered	cubierto 68
crazy	loco 36
creation	creación *(f.)* 86
credit	crédito *(m.)* 61
credit card	tarjeta *(f.)* de crédito 61
crew (airplane/ship)	tripulación *(f.)* 83
cross	cruz *(f.)* 41
cross (to ~)	atravesar 48

cross paths (to ~) cruzarse 57
crossing (intersection) cruce *(m.)* 38
crown (of the head) coronilla *(f.)* 87
cry (to ~) (weep) llorar 14
cuisine cocina *(f.)* 86
culture cultura *(f.)* 95
curiosity curiosidad *(f.)* 22
curious curioso 29
current corriente 13
curtain cortina *(f.)* 85
customer cliente *(m./f.)* 47
customs aduana *(f.)* 34
cut corte *(m.)* 76
cut (to ~) cortar 41
cut one's hair (to ~) cortarse el pelo 71

D

daily diario 80
dance baile *(m.)* 95
dance (to ~) bailar 95
danger peligro *(m.)* 38
dangerous peligroso 85
dare (to ~) desafiar 85
dark moreno 62
dashboard salpicadero *(m.)* 45
date (day) fecha *(f.)* 69
date (fruit) dátil *(m.)* 67
date (social engagement) cita *(f.)* 10
daughter hija *(f.)* 10
dawn alba* *(f.)* 65; albor *(m.)* 92
day día *(m.)* 1
day off día festivo *(m.)* 69
daybreak madrugada *(f.)* 65
deal negocio *(m.)* 26
death muerte *(f.)* 11
decide (to ~) decidir 70
decision decisión *(f.)* 48
deck chair tumbona *(f.)* 65
declare (to ~) declarar 34
decorate (to ~) decorar 85
dedicate (to ~) dedicar 15
deed acción *(f.)* 64
deep hondo 29
defy (to ~) desafiar 85
delay retraso *(m.)* 18
delay (to ~) tardar 24
deli (for cured meats) charcutería *(f.)* 52
delicate delicado 86
delight (to ~) encantar 36
delight in (to ~) deleitarse con 86
delighted encantado 36
demonstrate (to ~) demostrar, manifestar 90
deny (to ~) negar 90

department	sección *(f.)* 32
departure	salida *(f.)* 14
deposit	señal *(f.)* 72
depressed (to get ~)	deprimirse 85
descend (to ~)	bajar 27
desire	gana *(f.)* 51
desire (to ~)	desear 50
despite (in spite of)	a pesar de 38
dessert	postre *(m.)* 68
destination	destino *(m.)* 95
detail	detalle *(m.)* 78
devote (to ~)	dedicar 15
devote oneself (to ~)	dedicarse 15
dial (to ~)	marcar 54
dictate (to ~)	dictar 81
dictionary	diccionario *(m.)* 94
die (to ~)	morir 39
difference	diferencia *(f.)* 21
differently	de otra manera 90
difficult	duro 41; difícil 88
difficulty	dificultad *(f.)* 40
dine/have dinner (to ~)	cenar 16
dinner	cena *(f.)* 8
direct	directo 99
direct (to ~)	dirigir 40, 81
director	director/a *(m./f.)* 40
disadvantage	inconveniente *(m.)* 72
disaster	desastre *(m.)* 39
discuss (to ~)	discutir 27
display (to ~)	mostrar 90
distinguish (to ~)	distinguir 77
distribute (to ~)	distribuir 80
distrust	desconfianza *(f.)* 73
disturb (to ~)	molestar 45
diversity	diversidad *(f.)* 88
divide (to ~)	dividir 97
diving board	trampolín *(m.)* 37
dizzy	mareado 76
do (to ~)	hacer 8
doctor (medical)	médico/-a *(m./f.)* 29
doctor (someone with a doctorate)	doctor/a *(m./f.)* 29
doctor's office/surgery	consulta *(f.)* 29
dog	perro *(m.)* 34
domestic	doméstico 34
done	hecho 14
door	puerta *(f.)* 42
doormat	felpudo *(m.)* 90
double bed	cama de matrimonio *(f.)* 59
doubt	duda *(f.)* 57
doubt (to ~)	dudar 86
dozen	docena *(f.)* 52
draw (for a prize)	sorteo *(m.)* 85
draw (to ~) (end in a tie)	empatar 89

drawer	cajón *(m.)* 79
dress (to ~)	vestir 37
dressed	vestido 75
drink	bebida *(f.)* 61
drink (to ~)	beber 35
drive (fast) (to ~)	correr 38
drive (to ~)	circular 38; conducir 38, 77
drive crazy (to ~)	volver loco 36
drug	droga *(f.)* 31
drugstore	farmacia *(f.)* 29
dry cleaning	limpieza *(f.)* en seco 61
during	durante 84
dye (to ~)	teñir GA16
dynamic	dinámico 30

E

each	cada 30
eagle	águila* *(f.)* 93
early	temprano 65
earn (to ~)	ganar 26
earring	pendiente *(m.)* 44
earthworm	lombriz *(f.)* 46
east	oriente *(m.)* 93; este *(m.)* 97
eastern	oriental 93
easy	fácil 98
eat (to ~)	comer 13
economic	económico 92
ecosystem	ecosistema *(m.)* 93
effect	efecto *(m.)* 24
egg	huevo *(m.)* 52
either … or	ya… ya 70
elderly	mayor 38
elect (to ~)	elegir 81
election	elección *(f.)* 37
electronic	electrónico 50
elevator	ascensor *(m.)* 57
eliminate (to ~)	eliminar 89
e-mail	correo electrónico *(m.)* 50; emilio *(m.)* 59
embark (to ~)	embarcar 14
emerge (to ~)	surgir 95
emergency	emergencia *(f.)* 31
emergency exit	salida *(f.)* de socorro 43
emergency ward (hospital)	urgencias *(f.)* 29
emigrate (to ~)	emigrar 81
emphasize (to ~)	destacar 88
employee	empleado/-a *(m./f.)* 30
employment	empleo *(m.)* 41
empty	vacío 90
enchant (to ~)	encantar 36
end	fin *(m.)* 10; final *(m.)* 39; término *(m.)* 67
end (to ~)	acabar 13; terminar 55
end (to bring to an ~)	cerrar 67
ending (of a film/book etc.)	desenlace *(m.)* 39

endless number	sinnúmero *(m.)* 69
endure (to ~)	aguantar 27
energy	ánimo *(m.)* 20
engaged (phone)	comunicando 54
engine	motor *(m.)* 26
England	Inglaterra 30
English	inglés 2, 40
enjoy (to ~)	gozar 66
enter (to ~)	entrar 99
enter the fray (to ~)	entrar en liza 99
enthusiasm	entusiasmo *(m.)* 67
entrance	entrada *(f.)* 62
entranceway	portal *(m.)* 57
environment	ambiente *(m.)* 93
equal to the task (to be ~)	estar a la altura 100
escape (to ~)	escapar 99
euro	euro *(m.)* 1
Europe	Europa *(f.)* 93
European	europeo 80
evaluate (to ~)	evaluar 100
eve	víspera *(f.)* 67
even	mismo 1; todavía 8; incluso 40
even if/though	aunque 86
event	acontecimiento *(m.)*, manifestación *(f.)* 69
every	todo/-a/-os/-as 14
everything	todo 11
everywhere	en todas partes 29
exactly	exactamente 68
exaggerate (to ~)	exagerar 52
examine (to ~)	examinar 29
example	ejemplo *(m.)* 49
exceed (to ~)	superar 97
excellent	excelente 60
except for	quitando 73
exceptionally	excepcionalmente 86
excess	exceso *(m.)* 38
excited	excitado 89
excuse	excusa *(f.)* 69
excuse (to ~)	perdonar 5; disculpar 44
exercises (physical)	gimnasia *(f.)* 85
exhibit (to ~)	exponer 82
exhibition	exposición *(f.)* 82
existence	existencia *(f.)* 95
exit	salida *(f.)* 43
expensive	caro 52
experience	experiencia *(f.)* 41
expired	caducado 18
explain (to ~)	explicar 45
explanation	explicación *(f.)* 45
express (to ~)	expresar 95
express mail	correo urgente *(m.)* 50
expression	expresión *(f.)* 88
extent	amplitud *(f.)* 100

extinguish (to ~)	apagar 73
extraordinary	extraordinario 53
extreme	extremo 65
eye	ojo *(m.)* 24
eye-catching	llamativo 75

F

face	cara *(f.)* 11
face (to ~)	afrontar 100
faced with	frente a 90
fake	fraudulento 34
fall (to ~)	caer 55
familiar	familiar 100
family	familia *(f.)* 14
famous	famoso 100
fan (enthusiast)	fanático/-a *(m./f.)* 31; aficionado/-a *(m./f.)* 89
fanatic	fanático/-a *(m./f.)* 31
fantastic	estupendo 59
far	lejos 65
farmyard	corral *(m.)* 93
fashion	moda *(f.)* 76
fast (to ~)	ayunar 3
fasten (to ~)	abrochar 38
fat	gordo 85
fate	suerte *(f.)* 85
father	padre *(m.)* 27
favour	favor *(m.)* 75
favour (to do a ~)	hacer un favor 75
favourite	favorito 89
fear	miedo *(m.)* 99
fear (to ~)	temer 27
fed up	harto 87
feel (to ~)	sentirse 53
feel like (doing something) (to ~)	tener ganas 51
feel like (to ~)	apetecer 85
feeling	sentimiento *(m.)* 95
festive	festivo 69
fever	fiebre *(f.)* 68
feverishness	febrilidad *(f.)* 67
few (a ~)	unos/unas 71
field	campo *(m.)* 93
fig	higo *(m.)* 67
figure out (to ~)	descifrar 81
fill in/out (to ~)	rellenar 50
fillet	filete *(m.)* 68
film	filme *(m.)*, película *(f.)* 39
final	final *(f.)* 89
find (to ~)	encontrar 12; dar con, hallar 57
fine (penalty)	multa *(f.)* 38
fingerprint	huella dactilar/digital *(f.)* 65
finish (to ~)	acabar 13; terminar 55
fireworks	fuegos artificiales *(m.)* 67
firm	firma *(f.)* 40

first	primero 5; primer 14
first thing (the ~)	lo primero 41
fish (live)	pez *(m.)* 61
fish (seafood)	pescado *(m.)* 46
fish (to ~)	pescar 46
fish market	pescadería *(f.)* 61
fishing	pesca *(f.)* 46
fit (to ~)	caber 57
fix (to ~) (sort out)	arreglarse 75
fixed (unchanging)	fijo 53
flat	piso *(m.)* 85
flavour	sabor *(m.)* 86
flight attendant	auxiliar de vuelo *(m./f.)*, azafata *(f.)* 83
float (parade)	carroza *(f.)* 67
floor (ground)	suelo *(m.)* 65
floor (of a building)	piso *(m.)* 55
flower	flor *(f.)* 28
flutter (to ~)	revolotear 65
fly (to ~)	volar 83
focus (to ~)	concentrarse 61
follow (to ~)	seguir 84
food	comida *(f.)* 34
foot	pie *(m.)* 29
football (soccer)	fútbol *(m.)* 89
footwear	calzado *(m.)* 32
for	para 10, 85; por 36, 85
for (+ period of time)	hace *(+ time)* 71
forbidden	prohibido 37
foreigner	extranjero/-a *(m./f.)* 15
forest	bosque *(m.)* 48
forfeit	prenda *(f.)* 87
forget (to ~)	olvidar 6
fork	tenedor *(m.)* 68
form (shape)	forma *(f.)* 10
form (sheet)	impreso *(m.)* 50
form (to ~)	conformar 93
forward	adelante 28
frankly	francamente 40
free (available)	libre 15
free (of charge)	gratuito 82
free time	ocio *(m.)* 62
free-range	de corral 93
freeze (to ~)	congelar 61
freezer	congelador *(m.)* 61
French	francés 2
frequent (to ~)	frecuentar 80
Friday	viernes *(m.)* 14
friend	amigo/-a *(m./f.)* 4
friendly	acogedor 88
friendship	amistad *(f.)* 98
fries	patatas fritas *(f.)* 68
from	de 2; desde 37
from (originating ~)	procedente de 95

from now on	en adelante 100
front	frente *(m.)* 100
front of (in ~)	ante 90
frozen foods	congelados *(m.)* 61
fry (to ~)	freír 98
fulfill (to ~) (accomplish)	cumplir 23
full	completo 98
funeral	entierro *(m.)* 64
furniture (piece of ~)	mueble *(m.)* 26
future	futuro *(m.)* 12

G

game	juego *(m.)* 87
game (match)	partido *(m.)* 89
game (of cards)	partida *(f.)* 89
garden	jardín *(m.)* 38
garlic	ajo *(m.)* 52
gearstick	palanca *(f.)* de cambio 45
generous	generoso 64
gentleman	caballero *(m.)* 32; señor *(m.)* 44
geography	geografía *(f.)* 97
get (to ~)	sacar 82
get (to ~) (become)	ponerse 43
get (to ~) (fetch)	buscar 61
get dark (to ~)	anochecer 61
get ready (to ~)	disponer 31
get the chance (to ~)	aprovechar 76
get up (to ~)	levantarse 46
get up early (to ~)	madrugar 65
girl	muchacha *(f.)* 22; chica *(f.)* 46
girl (child)	niña *(f.)* 63
give (to ~)	dar 29
glance	ojeada *(f.)* 79
glass (for drinking)	copa *(f.)* 16; vaso *(m.)* 34
glasses (spectacles)	gafas *(f.)* 72
glossary	léxico *(m.)* 100
glove	guante *(m.)* 46
go (to ~)	ir 5
go (to ~) (with a specific purpose)	acudir 57
go away (to ~)	irse 4
go back (to ~)	volver 49
go back on (to ~) (reconsider)	echar marcha atrás 57
go down (to ~)	bajar 27
go into (to ~)	entrar 27
go out (to ~)	salir 6
go through (to ~)	atravesar 83
go to bed (to ~)	acostarse 60
go/be off (to ~)	irse 4
god	dios *(m.)* 36
gold	oro *(m.)* 86
good	bueno 4; buen 14
good morning ('good day')	buenos días 1
goodbye	adiós 1

goodbye (to say ~)	despedirse 94
good-looking	guapo 24
gourmet	gastrónomo/-a *(m./f.)* 86
grab (to ~)	agarrar 6; coger 33
grammar	gramática *(f.)* 100
grandchildren	nietos *(m.)* 38
grandfather/grandmother	abuelo/-a *(m./f.)* 24
grant (to ~)	conceder 59
graze (to ~)	pastar 91
great	estupendo 4; grande 14
greater	mayor 47
green	verde 32
greet (to ~)	saludar 57
grey	gris 35
grey-haired	canoso 75
grilled	a la plancha 62
groceries	comestibles *(m.)* 52
ground beef	carne picada *(f.)* 61
group	grupo *(m.)* 65
grow (to ~)	crecer 38
guarantee (to ~)	garantizar 83
guest	invitado/-a *(m./f.)* 70
guide	guía *(f.)* 62
guide (to ~)	orientar 82
guitar	guitarra *(f.)* 95
gulf	golfo *(m.)* 97
guy	tío *(m.)* 73
gypsy	gitano/-a *(m./f.)* 95

H

hair	pelo *(m.)* 71
hairdresser's	peluquería *(f.)* 71
half past	y media 17
ham	jamón *(m.)* 52
hammer	martillo *(m.)* 54
hand	mano *(f.)* 19
handball	balonmano *(m.)* 89
handful	puñado *(m.)* 65
handkerchief	pañuelo *(m.)* 34
handle	mango *(m.)* 68
hang (up) (to ~)	colgar 54
hang out (the laundry) (to ~)	tender (la ropa) 55
happen (to ~)	pasar 20; ocurrir 55
happiness	felicidad *(f.)* 23
happy	contento 9; alegre 65; feliz 66
hard	duro 41
hard disk	disco *(m.)* duro 94
hardship	pena *(f.)* 88
hardware shop	ferretería *(f.)* 78
harvest	cosecha *(f.)* 69
hat	sombrero *(m.)* 75
have (to ~) (available)	disponer de 83
have (to ~) (eat or drink)	tomar 33

have (to ~) (possess)	tener 1, 7
have + -ed (to ~)	haber *(auxiliary verb)* 3, 6, 7, 14
have a good/bad time (to ~)	pasár(se)lo bien/mal 88
have been + -ing (to ~)	llevar 60
have fun (to ~)	divertirse 98
have just + -ed (to ~)	acabar de *(+ infinitive)* 19
have to (to ~)	tener que 21; deber 54; hacer falta 90
he	él 7
head	cabeza *(f.)* 6
head office	casa central *(f.)* 75
head over to (to ~)	dirigirse 44
heads or tails (to toss for ~)	echar a cara o cruz 41
health	salud *(f.)* 98
hear (to ~)	oír 96
heart	corazón *(m.)* 29
heartbreaking	desgarrador 95
heat	calor *(m.)* 35
height	altura *(f.)* 100
hello	hola 2
help (to ~)	ayudar 53
help (to ~) (serve)	atender a 32
hen	gallina *(f.)* 52
her *(adj.)*	su/sus 28
her *(after prep.)*	ella 12
her *(indir. obj.)*	la, le 49
her *(dir. obj.)*	se 49
herbal tea	infusión *(f.)* 43
here	aquí 1
Here you go! *(informal/formal)*	¡Ten!/¡Tenga! 84
heritage	patrimonio *(m.)* 82
hers	suyo/-a/-os/-as 63
herself *(reflexive)*	se GA3
herself *(after prep.)*	sí 66
hesitate (to ~)	dudar en 86
hesitation	indecisión *(f.)* 41
hide (to ~)	esconder 79
high	alto 60
highlight (to ~)	destacar 88
hiking	senderismo *(m.)* 80
him *(after prep.)*	él 12
him *(dir./indir. obj.)*	le 49
him *(indir. obj.)*	se 49
him *(dir. obj.)*	lo 49
himself *(reflexive)*	se GA3
himself *(after prep.)*	sí 66
his *(adj.)*	su/sus 28
his *(pronoun)*	suyo/-a/-os/-as 63
historical	histórico 69
hobby	afición *(f.)* 89
hold (to ~) (have room for)	caber 57
hole	agujero *(m.)* 6
holiday	fiesta *(f.)* 23; día festivo *(m.)* 69
holidays	vacaciones *(f.)* 52

holy	santo 69
home	a casa, hogar *(m.)* 27
home (at ~)	en casa 27
honour	honor *(m.)* 40
honourable	honrado 57
hook (to ~)	enganchar 31
hopefully	ojalá 62
horn	cuerno *(m.)* 99
horse	caballo *(m.)* 32
hospital	hospital *(m.)* 29
hot (food or drink)	caliente 64
hot (weather)	calor *(m.)* 62
hotel	hotel *(m.)* 48
hour	hora *(f.)* 2, 11
hours (timetable)	horario *(m.)* 82
house	casa *(f.)* 1
how	cómo 96
How are you?	¿Qué tal? 3
how come	cómo así 30
how much	cuánto 10
huge	enorme 39
huge amount	barbaridad *(f.)* 52
humour	humor *(m.)* 35
hundred	cien/ciento 21
hurry	prisa *(f.)* 38
hurry (to be in a ~)	tener prisa 38
hurt (to ~) (have pain)	doler 29
husband	marido *(m.)* 25

I

I	yo 2
ice	hielo *(m.)* 67
ice cream	helado *(m.)* 85
idea	idea *(f.)* 4
idiot	cretino/-a *(m./f.)* 30
idle	desocupado, ocioso 62
if	si 12
if not	si no 18
ill	malo 43; enfermo 51
illiterate	analfabeto 81
imagine (to ~)	imaginar 66
imitation	imitación *(f.)* 34
immediately	ahora mismo, enseguida, en seguida 13; inmediatamente 31
importance	importancia *(f.)* 92
important	importante 26
important (it's not ~)	no importa 67
impossible	imposible 45
impressive	impresionante 88
in	en 6; por 10; dentro (de) 71
in front	delante 24
in order to	para 12
inadequate	deficiente 40

including	incluso 40; incluido 97
incomprehension	incomprensión *(f.)* 96
increase	aumento *(m.)* 92
increasingly	cada vez más 100
indeed	en efecto 92
independent	autónomo 83
indicate (to ~)	indicar 50
infinity	infinidad *(f.)* 69
inform (to ~)	advertir 48
information	información/informaciones *(f.)* 82
information (piece of ~)	dato *(m.)* 78
information technology (IT)	informática *(f.)* 84
inhabitant	habitante *(m./f.)* 97
initiatory	iniciático 80
injustice	injusticia *(f.)* 95
inn	albergue *(m.)* 80
innocence	inocencia *(f.)* 71
innocent	inocente 71
inside	dentro (de) 71
insist (to ~)	insistir 44
instant	instante *(m.)* 41
institute	instituto *(m.)* 41
instruction	indicación *(f.)* 82; instrucción *(f.)* 84
intelligence	inteligencia *(f.)* 88
intelligent	inteligente 42
intensity	intensidad *(f.)* 98
intensive	intensivo 40
interest	afición *(f.)* 80
interest (to ~)	interesar 66
interesting	interesante 41
international	internacional 92
interval	paréntesis *(m.)* 67
intimate	íntimo 95
introduce (to ~)	introducir 74
invitation	invitación *(f.)* 91
invite (to ~)	invitar 4
invoice	factura *(f.)* 90
involve (to ~)	conllevar 66
iron (the metal)	hierro *(m.)* 51
ironically	irónicamente 98
ironmonger's	ferretería *(f.)* 78
island	isla *(f.)* 72
issue	asunto *(m.)* 11
it *(dir./indir. obj.)*	le 49
it *(f.) (dir. obj.)*	la 49
it *(m.) (dir. obj.)*	lo 6
its	su/sus 28
it's been … (referring to time)	hace 16
itself *(reflexive)*	se GA3
itself *(after prep.)*	sí 66

J

jacket	chaqueta *(f.)* 38
jetty	malecón *(m.)* 65
Jewish	judío 95
job	trabajo *(m.)* 9; faena *(f.)* 72
join (to ~)	ligar 62
joke	broma *(f.)* 71
joker	bromista *(m./f.)* 54
journey	recorrido *(m.)* 80
joy	alegría *(f.)* 95
jubilation	algazara *(f.)* 67
judge (to ~)	juzgar 57
jug	jarra *(f.)* 68
juice	zumo *(m.)* 3
July	julio *(m.)* 63
jump (to ~)	saltar 38
just	por poco 11; justo 32
just in case	por si acaso 75

K

keep (to ~)	guardar 55
keep for oneself (to ~)	quedarse con 76
keep/stick to (to ~)	pegar 38
key	llave *(f.)* 6
key (principal)	principal 82
keyboard	teclado *(m.)* 94
kill (to ~)	matar 89
kilogram	kilo *(m.)* 75
kilometer	kilómetro *(m.)* 65
kind	tipo *(m.)* 69
king	rey *(m.)* 62
kiosk/stand	quiosco *(m.)* 54
kiss	beso *(m.)* 19
kiss (to ~)	besar 91
kitchen	cocina *(f.)* 86
knife	cuchillo *(m.)* 68
knight	caballero *(m.)* 32
know (to ~) (a fact or how to do something)	saber 5
know (to ~) (to be familiar with)	conocer 42
know of (to ~)	conocer, saber de 78
knowledge	conocimiento *(m.)* 100

L

lack	falta *(f.)* 90
lack (to ~)	faltar 79
lady	señora *(f.)* 49
land (to ~)	aterrizar 27
landscape	paisaje *(m.)* 93
language	idioma *(m.)* 40; lengua *(f.)* 72
laptop (computer)	ordenador portátil *(m.)* 94
large	importante 93
large (numerous)	numeroso 25

laser	láser *(m.)* 83
last (final)	último 18
last (referring to time)	pasado 10
last night	anoche 28
late	tarde 23
late (delayed)	con retraso 18
Latin American	latinoamericano 40
laugh (to ~)	reír(se) 98
launch (to ~)	lanzar 94
law	ley *(f.)* 90
lawyer	abogado/-a *(m./f.)* 100
laziness	pereza *(f.)* 90
lead (to ~)	llevar 60
leaf	hoja *(f.)* 91
leaflet	folleto *(m.)* 82
learn (to ~)	aprender 69
least	menor 57
leave (time off work)	permiso *(m.)* 59
leave (to ~)	salir 6, 91; irse, partir 27; dejar 31
leave behind (to ~) (accidentally)	dejarse 54
left (on the ~)	a la izquierda 32
left (to be/have ~) (remaining)	quedar 10
leg (animal or furniture)	pata *(f.)* 11
leg (part of the body)	pierna *(f.)* 29
leisure	ocio *(m.)* 62
lemon	limón *(m.)* 52
lend (to ~)	prestar 94
less	menos 17
less … than	menos… que 42
less and less	cada vez menos 47
lesser/smaller	menor 47
let (to ~) (allow)	dejar 35
let loose (to ~)	soltar 31
letter	carta *(f.)* 50
letterbox	buzón *(m.)* 50
level	nivel *(m.)* 92
library	biblioteca *(f.)* 94
licence	licencia *(f.)* 46; permiso *(m.)* 79
lie (falsehood)	mentira *(f.)* 28
lie (to ~)	mentir 22
life	vida *(f.)* 11
lifeguard	socorrista *(m./f.)* 37
lift	ascensor *(m.)* 57
like	como 13
like (to ~)	gustar 9; querer 19
like this/that	así 96
likewise	así mismo 100
lilac	lila *(f.)* 32
line	línea *(f.)* 54
line (of people)	cola *(f.)* 39
lip	labio *(m.)* 24
liqueur	licor *(m.)* 74
list	lista *(f.)* 61

listen (to ~)	oír 46; escuchar 75
literature	literatura *(f.)* 86
little	poco/-a/-os/-as 11; pequeño 25
little (by a ~)	por poco 11
live (to ~)	vivir 21
living (to do for a ~)	dedicarse 15
load (to ~)	cargar 67
lobby	hall *(m.)*, vestíbulo *(m.)* 48
local	local 54
logic	lógica *(f.)* 44
long	largo 36
look (at) (to ~)	mirar 13
look after (to ~)	ocuparse 81
look bad (to ~)	tener mal aspecto 77
look for (to ~)	buscar 42
look like (to ~)	parecerse 73
loose	suelto 6
lose (to ~)	perder 6
lose weight (to ~)	adelgazar 77
loss	pérdida *(f.)* 6
lottery	lotería *(f.)* 85
love	amor *(m.)* 9
love (to ~)	amar, querer 51
lover	amante *(m./f.)* 93
loving	amante 93
low	bajo 60
luck	fortuna *(f.)* 85; suerte *(f.)* 94
luggage	equipaje *(m.)* 33

M

machine	máquina *(f.)* 30
madam	señora *(f.)* 17
made	hecho 14
madness	locura *(f.)* 36
magazine	revista *(f.)* 99
magic	magia *(f.)* 95
mailbox	buzón *(m.)* 50
main	principal 82; mayor 93
main course	plato fuerte/segundo *(m.)* 68
mainly	principalmente 41
maintain (to ~)	mantener 66
major	mayor 93
make (to ~)	hacer 24
make do (to ~)	contentarse 74
make oneself (to ~)	ponerse 40
make up for (to ~)	compensar 60
man	hombre *(m.)* 12
manage (to ~)	arreglárselas 75
manage to (to ~)	conseguir, lograr 81
manager	director/a *(m./f.)* 75
manner	manera *(f.)* 100
many	muchos/-as 23
map	plano *(m.)* 82

Mardi Gras	carnaval *(m.)* 69
mark out (to ~)	jalonar 80
married couple	matrimonio *(m.)* 59
married man/woman	casado/-a *(m./f.)* 9
marry/get married (to ~)	casarse 12
marvel	maravilla *(f.)* 19
marvellously	estupendamente 47
master	dueño/-a *(m./f.)* 100
matter	problema *(m.)* 11
May	mayo *(m.)* 69
maybe	acaso, tal vez 85
mayor	alcalde *(m.)* 37
me	me 49
me *(after prep.)*	mí 14
meadow	pradera *(f.)* 35
meal	comida *(f.)* 34
mean (to ~)	querer decir, significar 55
means	medio *(m.)* 66
means (by ~ of)	por medio de 83; con motivo de 99
meantime (in the ~)	entretanto, mientras tanto 50
meanwhile	entretanto, mientras 50
measure (to ~)	medir 75, 100
meat	carne *(f.)* 61
meet (to ~) (a challenge)	afrontar 100
meet (to ~)	conocer 42
meet (to ~) (gather)	reunirse 66
meet (up) (to ~)	quedar 10
meeting	cita *(f.)* 10; reunión *(f.)* 63
melon	melón *(m.)* 52
member	miembro *(m.)* 83
member (of a club)	socio *(m.)* 89
member (of a political party)	afiliado/-a *(m./f.)* 89
menu	carta *(f.)* 74
menu (set menu)	menú *(m.)* 68
mess	lío *(m.)* 39
metre	metro *(m.)* 75
Mexican	mejicano 88
Mexico	Méjico 88
military	militar *(adj.)* 67
milk	leche *(f.)* 13
million	millón *(m.)* 92
mind (in ~)	en cuenta 52
mine	mío/-a/-os/-as 36
minister	ministro/-a *(m./f.)* 15
ministry	ministerio *(m.)* 59
minus	menos 17
minute	minuto *(m.)* 11
mirror	espejo *(m.)* 24
misdial (to ~)	confundirse de número 54
Miss	señorita *(f.)* 31
miss (to ~) (fail to catch)	perder 6
missing something (to be ~)	faltar 61
mission (commitment)	cometido *(m.)* 65

mistake	error *(m.)* 90; falta *(f.)* 100
mistake (to make a ~)	confundirse, equivocarse 54
mix up (to ~)	confundirse 54
mixture	mezcla *(f.)* 95
mobile phone	móvil *(m.)* 20
modern	moderno 76
moment	rato *(m.)* 15; momento *(m.)* 17
moment (brief ~)	ratito *(m.)* 22
Monday	lunes *(m.)* 10
money	dinero *(m.)* 6
month	mes *(m.)* 14
monument	monumento *(m.)* 82
more	más 33
more … than	más… que 42
more and more	cada vez más 36
more or less	más o menos 75
moreover	además 44
morning	mañana *(f.)* 10
morning (early ~)	madrugada *(f.)* 65
mother	madre *(f.)* 27
mother tongue (first language)	lengua *(f.)* materna 92
motion (progress)	marcha *(f.)* 43
motive	motivo *(m.)* 46
motorway/highway	autopista *(f.)*, autovía *(f.)* 38
mountain	montaña *(f.)* 91
mountain range	sierra *(f.)* 52
mountainous	montañoso 93
mouse	ratón *(m.)* 94
moustache	bigote *(m.)* 73
move (around) (to ~)	moverse 67, 88
Mr	señor *(m.)* 55
Mrs	señora *(f.)* 17
much	mucho/-a 9
mule	mula *(f.)* 60
multinational	multinacional *(adj.)* 30
multiplication	multiplicación *(f.)* 86
municipality	municipio *(m.)* 37
museum	museo *(m.)* 82
mushroom	champiñón *(m.)* 13
mushroom (wild)	seta *(f.)* 13
music	música *(f.)* 95
must (one ~)	hay que 90
my	mi/mis 28
my *(after noun)*	mío/-a/-os/-as 36
myriad	sinfín *(m.)* 69
myself	me 2, 10

N

naked	desnudo 46
name	nombre *(m.)* 30
name (family/last ~) (surname)	apellido *(m.)* 30
nap	siesta *(f.)* 28
napkin (table)	servilleta *(f.)* 62

narrow	estrecho 97
national	nacional 41
nature	naturaleza *(f.)* 80
navigate (to ~)	navegar 99
near	cerca 54
near (to ~)	acercarse 65
nearly	casi 41
necessary	necesario 82
necessary (it is ~)	hay que 9
necessary (to be ~)	hacer falta 75
need	necesidad *(f.)* 100
need (to ~)	necesitar 12; hacer falta 75
negotiate (to ~)	negociar 40
negotiation	negociación *(f.)* 40
neighbour	vecino/-a *(m./f.)* 59
neighbourhood	barrio *(m.)* 63
neither	ni 39; tampoco 52
network	red *(f.)* 38
never	jamás, nunca 13
never ever	nunca jamás 13
new	nuevo 26
newcomer	recién llegado/-a *(m./f.)* 44
newly	recién 9
news	noticias *(f.)* 81
news (piece of ~)	noticia *(f.)* 81
news (TV)	telediario *(m.)* 81
newspaper	periódico *(m.)* 39
next	próximo 14
next door	al lado 71
next to	junto a 30
next/following day (the ~)	al siguiente día 58
nice	simpático 7; amable 43
nice (weather)	bueno 62
night	noche *(f.)* 10
night (at ~)	de la noche 21
night club	discoteca *(f.)* 95
no	no 6; ningún/ninguno/-a/-os/-as 29, 57
no longer	ya no 58
nobody	nadie 43
noise	ruido *(m.)* 43
none	ningún/ninguno/-a/-os/-as 40
nonsense	bobada *(f.)* 79
north	norte *(m.)* 86
North American	norteamericano 40
nostril	nariz *(f.)* 87
not … any	ningún/ninguno/-a/-os/-as 57
not … anymore	ya no 63
not at all	en absoluto 40
not even	ni siquiera 39
note	nota *(f.)* 100
notes	apuntes *(m.)* 97
nothing	nada 5
nothing else/more	nada más 44

novel	novela *(f.)* 16
now	ahora 1
nowadays	hoy en día 80
nowhere	en ninguna parte 29
number	número *(m.)* 2

O

obey (to ~)	obedecer 90
obsess (to ~)	obsesionar 53
obtain (to ~)	conseguir 81
obvious	evidente 96
occasion	ocasión *(f.)* 100
occupy (to ~)	ocupar 97
occur (to ~)	ocurrir 55
occur (to one) (to ~)	ocurrirse 71
ocean	océano *(m.)* 97
o'clock	hora *(f.)* 21
odd	curioso 88
of	de 1
of course	por supuesto 66
of the	del 8
office (agency)	oficina *(f.)* 41
office (room)	despacho *(m.)* 59
oil (petroleum)	petróleo *(m.)* 62
ointment	pomada *(f.)* 62
OK	de acuerdo, bien 10
OK!	¡Vale! 10
old (former)	antiguo 58
older	mayor 38
omelette	tortilla *(f.)* 1
on	en 17; por 42; sobre 54
on board	a bordo 83
on the dot	en punto 18
on the one hand … on the other	ya sea… o ya sea 70
on time	a punto 71
on top of	encima 44
one	uno 8
oneself *(reflexive)*	se GA3
oneself *(after prep.)*	sí 66
onion	cebolla *(f.)* 52
only	sólo 26
only (unique)	único 53
only one (the ~)	el único 37
open	abierto 14
open (to ~)	abrir 14
opening	apertura *(f.)* 82
opening times	horario de apertura *(m.)* 61
operation/motion (in ~)	en marcha 33
opportunity	oportunidad *(f.)* 99
opposite	enfrente 54
or	o 11
orange	naranja *(f.)* 3
orange juice	zumo *(m.)* de naranja 3

orbit	órbita *(f.)* 23
order	orden *(m.)* 80
order (command)	orden *(f.)* 90
organic	biológico 52
organize (to ~)	organizar 69
orient oneself (to ~)	orientarse 82
origin	origen *(m.)* 69
original	original 99
other	otro 29; demás 93
otherwise	si no 18
our	nuestro/-a/-os/-as 28
ours	nuestro/-a/-os/-as 63
out	fuera 60
outrage	barbaridad *(f.)* 52
overcome (to ~)	superar 97
overtake (to ~)	adelantar 38
owe (to ~)	deber 76
owner	propietario/-a *(m./f.)* 78; dueño/-a *(m./f.)* 100

P

pacify (to ~)	apaciguar 77
pain	dolor *(m.)* 29
paint (to ~)	pintar 82
painting	cuadro *(m.)* 82
pair	par *(m.)* 32
palate	paladar *(m.)* 86
pale	pálido 43
panties	braga *(f.)* 87
paper	papel *(m.)* 34
parade	cabalgata *(f.)*, desfile *(m.)* 67
paradise	paraíso *(m.)* 93
parador (historic site renovated into a hotel)	parador *(m.)* 59
paradoxically	paradójicamente 98
parents	padres *(m.)* 38
park	parque *(m.)* 78
park (to ~)	aparcar 44
parking meter	parquímetro *(m.)* 38
part	parte *(f.)* 29
part (for his/her/its ~)	por su lado *(m.)* 81
particular	particular 38
particularly	particularmente 86
partner (business)	socio *(m.)* 89
party	fiesta *(f.)* 16
pass (by) (to ~)	pasar 36
pass someone (to ~)	adelantar 38
passenger	pasajero/-a *(m./f.)* 83
passport	pasaporte *(m.)* 18
past	pasado 10
pastime	afición *(f.)* 46
pastry	pasta *(f.)* 71
path	senda *(f.)*, sendero *(m.)* 57
patience	paciencia *(f.)* 90

paw	pata *(f.)* 11
pay (to ~)	pagar 13
peace	paz *(f.)* (Intro.)
peak	punta *(f.)* 2
pedal	pedal *(m.)* 45
pee (to ~)	hacer pis *(m.)* 37
peel (to ~)	pelar 67
pen	bolígrafo *(m.)* 50
pencil	lápiz *(m.)* 98
people (a specific or countable group)	personas *(f.) (pl.)* 78
people (general)	gente *(f.) (sing.)* 39
people (nation)	pueblo *(m.)* 92
perceive (to ~)	percibir 90
perceptiveness	lucidez *(f.)* 53
perfect	perfecto 71
perfectly	perfectamente 72
perhaps	a lo mejor 41; quizá(s) 68; igual, tal vez 85
period	temporada *(f.)* 60; período *(m.)* 69; época *(f.)* 86
permission	permiso *(m.)* 59
permit	licencia *(f.)* 46
permit (to ~)	permitir 48
perseverance	perseverancia *(f.)* 99
person	persona *(f.)* 21
personnel	personal *(m.)* 83
persuade (to ~)	persuadir 57
petition	petición *(f.)* 66
pharmacy	farmacia *(f.)* 29
phenomenon	fenómeno *(m.)* 86
photo	foto *(f.)* 88
phrase	frase *(f.)* 100
physical	físico 19
physics	física *(f.)* 2
pick someone up (to ~)	buscar 91
pick up (to ~) (collect)	recoger 77
pick up (to ~) (get together with someone)	ligar con 62
pilgrim	peregrino/-a *(m./f.)* 80
pilgrimage	peregrinación *(f.)* 69
pillow	almohada *(f.)* 53
pilot	piloto *(m./f.)* 83
piss (to ~)	mear 37
place	sitio *(m.)* 43; lugar *(m.)* 60
plan	proyecto *(m.)* 9
planned	previsto 46
plant	planta *(f.)* 38
plant (to ~)	plantar 90
plate	plato *(m.)* 68
play (to ~) (a game)	jugar 41, 87
play (to ~) (a musical instrument)	tocar 85
play (theatre)	obra *(f.)* 8
pleasant	agradable 82

please	por favor 1
pleased (to be ~)	complacerse 83
pleasure	gusto *(m.)* 9; placer *(m.)* 80
pleasure (to take ~)	complacerse 83
pocket	bolsillo *(m.)* 6
point	punto *(m.)* 100
point (tip or end)	punta *(f.)* 65
poisonous	venenoso 13
police station	comisaría *(f.)* 45
police/policewoman	policía *(f.)* 38
policeman	policía *(m.)* 38
political	político 92
poor	pobre 64
popcorn	palomitas *(f.)* de maíz 62
population	población *(f.)* 97
portion	ración *(f.)* 13
position	lugar *(m.)* 97
possible	posible 47
possibly	a lo mejor 41
post (mail)	correo *(m.)* 50
post (position)	puesto *(m.)* 41
post code	código postal *(m.)* 50
post office	correos *(m.)* 50
postcard	tarjeta *(f.)* postal 61
potato	patata *(f.)* 68
pour (to ~)	echar 34
practical	práctico 20
practice	práctica *(f.)* 99
practice (to ~)	practicar 70
prank	broma *(f.)* 71
prefer (to ~)	preferir 74
preference	preferencia *(f.)* 38
premises	recinto *(m.)* 37; local *(m.)* 57
prepare (to ~)	disponerse 31; preparar 55
present (gift)	regalo *(m.)* 23
present (to ~)	presentar 41
press (to ~)	apretar 29
pretty	bonito 36
prey	presa *(f.)* 93
price	precio *(m.)* 38
principle	principio *(m.)* 79
print (to ~)	imprimir GA8
printer	impresora *(f.)* 94
private (personal)	particular 40
probably	igual, probablemente 85
problem	problema *(m.)* 11
procession (religious)	romería *(f.)* 69
produce (to ~)	producir 74
product	producto *(m.)* 61
profession	profesión *(f.)* 15
profound	hondo 95
programme	programa *(m.)* 94
prompt (to ~)	empujar 64

proof of (to show ~)	dar pruebas/muestras de 90
proposal	petición *(f.)* 66
propose (to ~)	proponer 87
protagonist	protagonista *(m./f.)* 39
protect (to ~)	proteger 93
provide (to ~)	proporcionar 78
province	provincia *(f.)* 97
provocation	provocación *(f.)* 90
public	público *(m.)* 95
purchase	compra *(f.)* 76
push (to ~)	empujar 64
put (to ~)	poner 11
put on (a cream/lotion) (to ~)	echarse (crema) 62
put on (to ~)	ponerse 67
put on lipstick (to ~)	pintarse los labios 24
put on make-up (to ~)	maquillarse, pintarse 24
put oneself (to ~)	ponerse 42
puzzle	rompecabezas *(m.)* 72
pyjamas	pijama *(m.)* 48
pyramid	pirámide *(f.)* 88

Q

quality	calidad *(f.)* 68; cualidad *(f.)* 90
quarrel	bronca *(f.)* 55
quarter	cuarto *(m.)* 17
queasy (to feel ~)	marearse 43
question	pregunta *(f.)* 11
question (matter)	cuestión *(f.)* 11
queue	cola *(f.)* 39
quick	deprisa 6
quickly	rápido 21; enseguida 62
quiet	tranquilo 25

R

racket (din)	jaleo *(m.)* 39
radio	radio *(f.)* 45
radius	radio *(m.)* 45
railway	ferrocarril *(m.)* 43
rain (to ~)	llover 64
rainy	lluvioso 49
rare	raro 94
rate (pace)	ritmo *(m.)* 80
rather	bastante 40; más bien 75
ray	rayo *(m.)* 83
reach (to ~)	alcanzar 95
react (to ~)	reaccionar 90
read (to ~)	leer 16
reading	lectura *(f.)* 89
ready	listo 18
realize (to ~)	darse cuenta 87
rear	trasero 45
reason	motivo *(m.)* 46; razón *(f.)* 80
rebel (to ~)	sublevarse 90

receipt	recibo *(m.)* 21
receive (to ~)	recibir 75
recently	recién, recientemente 9
recipe	receta *(f.)* 86
recognize (to ~)	reconocer 60
recommend (to ~)	aconsejar 56; recomendar 68
record (to ~)	registrar 69
record (vinyl)	disco *(m.)* 47
red	rojo 5
red wine	vino tinto 74
reduce (to ~)	reducir 38
reel	rollo *(m.)* 39; carrete *(m.)* 46
reenactment	reconstitución *(f.)* 69
refined	fino 86
refund (to ~)	devolver 47
refuse (to ~)	negarse 90
regarding	con relación a, con respecto a 85
region	región *(f.)* 69
regular	asiduo 100
relationship	relación *(f.)* 92
relative	relativo 11
relief (topography)	relieve *(m.)* 97
religion	religión *(f.)* 48
religious	religioso 69
remain (to ~)	quedar 57
remember (to ~)	acordarse 63
remind (to ~)	recordar 83
remodel (to ~)	acondicionar 85
remote-controlled	teledirigido 83
remove (to ~)	quitar 45; retirar 52
rent (to ~)	alquilar 26
rental	alquiler *(m.)* 26
repair	arreglo *(m.)* 26
repair (to ~)	arreglar 26; reparar 94
repeat (to ~)	repetir 26
repeat something (to ~) (do again)	volver a *(+ infinitive)* 31
replace (to ~)	reponer 100
reply	respuesta *(f.)* 90
reply (to ~)	contestar 44
request	petición *(f.)* 66
request (to ~)	rogar 37; pedir 64
reread (to ~)	releer 81
resemblance	parecido *(m.)* 73
reservation	reserva *(f.)* 59
reserve (preserve)	coto *(m.)* 46
reserve (to ~)	reservar 78
reserved	reservado 44
resist (to ~)	resistir 64
resourceful	despabilado 81
respect (to ~)	respetar 38
responsibility	responsabilidad *(f.)* 66
rest (to ~)	descansar 65
restaurant	restaurante *(m.)* 44

restroom	servicio *(m.)* 37
result (to ~)	resultar 88
return	regreso *(m.)* 40
return (to ~)	regresar 49; volver 49, 70
return something (to ~)	devolver 47
review	repaso *(m.)* 7
review (to ~)	repasar 100
ribbon	cinta *(f.)* 33
rich	rico 12
rickety	bamboleante 65
ride a horse (to ~)	cabalgar 67; montar a caballo 78
right (on the ~)	a la derecha 5
right (prerogative)	derecho *(m.)* 79
right (to be ~)	tener razón GA10
right away	ahora mismo 1
right now	ahora mismo 31
ring (circle)	ruedo *(m.)* 99
ring (to ~)	sonar 31
rise (to ~)	levantarse 65
rise (to ~) (in height)	subir 65
river	río *(m.)* 97
road	calzada *(f.)* 38; camino *(m.)* 57; carretera *(f.)* 58
road sign	señal *(f.)* de tráfico 38
roast (to ~)	asar 62
roasted	asado 62
rob (to ~)	robar 45
rod (fishing ~)	caña *(f.)* 46
roll	rollo *(m.)* 39
room (bedroom or hotel room)	habitación *(f.)* 59
room (large)	sala *(f.)* 84
room (small)	cuarto *(m.)* 82
rooster	gallo *(m.)* 60
rosé wine	vino rosado 74
rough	accidentado 97
route	recorrido *(m.)* 67; ruta *(f.)* 80
rugged	agreste 93; accidentado 97
run (to ~) (a traffic light)	saltar 38
run (to ~)	correr 65
run around (to ~)	corretear 65
rural	campestre 93
rush hour	hora punta *(f.)* 2

S

sadness	tristeza *(f.)* 95
safety	seguridad *(f.)* 38
said	dicho 14
saint (patron ~)	patrón/a santo/-a *(m./f.)* 69
salad	ensalada *(f.)* 68
salesperson	vendedor/a *(m./f.)* 90
same	mismo 31; igual 68
same thing (the ~)	lo mismo 87
sand	arena *(f.)* 65
sandwich	bocadillo *(m.)* 3

Saturday	sábado *(m.)* 10
sauce	salsa *(f.)* 8
sausage (cured)	salchichón *(m.)* 52
savour (to ~)	paladear, saborear 86
saw (carpentry)	sierra *(f.)* 52
say (to ~)	decir 14
scarf	bufanda *(f.)* 67
scatter (to ~)	esparcir 77
school	colegio *(m.)* 25; escuela *(f.)* 40
scold (to ~)	reñir 98
screen	pantalla *(f.)* 94
screwdriver	destornillador *(m.)* 84
scribble	garabateo *(m.)* 81
sea	mar *(m.)* 97
seafood	mariscos *(m.)* 46
seafood counter	pescadería *(f.)* 61
seagull	gaviota *(f.)* 65
search (e.g. on the Internet)	consulta *(f.)* 94
search (through) (to ~)	registrar 79
seasick (to be ~)	marearse 43
season	temporada *(f.)* 60
seat	asiento *(m.)* 43
seat belt	cinturón *(m.)* 38
seated	sentado 43
second	segundo 8
second-hand	de ocasión 26
secret	secreto *(m.)* 100
section	sección *(f.)* 61
seduce (to ~)	seducir 74
see (to ~)	ver 9
seem (to ~)	parecer 10; resultar 88
seen	visto 14
self	mismo 40
sell (to ~)	vender 34
send (to ~)	enviar 31
seniority	antigüedad *(f.)* 86
sense	sentido *(m.)* 20
sentence	frase *(f.)* 26
separate (to ~)	separar 80
series	serie *(f.)* 82
serious	grave 11; serio 46
serve (to ~)	servir 13
server (computer)	servidor *(m.)* 94
servility	servilismo *(m.)* 90
set up (to ~)	disponer 65
settle (to ~)	establecerse 95
sew (to ~)	coser 30
shade	sombra *(f.)* 98
shake hands (to ~)	darse la mano 29
sharpen (to ~)	afilar 68
shawl	pañuelo *(m.)* 34
she	ella 7
sheep	oveja *(f.)* 91

shelter	refugio *(m.)* 80
shelter (to ~)	albergar 93
sherry	jerez *(m.)* 74
shine (to ~)	lucir GA16
ship	nave *(f.)* 83
shirt	camisa *(f.)* 35
shoe	zapato *(m.)* 32
shop	tienda *(f.)* 47
shopping	compras *(f.)* 76
shopping (to go ~)	ir de compras 76
shopping centre	centro comercial *(m.)* 61
shopping/errands (to do the ~)	hacer las compras 76
short	bajo 75
short (brief)	breve 83
short (in ~)	en suma 99
shot	tiro *(m.)* 39
should (one ~)	hay que 90
shoulder	hombro *(m.)* 43
shout	grito *(m.)* 43
shove (to ~)	empujar 64
show (performance)	espectáculo *(m.)* 95
show (to ~)	enseñar 46
show up (to ~)	aparecer 71
shower (to ~)	ducharse 46
shy away (to ~)	rehuir 100
sick	enfermo 43
side	lado *(m.)* 32
side (at the ~)	al lado 32
sidewalk	acera *(f.)* 54
sign	letrero *(m.)* 44; señal *(f.)* 72
sign (to ~)	firmar 25
signal	señal *(f.)* 72
signature	firma *(f.)* 40
signposting	señalización *(f.)* 72
simple	sencillo 72; simple 80
since	desde 67; ya que 83
since then	desde entonces 67
sing (to ~)	cantar 21
sir	señor *(m.)* 32
sister	hermana *(f.)* 63
sister-in-law	cuñada *(f.)* 63
sit down (to ~)	sentarse 40
site	sitio *(m.)* 29
situated	situado 97
situated (to be ~)	situarse 95
situation	situación *(f.)* 43
size	talla *(f.)* 76
ski	esquí *(m.)* 65
skin	piel *(f.)* 62
skirt	falda *(f.)* 35
sky	cielo *(m.)* 41
sleep	sueño *(m.)* 55
sleep (to ~)	dormir 3

sleepwalker	sonámbulo/-a *(m./f.)* 48
slice	raja *(f.)*, rebanada *(f.)* 52
slice (round)	rodaja *(f.)* 52
slice (thin)	loncha *(f.)* 52
slide	tobogán *(m.)* 63
slight	menudo 39
slip (to ~)	resbalar 57
slope	ladera *(f.)* 91
slowly	despacio 38
slush (crushed-ice drink)	granizado *(m.)* 76
sly	listo 74
small	pequeño 25; menudo 39; chico 46
smile (to ~)	sonreír 98
smiling	sonriente 9
smoke (to ~)	fumar 44
smoker	fumador/a *(m./f.)* 44
snack	merienda *(f.)* 7
snack (to ~)	merendar 4
snow	nieve *(f.)* 65
snow (to ~)	nevar 74
so	tan, tanto 11; así pues 66
so (that)	así que, conque, de manera que, de modo que 66
so much/many	tanto/-a/-os/-as 14
sock	calcetín *(m.)* 87
soda	gaseosa *(f.)* 74
solstice	solsticio *(m.)* 69
some	unos/unas 7; algún/alguno/-a/-os/-as 57
someone	alguien 47
something	algo 34
son	hijo *(m.)* 25
song	canto *(m.)* 60
soon	pronto 40
sophisticated	sofisticado 86
sorry (I'm ~)	lo siento 48
sorry (to be/feel ~)	sentir 48
sort (type)	especie *(f.)* 64
soul	alma* *(f.)* 24
south	sur *(m.)* 97
South American	sudamericano 40
space	espacio *(m.)* 83
Spanish	español 2
Spanish-speaking	hispanohablante 88
sparkling wine	cava *(m.)* 74
sparrow	gorrión *(m.)* 93
speak (to ~)	hablar 14
speak to someone (to go to ~)	dirigirse 81
special	extraordinario 85
specialist	especialista *(m./f.)* 53
speciality	especialidad *(f.)* 1
species	especie *(f.)* 93
specific	específico 69
spectator	espectador/a *(m./f.)* 39
speech	discurso *(m.)* 88

speed	velocidad *(f.)* 9
speed (to ~)	correr 42
spell	temporada *(f.)* 60
spell (magic)	hechizo *(m.)* 95
spend (to ~) (time)	pasar 87
spicy	picante 86
spin	vuelta *(f.)* 49
spirit	ánimo *(m.)* 20
spirit (magical creature)	duende *(m.)* 95
spiritual	espiritual 80
splinter	astilla *(f.)* 27
spoil (to ~)	amargarse 51
spontaneous	espontáneo 95
spool	carrete *(m.)* 46
spoon	cuchara *(f.)* 68
sport	deporte *(m.)* 89
sports shoes	zapatillas de deporte *(f.)* 75
sportsman/-woman	deportista *(m./f.)* 86
spouse (husband/wife)	esposo/-a *(m./f.)* 93
spread (diffusion)	difusión *(f.)* 92
spread out (to ~)	extender 62
spring	primavera *(f.)* 69
sprinkle (to ~)	esparcir 77
square	cuadrado 97
square (in a town)	plaza *(f.)* 67
stack (to ~)	apilar 65
stage (phase)	etapa *(f.)* 80
stained	manchado 91
stamp (postage)	sello *(m.)* 14
stand out (to ~)	destacar 88
star	estrella *(f.)* 48
start (to ~)	empezar 22; comenzar 42
start (to ~) (a car/computer)	arrancar 45
start up (to ~)	ponerse en marcha 33
station	estación *(f.)* 6
stay (to ~)	quedarse 10; permanecer 83
stay out all night (to ~)	trasnochar 16
stay/keep (to ~)	parar 67
steak	filete *(m.)* 68
steering wheel	volante *(m.)* 45
step/tread (to ~)	pisar 58
stick	palo *(m.)* 27
still	todavía 25; aún 72
still (immobile)	inmóvil 90
stocking	media *(f.)* 87
stomach	vientre *(m.)* 29
stop (for buses/taxis etc.)	parada *(f.)* 19
stop (to ~)	parar(se) 96
store	tienda *(f.)* 94
story	cuento *(m.)* 53; historia *(f.)* 79
strait	estrecho *(m.)* 97
stranded (to leave ~)	dejar plantado 90
strange	raro 17; extraño 29

street	calle *(f.)* 5
strength	fuerza *(f.)* 100
stress	estrés *(m.)* 60
strike	huelga *(f.)* 7
striking	llamativo 88
string (of identical things)	sarta *(f.)* 52
stripe	raya *(f.)* 32
strong	fuerte 68
studded	constelado 80
student	alumno/-a *(m./f.)* 97
study (to ~)	estudiar 22
stupid	tonto 12
style	estilo *(m.)* 2
style (model)	modelo *(m.)* 32
subscriber	abonado/-a *(m./f.)* 89
succeed in (to ~)	conseguir 81
success	éxito *(m.)* 99
successively	sucesivamente 87
such	tal 3, 27
suffering	sufrimiento *(m.)* 95
sufficient	suficiente 66
suggest (to ~)	proponer 25
suit	traje *(m.)* 77
suit (to ~)	ir 76
suit/not suit one (to ~)	sentar bien/mal 43
suitcase	maleta *(f.)* 18
summer	verano *(m.)* 40
sun	sol *(m.)* 65
sunburned (to get ~)	quemarse 62
Sunday	domingo *(m.)* 14
sunscreen	crema protectora *(f.)* 62
supermarket	supermercado *(m.)* 52
support (to ~)	mantener 66
suppose (to ~)	suponer 52
surcharge	suplemento *(m.)* 21
sure	seguro 40
surface area	superficie *(f.)* 93
surprise	sorpresa *(f.)* 19
surprise (to ~)	sorprender 91
surprised	extrañado 58
surrounding area	alrededores *(m.)* 78
suspect (to ~)	sospechar 57
suspicion	sospecha *(f.)* 57
swallow (bird)	golondrina *(f.)* 93
swallow (to ~)	tragar(se) 31, 73
swear (to ~)	jurar 72
sweet	caramelo *(m.)* 64; golosina *(f.)* 65
swim (to ~)	nadar 42
swimmer	bañista *(m./f.)* 37
swimming	natación *(f.)* 89
swimming (to go ~)	bañarse 46
swimming pool	piscina *(f.)* 27
switch off (to ~)	apagar 73

syllable	sílaba *(f.)* 2
system	sistema *(m.)* 83

T

table	mesa *(f.)* 14
table setting	cubierto *(m.)* 68
tag	etiqueta *(f.)* 76
take (a long) time (to ~)	tardar 61
take (to ~)	coger, tomar 6; quitar 45; llevar 55
take a shoe size (to ~)	calzar 32
take advantage (to ~)	aprovechar 26
take hold of (to ~)	coger 6
take off (to ~)	quitarse 87
take off one's clothes (to ~)	desvestirse 46
take out (to ~)	sacar 61
talk (to ~)	hablar 42
tall	alto 75
tan (to ~)	broncear 62
tape (adhesive)	cinta (adhesiva) *(f.)* 33
task	tarea *(f.)* 75
taste	gusto *(m.)* 69; paladar *(m.)* 86
taste (to ~)	probar 74; paladear 86
tasty	rico 86
taxi	taxi *(m.)* 18
taxi driver	taxista *(m./f.)* 19
tea	té *(m.)* 13
teach (to ~)	enseñar 46
teacher	maestro/-a *(m./f.)* 10; profesor/a *(m./f.)* 15
team	equipo *(m.)* 89
teaspoon	cucharilla *(f.)* 68
technician	técnico/-a *(m./f.)* 94
technology	tecnología *(f.)* 83
telephone	teléfono *(m.)* 2
telephone (to ~)	telefonear 4
telephone call	telefonazo *(m.)* 54
telephone card	tarjeta *(f.)* telefónica 61
television/TV	televisión/tele *(f.)* 31
tell (to ~)	decir 14, 22
tell (to ~) (recount)	contar 98
telling-off	bronca *(f.)* 55
tenacity	tenacidad *(f.)* 99
tennis	tenis *(m.)* 89
terminal	terminal *(m.)* 33
test	test *(m.)* 99
test (to ~)	probar 74
than	que 42
thank (to ~)	dar las gracias 63; agradecer 82
thank you	gracias 1
that	que 13
that (one) *(pronoun)*	ése/ésa 35
that (over there) *(adj.)*	aquel/aquella 35
that (over there) *(non-specific)*	aquello *(neuter)* 35
that *(adj.)*	ese/esa 35

that *(non-specific)*	eso *(neuter)* 35
that one (over there) *(pronoun)*	aquél/aquélla 35
the *(m. sing.)*	el 3
the *(f. sing.)*	la 4
the *(f. pl.)*	las 7
the *(m. pl.)*	los 4
the one(s) that	el/la/los/las que 32
theatre	teatro *(m.)* 8
their	su/sus 28
theirs	suyo/-a/-os/-as 63
them *(after prep.)*	ellos/ellas *(m./f.)* GA3
them *(dir./indir. obj.)*	les 49
them *(f.) (dir. obj.)*	las 49
them *(indir. obj.)*	se 49
them *(m.) (dir. obj.)*	los 49
themselves *(reflexive)*	se GA3
themselves *(after prep.)*	sí 66
then	luego 16
then (so)	entonces 25
there	ahí 33; allí 41
there is/are	hay 21
thermometer	termómetro *(m.)* 97
these (ones) *(pronoun)*	éstos/éstas 35
these *(adj.)*	estos/estas 35
they	ellos/ellas *(m./f.)* 7
thief	ladrón/ladrona *(m./f.)* 57
thing	cosa *(f.)* 13
think (to ~)	creer 11; pensar 40, 70; parecer 71
think about (to ~) (ponder)	pensar en 48
think of (to ~) (opinion)	pensar de 48
this (one) *(pronoun)*	éste/ésta 35
this *(adj.)*	este/esta 35
this *(non-specific)*	esto *(neuter)* 35
those (ones) *(pronoun)*	ésos/ésas 35
those (over there) *(adj.)*	aquellos/aquellas 35
those (over there) *(pronoun)*	aquéllos/aquéllas 35
those *(adj.)*	esos/esas 35
through	a través de 95
throw (to ~)	echar 34
throw oneself (to ~)	tirarse 68; echarse 99
Thursday	jueves *(m.)* 14
thus	así 92
ticket (for admission)	entrada *(f.)* 82
ticket (for transport)	billete *(m.)* 49
ticket (one-way/single ~)	ida *(f.)* 9
ticket (return ~)	ida y vuelta *(f.)* 9
tide	marea *(f.)* 65
tie (to ~)	ligar 62
tight	estrecho 97
till (cash register)	caja *(f.)* 76
time	hora *(f.)*, tiempo *(m.)* 10
time (occasion)	vez *(f.)* 36
tip (for service)	propina *(f.)* 21

tired	cansado 7
to	a 4; hasta 39
to the	al 4
toast	tostado *(m.)* 85
tobaconnist's/newsagent's	estanco *(m.)* 50
today	hoy 6; hoy día 80
together	juntos 16
toilet (lavatory)	servicio *(m.)* 37
token	ficha *(f.)* 61
tolerant	tolerante 90
tolerate (to ~)	aguantar 27
toll	peaje *(m.)* 38
tomato	tomate *(m.)* 61
tomorrow	mañana 10
tongue	lengua *(f.)* 92
too much	demasiado 33
tooth	diente *(m.)* 46
toothpaste	pasta *(f.)* de dientes 2
total (to ~)	sumar 97
totally	absolutamente 83
touch (to ~)	tocar 29
tour	gira *(f.)* 59
tourism	turismo *(m.)* 59
towards	hacia 80
towel	toalla *(f.)* 62
town	pueblo *(m.)* 69
town hall	alcaldía *(f.)*, ayuntamiento *(m.)* 37
track (footprint)	huella *(f.)* 65
trade (profession)	oficio *(m.)* 15
tradition	solera *(f.)*, tradición *(f.)* 86
traffic	tráfico *(m.)* 38
traffic jam	atasco *(m.)* 18
traffic light	semáforo *(m.)* 5
train	tren *(m.)* 11
translate (to ~)	traducir 74
travel (to ~)	viajar 43
tree	árbol *(m.)* 41
trip (voyage)	viaje *(m.)* 23
trophy	trofeo *(m.)* 97
trouble (in ~)	apañado 17
trouble (to ~)	molestar 45
trousers	pantalón/pantalones *(m.)* 76
true	verdad *(f.)* 9; verdadero 99
trunk (of a car)	maletero *(m.)* 57
trust (to ~)	confiar 40
truth	verdad *(f.)* 9
try (on) (to ~)	probar 32
try to (to ~)	tratar de 99
T-shirt	camiseta *(f.)* 87
Tuesday	martes *(m.)* 14
turn	vuelta *(f.)* 49
turn (in a game/line)	turno *(m.)* 50
turn (in line)	vez *(f.)* 71

turn (to be one's ~)	tocar 50
turn around (to ~)	darse la vuelta 29
turn out (to be) (to ~)	resultar 88
turn/switch on (to ~)	encender 45
two	dos 1
type	tipo *(m.)* 43
typical	propio 95
typically	típicamente 86

U

ugly	feo 53
umbrella	paraguas *(m.)* 46
uncle	tío *(m.)* 73
underline (to ~)	subrayar 88
underneath	debajo de 90
underpants	calzoncillo *(m.)* 87
understand (to ~)	comprender 43; entender 96
underwear	ropa interior *(f.)* 55
undress (to ~)	desnudarse 46
unemployment	paro *(m.)* 41
unexpected	imprevisto 100
unforgettable	inolvidable 80
unique	singular 97
universally	universalmente 95
university	universidad *(f.)* 46
unleash (to ~)	desatar 67
unlikely	inverosímil 73
until	mientras 71; hasta 82
up to	hasta 87
upset/embittered (to become ~)	amargarse 51
urban area	aglomeración *(f.)* 69
us *(after prep.)*	nosotros/-as GA3
us *(dir./indir. obj.)*	nos 49
used to (to be ~)	soler 43
usually do something (to ~)	soler 43

V

vacant	vacío 43
vacation	vacaciones *(f.)* 52
value	valor *(m.)* 35
variant	variante *(f.)* 95
varied	diverso 78; variado 86
veal	ternera *(f.)* 68
vegetarian	vegetariano/-a *(m./f.)* 100
verge on (to ~)	rozar 97
version	versión *(f.)* 99
very	muy 3
very bad	malísimo 8
very good	buenísimo 8
very much	muchísimo 25
vicinity	alrededores *(m.)* 78
video	vídeo *(m.)* 47
view	vista *(f.)* 100

wetland	humedal *(m.)* 93
what	cómo, cuál 2; lo que 29
What?	¿Qué? 3
whatever	cualquiera (que) 48
when	cuando 29
where	adonde/a donde, en donde 5; donde 70
where (in which)	en el que, en que 65
Where? *(with movement)*	¿Adónde? 5
Where? *(without movement)*	¿Dónde? 5
whether … or	bien… o bien 70
which	cuál 15
while	mientras 50
whistle (to ~)	silbotear 65
white	blanco 32
who	quien/quienes 12
whom (from ~)	del que 81
whom (of ~)	de quien 81
whose (of which)	cuyo/-a/-os/-as 91
why	por qué 12
wife	mujer *(f.)* 100
wild	agreste, salvaje 93
wild animal	fiera *(f.)* 60
win (to ~)	ganar 97
wind	viento *(m.)* 62
window	ventana *(f.)* 28
window (car/counter etc.)	ventanilla *(f.)* 28
window-shopping (to go ~)	ir de escaparates 76
wine	vino *(m.)* 16
wine list	carta de vinos *(f.)* 74
winner	vencedor/a *(m./f.)* 86
winter	invierno *(m.)* 97
wish (to ~)	desear 82
with	con 3
with himself/herself/itself/ oneself/yourself *(formal)*/ themselves	consigo 66
with me	conmigo 12
with you *(informal sing.)*	contigo 12
withdraw (to ~)	retirar 52
within	dentro (de) 71
without	sin 36
wizard/witch	brujo/-a *(m.)* 95
woman	mujer *(f.)* 14
wonder	maravilla *(f.)* 82
wonder (to ~)	preguntarse 96
wonderful	maravilloso 36
wonderfully	de maravilla 49
wood (the material)	madera *(f.)* 68
woodcutter	leñador/a *(m./f.)* 41
wool	lana *(f.)* 75
woollen	de lana 75
word	palabra *(f.)* 98
work	trabajo *(m.)* 15

yourself *(reflexive) (formal)* se 45
yourself *(formal) (after prep.)* sí 40
yourself *(informal sing.)* te 2
yourselves *(formal) (after prep.)* sí 66

Z

zero cero *(m.)* 54
zone zona *(f.)* 38